Nation-Building and Turkish Modernization

Nation-Building and Turkish Modernization

Islam, Islamism, and Nationalism in Turkey

Rasim Özgür Dönmez
Ali Yaman

LEXINGTON BOOKS
Lanham • Boulder • New York • London

Published by Lexington Books
An imprint of The Rowman & Littlefield Publishing Group, Inc.
4501 Forbes Boulevard, Suite 200, Lanham, Maryland 20706
www.rowman.com

6 Tinworth Street, London SE11 5AL, United Kingdom

British Library Cataloguing in Publication Information Available

Library of Congress Cataloging-in-Publication Data

Names: Donmez, Rasim Ozgur, editor. | Yaman, Ali, editor.
Title: Nation-building and Turkish modernization : Islam, Islamism, and
    nationalism in Turkey / edited by Rasim Ozgur Donmez and Ali Yaman.
Description: Lanham, Maryland ; Boulder : Lexington Books, 2019. | Includes
    bibliographical references and index.
Identifiers: LCCN 2018059829 (print) | LCCN 2019005148 (ebook) | ISBN
    9781498579407 (Electronic) | ISBN 9781498579391 | ISBN
    9781498579391(cloth : alk. paper) | ISBN 9781498579414 (pbk : alk. paper)
Subjects: LCSH: Nationalism—Turkey—History. | Islam and politics—Turkey. |
    Turkey—Politics and government. | AK Parti (Turkey)—History.
Classification: LCC DR440 (ebook) | LCC DR440 .N38 2019 (print) | DDC
    306.209561—dc23
LC record available at https://lccn.loc.gov/2018059829

♾ᵀᴹ The paper used in this publication meets the minimum requirements of
American National Standard for Information Sciences—Permanence of Paper
for Printed Library Materials, ANSI/NISO Z39.48-1992.

Printed in the United States of America

Contents

Acknowledgments

This book was born from the discussions on the center–periphery relations in Turkey for explaining Turkish modernization. These questions led us to discuss the structure of modernization and the nation-building process in Turkey. We tried to understand how the nation-building process has affected center–periphery relations and state-making in the country. We tried to reveal as many sociopolitical dimensions of nation-building of Turkey as we can. In this long and hard process, we would like to give thanks to our families for encouraging us to prepare this book. This book is dedicated to Farah, Mehmet, and Doğa.

Introduction

Turkey, as a sociocultural and political bridge between the East and the West, has always experienced structural political conflict since its establishment. Unlike its Western counterparts, the country could not stay stable in socioeconomic and political terms. Many white-collar workers migrated from Turkey to the West because of restrictions to their freedom and the loss of their cultural hegemony in the system. In addition, many surveys have shown a high polarization between the Europeanized and traditional segments of Turkish society as represented by the Justice and Development Party (JDP). Nowadays, an important question is continuously asked by Turkish people: What made the Turkish nation stick together? This study tries to answer this question by describing how nation-building has occurred in the Turkish case. To understand the neoconservative or the pro-Islamist JDP periods, it is crucial to understand the nation-building process since the late Ottoman Empire period.

The concept of nation-building is used in different contexts. The term roughly means "to transform and integrate diverse and localized societies into the nation." This process has been ongoing in numerous societies. The term is basically used in the literature in two ways. The first became popular in the 1960s in modernization theory. The term was normatively used as a strategy for development necessitating some political preconditions such as functioning state institutions for change and development. The theory also required the integration of societies along national lines by overcoming tribal and primordial ties. Thus nation-building signified a strategy toward economic and political development.[1] The second usage is linked with political dominance; it is here that the term is used by domestic actors to foster their own power or by external actors to influence foreign societies and states by the help of nation-building "with deciding on models, structures and personnel."[2]

In other words, external actors shape the framework and structure of another country's nation-building process. All these usages of the term appear in this study to some extent.

In this regard, what makes the Turkish case unique is the country's imperial past, and since the country has not been colonized before, its understanding of nationalism is quite different than those of colonized and Western countries. These features gave a modernist character to Turkish national identity, and the political elite chose modernist nationalism in forging nation-building rather than ethnic and racial purity or civic understanding. While ethnic nationalism envisions an ethno-racial image of nation-building, civic nationalism asserts to rally people around a joint ideal.

According to Ayhan Akman, modernist nationalism, to an extent, resembles ethnic nationalism "with substantive claims regarding the identity of members comprising the nation."[3] On the other hand, modernist nationalism avoids adopting an ethnic or racial criterion in its vision of nation-building. Modernist nationalism's goal of commonality among its members is different than that of the ethnic-nationalist model, which is derived from some features of the Western cultural model applicable to the country's native features. Modernist nationalism also diverges from civic nationalism by not relying on popular participation.[4] It finds democratic participation risky because "it restricts political and cultural expression of nonconforming, traditional, religious, or local identities."[5]

While modernist nationalism explains the pre-JDP period succinctly— from the establishment of the country to the JDP's rise to power—the theory fell short in explaining the nation-building process *during* the JDP period. Although the JDP period continues the same essences of traditional nation-building since the late Ottoman Empire period, such as the role of the state—namely, state-led developmentalism—and nationalism and the strong role of Islam in the creation of the nation, it differs in that the JDP, to a great extent, otherizes the West in their narratives, particularly during the Arab Spring and onward. This period hindered the state and societal structure of the country, which was directly involved in the Syrian conflict. In this regard, the nationalism of the JDP resembles postcolonial nationalism discursively and in the symbolic sphere in that the party tries to apply modernism without following the route of Western modernization and essentialist understanding—namely, claiming to be the representative of Islam and excluding the West in its discourse. As Jenny B. White claims, the JDP's national identity or nation-building vision can be described as "Muslim nationalism," a majority nationalism that patterns itself on dominant majorities with arithmetical advantage and control of a state.

By addressing these facts, this study evaluates the nation-building process of Turkey. In fact, there are very successful studies about the subject, such as Erik Jan Zürcher's *The Young Turk Legacy and Nation Building: From the Ottoman Empire to Atatürk's Turkey*[6], Alexandros Lamprou's *Nation-Building in Modern Turkey: The "People's Houses," the State and the Citizen*[7], Karen Barkey and Mark Von Hagen's *After Empire: Multiethnic Societies and Nation-Building: The Soviet Union and the Russian, Ottoman, and Habsburg Empires*[8], and Reşat Kasaba and Sibel Bozdoğan's *Rethinking Modernity and National Identity in Turkey.*[9] However, these studies focus on the late Ottoman Empire period and the early years of the Turkish Republic and do not explain the late Republican years, including the JDP period. Jenny B. White's *Muslim Nationalism and the New Turks*, while essential in understanding the national identity during the JDP period, does not comprehensively compare and contrast the previous periods and has a perspective that is restricted by anthropological views.

This book evaluates the nation-building process of Turkey since the late Ottoman Empire period to the current period, namely, the post-Islamist or neoconservative JDP period. The articles in this book give insight into how nation-building occurs at the micro and macro levels. In other words, while some chapters in the book deal with micro politics, such as Seren Selvin Korkmaz's chapter on architectural style reflecting JDP's ideological stance, some articles, such as that of Rasim Özgür Dönmez, focuses on the international community's influence on nation-building in Turkey. This book aims to provide a picture of Turkish nation-building by comparing and contrasting the pre-JDP and JDP periods. In doing so, some chapters were intentionally made long and descriptive so that readers grasp how macro and micro power relations are entrenched in the country's nation-building process. This will show Turkish, Middle East, and nationalism scholars how nation-building has been realized in a Muslim country with an imperialist, noncolonial past.

This book consists of eight chapters. Rasim Özgür Dönmez's chapter analyzes the role of Islam in the nation-building process and examines how Islamists contribute to such process through their interaction with the international community. The second chapter, written by Büke Koyuncu, evaluates how the nation-building process in Turkey gave rise to dialectical or antagonistic sociopolitical actors in the system as well as the role of Islam in the creation of these dialectics. The third chapter, written by Ali Yaman, analyzes the role of the Presidency of Religion Affairs in the nation-building process. Edgar Şar, in the fourth chapter, evaluates desecularization processes during the JDP period.

Senem Kurt Topuz's chapter concentrates on the role of women in Turkey's nation-building process. The sixth chapter, written by Béatrice Hendrich, argues how national identity is perceived by the founders of the Turkish Republic by elaborating on the intersectionality of racism and state feminism in the work of Afet İnan (1908–1985). İnan, an anthropologist and historiographer and one of Atatürk's adopted daughters, was haunted by the fear of being nonwhite and thus culturally and physically inferior to Westerners. Instead of developing independent, self-reliant individuals and a collective identity, the heritage of the aggressively masculine military state had already prepared a solution, which is the creation of a super-ethnicity in the form of women-like men (chaste girl), since the state did not offer a place for feminist women. In the seventh chapter, Gül Arıkan Akdağ investigates how gender roles are constructed in secondary school textbooks to understand the JDP's formation of the role of women in their nation-building process. In the final chapter, Seren Selvin Korkmaz examines the reconstruction of the JDP's national identity through urban space.

NOTES

1. Jochen Hippler, "Ethnicity, State, and Nation-Building-Experiences, Policies and Conceptualization," http://www.jochenhippler.de/html/ethnicity-_state-_and_nation-building.html.
2. İbid.
3. Ayhan Akman, "Modernist Nationalism:Statism and National Identity in Turkey," *Nationalities Papers* 32, no. 1 (2004): 25.
4. Ibid.
5. İbid.
6. Erik Jan Zürcher, *The Young Turk Legacy and Nation Building From the Ottoman Empire to Atatürk's Turkey* (London: I.B. Tauris, 2010).
7. Alexandros Lamprou, *Nation-Building in Modern Turkey: The 'People's Houses', The State and the Citizen* (London: I. B. Tauris, 2015).
8. Karen Barkey and Mark Von Hagen, *After Empire: Multiethnic Societies and Nation-Building: The Soviet Union and the Russian, Ottoman, and Habsburg Empires* (Boulder, CO: Westview Press, 1997).
9. Sibel Bozdoğan and Reşat Kasaba, *Rethinking Modernity and National Identity in Turkey* (Seattle: University of Washington Press, 1997).

REFERENCES

Akman, Ayhan. "Modernist Nationalism:Statism and National Identity in Turkey," *Nationalities Papers* 32, no. 1 (2004): 23–51.
Barkey, Karen and Hagen, Mark Von. *After Empire: Multiethnic Societies and Nation-Building: The Soviet Union and the Russian, Ottoman, and Habsburg Empires.* Boulder, CO:Westview Press, 1997.
Bozdoğan, Sibel and Kasaba, Reşat. *Rethinking Modernity and National Identity in Turkey.* Seattle: University of Washington Press, 1997.

Hippler, Jochen. "Ethnicity, State, and Nation-Building-Experiences, Policies and Conceptualization", http://www.jochenhippler.de/html/ethnicity-_state-_and_nation-building.html (accessed June 5, 2018).

Lamprou, Alexandros. *Nation-Building in Modern Turkey: The 'People's Houses', The State and the Citizen.* London: I. B. Tauris, 2015.

Zürcher, Erik Jan. *The Young Turk Legacy and Nation Building From the Ottoman Empire to Atatürk's Turkey.* London: I. B. Tauris, 2010.

Chapter One

The Relationship between Nation-Building, Islam, and Islamism in Turkey

Rasim Özgür Dönmez

The relationship between nation-building and Islam in Turkey regarding modernization has already been evaluated in the extant literature. Studies have focused on the nationalization and modernization efforts of the Otto-man Empire and its continuation, the nation-state of the Turkish Republic, in relation to domestic and international actors. These studies have evaluated the role of Islam and secularism in these processes but have given little consid-eration to the conditions, roles, actions, and perspective of Islamists in these processes.[1] Thus, it is extremely difficult to analyze Islamism in the Turkish Republic without understanding the role that Islamism and Islamists played in the political life of the Ottoman Empire.

In this sense, most of these studies did not shed light on the dynamics of the interactions between the international and domestic sphere from a histori-cal perspective, which ultimately led to the Justice and Development Party's (JDP) rise to power. These studies generally perceive the JDP's 2002 victory from two different perspectives. The first perspective perceives the success of the Islamists as the failure of the secular government and its social habitus to realize the political and social demands of Turkish society. Hence, these scholars blame the victory of the Islamists on the secular government and military.[2] The second perspective focuses on the Islamists' successful mo-bilization and political strategies, which have allowed them to connect with the majority of the population.[3] Although both perspectives explain to some extent the victory of the JDP, they ignore two important points. The first is the strong role of Islam in the creation of the Turkish state and the Turkish national identity, which has made Islamists essential actors in nation-building and state-making. The second is the strong cooperation of Islamists with the Western international sphere.

In this vein, this study evaluates the process of nation-building in Turkey in regard to the role of Islam by comparing and contrasting the conditions since the late Ottoman period to those in the post-Islamist JDP period. The study comprises four sections. The first section evaluates the connections among nation-building, non-Western societies, and international sphere. The second section analyses the relationship of the nation-building process with Islam and Islamists from the late Ottoman Empire to the modern-day Turkish Republic (founded in 1923), taking into consideration the Western international sphere. The third section evaluates the relationship of Islamists with the state and the international society in regard to the political and social conditions of Turkey from the establishment of the Turkish Republic until the JDP period by evaluating the nation-building in the JDP period in terms of its relationship with the international sphere.

NATION-BUILDING, NON-WESTERN SOCIETIES, AND SOCIOPOLITICAL STRUGGLES

The concept of nation-building gained popularity after the 9/11 terrorist attacks in the United States. The North Atlantic Alliance's (NATO) war against weak and rough states introduced to the literature the concept of rebuilding these states with the help of global and regional actors. However, the entry of this topic to the political science literature can be traced back to the early twentieth century, at which time it indicated the transformation of a society from a community to a society—*Gemeinschaft* to *Gesellschaft*, in Tönnies's terms[4]—by means of the nation-state. In this regard, this concept of nation-building is widely used in two different categories of the literature.

In the first category, this concept refers to the historical, social, and political processes that act to transform different ethnic or ethno-religious groups loosely connected to each other through modern society—*Gesellschaft*—by means of the nation-state. This category frames nation-building as the homogenization of a population by means of national education, a military system, citizenship policies, centralization, and bureaucratic control of the country.[5] The studies in this category focus on nation-building in Europe and the third world, evaluating key actors, political and social structures, and socioeconomic processes such as citizenship and education policies and the role of colonialism.

The second category sees nation-building as a strategy for both international and domestic actors to reach political targets. Hence, these studies focus to a great extent on the international actors in nation-building and state-making.[6] These studies mushroomed significantly after the "War on Terror" following 9/11.

However, neither category is sufficient to explain the nation-building process in Turkey. The first category examines the topic by considering domestic actors and largely ignores the role of international actors in the nation-building process. The second category can be applied to Turkey due to the features of the country, as it did not experience a colonial past. This category is applied more to studies on the democracy and democratization of Turkey, particularly on the effects of the Europeanization process on Turkish society. In this regard, this study tries to reveal the symbiotic relationship between international and domestic actors in the relationship between Islam, Islamism, and nation-building.

NATION-BUILDING, THE INTERNATIONAL SYSTEM, AND NON-WESTERN SOCIETIES

The argument of the influential role of the international system on domestic politics, particularly on democracies patterned on Peter Gourevitch's study "Revisiting Second Image Reversed" was a cornerstone for similar future studies.[7] According to Gourevitch, two main dimensions of the international system influence states on the domestic level: war and trade patterning on the allocation of power and wealth.[8] His focal point is to focus on regime type and coalition pattern as the dependent variables. He argues that "enduring features of a given political system, ones which operate over time to shape behaviour at specific moments of decision, events, or policy formation."[9] However, his theory ignores the perspective of the culture or the identity feature of the international system. To understand the nation-building process in Turkey, it is essential to understand the structure of the international system and its image of non-Western societies in this system.

Another example of a theory regarding the international system, culture, and identity is found in Samuel Huntington's groundbreaking study entitled "Clash of Civilizations."[10] Before the Cold War, societies were divided along ideological lines, such as the struggle between democracy and communism. Huntington's main thesis argues that "the most important distinctions among peoples are [no-longer] ideological, political, or economic. They are cultural,"[11] and new patterns of conflict will occur along different cultures. The study focuses on macro-level sociocultural patterns that have been employed in an attempt to fix this gap, as well as on the perception of the international system from the perspective of civilization, but it contains a noticeable weakness: Huntington perceives religion as monolithic and static. His understanding of the international system is static and deterministic, which cannot be applied to the current study. Although other bodies of work focusing on the effects of socialization on the international system, such as the

English school, constructivism, critical theory, and so on, are concerned with "moving beyond the positivist and materialist accounts" in mainstream IR to understand the common ancestral features among states,[12] all these theories focus more on "how the international society shapes states as actors in the international society" and less "on domestic implications."[13]

In her groundbreaking book, *After Defeat: How the East Learned to Live with the West*, Ayşe Zarakol closes this gap and focuses more on the impact of the international society on domestic politics and the nation-building process. The author merges Norbert Elias's discussion of the established outsider with Erving Goffman's notion of "stigmata" to analyze the polity physiology of some non-Western countries, namely Turkey, Russia, and Japan. The author's argument is based on the hierarchy of the international society and poses the question of why some non-Western states' defeats in terms of politics and military lead to a sense of both inferiority and anger.[14]

According to Zarakol, the defeat of some non-Western empires, such as the Ottoman Empire, led to trauma in their national identities. All these countries are torn between the East and the West, and the elites in these countries perceive this as a weakness to overcome or use this situation to their own benefit by, for example, acting as a bridge or a gate between the two.[15] This perspective is also supported by Partha Chatterjee's Eastern nationalism, or postcolonial nationalism, perspective. According to him, while Eastern nationalism admires Western values, it simultaneously paints it as the "other."[16]

However, Zarakol goes beyond Chatterjee and pinpoints the material patterns of stigmatization by recalling Elias's notion of the "established outsider." The notion indicates that, through stigmatization, the superior actor may cause the less powerful to feel "that they lack virtue and they are inferior in human terms." In this regard, non-Western countries, such as the Ottoman Empire, Russia, and Japan, constitute the "established outsiders" of the international society. Before they were unified with the Westphalian system, they were empires that produced wide-ranging worldviews by which they defined themselves as "normal" and others as different or "inferior."[17] However, the incorporation of these pre-modern empires into the Westphalian system has led them to leave their privileged positions and compromise with an outsider position. Zarakol states:

> This new position did not square well with self-understanding shaped by centuries of being masters of their own domains. Furthermore, because they joined the original incarnation of the international system, the European society of states, as autonomous entities, their position of inferiority was not overtly forced on them, as it was in the case of colonized peoples—they came to an awareness about their inferiority.[18]

Unlike colonial states, these states compromise with the values of Western modernity by not denying them as a hostile foreign imposition. Hence, they perceive these values as elements that should be absorbed to regain their past privileged position in the new, normative world.

However, social hierarchies of the international system both affect states' behaviour and the characteristics of domestic politics, particularly the identity formation of social classes in the nation-building process. In other words, the normative standards of the international society create domestic groups' missions, identities, and sentiments of opposition. In the non-colonized and non-Western countries mentioned above, the nation-building process merged with state-making patterns in state-led development, which enabled them to create their own middle class consisting of bureaucrats and others funded by the state and sharing the same world vision. This vision consists of a developmentalist, modernist view that positions the country in the modern and civilized world and engaged with the modern norms of international society. These middle classes use their education and lifestyle to assume a privileged position against other social classes, defined as ignorant, traditional, and backward. In this context, state-building and citizenship regimes are used as an inclusion/exclusion mechanism for these social classes, which makes the reconciliation of these actors in these areas almost as impossible as in these states in Western counterparts. [19]

This new middle class, previously poor urban suburbs of the cities, not sharing with the same worldview of sociopolitics and the democratization process in their countries, is seen as distrustful by the dominant social classes (statist middle classes), on the premise that it is not capable of ruling the country and may serve as a tool of the West to dismantle the country's dominance in the international system. However, they are not willing to decline economic and political liberalization entirely. As Zarakol describes, they are their own gravediggers in which their attitudes open a space to emerge a new middle class sharing cultural values with the urban poor and peasants that followed the same route with statist middle classes, including developing a strong relationship with the international order so as to suppress the statist middle classes.[20] This fact naturally created antagonisms within society and among the middle classes.

Although this perspective is used in this study to understand the symbiotic relationship between state elite and Islamists in nation-building, it ignores the active role of the Western hegemony in turning different social classes against each other and motivating them to clash in the name of democratization. These social classes cooperate with the West to increase their territory both in the political and public spheres and to gain additional power. Here, the term hegemony is used "as the exercise of leadership within historical blocks within a particular world order."[21] Hegemony indicates a sense of some paramount state power in the world system while conveying a more specific sense of the establishment of consent or ideological leadership around a particular historical project.[22] While Great Britain was able to achieve international hegemony in the eighteenth century via its military, the United States has achieved this objective in the post-World War II era through its global economy.

THE OTTOMAN EMPIRE, NATION-BUILDING PROJECTS, AND ISLAM/ISLAMISTS

The nation-building process of Turkey can be traced back to the Ottoman Empire period, particularly the period initiating its decline of power: the late sixteenth century. The Empire's position in the global social hierarchy began to be intensively questioned in the late seventeenth and eighteenth century by both the European international system and its own internal administrative system. Recalling Zarakol's words, the Ottoman Empire's entering into the European state system was simultaneously "stigmatized." The stigmatization of the Empire led the elite to contemplate how the Empire could compete with European states on the economic, technological, and administrative levels.

These policies also reflect domestic politics, in which efforts to protect the lands of the Empire led to the emergence of two important processes: strong centralization and the forming of a Muslim nation. The policies reinforcing the center were realized through the nation-building process and the citizenship regime. Heterodox Islamic institutions, namely sects, were always perceived as either strong lobbies that helped the sultan stay in power or actors that worked to dethrone the sultan. In this regard, this section evaluates the relationship between stigmatization, nation-building, and Islam. The other question is where Islamists positioned themselves in this process.

The Question of How We Can Rescue the Empire, Stigmatization, Islam, and Nation-building

The declining power of the Ottoman Empire since the sixteenth century led the Ottoman bureaucracy to begin voicing the decline. Prominent bureaucrats such as Gelibolulu Mustafa Ali and Koçi Bey began to write treatises on the deterioration of the socioeconomic and administrative system of the Empire, and other bureaucrats in subsequent centuries followed suit. Starting at the beginning of the eighteenth century, their solution was to wait for an authoritarian and virtuous sultan to control the chaos in the society.[23]

At the beginning of the eighteenth century, the decline began to be interpreted in reference to Ibni Khaldun's *Muqaddimah*. The explanation was simply based on the evolution of states and society. According to Khaldun, nomad societies are egalitarian, dynamic, and belligerent. The transformation to civilized life brings social stratification, societal hierarchy, and the division of labor, which lead to prosperity but also to the loss of dynamism and belligerency. Every state named this transformation process birth, youth, maturity, and senility. Finally, a new dynamic, nomadic society raids and demolishes the current state, establishing a new one. [24] This perspective can be reread as the normalization of the decline of power in the eyes of the Ottoman bureaucracy. The military defeats deepened the Empire's dissolution concerns at the end of the eighteenth century, particularly the defeat against Russia and the loss of Crimea. The Ottomanism has not been sufficient to attach different non-Muslim communities in the Empire. The imperial countries became porters of minorities, closing themselves off to separate themselves from the Ottoman Empire, known as the "Eastern Problem" in Turkish politics. The dissolution of the Empire stigmatized it from the international sphere and forced it to question why it had declined in the global hierarchy.[25]

This process forced the Ottoman elite to rethink the reasons for the dissolution and to compare the position of the Ottoman Empire to those of its Western counterparts. In the late eighteenth century, the high Ottoman elite believed the solution to the Empire's problems, in the context of Ottoman Islamic thought, was to return to the ancient order of the Ottoman Empire (from its initial years to the period of Suleiman the Magnificent).In this sense, they initiated the circulation of a new discourse, "renewing" (*tecdid*) to fix the problems of the Empire to signify the restoration of the power of the Sultan as the sole power. To return to the powerful years of the Empire, they were not hesitant to imitate Western military organization and technology.[26]

The deterioration of the millet system in the eighteenth century due to the declining prosperity of the Empire led Christian minorities to close in on themselves and demarcate their borders against the center. This process was also reinforced by the Empire's citizenship policies, which prioritized Muslims over non-Muslims. The self-determination of the Christian minorities, namely the Serbs and Greeks, in the nineteenth century forced the sultans to develop two important policies. The first was state-building through a process of modernization, and the second was the renewal of the social contract based on the principles of the Islam and Muslim identity, not Ottomanism. The modernization efforts of the Ottoman Empire accelerated this process.

The modernization project, beginning in the military, inevitably led the Ottoman Empire to pattern its nation-building process on Muslim identity. The modernization project was first initiated by Sultan Selim III through his attempts to modernize the army. He brought commanders from France and Sweden, adopted the modern military system, and abolished the guild of the Janissaries—the traditional Ottoman army.[27] Sultan Mahmud II (1808–1839) continued the modernization project and dismantled all actors that could prove to be obstacles for the center. He dismantled both the Janissaries and the local notables (Ayans), establishing different extents of administrative control over society and politics in the Ottoman Empire from the sixteenth to the early nineteenth century. He also altered Islamic waqfs by placing a government agency over the administration for diminishing the power of the ulama, whom he saw as a potential obstacle for the center.[28]

The radical modernization policy of Sultan Mahmud II was followed by the dismantlement of the Janissaries and replaced with a compulsory military duty policy that recruited Muslims to the military without their consent. The army recruited Muslim subjects by forcefully removing them from their families for as long as ten years.[29] This radical centralization and Westernization policy had two results: first, the transformation of the Empire was a more laicized version of state interpretation; and second, these policies can be interpreted as the first steps of Muslim-based nation-building. In other words, the answer to how to save the Empire was through the restoration of both the power of the Sultan and the secular power as well as the mandatory Westernization of the Empire.

However, this nation-building process was painful. The compulsory military policy led to the Muslim population diminishing because those serving in the military could not get married for decades, and many recruits died from starvation or epidemic disease. In addition, the culmination of poverty in the society led the Muslim population to lose trust in the political system.[30] Although Ottomanism was still coherently followed by the palace during these periods, both Muslims and non-Muslims lacked confidence in the center.

In addition, the philosophy of the French Revolution had embodied itself in the principles of equality, nationality, freedom, and justice and had an impact on the non-Muslim minority of the Empire, especially those in the Balkans. These principles motivated their self-determination struggles, which forced Sultan Mahmud II to abandon the idea of Ottomanism inspired by the hierarchical dominance of the Muslim population (Muslim millet[31]) and pursue the idea of Ottomanism inspired by the equality of citizens regardless of religious or ethnic identity. Sultan Mahmud II laid the footprints of modern citizenship of the country, which would later be completed by Sultan Abdulmejid I.[32] For example, the traditional law of compulsory clothing for the millets was lifted by Sultan Mahmud II on the premise of providing equality across the different millets. All these reforms, inherited from the West, were the answers to the culminating loss of land and the declining power of the Empire to save the Empire from stigmatization in the global hierarchy.

These ideas were put into action by Sultan Abdulmejid I, who came to power after Sultan Mahmud II. With the proclamation of an imperial edict of reforms, the Gülhane Hatt-ı Şerif (Supreme Edict of the Rosehouse) opened a new era on November 3, 1839. After a public proclamation before an assembly of diplomats and Ottoman notables, the edict was sworn to by Sultan Abdulmejid I and his high officials. According to Roderic Davison, much of the Gülhane Hatt-ı Şerif had a strong Muslim ring. It perceived the decline of the Empire to the defiance of the principles of the Koran but proposed the equality of Muslims and non-Muslims in the public and state sphere.[33] The security of life, honor, and property was guaranteed, and reforms enacted in taxing and conscription methods were enacted. The new policy was confirmed in the more extensive Hatt-i humayun of 1856, which promised the equal treatment of individuals of all faiths in various matters, such as educational opportunities, the appointment of governmental posts, and the administration of justice, in addition to taxation and military service.[34]

In other words, the Hatt-i humayun can be perceived as a social contract that proposed nation-building based on the idea of modern and equal citizenship. Sultan Abdulmejid I tried to reconcile Muslim traditions and progress, promising to create new institutions in line with the demands of the population that would not contravene with Muslim law. However, this solution satisfied neither Muslim nor non-Muslim residents of the Empire.[35]

There were three main reasons why Muslims were not satisfied with the contract. The first one was that the Westernization of laws and emerging new actors contributed to the deterioration of the traditional structures of the society. The dominance of modern bureaucracy had become more visible and constituted a power vacuum in society.[36] According to Şerif Mardin, when the ulama's traditional distributive power was eliminated and they could not engage in conflict resolution, the result was a power vacuum. The Westernized bureaucracy could not fill this vacuum, leading to a legitimacy crisis.[37]

Second, Muslims felt that their dominant position was being undermined and the demarcation lines of the millets being blurred, which led Muslims to question why they were equal to non-Muslims when only they were dying for the Empire. Similarly, this contract did not satisfy the non-Muslim *tebaas* (subjects) because they did not want to stay within the Empire's borders, instead wishing to set up their own nation-states. The imperial powers manipulated and urged these non-Muslim minorities to revolt against Istanbul. This situation made Muslim subjects anxious about losing their land, creating tension between Muslims and non-Muslims. The Muslim community also felt angry and anguished about non-Muslims forcing the Empire to give up privileges to European countries. Lastly, the state did not act coherently in terms of Ottomanism. For example, the bureaucrats always stressed that the state religion was Islam, but both the religious and secular courts operated at the same time.[38]

The role of the international society was also essential in the adaptation of Ottomanism. The Ottoman Empire as the part of the international society acted to stop the penetration of imperial powers such as Russia, the United Kingdom, and France. Although the international society was relatively fragmented in comparison to today and lived with the power balances rather than adopting a common set of rules and procedures, its common other was the Ottoman Empire due to its financial and military weakness, which made it open for invasion. Hence, the non-Muslims' self-determination demands were used to penetrate and conquer the lands of the Ottoman Empire by the imperial powers. [39]

The modernization and Westernization of the Empire, during which Westernized secular schools were opened and Western thought circulated, led to the appearance of new intellectuals known as "Young Ottomans." They were ex-state bureaucrats who now worked for newspapers or as writers. They strongly opposed the Tanzimât reforms and the high bureaucrats' importing of the Western style of modernization to the country. They had witnessed the financial poverty of the Empire and the capitulation effects that had weakened the Ottoman economy, leading to higher unemployment. They perceived the high bureaucrats' Westernization policies as executing the interests of Western powers inside the Ottoman Empire and strengthening their positions.[40]

These intellectuals, including Şinasi, Ziya Paşa, Ali Suavi, and Namık Kemal, were strongly opposed to the government (the high bureaucrats and the governing style of the sultan) and the Ottomanism that prevailed in the Tanzimât era because they had lifted the dominant millet status of Muslims. The Young Ottomans, conversely, offered a new modern monarchy patterned on Islam and the parliamentary system. They thought Islam was the sole and strongest foundation that bound the Empire's Muslims, who comprised the majority of the country. In this vein, they wished to influence the Muslim population in foreign policy outside of the Empire through the caliphate status of the sultan. Thus, they envisioned a new political system patterned on Muslim dominance but blending with modernization/Westernization and nativism.[41]

The Young Ottomans adopted terms of Western enlightenment, such as modernization, progress, and democracy, and integrated them with Islamic concepts. They perceived Islam as essentially containing democracy (*meşveret*) and contracts (*biat*), which rendered the participation and legitimacy of the people essential for the political system. In other words, the New Ottomans offered a new national contract built on modern Muslim identity. However, they emphasized Ottomanism in the public sphere to garner support from the minorities who opposed the government.[42] These intellectuals believed that nation-building patterned on modernization and Muslim dominance would strengthen the country and would prevent European penetration to politics. In fact, their effort was to stick the country to international order through the country's native features.

The continuation of the decline of the Empire led to Islamism emerging among the "Young Turks," reflecting the mindset of Muslim subjects in the Empire, whose perspective would later be shared by Sultan Abdülhamid II (1876–1908). Unlike the Young Turks' grassroots perspective about nation-building and Islam, Sultan Abdülhamid II implied Pan-Islamism in international relations as a radical measure in his state project. The main reason for Sultan Abdülhamid's choice stemmed from the defeat of the Ottoman Empire in the Russian–Ottoman War (1806–1812) and the revolts of the non-Muslims in the Balkans against the Empire, which had led hundreds of thousands of Ottoman Muslims to emigrate. This development forced Sultan Abdülhamid II to demarcate the Ottoman identity on the grounds of Islam and the Muslim identity. However, he did so via authoritarian policies such as sustaining the assembly and the constitution and enacting strict police-state policies.[43]

On the other hand, the Ottoman Empire put great effort into establishing legitimacy in the international sphere to avoid stigmatization by the international community. The adoption of international law and its interpreted support of the Ottoman state can serve as an example. The Empire also found new policies and new traditions to be an influential player in the international sphere. Sultan Abdülhamid II's pan-Islamist policies can be perceived as an effort to forge new traditions. He tried to create "imaginary communities" using the Empire's status as a caliphate to impact all Muslims. As Selim Deringil remarked, this highly secular policy allowed the Empire to compete in the international sphere using religious symbols.[44]

Both the sultan's pan-Islamist policy and the Muslim millet's anxiety about losing land strengthened Abdülhamid II's seat. The sultan enacted authoritarian policies in an attempt to acquire additional power for the center. These actions led to two important developments: the oppression of non-Muslim minorities, particularly Armenians in the Empire, and the emergence of a strong opposition against Abdülhamid II's monarchy. In other words, while the sultan was increasing his power—making centralization efforts—to demarcate the Ottoman identity on the grounds of Muslimhood, the ideas of modernity and Westernization affected the Ottoman citizens, including the Muslims. More specifically, the Young Turks demanded the democratization of the Empire. In this regard, the oppression of the Armenians in eastern Anatolia was exceptionally important for the regime to reinforce itself.

The potential risk of Russia invading and helping to set up an Armenian state in the eastern part of modern-day Turkey worried both Kurdish tribes living in the same region and Sultan Abdülhamid II. Kurds living in the region comprised the majority of the population and were afraid of losing their land through the self-determination of the Armenians. The anxiety of the Kurds motivated Abdülhamid II to form the "Hamidiye Light Cavalry" from sixty regiments of the Sunni Kurdish militia. Abdülhamid II had three reasons for setting up the cavalry: to set up an irregular force to help the Ottoman military prevent a Russian invasion and to protect the borders of the Empire; to suppress a potential Armenian rebellion; and to govern the Kurdish region with a Kurdish cavalry, thereby suppressing Kurdish irredentism. The cavalry was successful in suppressing Armenian rebels, and the expropriation of Armenian property began with the entry of the cavalry to the region. This event is crucial to the topic of this paper because this policy reinforced the Muslim foundation of the Empire's identity.[45]

Paradoxically, strong opposition from all sections of society emerged against the monarchy. The leading actor of the opposition was the "Young Turks" movement, populated by members who had graduated from the modern schools established by Sultan Abdülhamid II. The movement was first established by medical students from border cities that had experienced civil wars with Christians. The organization was founded by an Albanian (İbrahim Temo), a Circassian, and the two Kurdish medical students, and as understood from their background, the Ottomanist vein of the organization was powerful. Although this mindset changed slightly when the organization assumed the name "Union and Progress" in 1908, it still followed Ottomanism to cooperate with non-Muslims against the monarchy. The movement's approach was grounded in pragmatic reasons to unite all opposition against the monarchy. For example, Union and Progress cooperated with Albanians, Jews, and the Armenian nationalist organizations Hınçak (Social Democrat Party) and Tasnakyutsan against Sultan Abdülhamid II's regime.[46]

Relating to the topic of this paper, not only the monarchy itself, but also the opposition required support and legitimacy from the international society to implement their own projects and to save the country from stigmatization, which distorted the demarcation efforts of Sultan Abdülhamid II. These efforts can also be perceived as the internalization and modernization efforts of the opposition embodied in demands for an open parliament and the restriction of the sultan's power.

However, Union and Progress's emphasis on Ottomanism and cooperation with different factions of society and sectors of the state ended after the organization dethroned Abdülhamid II (July 23, 1908) and reopened the Chamber of Deputies (*Meclis-i Mebusân*). The dramatic defeat of the Ottoman Empire in various wars and the separation of various millets from the Empire nurtured the Turkish vein of Union and Progress. The milestone of the emerging Turkism was first voiced by Yusuf Akçura, a Kazan Tatar who had immigrated to Anatolia and was a close friend of Atatürk. In his ground-breaking article "Three Genres of Politics" (Üç–Tarzı Siyaset), published in a newspaper called *Turk* in Cairo in 1904, Akçura discussed the fundamental Ottoman state policies: Ottomanism, Pan-Islamism, and Pan-Turkism. The article stressed that the first two currents of thought had not been sufficient enough to attach the different millets of the Empire. The final ideological current that Akçura brought to the forefront differed from the previous ones in that it had not been implemented before and did not have a strong base in the Empire. This current was the "Unification of the Turks" and would, as Akçura described it, attach all Turkic peoples, including those in Asia, and could include non-Turkic peoples, who would become "Turkified."[47]

Contrary to Akçura's expectations, there was no widespread support for Turkism in the Ottoman Empire. However, with the Balkan Wars (1912–1913) and the independence of the Albanians (October 2, 1912), one of the first Muslim millets separated from the Empire and strengthened the Turkish vein of Union and Progress. Medical doctors Dr. Behaeddin Shakir and Dr. Nâzım, the most action-oriented members of the Union, who supported Turkish dominance in the Empire, gained prominence in the Union and Progress movement. This clique pacified the Ottomanist clique in the organization and reunified with the middle-rank soldiers in the Balkans, such as Enver Pasha and Atatürk.[48]

The Balkan Wars strengthened the Islamization and Turkification process of Union and Progress. Although Islamization and Turkification policies had been initiated by Sultan Abdülhamid II to place non-Turkish immigrant ethnic groups, such as the Bosniaks, Pomaks, and Circassians, in strategic locations of the Empire, the organization vigorously continued its population engineering to prevent the loss of territory. The widespread migration of Muslims to the Ottoman Empire after the Balkan Wars offered the government a convenient population for Turkification, which reinforced these settlement policies of the government and Union and Progress. The Armenian resettlement and the Greek minority's forced migration from the Aegean region of the country to Greek islands were part of Union and Progress's Turkification policies, and in return, non-Muslim mobs forced Balkan Muslims to migrate from their homes in the Balkans to Anatolia. Parallel to this action, Union and Progress radically continued its modernization project in every facet of life, including law, politics, and military.[49]

As mentioned previously, the nation-building process in the Empire transitioned from the question of how to return to the Empire's golden age to one of how to prevent the loss of territory. This transformation cannot be separated from international relations and the international community. Although the Ottoman Empire initiated modernization policies against the West, its political, economic, and social sphere merged with the West. While the country demarcated its cultural, political, and economic boundaries to create a national identity, it still tried to attach itself to the international sphere. For example, there existed close bonds between the Salonican Young Turks members—then Union and Progress committee members—and Italian Freemasonry, and Union and Progress was also influenced by the Constitutionalism Movement of Europe, which was strongly motivated by the European lodges, particularly those of the Italian Freemasonry.[50] The question was still how the Empire could save itself from stigmatization while adopting the European nation-state system.

A Brief Overview of Islamism and Islamists in Ottoman Nation-Building

In terms of Islam, the Ottoman Empire was traditionally divided by two main actors. The "ilmiye" class represented the state of Islam and was an important actor in the state organization, and the other actor represented heterodox Islam, mainly organized by Sufi orders such as the Bektashi and Naqshbandi Sufi orders, which mushroomed in civil society but retained strong links with the state sphere. The palace tried to monitor and govern society through these two actors. From the beginning to the late nineteenth century to the early twentieth century, these two actors maintained a symbiotic and sometimes antagonistic relationship. However, they both had a strong influence on the palace and society.

The Sufi orders had always aimed to obtain power from the state and be part of the Ottoman administration. In this vein, they sometimes brought down sultans. Although the Ottoman administration used the Sufi orders to help govern society, the orders were also always the object of security measures in the palace. For example, Sultan Mehmed the Conqueror was under the effect of the Hurufi order, one of the Bektashi branches, which began to influence Fatih the Conqueror and to dominate bureaucracy. The order began to be perceived as a security threat by the Ottoman bureaucracy, the order was dismantled, and their members were executed by the authorization of Fatih the Conqueror.[51]

By the beginning of the eighteenth century, namely with Sultan Mahmud II, the power of the ilmiye had been, to a great extent, restricted, and secular bureaucracy was being prioritized.[52] With the dismantlement of the Janissaries in 1826 under the strong influence of the Bektashi order, the order was oppressed, and there was widespread deportation and forced resettlement of the order's members. The Naqshbandi sheiks were appointed to some Bektashi foundations, and the Naqshbandi and the Mevlevis were relocated to the places the Bektashis had left.[53] As explained below, many Bektashis would enter masonry lounges and become influenced by Western ideologies such as liberalism and nationalism. They would become agents of these ideologies; examples include Namık Kemal, Ziya Gökalp.[54]

With the dawn of the nineteenth century, all Sufi orders were incrementally integrated into the Ottoman government. The foundation of the Assembly of Sheikhs (*Meclis-i Meşayıh*) in 1866 was orchestrated by the palace, and entrants to the assembly strongly required both secular and religious skills.[55] The Assembly was tied to the office of the Sheikhul-Islam and represented all Sufi lodges from Istanbul. In addition, all financial and fiscal assets of the Sufi orders were registered and controlled by the state. In other words, in the nineteenth century, religion largely became part of a state apparatus.[56] Although some Nakshbendi Halidiye branches, particularly the ones in the Kurdish region of the Empire, such as that led by Sheikh Ubeydullah, rebelled in 1880–1882 against the Istanbul government to separate from the Empire and form an independent Kurdish nation-state, these actions cannot be attributed to the Naqshbandi order as a whole.[57]

The Nakshbendi order was the most widespread order after the Bektashi order was abolished.[58] Although Sultan Mahmud II (1808–1839) banned the Halidi-Naqshbandi Sufi order[59] and exiled their leaders in Istanbul, Sultans Abdülmecit (1839–1861), Abdülaziz (1861–1876), and Abdülhamid II (1976–1909) all opened spaces for them to organize in civil society to make them mediator between society and the state. In other words, the government and the Sultan used them as interpreters to the people. They discovered new Islamic activism by interpreting economic and political events through the lens of Sharia and Sunna. They even directly participated in the Russian–Ottoman War (1877–1878) and helped the palace mobilize the people in the war.[60]

The order was generally organized in cities, and their members were comprised of elites such as bureaucrats, merchants, and educated people. They played a key role in preparing the political and social base and supporting constitutionalism and human rights in the Empire. More importantly, the Naqshbandi functioned as de facto guilds or networks to protect themselves from the effects of capitalism and foreign investment. In other words, Sufi orders such as the Naqshbandi order played a key role in the transformation of Muslims during the strong modernization and Westernization process.[61]

In terms of the nation-building process, the sultans backed the Halidi-Naqshbandi order as a means of achieving the Muslimization of the nation and to control the society by means of their connections. In the Balkans, conversely, many Orthodox Christians shared both Orthodox and Bektashi beliefs, and the philosophy of Bektashism, patterned on the principle of *Wahdat al-Wujud* (Vahdet-i Vücud), implied that the unity of existence allows different religions to coexist peacefully.[62] According to Christos Retoulas, there exist philosophically parallel views between Orthodox Christianity and Bektashism regarding rationality, the existence of God, the nature of man, and so on. The demolishment of the Bektashi order and the strengthening of Naqshbandism indicate the culmination of *Wahdat al-Shuhüd*, signifying the unity of the Islamic testimony of faith. More explicitly, this philosophy excluded all religions other than Islam. In this sense, the backing of Sunni Sufi orders by the palace signified the Muslimization of the nation-building project rather than Ottomanism, despite the center's strong emphasis on Ottomanism.[63]

Apart from these two versions of traditional Islamic understanding, a new understanding—modern Islamism—mushroomed in the Empire. As stated above, the Young Ottomans had graduated from modern schools of the Ottoman Empire. Unlike the ulama, who had identified with the state, they were independent intellectuals. Their epistemological concern was how to save the Empire. Their answer was to reinterpret the world and politics through Islam, more specifically through *fiqh*.[64] They were strongly opposed to the secularization of law, favoring Islamic law and jurisprudence, because they did not believe that law could be patterned on morality. Rather, they thought justice should be based on religion.[65]

Unlike the traditional ulama, the Young Ottomans were not directly opposed to the West and Western values. While they accepted the dominance of Western technology, they wished to reestablish Western political concepts, such as a representative government, leader, and constitution through Islamic concepts *meşveret*, *imam*, and *kanun-i esasi*, respectively. Some Young Ottomans, such as Namık Kemal and Suavi, lived in Europe and were members of masonry lodges.[66] Thus, they had strong ties to the West. They were keen on the concepts of freedom, liberty, and democracy, and they believed that these concepts already existed in Islam. In other words, they envisioned a modern state that retained the essence of Islam and Islamic values but that accommodated Christians to prevent Western invasions.[67] In this regard, they believed in the unity of Muslims and devoted themselves to solving the problems of the Muslim world. According to Akçura, Islamism as a salvative and redemptive ideology was the precursor to nationalism in the Empire.[68] The Young Ottomans were the pioneers of Turkish nationalism and eventually left their ideas to Union and Progress and Mustafa Kemal. Mustafa Kemal commented on this situation, stating, "The father of my feelings is Namık Kemal, and the father of my thoughts is Ziya Gökalp."[69]

As stated above, the conditions of the Empire resulted in the independence of the Muslim millets, such as the Arabs and Albanians, strengthened the pro-nationalist movement—namely Union and Progress—and prevented Islamist projects from being implemented in the Empire. Prominent and influential Islamists, such as Ahmet Cevdet Pasha and Eşref Edip, began to use the nation not as a Muslim *umma* but rather as the Turkish nation. [70]

THE TURKISH REPUBLIC, NATION-BUILDING PROJECTS, AND ISLAM/ISLAMISTS

The nation-building process in Turkey has always taken place in relation to state-making, and unlike the Western world, parliamentary democracy in Turkey has been an agent in the state-making and nation-building processes. In this context, the interpretation of Islam and nationalism were always fault lines in the state- and nation-building processes between antagonistic actors. While the internalization of international norms and values has been necessary to be accepted in the global hierarchy, Islam and nationalism have also been used in society legitimization.

Therefore, the content of these two concepts—Islam and nationalism—changes in relation with domestic actors and, of course, with the influence of the Western international community in both state-making and nation-building. In other words, the international community has affected the inclusion/exclusion mechanisms of nation-building in Turkey. In terms of the role of Islamists, there are mainly three periods in the nation-building process in the Republican era. In the first period (1923–1950), Islamists went underground and disappeared from the public view. In the second period (1950–2001), they began to penetrate the political and social life, particularly with the urbanization of the country and the admission of Turkey to NATO. In the last period (2001–present), the Islamists have broken the hegemony of Kemalism and secular establishment and have become a leading actor on the political stage.

The First Period (1923–1950)

The nation-building process in this period was carried out radically by the Turkish elite to transform the former Ottoman Empire into a modern nation-state. Although this process can be traced back to the Tanzimat period, radical policies were implemented to create a modern and Westernized nation without losing its Turkish traits. Thus, the Republican elite made great efforts to place the new country on equal footing with other European states in the international order.

In this regard, the victory in the Turkish War of Independence (1919–1923) was a milestone for the Republican elite, which opened a new era in the Turkish nation-building process. The Muslim immigration from the Balkans and Caucasus gave new impetus to the Committee of Union and Progress, and Mustafa Kemal mobilized them on the premises of saving the Turkish/ Islamic identity and the Caliphate from the Christian West.[71] The Armenian resettlement ended in 1922, and after the Lozan Peace Agreement (July 24th, 1923), the Turkish–Greek population exchange homogenized and shaped the Turkish/Muslim population to a great extent.

After the victory in the War of Independence, the Republican elite found that the status of the Caliphate was an obstacle against creating a new nation-state and placing the country among the European nations. In other words, the country could not continue to live by a meta-ideology, namely Islam, in the new international order created to a great extent by secular nation-states. Therefore, the Republican elite mobilized the Turkish citizens to rescue the country and get rid of the Caliphate in order to transform *umma* into a nation.[72]

Another belief of the Republican elite was that the new country could be saved from the deficiencies of the Ottoman Empire and from international stigmatization by the modernization of society and the political sphere. In this regard, the elite tried to create a modern and Westernized public sphere along a nationalist ideology. According to Bernard Lewis, the reason for that is the transformation of an Islamic Empire patterned on theocracy into a modern national state patterned on capitalism.[73]

However, there were two legacies of the Ottoman Empire transmitted to the Republic: the strong state tradition, where the unity of state and society was crucial in the survival of the regime, and the center–periphery dichotomy. The strong state tradition legacy can be traced back to the old Turkish idea of supreme law (*yasa*). According to Metin Heper, the Ottomans implemented the supreme law according to which the ruler should act in the context of equity and justice rather than his personal choice, calling it the notion of örf-i sultani.[74] The notion indicates that the government acts should be modeled on "measuring rods of necessity and reason and not on the personal whims of the sultans," which led to the emergence of a state-oriented tradition.[75] This was also called *adab*, a tradition developed as a consequence of the efforts "to identify government with the newly adopted norms formulated independently of civil societal elements."[76] The bureaucratic elites instilled these ideals and values through their organizational socialization.[77] This legacy was transmitted to the Republic, as Mustafa Kemal also undertook the mission of institutionalizing the *adab* tradition to an extent. Therefore, the strong state tradition was employed in the state-building process in the Republican period.[78]

Strongly related to the first legacy is the center–periphery discrepancy.[79] In the early part of the nineteenth century, the civilian bureaucratic elite took over much of the sultan's role, becoming an actor solely guided by state interests. This prevalence of the state bureaucracy led to the emergence of a center–periphery division along cultural lines. Those belonging to the ruling class were visibly distinct from the rest of the population relating to cultural orientation. Their engagement with the *adab* tradition led to their having an excellent understanding of the system of customs, behavior, and language. This complicated custom system included teachings of orthodox Islam and the use of a language infused with Arabic and Persian words. The "little culture" of the people was shaped by loyalty to various heterodox Islamic groups and the use of the Turkish dialect. From the nineteenth century onward, the cultural disparity between the elite and ordinary people intensified as the elite became increasingly familiar with Western culture.[80] The sociopolitical sphere continued to be shaped by the discrepancy between the more modern, Western-oriented, and secular "center" formed mainly by the state bureaucrats and the more traditional, religious "periphery" in the Turkish Republic.[81]

The Republican elite envisioned a modern public sphere willing to dismantle all the symbols and institutions not belonging to the framework of the state. Their project was to construct a modern country through strong state mechanisms and a one-party system, the Republican People's Party (RPP).[82] The elite's mindset—shaped by positivism— influenced their molding of a society compromised by the periphery to a great extent—approximately 88 percent of the population worked in agriculture between 1924 and 1939.[83] Although this perspective would be a stimulus for many Middle Eastern regimes such as Nasser's Arab socialism in Egypt or Shah Rıza Pehlevi's rule in Iran, the Turkish Westernization and modernization processes were more radical.

Here the relationship between the function of Islam and the elite was important. Prominent names of the Turkish elite were members of the Bektashi order and were influenced to a great extent by Western political ideas such as the French positivism, English liberalism, or the Italian revolutionary movement, namely the Mazzini and Garibaldi movements.[84] The Bektashi order and the West had a strong relationship thanks to the freemasonry orders both outside and inside the Empire, which relayed many Western political ideas to Bektashi adepts, who in turn acted as proponents of these ideas in the Empire. After the dismantlement of the Bektashi order, these elites—strongly influenced by Western enlightening ideas such as nationalism and liberalism—transformed their spiritual religion into a political one, namely nationalism and statism.[85]

In contrast to Gökhan Çetinsaya's argument claiming that the Kemalist establishment's perspective on nationalism found nationalism and Islam incompatible, Islam had always been a prominent implicit element of the Turkish national identity.[86] According to Retoulas, the Republican elite, Mustafa Kemal in particular, objected to setting up a sociopolitical sphere modeled on *Wahdat al-Wujud* to include all Muslims in the secular regime, and Mustafa Kemal tried to erase all the symbols and political divisions that could potentially distract from this vision.[87] His envisioning of laicism was quite different from its Western counterparts—the West removed religion from the public and state spheres, while in Turkey, this did not happen. Rather, religion was organized and controlled by the state—not to revive the former regime—particularly by the Directorate of Religious Affairs (*Diyanet İşleri Başkanlığı*), indicating the existence of Islam in the public sphere and making Islam a national religion. In other words, Islam was reinterpreted and set up by laicism and nationalism. Here, the elite's objective was to use Islam as a stimulus mechanism both in the political and public spheres to educate and protect the periphery, particularly from the heterodox version of Islam. The primary task of the elite was to create rational and secular citizens; therefore, the translation of the Koran or reciting *Ezan* (the call to worship) in Turkish were attempts to achieve this objective. In other words, the Republican elite tried to reform Islam.[88]

There were strongly organized heterodox Islamic groups, particularly the Naqshbandi order, which were highly powerful both in the social and state spheres in the last decades of the empire, particularly after the dismantlement of the Bektashi order, and did not approve of this interpretation of Islam and the centralization—as the nature of nation-state—of the Turkish state. This upheaval intensified after the abolishment of the Caliphate on March 3, 1924. There were many rebellions against the Ankara government organized by the Naqshbandi order, such as the Sheikh Said Rebellion (February–April 1925) and the Menemen Incident (April 23, 1930). These events led the Republican elite to suppress the Naqshbandi order and banits dervish lodges; as a result, the order went underground.[89] Bedri Gencer remarks that Bektashism transformed into a political religion as Kemalism and Nasserism took revenge from Naqshbandi in the Republican era, which was grasped as a secularism–Islam antagonism by the public.[90] Çetinsaya depicts the conditions of Islamist, particularly the Islamic orders:

> ... some of the Islamists went to Egypt, some stayed home for twenty-five years, and some accepted positions under the new regime, hoping that they could do some "good" for the Muslims, as far as circumstances allowed. There appeared only a secret Qur'an-teaching movement by conservative ulama, centered largely in remote areas of the Black Sea and Eastern Anatolia.[91]

However, the Republican elite did not carry out its policies unchallenged. The Islamic conservative deputies and bureaucrats, such as the prominent military general Kazım Karabekir and Trabzon MP Ali Şükrü, were opposed to secularization policies, particularly the abolishment of the Caliphate. In this regard, Islam became a catalyst that distinguished the center from the periphery because the counter-elites vision of nation-building was molded to a greater extent on Islam rather than Westernization and nationalism.[92]

However, the opposition was suppressed by the center until the Democrat Party's establishment in 1945. The Republican elite, particularly under Prime Minister İsmet İnönü, tried to build an organic society reliant on the state and were not interested in any political and societal diversity that could pose a threat to the unity of the state–society relationship. In this regard, any opposition such as liberal, socialist, or other movements independent from the state—such as the nationalist Turkish Hearts—was closed down. The elite wanted to set up a nation of nationalist, essentialist, statist, and moral citizens working for the common good without regarding men or women loyal to the state.[93] In fact, the Turkish type of Republicanism became a civil religion for the new nation-building process.

The Second Period (1950–2001)

The second period can be divided into two sub-periods, according to the role of Islamists in the nation-building process: 1950–1980 and 1980–2001. The Islamists became visible with the transformation of the single-party system to a multiparty one and began to strengthen their place in society and politics due to the threat of Communism. With the change from state-led development to a free-market economy, the Islamists became one of the leading actors of Turkish politics, but they acted within the context of the secular Kemalist establishment. The 1950–1980 period was marked by two important events: the transition from the one-party system to a multiparty one and Turkey's membership to the North Atlantic Treaty Organization (NATO).

The Republican elite were obliged to adopt the multiparty system. There were two reasons for it. First, the elite perceived that there was visible unrest in the society, particularly in rural areas. Second, parliamentary democracy became *sine qua non* in Europe, and the elite wanted the country to integrate into the international community.[94] The Democrat Party (DP) was established in 1946 mostly by agrarian elite representatives who were ex-members of the RPP, and the DP understood the language of the villagers and small merchants better than the RPP, which was made up by highly placed bureaucrats. The party came to power in 1950 and relatively liberalized the political environment for Sufi orders and other Islamists, namely Naqshbandi and the Nurcu Movement founded by Said Nursî. Although the DP's perceptions about the Sufi orders were not radically different from the Kemalist establishment's ones, the orders found it easy to establish themselves in social and political life. In other words, the center began to connect with the periphery and vice versa (i.e., the Sufi orders started to infiltrate the center).[95]

However, two important developments increased the power of Islamism in Turkey. First, Turkey's entry in NATO in 1952 reshaped the state-making process and led the state to increase the dosage of Islamism in its national identity. This was part of the US policy after World War II in that Washington encouraged setting up and organizing Islamic movements against radical secular nationalist regimes that could damage US interests in the region, such as Nasser's Arab Socialism and the Communist threat in other countries.[96] Second, Ankara received aide via the Marshall Plan, which helped with the urbanization of the country, creating a fertile ground for Islamists to establish themselves among immigrants from rural areas to urban centers.

The Cold War forced Turkey to enter NATO, which started the modernization of the military and, therefore, the reshaping of the state institutions. The global Communism threat forced the United States to influence the allied states by forming intelligence and security services that strengthened the central institutions in these countries. The Turkish intelligence services and many state- and NATO-led security organizations were set up during these years.[97] The military coup on May 27, 1960, which was neither prevented nor encouraged by the United States[98]—resulting in the banning of the DP and the execution of some of its prominent leaders, such as Adnan Menderes, Fatih Rüştü Zorlu, and Hasan Polatkan—reinforced this process.[99] The 1961 Constitution, enacted during the aftermath of the coup, strengthened the role of the military in both social and political spheres, and it empowered them to intervene in Turkish politics.

While the secular establishment was happy to be a part of the Western international community, the other side of the coin was the perception of Islamism as the return of Turkey's ancient regime. In fact, Turkey was part of the US-centered hegemonic system in Gramscian terms, in that many youth organizations, including Islamist youth organizations such as İlim Yayma Cemiyeti (the Society to Disseminate Science), *Türk Milli Talebe Birliği* (the National Turkish Students Association), and *Komunizmle Savaşanlar Derneği* (the Association for Combating Communism), would be set up as a result of Turkey's admission into the Western international security system.[100] There was no stigma attached to it because to be against the Communist bloc meant to be part of the West during the Cold War. This fact was a strong stimulus in regenerating the nation-building process. The Marxist leftwing began to be perceived as a security threat against the political system, so the social and political system excluded Marxist left-wing citizens, who were middle-class, patriotic youth who supported an independent Turkey in the international sphere—a youth phenomenon that started in the 1960s and continued into the 1970s.[101] The systematic suppression of the Marxist left by the state and state-led counter-organizations, such as the ultra-nationalist youth organization Grey Wolves, was similar to what was happening in European countries like Germany, Italy, Greece, and so on.

The second development was the immigration of the masses from rural to urban areas, especially big cities such as Istanbul, Ankara, and so on, due to the Marshall Plan, which aided the urbanization of the country. This new social development helped the Naqshbandi order, one of the strongest peripheral players predominant in Anatolia, as they were willing to integrate themselves into the society. The reason for that was that the order cohabited peacefully with the Republican regime, which led to its secularization.[102]

The order's view of nation-building was not much different from the secular establishment's, except for its demand to increase the role of Islam and confine the Western culture penetration into the social life.[103] This stemmed from the nature of the Kemalist regime, which allowed them to integrate into the system. Hence, Naqshbandi's modern ideological stance started with the Gümüşhanevi branch, led by Mehmet Zaid Kotku, who praised modernity and glorified the technological power of the West, thus perceiving the state in the context of constitutional legitimacy. Unlike Salafism, the order had never perceived the state as an absolute evil; rather, it merged nationalism with Islamic values.[104] During these years, the Islamists began to infiltrate the state and political spheres via right-wing parties, who perceived them as wielding great voting power and gave them many incentives to survive in the political and socioeconomic spheres.

The Sufi orders created their own societies and borrowed the rationality, free-market economy, and utilitarianism principles. This was solidified with the emergence of Islamist-oriented businessmen and the setting up of the first Islamist political party—the National Salvation Party (NSP)—by Necmettin Erbakan in the 1970s, who was a member of the Naqshbandi order.[105] This would be followed by another Naqshbandi, Turgut Özal, who founded the Motherland Party in the 1980s, and Tayyip Erdoğan, with his Justice and Development Party (JDP). These all created a new type of Islamist who tried to synthesize Islam, nationalism, and modernity, such as Neci Fazıl Kısakürek, Nurettin Topçu, and so on.

The grassroots-level integration of Islamists was derived from the security concerns of the state and NATO. This would be accomplished to a great extent by the United States's anti-Communism agenda implemented between the 1950s and 1970s, with the help of the anti-Marxism alliance of NATO, Saudi money, Turkish conglomerates, and the state.[106] Another alliance stemmed from counter-terrorism needs—the state needed paramilitary organizations at the grassroots level. This was the alliance against the Marxist left between Islamists and ultra-nationalists based on the Turkish-Islamic synthesis that was believed to be the shortcut to the integration into the state.[107]

As a matter of fact, the founding fathers of the modern grassroots Turkish–Islamic synthesis were Naqshbandi order members, such as Seyyid Abdülhakim Arvasi (1865–1943) and Seyyid Ahmet Arvasi (1932–1988), and this new system was a hybrid interpretation of Kemalism, nationalism, and Islamism.[108] For example, Ahmet Arvasi's ideas were important in the mobilization of the ultra-nationalist youth. Arvasi considered that the Turks had the mission of defending the cause of Islam on Earth. This perspective was the motive for the ultra-nationalist right wing and Islamists to fight against Marxism.

In this regard, the new nation-building process was established by excluding Marxists, socialist Alavi, Kurdish nationalists, and Kurdish socialists from the political and social spheres, and it revitalized a new right, namely the Turkish–Islam synthesis by bringing together the Naqshbandi and Nurcu orders with NATO.[109]

On the other hand, the state directly supported a group of nationalist-conservative intellectuals, such as İbrahim Kafesoğlu and Nevzat Yalçıntaş, who called themselves "The Heart of the Enlightened" (*Aydınlar Ocağı*). The group was founded in 1969 to spread the Turkish–Islamic synthesis. Some of its members, such as Nevzat Yalçıntaş, had connections with the Naqshbandi order. According to Aydınlar Ocağı, Islam is more important than Turkish identity, but without the Turks and the Turkish culture, Islam can never exist.[110] However, Aydınlar Ocağı—and to a great extent, Turkish Islamists—and the Kemalist secular establishment, namely the military and the circles close to them, shared a common intellectual heritage. According to Duran and Aydın, Islamists have never entirely rejected the West, and Kemalists have never been a copycat of the West either. For the authors, both Kemalism and Islamism belonged to the same epistemological universe, molding themselves on West/East dichotomy and recognizing the superiority of the West but reinterpreting elements of Western-oriented concepts and values according to their own cultural and national framework.[111] It is not wrong to point out that Aydınlar Ocağı and the Turkish Islamists came from the similar thought heritage of the Young Ottomans. Both the secular establishment and the Islamic episteme were shaped by the question of how they would avoid stigmatization from the international community and, particularly for Islamists, how they could go back to the golden age of the past.

With this relative exception, the state and these intellectuals were united against Communism in the protection of the state security. Aydınlar Ocağı became a mediator for the state and a ground where nationalists, Islamists, and nationalist-conservative intellectuals/parties met. It also reinforced the content of the ideology of the state, which did not have powerful, organic intellectuals and a good discourse to fight Communism.[112] These developments shifted the center towards the demands of the periphery, and the center began to be hybridized, at least in sociopolitical terms.

This process culminated with the January 24, 1980 coup d'état, whose alleged objective was to carry out economic decisions that can shortly be summarized as the recipe for transitioning Turkey's economic structure from state-led development to a free market economy.[113] Although the military carried out the coup to restore Kemalism, the new state ideology was shaped on Aydınlar Ocağı's ideas (i.e., the Turkish–Islamic synthesis). The coup was encouraged by the United States, and the plotters tried to preserve Turkey's place in the Western community by changing the content of the state ideology from secular Kemalism to Kemalism patterned on the Turkish–Islamic synthesis to control the spread of Communism and secular, radical Turkish nationalism in the society.[114] The coup set to eliminate all the obstacles, namely the left wing and the nationalists, by imprisoning or executing them.[115] Hence, it tried to achieve a nation-building process by individuals loyal to the state and by inculcating national and Islamic values. The leader of the Grey Wolves, Alparslan Türkeş, who was imprisoned during the 1980 coup d'état, expressed this situation succinctly: "We are in prison, but our ideas are in power [in the political and social sphere]."[116] Although the secular establishment began to adopt the values of the Turkish–Islamic synthesis, the aim of the coup was to dismantle all the ideological, ethnic, and religious diversity, such as the Alevi movement, ultra-Turkish nationalists, Kurdish nationalists, and Islamists opposed to the free-market economy, which could pose a threat to the unity of the country and the free-market economy.

The 1980 military intervention was aimed at restoring the center. The state elite wanted to establish the regime on the premise of the Turkish–Islamic synthesis. As a result of ideological convergence, religious schools and universities flourished, and religious lessons became compulsory in primary and secondary schools. The state ideology, Kemalism, blended with the Turkish–Islamic synthesis.[117] Islamists and Sunni sects found their place in this new environment. The state elite's objective in imposing Islam was to support concepts such as civilization, positivism, and secularism as a basis for the regime's secular and modernizing goals through Islam.[118] The transition from a military to a civilian regime was also successful from the viewpoint of the state elite in that the Motherland Party became successful in adopting the ideological movements by integrating the Islamists into the system. In other words, the party was an important player that helped close the gap between the center and the periphery. Although the right-wing parties also helped to achieve this, the Motherland Party was unique because it was a party in power that was set up by a Naqshbandi member, Turgut Özal.[119]

Although the 1982 Constitution reinforced the place of the military in the political and social systems and strengthened the condition for a free-market economy to preserve the country's place within the international community, Turkey's geopolitical location began to be questioned by the West, and Turkey was less perceived as a Western state compared to during the Cold War period. Turkey again began to be stigmatized by the West, and the country's entry into the European Union (EU) was blocked. The independence of Turkish Republics from the USSR gave Turkey a chance to relocate itself on the international stage as a bridge between Europe (the EU) and central Asia. This view strengthened the Turkish–Islamic identity of the state, referred to as Neo-Ottomanism by Hakan Yavuz, and led to the opening of schools in Central Asia and all over the world by Sufi orders, particularly the Gülen community, with, of course, the help of the United States.[120]

Moreover, Sufi orders began to organize themselves within the state and society, for example, Fethullah Gülen, a Nurcu sect, or Naqshbandi sects, such as Işıkcılar, Süleymancılar, İskenderpaşa, and so on. At the same time, they began to operate both in civil society and the economic sphere so that they became prominent players on the political scene by means of their economic and social power. Many right- and left-wing politicians helped these groups in their integration into the state and economic spheres.

It should be remarked that while some state sectors perceived Islamism as a threat to the secular, Westernized nature of the state, they employed Islamists on the grounds of their loyalty to the state. This reinforced the Islamists' organizational power both in civil society and the economic sphere. They set up their businessmen association (*MÜSİAD*) to compete against the secular establishment's business association (TÜSİAD). Hence, they had strong transnational connections to put pressure on the secular elite, which was not lost on the Islamist political factions. The Islamists split from the Motherland Party and set up their own Islamic parties—the Welfare Party (*Refah Partisi*) and the Virtue Party (*Saadet Partisi*)—founded by Naqshbandi members such as Necmettin Erbakan, Recai Kutan, and so on. These parties played a great role in the political sphere due to their social power and transnational connections, particularly with Saudi Arabia. On the other hand, the West, namely the United States and some other Western countries, implicitly supported the Islamist parties to balance the power between the secular establishment and Islamists.[121] The Nur movement, particularly the Gülen community, stayed out of politics and infiltrated the bureaucratic apparatus with the assistance of the international community and the West-oriented state elite.[122] The reason for the international community's playing this balancing game was twofold. First, they perceived the Islamists' strong mobilization potential; therefore, foreseeing their success in the future, the Western governments wanted to ally themselves with the winner in order to shape Turkey's policies. Second, the West used the Islamists against the secular establishment when their relationship with that establishment was blocked.

Thus, the nation-building process in Turkey was mainly based on the Turkish–Islamic synthesis. There were many common grounds between central-right, nationalist, and Islamist parties, namely the Turkish–Islamic synthesis. However, the Islamists were not the most prominent player in the system, which was still guarded by the secular modernist bureaucrats and politicians in the name of the guardianship of Kemalism and to keep the country in the Western international sphere.

However, the February 27, 1997 coup against the Islamists[123] and the 2001 economic crisis led to the collapse of the central political system and brought in a new neo-Islamist party, the Justice and Development Party (JDP), a coalition between Naqshbandi politicians and the Gülen movement. The party's leaders, Recep Tayyip Erdoğan, Abdullah Gül, and Bülent Arınç, had Naqshbandi origins and came to power in 2002 in coalition with the Gülen movement, being backed by the international community to dismantle the secular establishment's bureaucratic power.

The Third Period (2001–present)

In the third period, the Islamists penetrated and captured the center. In terms of the nation-building process, this period can be divided into two sub-periods: 2002–2011, marked by the JDP, liberals, and the Gülen community's alliance to dismantle the secular establishment's bureaucratic power and to integrate the country into the neoliberalism and international order; and 2011–present, marked by the Arab Spring, a change in alliances, a slowdown in the process of integration into the international society, and a clearer demarcation of Turkish national identity.

In the first sub-period, the JDP's foreign policy influenced the domestic politics directly. The party's effort to adapt to the EU legislation regarding human rights, democracy, and so on and to integrate the country into international alliances made the party visibly more powerful against the secular establishment. The party's neo-Ottoman foreign policy aiming at "zero problems" with its neighbors and surrounding regions made the domestic policies more flexible.[124] Unlike the secular establishment's Westernized and strict secular-oriented policies, the JDP elite supported the integration into the international order by preserving an authentic identity of the country,[125] namely by Muslim nationalism. Jenny White describes it as "distinctly Turkish post-Imperial sensibility" that the Islamic and Ottoman past was romanticized and used as a soft power tool in foreign policy and a tool for demarcating the conservative electorates.[126]

While this post-imperial sensibility required the integration of authoritarian Middle Eastern states into the international order by using Turkey's strategic and historical depth, this policy entailed the Islamization of the Turkish identity—increasing the Sunni- Hanafi identity—to be the center of the Middle East. Relating to domestic politics, the new intellectuals of the party rewrote a fictive Ottoman history that reinforced the legitimization of the current party's Turkish–Ottoman–Islamic position.[127] By means of these policies, the JDP elite and its circles believed that neo-Ottomanism would take Turkey to the high ranks of global hierarchy.

In this vein, the party loosened ties with the French type of secularism that opened the space to Sufi orders and their conservative base and softened its nationalism viewpoint. For this reason, the party allied itself with the classical "others" of the Turkish social system to extend the coalition against the secular establishment and strengthen the support of the international community. The party made efforts to establish peace with the Alavis, Kurds, and minorities such as Armenians, Greeks, and so on, on the basis of religious brother and sisterhood.

Although the party followed the central-right parties' definition of the nation, the JDP prioritized Islam in the political and social contract rather than nationalism. The JDP marked the secular establishment, the left wing, and the Marxist Alavi and Kurds as "others" for the new nation-building. The JDP elite believed that they should homogenize the periphery on the grounds of religion, albeit many dichotomies existed in the periphery not directly relating with Islam. The party tried to deconstruct the French type of secularism and altered laws to control the bureaucracy. They did this by implementing major changes in the economy and by changing the amendments to the Constitution to reorganize the civil service—which was formed to a great extent by Islamic conservatives and Sufi members.

The second sub-period began with the Arab Spring. Turkey's transformative role in the Arab Spring, particularly in the Syrian regime change, and the two historical trials against the military—"Balyoz" and "Sledgehammer"—proved too much for the JDP and its allies. Although these policies and trials would have pushed Turkey toward the center of the world, the state could not carry the weight of the cases for the liberal Islamists that this situation stopped Ankara's Syrian politics. In addition, the alliance of the JDP, liberals, and the Gülen movement floundered during the Arab Spring.[128]

In the second sub-period, Turkey found a new foreign policy role—as a buffer state. According to E. Fuat Keyman, the buffer-state role of the country was not new; it was a continuation of Turkey's cardinal foreign policy identity and behavior in the Cold War era.[129] The present role of Turkey as a buffer state is also similar to the Cold War in that it is patterned on security-driven and controlling ideas. More specifically, Ankara's role is "(1) to contain refugees in Turkey; (2) to contain the ISIL problem in the MENA region, mainly in Syria and Iraq; and (3) to balance Iran's regional hegemonic aspirations."[130]

With the change in foreign policy, the JDP began to clash with its ex-allies in the bureaucratic, economic, and political spheres. The police and the judiciary that were affiliated with the Gülen movement tried to topple Prime Minister Erdoğan from power by means of corruption allegations on December 17–25, 2013. This attempt was perceived as a coup both in the social and state spheres, triggering the state's fight against the Gülen movement. The final attempt of the Gülen movement was the July 15, 2016 coup, which resulted in 250 deaths, and it made the movement a security threat and framed it as a FETÖ terror organization. As a result, JDP changed its partners and allied itself with nationalists and members of the secular Kemalist establishment.

If the previous alliance could be defined as moderate Islamism, the new nation-building process was shaped by a Muslim identity–nationalism synthesis in which the latter principle was as important as the first one. The concept represents the right-wing electorate's perspective, which represents the majority of the Turkish population. In fact, Muslim nationalism is a form of majority nationalism that patterns itself on dominant majorities' having a numerical advantage and enjoying the control of the state. Unlike minority nationalism, Muslim nationalism's objective as majority nationalism is to protect the already-achieved state sovereignty, preserve the majority group's national culture, and defend the major ethnic civilian populations from terrorism.[131]

Hence, the JDP's and Kemalists' viewpoints on security were largely similar, which shaped the nation-building process in this period: the external threat paradigm, a belief in the effectiveness of social engineering, suspicion of foreigners irrespective of their identity, and perceiving an internal/external enemy as opposing state policies. In other words, any identity that is considered a threat can be perceived as a security threat (for example, Kurdish nationalists, Islamic cults and orders opposing the government, Marxists, etc.). Unlike the previous sub-period, the JDP defined its actions on the grounds of struggle and distinction between friend and foe, rather than making peace with foes.

CONCLUSION

The nation-building process of non-European empires such as the Ottoman Empire, Russia, and Japan was painful. The transformation from an empire to a nation-state stemmed from their defeat, which excluded them from the top segments of the global hierarchy and forced them to adopt modern, Western standards that were not entirely compatible with their political and social culture. Although this created trauma and stigma in these countries, they adopted the standards of modernity to protect their place in the hierarchy. Hence, the elites of these countries emerging from state-led development and internalized enlightenment's cultural values adopted the principles of liberalism and democratization to integrate the countries into the international order. However, this led to the emergence of new middle classes and antagonism towards each other in the society.

The elites in the Ottoman Empire began to ask the epistemological and ontological question of how the Ottoman Empire could return to its golden age of the sixteenth century. The continuous defeats in the seventeenth and eighteenth centuries, coupled with the independence of non-Muslim subjects, deepened this problem. In addition, the Ottoman Empire's closer integration into the international community deepened the feeling of stigmatization of the country. This made Muslims prominent actors on the imperial stage since the nineteenth century, so that Islam became the sole cement that kept the Empire together, notwithstanding the tactical Ottoman views of the elites. Besides, the Sufi orders had always been a part of the political and social spheres so that the sultans tried to use them to control these spheres. The Tanzimat period was a solid example of the process of building a nation on the ideological patterns of Ottomanism and the incorporation of modern Western ideas to integrate all the non-Muslim subjects into the Empire. However, this process failed, as it did not satisfy both Muslims and non-Muslims of the Empire.

The ideology of Islamism was first founded in the Empire by the "New Ottomans" reformists in Turkish-speaking regions as a reaction to the Tanzimat reforms. Although the New Ottomans had strong connections with Europe and adopted Western values, they supported Islamism and tried to mingle Islamism with Western values. Their perspective was to create a nation patterned on Islam. On the other hand, the dismantlement of different powers such as the Bektashi order by Sultan Mahmud led to a centralization and culmination of the power of Islamism in the Empire. The politics of Islamism was continued by Sultan Abdülhamid II as a state project, but his authoritarian policies and the defeat of the Ottomans by the Russians led to his losing the throne.

The Committee of Union and Progress established in 1889 held power between 1908 and 1918 and continued Islamist policies, but the independence of Albania changed their mindset regarding nationalism and the nation-state. They were strongly influenced by European movements and their strong connections with European freemasonry lodges. World War I gave them a chance to set up the Turkish nation-state. Mustafa Kemal, a leader of the War of Independence, created the Turkish modern state in 1923.

The founders of the Turkish state wanted a strong modernization and transformed the country from an empire to a nation-state. They proposed to overcome stigmatization from the international community by incorporating Western modernity, albeit the imperialist face of the West. They envisioned creating modern, rational, essentialist, and nationalist individuals. However, these policies fell short from being embraced by the majority of the population, as almost 90 percent lived in rural areas.

The Turkish nation-state inherited the center–periphery relationship from the Ottoman Empire and chose to suppress the peripheral players that could pose a threat to the center, such as the Naqshbandi and Nur orders. However, the orders adapted themselves to democracy and the nation-state and have played an active role in the social and political spheres since the 1950s. The Naqshbandi order transformed itself from a religious order to a party—the Welfare Party—and became the voice of those who migrated from rural areas to the cities. They demanded to be recognized in the political sphere.

The integration of religious groups into the political system intensified after the 1980 coup d'état. Turgut Özal, a member of the Naqshbandi order and an ex-bureaucrat of the World Bank, signified a successful profile of hybridization of the West and the East. While he liberalized and integrated the economy into the global neoliberalism, he also employed a great number of members from the Naqshbandi and Nur movements. He liberalized the society and economy, which left room for Islamists to find their own place in these spheres. On the other hand, he continued to mold the nation-building process on the Islamization and Turkification of the Turkish national identity.

While the police and the judiciary perceived Islamism as a treat to the unity of the country, NATO and the Western-oriented elites in Turkey used Islamism to strengthen the state against the secular establishment in Gramscian terms. This fact intensified the antagonism between the center and the periphery in the country. While the peripherization of the state and the nation-building process was strongly visible, the center and the statist middle class tried to control the Islamist politics. From Özal onwards, the dominance of the right wing, particularly Islamists, accelerated the Islamization and Turkification of the nation-building process and the integration into the global neoliberal system.

The JDP's coming to power in 2002 was heralded as a new era in which Islamism, until then a secondary player, became the main actor on the Turkish political stage. The JDP's alliance with the Gülen movement and the liberals pushed the country towards a liberal or moderate Islamism that excluded the secular establishment, the left wing, and the Kurdish nationalists. Islam was for the first time the strongest agent of the nation-building process. However, the Arab Spring, particularly the war in Syria and Turkey's intervention into the conflict, overloaded Turkey's capacity and deteriorated the alliance between the JDP, the Gülen movement, and the liberals. The nation-building process based on moderate Islamism ended. The JDP established a new alliance with nationalists and, to an extent, the secular establishment against the pro-West elites—both secular and Islamists—and made foreign policies more nation-state–oriented; namely, it followed the Kemalist foreign policy. In this respect, this new coalition based the nation-building process on the principle of majority (i.e., Muslim nationalism).

Hence, the JDP's and Kemalists' viewpoints on security were largely similar, which shaped the nation-building process in this period: the external threat paradigm, a belief in the effectiveness of social engineering, suspicion of foreigners irrespective of their identity, and perceiving an internal/external enemy as opposing state policies.

NOTES

1. See Sibel Bozdoğan and Reşat Kasaba, *Rethinking Modernity and National Identity in Turkey* (Seattle and London:University of Washington Press, 1997).

2. See M. H. Yavuz and M. R. Khan, "Turkey's Fault Lines and the Crisis of Kemalism" *Current History* 99, no. 633 (2000), 33–38.

3. See Jenny B.White, *Islamist Mobilization in Turkey: A Study in Vernacular Politics* (Seattle:University of Washington Press, 2002).

4. Niall Bond, *Understanding Ferdinand Tönnies's 'Community and Society'* (Zürich-Berlin: Lit, 2013).

5. Jochen Hippler, *Ulus İnşası* (İstanbul:Versus, 2007), 11..

6. Ibid.

7. Peter Gourevitch, "The Second Image Reversed: The International Sources of Domestic Politics," *International Organization* 32, no.4 (1978): 881–912.

8. İbid, 883.

9. İbid.

10. Samuel P. Huntington, "The Clash of Civilizations," *Foreign Affairs* 72, no.3 (Summer 1993): 22–49.

11. Samuel P. Huntington, *The Clash of Civilizations and the Remaking of World Order* (New York, London, Toronto, and Sydney: Simon & Schuster, 1996): 21.

12. Ayşe Zarakol, "Revisiting Second Image Reversed: Lessons from Turkey and Thailand," *International Studies Quarterly* 57, no. 1 (2013): 151.

13. İbid.

14. Ayşe Zarakol, *After Defeat:How the East Learned to Live with the West* (Cambridge: University of Cambridge Press, 2011).

15. İbid., 3–59.

16. Partha Chatterjee, *Nationalist Thought and the Colonial World: A Derviative Discourse* (Delhi: Zed Books, 1986), 38.

17. Zarakol, *After Defeat,* 49–71.

18. İbid., 10.

19. Zarakol, "Revisiting Second Image."

20. İbid.

21. Robinson, William I., "Gramsci and Globalisation:From Nation-State to Transnational Hegemony," *Critical Review of International Social and Political Philosophy* 8, no. 4 (2005): 2.

22. İbid.

23. "Osmanlı'da Gerilemeyi İlk Bürokratlar Gördü," in *Karar Gazatesi*, February 23, 2018, 11.

24. Cited in Ibid.

25. İbid.

26. İbid.

27. İbid.

28. İbid.

29. İbid.

30. İbid.; see Gültekin Yıldız, *Osmanlı Askeri Tarihi* (İstanbul: Timaş Yayınları, 2017).

31. The concept of "millet" encompasses various ethnic and ethno-religious communities of the Ottoman Empire bounding the Empire.

32. Barış Ünlü, *Türklük Sözleşmesi* (Dipnot Yayınları: Ankara, 2018), 84–85.

33. Roderic H. Davison, "Turkish Attitudes Concerning Christian–Muslim Equality in the Nineteenth Century," *The American Historical Review* 59, no. 4 (1954): 847.

34. İbid.

35. Ünlü, *Türklük,* 86–88.

36. İbid.

37. Şerif Mardin, *Türkiye, İslam ve Sekülarizm* (İstanbul: İletişim Yayınları, 2011), 52–54.

38. Ünlü, *Türklük,* 88; "Osmanlı'da Gerilemeyi."

39. Ünlü, *Türklük,* 88.

40. Halil İnalcık, *Osmanlı Tarihinde İslamiyet ve Devlet* (İstanbul: İşbankası Yayınları, 2016), 144.

41. Ünlü, *Türklük,* 90–91.

42. İbid., 91–92.

43. Erik Jan Zürcher, *Modernleşen Türkiye'nin Tarihi* (İstanbul: İletişim Yayınları, 1995), 120.

44. Selim Deringil, *Simgeden Millete* (İstanbul: İletişim Yayınları, 2007), 30.

45. Ünlü, *Türklük,* 97.

46. Zürcher, *Modernleşen Türkiye'nin,* 133–34.

47. Ünlü, *Türklük,* 104–5.

48. İbid., 107.

49. İbid., 121.

50. Ozan Arslan and Çınar Özen, "The Rebirth Of The Ottoman Committee Of Union And Progress In Macedonia through The Italian Freemasonry," *Oriente Moderno, Nuova Serie* 24, no. 1 (2005): 93–115.

51. Murat Bardakçı, "Fatih'in yaktığı Matrix Tarikatı," *Sabah,* March 31, 2007.

52. Şerif Mardin, *Türkiye'de Din ve Siyaset* (İstanbul: İletişim Yayınları, 2004), 13–14.

53. Butrus Abu-Manneh, "The Naqshbandiyya-Mujaddidiyya in the Ottoman Lands in the Early 19th Century," *Die Welt des Islams* 22 (1984): 1–36.

54. *Masonlar Org.* https://masonlar.org/masonlar_forum/index.php?topic=3538.0, accessed February 15, 2018.

55. For example, Sufi Sheikh Huseyin Şerafeddin, who was born in 1872, graduated from mekteb-i Mülkiye-i Şahane, and worked for the Ministry of Justice, could speak Turkish, French, Greek, and Arabic.

56. Brian Silverstein, "Sufism and Govermentality in the Late Ottoman Empire," *Comparative Studies of South Asia, Africa and the Middle East* 29, no. 2 (2009): 173–76.

57. Martin Van Bruinessen, "Mevlana Halid:Bir Sünni Milliyetçisi," *Kürt Tarihi* no. 30 (2017): 12–13.

58. In the nineteenth century, the Kadiri order was the most widespread order, and leadership was passed down through the leading family. The Nakshbendi democratized Sufi orders by lifting the requisite of genealogy in the leadership, which made them the largest and widespread Sufi group in the Empire.

59. Bruinessen, "Mevlana Halid," 12–13.

60. Silverstein, "Sufism," 171–85.

61. Hakan Yavuz, *Modernleşen Müslümanlar:Nurcular, Nakşiler, Milli Görüş ve AK Parti* (İstanbul: Kitap Yayınevi, 2005): 186–88.

62. The doctrine of *Wahdat al-Wujud* asserts that "everything that exists can only exist because it is an aspect of Divine Reality, hence an aspect of Divine Unity itself. ... God remains supremely transcendent, even though everything which arises and exists resembles him (*tashbih*). He resembles nothing but himself" (Masood Steven " *Wahdat Al-Wujud*: A Fundemental Doctrine in Sufism," http://www.stevenmasood.org/article/wahdat-al-wujud-fundamental-doctrine-sufism, accessed February 2, 2018).

63. Christos Retoulas "Laiklik, Vahdet-i Vücud felsefesiyle şekillendi," *Akşam,* January 29, 2013, accessed March 14, 2018.

64. Islamic jurisprudence.

65. Mardin, *Türkiye'de İslam,* 21–22; Recep Şentürk, "Fıkıh ve Sosyal Bilimler Arasında Son Dönem Osmanlı Aydını," *İslam Araştırmalar Dergisi* no. 4 (2000): 152–53.

66. Ali Suavi was pro-British Empire, and his wife was British.

67. Şentürk, "Fıkıh," 153.

68. Yusuf Akçura, Üç Tarz-ı Siyaset (İstanbul: Andaç Kitabevi, 2015), 21.

69. These two prominent thinkers thought the Turks had gained their independence and political freedom by means of Islam. Moreover, they created a community based on the ideals of a cosmopolis (*nizam-ı alem*), which made Turks and Islam synonymous with each other. Namık Kemal's perception of Islam as a civilization or a cosmopolis representing liberty and freedom was an ideal for Mustafa Kemal. But, in reality, he followed Ziya Gökalp's thought of the Turkish nation-state nationalism. Gökalp indeed supported Pan-Turkism, but he believed that it was impossible to set up Pan-Turkism in the era of nation-states. See Bedri Gencer, İslam'da Modernleşme (Ankara: DoğuBatı Yayınları, 2014).

70. Mardin, *Türkiye'de İslam,* 54–55.

71. S. Sayyid, *Fundementalizm Korkusu* (Ankara: Vadi Yayınları, 2000), 84.

72. İbid.

73. Bernard Lewis, *The Emergence of Modern Turkey,* (Newyork-Glosgow:University of Oxford Press, 2001),474.

74. Metin Heper, "The Strong State as a Problem for the Consolidation of Democracy," *Comparative Political Studies* 25, no. 2 (1992): 174.

75. İbid.

76. İbid.

77. İbid.

78. İbid., 175.

79. Şerif Mardin, "Center-Periphery Relations: A Key To Turkish Politcs," *Dedalus* 102, no. 1 (1973): 169–90.

80. Metin Heper, "The Ottoman Legacy and Turkish Politics," *Journal of International Affairs* 54, no. 1 (2000): 65–67.

81. Paul Kubicek, "The European Union and Political Cleavages in Turkey," *Insight Turkey* 11, no. 3 (2009): 110.

82. Mehmet Kaya, "Turkey's Vain Struggle to Create a Homogeneous Nation," *Middle East Policy* 25, no. 2 (2018): 124.

83. Yunus Kaya, "Türkiye Ekonomisinin Dönüşümleri Işığında Tabakalaşma," in *Türkiye'de Toplumsal Değişim,* eds.Lütfi Sunar(Ankara:Nobel Yayınevi), 160.

84. Veronica Musardo, *Secret Connections in Constantinopole* (Istanbul: Limra Yayınevi, 2015).

85. Thierry Zarcone, İslam'da Sır ve Gizli Cemiyetler (İstanbul: Kabalcı Yayınevi, 2011).

86. Gökhan Çetinsaya, "Rethinking Nationalism and Islam: Some Preliminary Notes on the Roots of "Turkish-Islamic Synthesis" in Modern Turkish Politcal Thought," *Muslim World* 89, no. 3–4 (1999): 363.

87. Retoulas "Laiklik, Vahdet-i Vücud."

88. İbid.

89. Hulusi Şentürk, *Türkiye'de İslami Oluşumlar ve Siyaset:* İslamcılık (İstabul: Çıra Yayınevi, 2011), 144–49.

90. Gencer, İslam'da Modernleşme, 798.

91. Çetinsaya, "Rethinking Nationalism," 364.

92. Zürcher, *Modernleşen Türkiye'nin.*

93. İbid.

94. Zürcher, *Modernleşen Türkiye'nin*, 302.

95. Şentürk, *Türkiye'de İslami*, 216.

96. Soner Yalçın, "Bilerek Yanıltıyorlar," *Sözcü*, November 29, 2017: https://www.sozcu.com.tr/2017/yazarlar/soner-yalcin/bilerek-yaniltiyorlar-2109651/, accessed February 12, 2018). The Nazis set up Muslim troops, known as *Ost-Bataillone*, in the Middle East and Balkans against the Western alliance in World War II. The architects of this project were not only Germans, but also prominent Muslim elites, such as Jerulaslam Mufti Hacı Emin el-Hüseyin. The center of this formation was the founder, Ihvan-i Muslim Hasan el-Benna. After World War II, the United States took over these organizations and used them against Communism and radical secular nation-states in the Middle East, risking the US and Western interests in the region. Ibid.; See Enver Altaylı and Ruzi Nazar, *CIA'nın Türk Casusu* (Istanbul: Doğankitap, 2013), 83–437.

97. "Abdülhamid'den Hakan Fidan'a MİT'in tarihi," *Haber7.com*, March 14, 2014, http://www.haber7.com/guncel/haber/1137120-abdulhamidden-hakan-fidana-mitin-tarihi, accessed April 14, 2018.

98. See Christopher Gunn, "The 1960 Coup in Turkey: A U.S. Intelligence Failure or a Successful 'Intervention,'" *Journal of Cold War Studies* 17, no. 2 (2015): 103–39.

99. "15 Temmuz Darbe Girişimi Darbeler ve ABD," *Aljazeera Turk,* http://www.aljazeera.com.tr/haber/darbeler-ve-abd, accessed March 15, 2018.

100. Ertuğrul Meşe, *Komünizmle Mücadele Dernekleri* (İstanbul: İletişim Yayınları, 2016).

101. See Murat Belge, "Türkiye'de Sosyalizm Tarihinin Ana Çizgileri," in *Modern Türkiye'de Siyasi Düşünce:Sol*, edited by Murat Gültekingil (İstanbul: İletişim Yayınları), 19–49.

102. Şentürk, *Türkiye'de İslami*, 505–7.

103. Burhanettin Duran and Cemal Aydın, "Competing Occidentalisms of Modern Islamist Thought: Necip Fazıl Kısakürek and Nurettin Topçu on Christianity, the West and Modernity," *Muslim World* 103, no. 4 (2013): 479–500.

104. Şerif Mardin, "Operasyonel Kodlarda Süreklilik, Kırılma ve Yeniden İnşa: Dün ve Bugün Türk İslami İstisnacılığı," *Doğu Batı* 31, no. 8 (2005): 48–49.

105. Rasim Özgür Dönmez, "Adalet ve Kalkınma Partisi: İslamcılıktan Post Kemalist Bir Anlatıya Doğru," *Doğu Batı* 14, no. 58 (2011): 42–43

106. Washington began to support Islamists in the Middle East against Communism. The project was officially initiated by Zibigniew Brezinski, the national security advisor of the United States in Afghanistan against the USSR. The mujahid were supported against Moscow. See Oliver Roy, *Siyasal İslamın İflası* (İstanbul: Metis Yayınları, 1994); and Oliver Roy, *Küreselleşen İslam* (İstanbul: Metis Yayınları, 2016).

107. Serdar Akinan, *Buzdağı* (İstanbul: Kırmızı Kedi Yayınevi, 2017), 90–106.

108. Duran and Aydın, "Competing Occidentalisms," 479–500.

109. See Akinan, *Buzdağı,* 112–40; See Soner Yalçın, "Oyun Masası," *Sözcü,* February 13, 2015.

110. Ettiene Copeaux, *Turk Tarih Tezinden Turk Islam Sentezine* (Istanbul: Tarih Vakfi Yurt Yayinlari, 1998), 55–57.

111. See Duran and Cemal Aydın, "Competing Occidentalisms."

112. Fatih Yaşlı, "12 Eylül 37 yıldır sürüyor," *Birgün,* September 13, 2017. https://www.birgun.net/haber-detay/12-eylul-37-yildir-suruyor-179122.html, accessed June 15, 2018.

113. See Ebru Deniz Ozan, *Gülme Sırası Bizde* (İstanbul: Metis Yayınları, 2012).

114. See Mehmet Akif Okur, "Türkiye-ABD İlişkilerinin 12 Eylül Kavşağı: Amerikan Belgeleri Darbe Hakkında Ne Anlatıyor," *Uluslararası Hukuk ve Politika* 10, no. 40 (2014): 67–93; "ABD Gizli Diplomatik Belgelerinde 12 Eylül Darbesi: 'Askeri Liderleri İyi Tanıyoruz, Endişelenmek İçin Neden Yok'," *BBC Türkçe,* September 12, 2018, https://www.bbc.com/turkce/haberler-dunya-45486144 (Acessed September 14, 2018).

115. See Zürcher, *Modernleşen,* 407–8.

116. "Alparslan Türkeş 12 Eylül'le helalleşmiş!" *Evrensel,* April 30, 2012, https://www.evrensel.net/haber/28102/alparslan-turkes-12-eylulle-helallesmis, accessed January 10, 2018.

117. Gunter Seufert, "Milliyetci Soylemlerin Sivil Toplum Uzerindeki Etkisi (The Effects of Nationalist Discourses on Civil Society)," in *Turkiye'de Sivil Toplum ve Milliyetcilik (Civil Society and Nationalism in Turkey),* (Istanbul: Iletisim Yayinlari, 2001), 30.

118. Umit Cizre Sakallioglu, "Parameters and Strategies of Islam-State Interaction in Republican Turkey," *Internal Journal of Middle East Studies* 28, no. 2 (May 1996): 246.

119. See Rasim Özgür Dönmez, "Nationalisms in Turkey: Political Violence and Identity," *Ethnopolitcs* 6, no. 1 (2007): 43–65.

120. Hakan Yavuz, "Turkish Identity and Foreign Policy in Flux: The Rise of Neo–Ottomanism," *Critique: Critical Middle Eastern Studies* 7, no. 2 (2007): 19–41.

121. See Akinan, *Buzdağı,* 98–115.

122. See "Bedrettin Dalan'dan kritik Gülen ve Özal İddiası," İnternet Haber, May 18, 2015, http://www.internethaber.com/bedrettin-dalandan-kritik-gulen-ve-ozal-iddiasi-788484h.htm.

123. The coup was realised both by the help of international community and was due to the anti-capitalist and nationalist stance of the Welfare Party that gave little room to impose neoliberalism on Turkey; Soner Yalçın, "28 Şubat Hala İktidarda," *Sözcü,* March 1 2017, https://www.sozcu.com.tr/2017/yazarlar/soner-yalcin/28-subat-hala-iktidarda-1706228/, accessed March 15, 2018.

124. Tarık Oğuzlu, "Komşularla Sıfır Sorun Politikası: Kavramsal bir Analiz," *Ortadoğu Analiz* 4, no. 42 (2012): 8–17.

125. Hasan Kösebalaban, "The Permanent 'Other'? Turkey and the Question of European Identity," *Mediterranean Quarterly* 18, no. 4 (2007): 96.

126. Jenny B.White, *Muslim Nationalism and the New Turks* (Princeton-Oxford: Princeton University Press, 2013), 9.

44   *Rasim Özgür Dönmez*

127. See Fatih Yaşlı, *AKP, Cemaat, Sünni-Ulus* (İstanbul: Yordam Kitap, 2015).
128. See Rasim Özgür Dönmez, *Neo-Osmanlıcılığın Sosyo-Politiği* (Bursa: Dora Yayınevi, 2015).
129. E. Fuat Keyman, "Turkish Foreign Policy İn The Post-Arab Spring Era:From Proactive To Buffer State," *Third World Quarterly*, 37, no. 12 (2016): 7.
130. İbid.
131. Neophytos Loizides, *The Politics of Majority Nationalism* (Palo Alto, CA: Stanford University Press, 2015), 2.

RESOURCES

"Abdülhamid'den Hakan Fidan'a MİT'in tarihi." *Haber7.com.* March 14 2014. http://www.haber7.com/guncel/haber/1137120-abdulhamidden-hakan-fidana-mitin-tarihi. Accessed April 14, 2018.
"Alparslan Türkeş 12 Eylül'le helalleşmiş!" *Evrensel.* April 30, 2012. https://www.evrensel.net/haber/28102/alparslan-turkes-12-eylulle-helallesmis. Accessed January 10, 2018.
"Bedrettin Dalan'dan kritik Gülen ve Özal İddiası." İnternet Haber. May 18, 2015. http://www.internethaber.com/bedrettin-dalandan-kritik-gulen-ve-ozal-iddiasi-788484h.html. Accessed February 15, 2018.
"Laiklik, Vahdet-i Vücud felsefesiyle şekillendi." *Akşam.* January 29, 2013. https://www.aksam.com.tr/roportaj/laiklik-vahdeti-vucud-felsefesiyle-sekillendi/haber-167704. Accessed March 15, 2018.
"Namık Kemal'in Bektaşiliği ve Masonluğu II." *Masonlar.Org.* https://masonlar.org/masonlar_forum/index.php?topic=11018.0.
"Osmanlı'da Gerilemeyi İlk Bürokratlar Gördü." *Karar Gazetesi.* February 23, 2018. http://www.karar.com/gorusler/osmanlidaki-gerilemeyi-ilk-burokratlar-gordu-764927#. Accessed February 4, 2018.
Abu-Manneh, Butrus. "The Naqshbandiyya-Mujaddidiyya in the Ottoman Lands in the Early 19th Century." *Die Welt des Islams* 22, (1984): 1–36.
Akçura, Yusuf. Üç Tarz-ı Siyaset. İstanbul: Andaç Kitabevi, 2015.
Akinan, Serdar. *Buzdağı.* İstanbul: Kırmızı Kedi Yayınevi, 2017.
Altaylı, Enver. *Ruzi Nazar; CIA'nın Türk Casusu.* İstanbul: Doğan Kitap, 2013
Arslan, Ozan, and Çınar Özen. "The Rebirth of the Ottoman Committee of Union And Progress in Macedonia through the Italian Freemasonry." *Oriente Moderno, Nuova Serie* 24, no. 1 (2005): 93–115.
Bardakçı, Murat. "Fatih'in yaktığı Matrix Tarikatı." *Sabah.* March 31 2007. http://arsiv.sabah.com.tr/ozel/matrix3615/dosya_3615.html. Accessed March 5, 2018.
Belge, Murat. "Türkiye'de Sosyalizm Tarihinin Ana Çizgileri." in *Modern Türkiye'de Siyasi Düşünce:Sol,* edited by Murat Gültekingil, 19–49. İstanbul: İletişim Yayınları, yıl.
Bond, Niall. *Understanding Ferdinand Tönnies's Community and Society.* Zürich-Berlin: Lit, 2013.

Bozdoğan, Sibel, and Reşat Kasaba. *Rethinking Modernity and National Identity in Turkey*. Seattle and London: University of Washington Press, 1997.

Bruinessen, Martin Van. "Mevlana Halid: Bir Sünni Milliyetçisi." *Kürt Tarihi* no. 30 (2017): 12–13.

Cevahiroğlu Ömür, E. Melek. "The Sufi Orders in a Modernizing Empire: 1808—1876." *Tarih:Graduate History Journal* 1, no. 1 (2009): 70–93.

Chatterjee, Partha. *Nationalist Thought and the Colonial World*. Delhi: Zed Books, 1986.

Copeaux, Ettiene. *Türk Tarih Tezinden Türk İslam Sentezine*. İstanbul: Tarih Vakfı Yurt Yayınları, 1998.

Çetinsaya, Gökhan. "Rethinking Nationalism and Islam: Some Preliminary Notes on the Roots of 'Turkish–Islamic Synthesis' in Modern Turkish Political Thought." *Muslim World* 89, no. 3–4 (1999): 352–76.

Davison, Roderic H. "Turkish Attitudes Concerning Christian–Muslim Equality in the Nineteenth Century." *The American Historical Review* 59, no. 4 (1954): 844–64.

Deringil, Selim. *Simgeden Millete*. İstanbul: İletişim Yayınları, 2007.

Dönmez, Rasim Özgür. "Adalet ve Kalkınma Partisi: İslamcılıktan Post Kemalist Bir Anlatıya Doğru." *Doğu Batı* 14, no. 58 (2011): 37–59.

———. "Beyond State Led Nationalism in Turkey." In *Societal Peace and Ideal Citizenship in Turkey*, edited by Rasim Özgür Dönmez and Pınar Enneli, 1–27. Lanham, MD: Lexington Books, 2011.

———. "Nationalisms in Turkey: Political Violence and Identity." *Ethnopolitcs* 6, no.1 (2007): 43–65.

———. *Neo-Osmanlıcılığın Sosyo-Politiği*. Bursa: Dora Yayınevi, 2015.

Duran, Burhanettin, and Cemal Aydın. "Competing Occidentalisms of Modern Islamist Thought: Necip Fazıl Kısakürek and Nurettin Topçu on Christianity, the West and Modernity." *Muslim World* 103, no.4 (2013): 479–500.

Gencer, Bedri. *İslam'da Modernleşme*. Ankara: Doğu Batı Yayınları, 2014.

Gourevitch, Peter. "The Second Image Reversed: The International Sources of Domestic Politics." *International Organization* 32, no. 4 (1978): 881–912.

Gunn, Christopher. "The 1960 Coup in Turkey: A U.S. Intelligence Failure or a Successful 'Intervention.'" *Journal of Cold War Studies* 17, no. 2 (2015): 103–39.

Heper, Metin. "The Strong State as a Problem for the Consolidation of Democracy." *Comparative Political Studies* 25, no. 2 (1992): 169–94.

———. "The Ottoman Legacy and Turkish Politics." *Journal of International Affairs* 54, no. 1 (2000): 63–82.

Hippler, Jochen. *Ulus İnşası*. İstanbul: Versus, 2007.

Huntington, Samuel P. "The Clash of Civilizations." *Foreign Affairs* 72, no. 3 (Summer 1993): 22–49.

İnalcık, Halil. *Osmanlı Tarihinde İslamiyet ve Devlet*. İstanbul: İş Bankası Yayınları, 2016.

Kaya, Mehmet S. "Turkey's Vain Struggle to Create a Homogeneous Nation." *Middle East* Policy 25, no. 2 (2018): 121–35.

Kaya, Yunus. "Türkiye Ekonomisinin Dönüşümleri Işığında Tabakalaşma." In *Türkiye'de Toplumsal Değişim*, edited by Lütfi Sunar, 155–77. Ankara: Nobel Yayınevi, 2016.

Keyman, E. Fuat. "Turkish Foreign Policy in the Post-Arab Spring Era: From Proactive to Buffer State." *Third World Quarterly* 37, no. 12 (2016): 2274–87.

Kösebalaban, Hasan. "The Permanent 'Other'?: Turkey and the Question of European Identity." *Mediterranean Quarterly* 18, no .4 (2007): 87–111.

Kubicek, Paul. "The European Union and Political Cleavages in Turkey." *Insight Turkey* 11, no. 3 (2009): 109–26.

Lewis, Bernard. *The Emergence of Modern Turkey.* New York: Oxford University Press, 2001.

Loizides, Neophytos. *The Politics of Majority Nationalism.* Palo Alto, CA: Stanford University Press, 2015.

Mardin, Şerif. "Operasyonel Kodlarda Süreklilik, Kırılma ve Yeniden İnşa: Dün ve Bugün Türk İslami İstisnacılığı." *Doğu Batı* 31, no. 8 (2005): 48–49.

———. *Türkiye, İslam ve Sekülarizm.* İstanbul: İletişim Yayınları, 2011.

———. *Türkiye'de Din ve Siyaset.* İstanbul: İletişim Yayınları, 2004.

Masonlar Org. https://masonlar.org/masonlar_forum/index.php?topic=3538.0. Accessed February 15, 2018.

Meşe, Ertuğrul. *Komünizmle Mücadele Dernekleri.* İstanbul: İletişim Yayınları, 2016.

Musardo, Veronica. *Secret Connections in Constantinople.* İstanbul: Limra Yayınevi, 2015.

Oğuzlu, Tarık. "Komşularla Sıfır Sorun Politikası: Kavramsal bir Analiz." *Ortadoğu Analiz* 4, no. 42 (2012): 8–17.

Okur, Mehmet Akif. "Türkiye-ABD İlişkilerinin 12 Eylül Kavşağı: Amerikan Belgeleri Darbe Hakkında Ne Anlatıyor." *Uluslararası Hukuk ve Politika* 10, no. 40 (2014): 67–93.

Retoulas, Christos. "Laiklik, Vahdet-i Vücud felsefesiyle şekillendi." *Akşam.* January 29, 2013. Accessed March 14, 2018.

Robinson, William I. "Gramsci and Globalisation: From Nation-State to Transnational Hegemony." *Critical Review of International Social and Political Philosophy* 8, no. 4 (2005): 1–16.

Roy, Oliver. *Siyasal İslamın İflası.* İstanbul: Metis Yayınları, 1994.

Sakallioglu, Ümit Cizre. "Islam-State Interaction in Turkey." *Internal Journal of Middle East Studies* 28, no. 2 (1996): 231–51.

Sayyid, Selman. *Fundementalizm Korkusu.* Ankara: Vadi Yayınları, 2000.

Seufert, G. "Milliyetçi Söylemlerin Sivil Toplum Üzerindeki Etkisi." In *Türkiye'de Sivil Toplum ve Milliyetçilik,* edited by Stefanos Yerasimos, 25–44. İstanbul: İletişim Yayınları, 2001.

Silverstein, Brian. "Sufism and Governmentality in the Late Ottoman Empire." *Comparative Studies of South Asia, Africa and the Middle East* 29, no. 2 (2009): 171–85.

Şentürk, Hulusi. *Türkiye'de İslami Oluşumlar ve Siyaset: İslamcılık.* İstabul: Çıra Yayınevi, 2011.

Şentürk, Recep. "Fıkıh ve Sosyal Bilimler Arasında Son Dönem Osmanlı Aydını." *İslam Araştırmalar Dergisi* no. 4 (2000): 133–71.

Ünlü, Barış. *Türklük Sözleşmesi.* Dipnot Yayınları: Ankara, 2018.

Watson, J. H. Adam. *Hegemony and History.* London and New York: Routledge, 2007.

White, Jenny B. *Islamist Mobilization in Turkey: A Study in Vernacular Politics.* Seattle: University of Washington Press, 2002.

———. *Muslim Nationalism and the New Turks.* Princeton and Oxford: Princeton University Press, 2013.

Yalçın, Soner. "28 Şubat Hala İktidarda," *Sözcü.* March 1 2017, https://www.sozcu. com.tr/2017/yazarlar/soner-yalcin/28-subat-hala-iktidarda-1706228/. Accessed March 15, 2018.

———. "Bilerek Yanıltıyorlar." *Sözcü.* November 29, 2017. https://www.sozcu.com. tr/2017/yazarlar/soner-yalcin/bilerek-yaniltiyorlar-2109651/. Accessed February 12, 2018.

———. "Oyun Masası." *Sözcü Gazetesi.* February 13, 2015. https://www.sozcu.com. tr/2015/yazarlar/soner-yalcin/oyun-masasi-741905/. Accessed February 15, 2018.

Yaşlı, Fatih. "12 Eylül 37 yıldır sürüyor." *Birgün Gazetesi.* September 13, 2017. https://www.birgun.net/haber-detay/12-eylul-37-yildir-suruyor-179122.html. Accessed June 15, 2018.

———. *AKP, Cemaat, Sünni-Ulus.* İstanbul: Yordam Kitap, 2015.

Yavuz, Hakan and Mujeeb R. Khan. "Turkey's Fault Lines and the Crisis of Kemalism." *Current History* 99, no. 633 (2000): 33–38.

———. "Turkish Identity and Foreign Policy in Flux: The Rise of Neo-Ottomanism." *Critique: Critical Middle Eastern Studies* 7, no. 2 (2007): 19–41.

———. *Modernleşen Müslümanlar: Nurcular, Nakşiler, Milli Görüş ve AK Parti.* İstanbul: Kitap Yayınevi, 2005: 186–88.

Yıldız, Gültekin. *Osmanlı Askeri Tarih.* İstanbul: Timaş Yayınları, 2017.

Zarakol, Ayşe. *After Defeat: How the East Learned to Live with the West.* Cambridge: University of Cambridge Press, 2011.

———. "Revisiting Second Image Reversed: Lessons from Turkey and Thailand." *International Studies Quarterly* 57, no. 1 (2013): 150–62.

Zarcone, Thierry. *İslam'da Sır ve Gizli Cemiyetler.* İstanbul: Kabalcı Yayınevi, 2011.

Zürcher, Erik Jan. *Modernleşen Türkiye'nin Tarihi.* İstanbul: İletişim Yayınları, 1995.

Chapter Two

Religion in the Dialectic of Turkish Nation-Building and the Case of the Justice and Development Party

Büke Koyuncu

Observing Turkish politics dominated by the Justice and Development Party (JDP) for sixteen years now, many claim that Turkish society has gradually become more religious in the last twenty years. However, what seems like the Turkish society getting more and more religious is, in fact, the Islamization of Turkish national identity. These two may affect each other, one enforcing or weakening the other, but they are still two very different propositions; the former remains beyond the scope of this work. Another frequently mentioned allegation linked to the previous one is the manifestation of an Islamist revolution against the Republican one. Yet, the Islamization of Turkish national identity does not necessarily mean the overthrow of the Republic. Such an approach overlooks the continuity between the late Ottoman, the early Republican, and the current Turkish politics. What we see when we overview these periods is, indeed, the reflection of an on-going nation-building process and the wrestling over the possession of nationhood.

The most recent presidential and parliamentary elections on June 24, 2018, may also be considered as an appearance of this process. The strongest opponents competing for power were the two electoral alliances created by various political parties. On one side, there was the People's Alliance (*Cumhur İttifakı*) formed by the Justice and Development Party (JDP), the Nationalist Movement Party (NMP), and the Great Union Party (GUP); on the other side was the Nation Alliance (*Millet İttifakı*) consisting of the Republican People's Party (RPP), the Good Party (GP), the Felicity Party (FP), and the Democratic Party (DP). Even the names of these alliances themselves are capable of pointing out the continuing nation-building process.

National identities are never solid, fixed entities. They are rather dialectic processes between the "us" and the "other." Moreover, as they define whom to be included and whom to be excluded and to what extent, they are closely linked to the sociopolitical power struggles within nation-states. In this sense, they are fields of conflict and reconciliation. Still, in many cases, as in Western European countries, there is a relatively established consensus, abiding undisputed except for particular occasions as the European Union (EU) or immigration regulations. However, in our example, the fight over the possession of nationhood proves that the Turkish national identity has not been really consolidated yet and the nation-building process is still very alive; it is a situation that also causes most social conflicts to be translated into patriotic controversies, frequently blurring the real problems.

It we have a closer look at the Islamic references in the discourses and policies of the JDP, we see that they are far from offering a coherent and encompassing frame defining the ideology of the party; rather, they are used as legitimizers and support for the claim to the possession of nationhood. The adoption of laicity by most of the adherents of the main opposition party, the RPP is a similar one. The text you are reading focuses primarily on this long-established attribute of Turkish politics. It proposes that the representations of laicity and Islam in Turkish politics serve as a benchmark in the dialectic of Turkish nation-building.

It's possible to follow the Turkish nation-building process, encountering all its conflicts and reconciliations, from the nineteenth century until today. Unfortunately, that kind of journey would transcend the limits of this work. Instead, we will start with a quick look at the late Ottoman and early Republican periods to show how laicity and Islam became symbolic capitals in the sense Pierre Bourdieu uses the terms.[1] Then, we'll stop by some crossroads throughout the Republican history to see how they have paved the way for today's politics. Finally, we will focus on the JDP period, giving some examples of its nation-building practices, and finish with a discussion on the last elections, evaluating it in the context of national identity formation.

LAICITY AND ISLAM BECOMING SYMBOLIC CAPITALS IN THE DIALECTIC OF TURKISH NATION-BUILDING

Turkish political culture is rooted in the Ottoman modernization period (roughly from the 1720s through the 1910s), a time when, after successive military defeats, the state was trying to empower itself with a set of reforms. In the nineteenth century, these reforms included an effort to promote a common identity—a proto-national one—to avoid separatist movements within the Empire. First, the state had some attempts to create a religiously heterogeneous Ottoman identity. Yet, in a very short amount of time, it became clear that this wouldn't be succeeded. By the beginning of the twentieth century, the Empire had recognized the independence of Greece (1832), Serbia (1878), and Bulgaria (1908); these three communities had constituted a big part of the Ottoman Orthodox population.[2]

After these incidents, Muslim statesmen, who were already discontent for having lost their privileged places as a result of the reforms that were trying to ensure equal citizenship among different religious groups, started defending more strongly the need for a religiously homogeneous identity. During the reign of Abdul Hamid II (1876–1909), Islamic identity was far more promoted, this time, to avoid Arab separatism. However, this effort was far from having popular roots. The Ottoman Empire had long been, until the nineteenth century, a multi-religious empire granting the main religious groups, such as Jews, Orthodox Greeks, and Gregorian Armenians, autonomy in their internal affairs.[3] These religious groups were also functioning as administrative units. Islam was the religion of the sovereigns; however, it is hard to say that religious doctrine was unexceptionally dominant in state affairs. Most of the time it was used as a legitimizer of state policies; the sultan obtained fatwas from Shaykh al-Islām, who was actually a state official himself, to support his decisions. Muslim subjects who substantially lived in rural areas were not only ethnically diverse but also heterogeneous in their lifestyles, beliefs, and religious practices. In short, Islam was more of a symbolic capital giving power to Ottoman rulers and prestige to their Muslim subjects, particularly to the ones who had access to the "high" Islamic culture. It was not an encompassing source of ethics and aesthetics that would naturally unite all Muslims of the empire regardless of their social positions.

Besides, as Arab nationalism enhanced, it became clearer that the unifying identity could not depend on Islam alone. Çağlar Keyder explains how, at this point, the Ottoman reformists discovered that there was a considerably large population who was ethnically Turk within the borders of the empire. But Turkism had even weaker popular roots than Islamism. Before then, "Turk" was only a label that was used to refer to the Anatolian peasantry. The Ottoman reformers were inspired by the works of Turkish nationalists within the Austro-Hungarian and Russian Empires. Their approach had to exclude the idea of ethnic purity, since the population they were dealing with, as well as themselves, was far from being ethnically pure.[4] Meanwhile, in 1912, the Balkan War I took place between the Ottoman State and the Balkan League. The members of the Balkan League—Serbia, Bulgaria, Greece, and Montenegro—were former Orthodox subjects of the Ottoman Empire, and religion was an important part of their nationalism. So when Turkism became the dominant ideology of the Party of Union and Progress (PUP), who took control of the state in 1913, their imagination of Turkishness reciprocally included Muslimhood.[5] Ottoman reformists, including the members of the

PUP, were coming from diverse backgrounds and were accordingly varied in their affiliations to Islamic and Western cultures. The presupposition that Turks were Muslims was now dominant among them. However, how to situate the imagined Muslim Turkishness vis-à-vis Western and Islamic cultures was an issue of debate.

During World War I (1914–1918) and the War of Independence (1919–1923), these debates fell to the wayside. However, after the Turkish War of Independence, the leaders of the military success became the privileged ones to impose their definition of national identity. This group, led by Mustafa Kemal Atatürk, was closer to the Western culture, particularly to the French one.[6]

The balance between Westernization and autonomization has always been a tricky issue for Ottoman/Turkish nation-building since the nineteenth century. Due to the traumatic loss of power and late modernization experienced by the Empire, the "West" had become at the same time both the ideal to pursue as well as a source of a strong inferiority complex.[7] The imagination of a golden Islamic era and efforts to return to that era with a set of reforms, such as seen in the example of Islamism in the nineteenth century, was one way to deal with this dilemma. Here, it is important to point out that this inferiority complex is likely to be triggered particularly in times of national insecurity. Having gained a victory against the Western occupiers, the young Republic had high self-esteem and a strong belief that Turkey could be a part of the European World. So the "West" did not really appear as "the other" against which "us" would be constituted. However, what was perceived as a threat, this time, were the un-Westernized masses and the traditional culture that could be an obstacle against becoming a part of the European World.

On the other hand, Islamic culture was not also believed to be consistent with the European culture and modern life. Most importantly, it symbolized the Ottoman past. Bourdieu indicates that defining the values of cultural capitals in the context of a social field means to define the power hierarchy (high) among different groups owing these capitals. Conversely, the power hierarchy itself determines the values of different types of cultural capitals.[8] There, he gives the example of French nationalism after the Revolution where the bourgeoisie embraced laicity against Catholic culture that was mostly owned by the aristocracy.[9] A similar interpretation may be operative in the case of Turkey. Laicity became a symbol for the promoted national culture by the founders of the modern state where symbols of Islamic culture were alienated as the leftovers of the detached Ottoman dynasty.[10]

However, the unwritten presupposition that Turks were Muslims endured. It defined the post-war population exchanges, caused many discriminating politics aimed at non-Muslim citizens, and, ultimately, made millions of them abandon the country, leaving it with a much more religiously homogeneous population.[11] This was clearly contradicting the principle of laicity, leaving it crippled. As a result, laicism became a symbolic capital, granting its adherents the etiquette of modernity and a higher status in society stemming from their loyalty to the Republic and to its promoted national identity. Meanwhile, Turkey missed the opportunity to discuss and deepen laicity as a political principle that involves the secularization of the state as a means of democratization.[12]

While laicity was interpreted as loyalty to the state, Islamism started to operate as the counterpart. Thus many opposition movements of the time got recorded in the official history as "Islamist movements backed by foreign forces." Being defined in such a manner, these movements also started to lose their diversity. Moreover, as Islamic culture was excluded from intellectual circles and city life, Islamist approaches also lost, to a large extent, their opportunities to sophisticate their philosophical dimensions.[13] In the end, Islamist discourse mostly became a pragmatic opposition tool in the context of everyday politics.

SOME CONFLICT AND RECONCILIATION MILESTONES

When Turkey passed to a multi-party regime in 1946, the inherited political culture encouraged the opposition party (the Democratic Party) to transfer all class-related, regional, and even ethnic issues to a cultural dichotomy between the laisists and the devotees. It is important to point out that what DP situated against "laicism" was mostly the traditional lifestyle of the groups who felt excluded from the circle of modernity; it was not Islamism as an encompassing ideology. As mentioned before, the late Ottoman nation-building process had been marked by a dialectic wavering between "Westernization" and "autonomization." Now, "Western" was an embraced lifestyle within the nation, it was one that was promoted by the state through all its institutions, and it was one that was granting its adherents national belonging. As a larger population with traditional lifestyles was being nationalized, a new encounter was being experienced. The DP promised the newcomers inclusion, using the motto: "Enough! The nation has the say."

In fact, DP differed from its opponent mainly with its liberal economy politics. However, this difference did not mean much for most of the voters. Yüksel Taşkın points out that, unfortunately, the party missed the opportunity to create a class-based basis that would embrace cultural elements both from the periphery and the center. Hence, Turkey got caught in a vicious cycle of culturist and essentialist approaches that would mark its future political life.[14]

In 1960, Turkey witnessed its first military coup. The DP was abolished, and many of its members were brought to trial. Three ministers, including the Prime Minister, Adnan Menderes, were executed. The reasons behind the coup are multidimensional and still very controversial. However, the main ones may be summarized as the inner dynamics of the army, the economic crisis of the time, the social problems growing due to migration to cities, the policies of the DP deviating from the strict "laicism" of the one-party rule, the DP's autocratic measures against its opponents, and, last but not the least, the immature democratic culture of the country.

The coup also reminds us of Bourdieu's explanations about the functioning of a social field. According to Bourdieu, actors who are in advantageous positions in a social field tend to protect their places by not letting in newcomers. They do this either by establishing a monopoly over the valuable capitals (economic, social, or, as in our case, cultural) within the field or by enhancing the value of the capitals they already own.[15] The DP's promotion of the traditional lifestyle under the name of religion and its emphasis on economic capital could have threatened the social status of the fresh elites whose eliteness came primarily from their loyalty to the values of the Republic. When this disturbance came together with the conditions mentioned previously, it could have contributed to a favorable atmosphere for the coup.[16]

In the end, although Menderes himself had a Western lifestyle, his execution easily became the symbol of the suppression of "piety" and "vernacularity." Ironically, this anti-democratic coup resulted in the most democratic constitution in Turkish history, opening the door to a new perception of modernity based on democracy and freedoms.

It's important to note that one may easily lose track if one tries to follow the Turkish history focusing on actors. Instead, what are at stake are the symbolic capitals emphasized by various actors through the nation-building process. The struggle between different kinds of cultural capitals and also the one between the cultural and the economic capital reflect much better the power battles in Turkish politics.[17] Thus, in less than ten years, Süleyman Demirel, the leader of the Justice Party (JP), which was founded as the successor of the DP, became the one to be accused of representing the elites. In 1969, when Demirel was the prime minister, Necmettin Erbakan, a successful engineer and academician with Islamist tendencies, became the president of the Union of Chambers. Erbakan was supporting small- and medium-scale enterprises and working in their favor, whereas Demirel had close relations with big industrial circles. A conflict between them resulted in Erbakan's dismissal. In 1970, Erbakan founded Turkey's first Islamist Party, the National Order Party (NOP).[18]

Erbakan's teachings, which defined the ideological stance of the NOP and its successors, were referred to as the "National Vision" (*Milli Görüş*). The National Vision was transferring nineteenth-century Islamism to modern Turkish politics. The electoral base of the movement was mostly constituted of the peripheral merchants and small- and medium-scale entrepreneurs who felt excluded from the national power field because of their traditional culture. It was here that Islamism was being reformulated to serve as a source of authenticity that would give its adherents the right to demand a higher position in the social hierarchy. The National Vision parties promised them support against what they called the Western–Jewish–Masonic alliance. The "West," Jews, and freemasons constituted the ultimate "other" for the National Vision. Big industrial circles and the elites of the Republic were accused of being their collaborators.[19] This was ironic because a considerable amount of nineteenth century Islamists were, in fact, masons[20]; this showed how Islamism, as it lost its legitimacy in the center, became a peripheral cultural capital. What Islam was symbolizing here was again "the vernacular." New actors were emerging in the national economic field. Moreover, their discursive legitimization was trying to be ensured by the National Vision through a projection of authentic economic progress situated against the "Westerns" inside and outside of the country.

On the other hand, the 1960s were also the flourishing and diversification years of the Turkish left. Although the military intervention of March 12, 1971, ended the legal opportunities of the 1960s, the workers' movement continued to be active for another decade. This caused a counter-reaction, uniting once again the right-wing parties in coalitions as exemplified in the First (1975) and Second (1977) National Front governments. The First National Front government consisted of the National Salvation Party (NSP), successor of NOP; the Justice Party (JP); the National Movement Party (NMP), a Turkish nationalist party; and the Republican Trust Party (RTP) that was founded by former members of the RPP who left that party when it adopted a relatively leftist approach. The latter included only the first three of these parties mentioned.

This ideological cleavage, although it still contained strong cultural references, was perhaps the most class-based one in Turkish history. However, the democratic culture had not been consolidated enough to bear reconciliation and transformation from such an era. What ended the conflicts was again a military coup with which Turkey missed its second important chance to transcend culturist and essentialist politics. The 1980s starting with this military coup, and the continued rule of the Motherland Party (MP) became very definitive for Turkey's years to come. The altering of the international power relations after the Cold War period shaped the approach of the armed forces. This time, the army was for a more religious definition of national identity and a light version of Islamism that was legitimized as an antidote of Communism. Leftist politics were delegitimized as "alien" to the "national" culture. Moreover, at the time, the Turkish state was much more enthusiastic about being the ally of United States than being a part of Europe. Economic liberalization and technological development defined the American way of modernization and Westernization, which was less contradicting with Islamic or traditional cultural elements. After a period of military rule, the country underwent a very rapid liberalization process under the rule of the MP, which was led by Turgut Özal, a civilian who had also served in the military government from 1980–1982 as the deputy prime minister for economic affairs.[21]

As a result of the 1980s, Islamism gained a double function in Turkey. First, it started to serve as an ethical resistance point against the aggressive capitalist culture. As Islamist circles were much freer under the rule of MP, Islamist intellectual activity found the chance to accelerate and diversify. In the 1990s, Islamist intellectuals criticizing the individualism of capitalism and the universal values of Western modernity multiplied. Their engagement in postmodern thought partly legitimated their presence in the intellectual field and enhanced their development. There were huge masses left out of the neoliberal growth taking place, and class politics, particularly the workers' movements, had lost their popularity and organizational power after the coup. These masses now found the chance to express their uneasiness through the Islamist discourse.[22] They were substantially supporting the successor of Turkey's first Islamist party, the WP, who were against the EU, the United States, and the big capital owners. The WP took 21 percent of the votes in the national election of 1995[23] and formed a coalition government with a center-right party. However, the party's antagonistic approach towards the West and strong emphasize on Islamist policies caused unrest. On February 28, 1997, the armed forces published a declaration on its official website hinting at its members' worries about the policies of the WP. This was interpreted as a "postmodern coup." The government had to resign, and the WP was banned by the Constitutional Court.

Secondly, and to some extent contradictorily, Islamism was providing the necessary networks for the economic development of a group of people. During the liberalization process in the 1980s, Özal collaborated with medium- and small-scale producers from Anatolia for whom adaptation to the new economic regulations was much easier because they were supported by the rural, communal, and religious networks. In the meantime, the religious organizations that also served as business networks became stronger, both by the economic advance of their participants and by the liberal and populist approaches of the state. To be able to climb up the social hierarchies, this group needed to combine its economic capital with valued cultural capital. Until then, social mobility had been relatively gradual letting balance between these two. However, for most of the new bourgeois of the 1990s, particularly for the ones coming from religious networks, the dominant cultural capital was foreign. The 1990s were years when "the nouveau riches" were highly caricatured in the media as having economic capital and lacking the legitimate cultural capital. Partly as a response, Islam started to be transformed into a new cultural reference point in a way compatible with the liberal approaches of this new middle class. This trend had already started with the National Vision movement. However, the base of the movement was now much stronger economically. The new cultural ideal combined liberal philosophy with Islamic doctrines and was completed with a rearticulated version of the Ottoman past, stressing on the high Ottoman culture. The Ottoman culture was again serving as a source of authenticity and vernacularity against Western culture, which was inevitably infusing to the lives of new rich through new modes of consummation.[24] Towards the end of the 1990s, Islamic five-star hotels or fashion shows with Ottoman features had taken their place in the public sphere.[25]

The postmodern coup on February 28, 1997, caused the equilibrium between these two functions of Islamism to change in favor of the latter. Islamism once again got squeezed into the Western/vernacular dichotomy of the 1950s. Its critical approach weakened whereas its function as a source of authenticity strengthened for those who were excluded once more from the national power field through the postmodern coup.

THE JUSTICE AND DEVELOPMENT PARTY

This new situation was embodied in the JDP, founded in 2001 by a group of young politicians leaving the WP. The party declared itself to be a conservative democrat party instead of an Islamist one. One of the ideologues of the party, Yalçın Akdoğan, wrote in his book *Conservative Democracy* that the JDP was not an Islamist party because an Islamist party would pursue identity politics whereas the JDP aimed to encompass the whole nation. According to him and to the founders of the party, they were just advocating the genuine values of the nation, one of which was religion.[26] Recep Tayyip Erdoğan, Turkey's current president and the founder of the JDP, defined "conservative democracy" as "an attempt to fulfill the demand of a modernity that did not exclude tradition, a universality that admitted locality, a rationality that did not refuse meaning and a transformation that was not radical."[27] This positioning was also nourished with the anti-elitist discourse accusing the RPP, the founding party and the main opposition, of being elites alienated from their own nation. After coming to power, Erdoğan declared in many of his speeches that elites were no longer in power and now "his nation" had the say.[28]

The year 2007 was an important crossroad in the JDP's journey. On one hand, the successful results in the local elections of 2004 and the commencement of the negotiations with the EU on October 3, 2005 had strengthened the party even more. On the other hand, a sequence of shady events had tensed up the political arena enormously. There was the bombing of a bookstore owned by a former Kurdistan Workers Party (KWP; widely known as PKK) member by a truck that later turned out to belong to the gendarme. There was also the murder of the priest of the Santa Maria Church in Trabzon and an attack on the members of the State Council that can be regarded among these events. The convicts and the legal outcomes of these incidents are beyond the limits of this work. However, what is important is that all of these events were leading to an atmosphere of chaos, inflaming the nationalist reactions of political opposition, particularly of the RPP electorate. Towards the end of 2006, discussions on Cyprus in the context of the EU process provoked the nationalist reactions of the opposition even more. A part of the opposition took position against EU membership.

This may seem ironic since the RPP is known to be much more sympathetic towards the West then the JDP. However, the irony here reveals once more the ambivalence of the Turkish nation-building process. The first years of the 2000s were years when the JDP had high self-esteem due to electoral success, foreign support (particularly from the West), and progress in the EU process. Whereas the opposition, particularly, the electorate of the RPP, was feeling insecure, disappointed about the support given to the JDP by the West. The JDP was even accused of collaborating with the West against national interests. This shows that the attitude of Turkish power parties towards the West is far from being fixed; it is rather dialectical. The course of the relations between Turkey and the West, particularly Europe, as well as the relations between the "Western" and "vernacular" within the country, determine this attitude.

The unrest of the RPP electorate, which had started with the local elections in 1994 when the WP won the mayorship of the big cities like İstanbul and Ankara that led to the February 28 postmodern coup, peaked with the victories of the JDP and the incidents in 2005 and 2006 that found its last straw during the presidential elections of 2007. When the term of office of President Ahmet Necdet Sezer was approaching its end, the possibility that the JDP would nominate an Islamist politician as candidate led to discussions. Big demonstrations were organized under the name of "The Republic Meetings."

Although it was claimed that these meetings were backed by armed forces as a part of a plan to overthrow the government, it is a fact that there was an enormous civil participation, particularly from middle-class RPP electorate for whom this kind of political activity was new. Ten days after the first Republic Meeting, Erdoğan nominated Abdullah Gül, who was the former prime minister and one of the founders of the JDP, as president. While the RPP boycotted the elections, aiming to rend the elections invalid, the armed forces, on the night of the elections, issued a declaration on its website warning the government about its Islamist activities. However, the government did not back off this time and declared a counter statement; it was a very hard one, underlining the fact that the military was an institution under the rule of the government and was responsible to the prime minister in its duties and exercise of power. It also included a warning that those who harmed the trust and stability should face the negative consequences.[29] This was a threshold in the Turkish history where the armed forces lost its position as the warning institution and became, instead, the warned one.

In the meantime, discussions were going on about the validity of the election. Some claimed that number of deputies that participated (354) were not enough to run the election. So the RPP took the issue to the Constitutional Court, and the court gave a contentious decision in cancelling the election and giving way to the renewal of parliamentary elections.

The pre-election period for 2007 Parliamentary Elections exemplifies perfectly how the dialectic of nation-building had been working in Turkey. After the cancellation of the presidential election, the Foundation of Turkish Voluntary Organizations (an association that brought together various Islamic organizations) issued a declaration in popular newspapers. In the declaration, three leaders—Menderes, Özal, and Erdoğan—were presented as "the stars of democracy." The text under the heading stated: "They are the symbols of the democracy path opened by Atatürk. They are the shining stars in the horizon of democracy."[30]

Although the president of the Foundation stated that they issued this declaration not to support the JDP[31] but to show their reaction against the Republic meetings and the attitude of the armed forces, on April 27, their declaration inspired the party's new campaign.

About ten days later, a very smilar post was published by the Association of Legal Research, also known for its Islamic tendencies; this time, they presented the same three leaders as "The Nation's Men." In a very short time, this label started to take place in the JDP's election campaign. For example, postcards with Menderes, Özal, and Erdoğan's photos on them were printed and delivered. The text on the postcards stated: "They are the symbol names for the love of the nation strengthed by Atatürk. They are the voice, conscience, and progressive spirit of this land. The nation is in their hearts; they are in the nation's heart. They are the nation's men."[32]

From that point on, this discourse became the main element not only in the campaign for the 2007 Parliamentary Elections, which the JDP won taking 46.47 percent of the votes,[33] but also in the following campaigns, such as the one for the 2007 Referendum or the 2011 Local Elections. With this discourse, Erdoğan situated himself and his party in a dichotomic narration of Turkish history. On one side, there was Atatürk, Menderes, Özal, and Erdoğan, "the rescuers and founders of the nation"; on the other side, there were the elites collaborating with the "foreign forces" against the interests of the nation. Erdoğan had realized many speeches to exemplify this narration. For example, in one of them that took place during a parliamentary group meeting in 2007, he said:

> There were people who were against Atatürk while he was founding Turkey. Menderes and Özal both experienced the same thing. We experience the same. The story is the same, only the actors are changing. . . . The ones who resist change and transformation are working on their own interests, and they will not succeed.[34]

His self-identification with Atatürk, the founder of Turkey, demonstrates how he and this party stake their claim to the possession of the nation-sate. With this discourse, the RPP's and its electorate's monopoly on the Atatürk symbol had been representative of their loyalty and belonging to the nation-state since the Early Republic was shaken. Erdoğan's approach, which manifested in these speeches, cannot be evaluated independently from the February 28 incident, the Republic Meetings, or the cancellation of the presidential election. It can be said that, each act of exclusion starting from February 28 on, led the JDP cadres to adapt themselves more and more to the dominant philosophy of the state, but at the same time, to become more aggressive and exclusionary in their claim to the ownership of the Turkish nation-state and national identity.

One way of doing this has been through the national rituals, which are one of the most powerful nation-building instruments. It was explained in the previous paragraphs how Islam had become a symbolic capital used in social power struggles in Turkish politics. Correspondingly, in the JDP's case, it has also served as an important reference in the reshaping of national rituals. The JDP period is full of such examples; however, in the limits of this work, it will be possible to focus on just two of them, one representing the Islamization of a previously secular national ritual and the other revealing the nationalization of a religious one.[35]

The first example is about National Anthem Day. The national anthem is clearly one of the main national symbols. However, the lyrics of the Turkish National Anthem belong to an Islamist poet, Mehmet Âkif Ersoy (1873–1936). That is why, although the anthem was embraced by the young Republic, there had not been too much emphasis on the lyricist. Contrarily, the poet had always been favored by the conservative right and commemorations for him had been organized by nongovernmental foundations. The first time Ersoy was used as a national figure was when Ersoy's picture was put on Turkish banknotes during Özal's government.

After the JDP came to power, the government officials started to participate in the commemorations organized for Ersoy. They also announced that this previously ignored national figure would have the respect he deserved. Governmental commemoration activities for the poet started to be organized on the adoption day of the national anthem. In 2007, a law proclaiming March 12 as the "Adoption of National Anthem and Mehmet Âkif Ersoy Memorial Day" passed. The prime minister declared 2011 as the year of Mehmet Âkif Ersoy. Throughout that year, the Ministry of Culture and Tourism organized various activities. Moreover, the Ministry of National Education reserved two issues of its journal to introduce Ersoy. These issues promoted, particularly, the religious character of Ersoy, linking his piety to his patriotism, naming him the "poet of the nation," and advising children to be just like him.

In short, it can be said that the government, with its discourses and activities around the national anthem and its lyricist, reproduced and reshaped nationalism, enforcing and at the same time Islamizing a national symbol.

The second example, on the other hand, is about the nationalization of a religious ritual: the Holy Birth Week. The Holy Birth Week is the week during which various activities are organized to celebrate the birth of the Prophet Muhammad. In fact, the birth of Muhammad (*Mawlid*) has been commemorated for a very long time in the Muslim world. During the early Republic, although the tradition of celebrating *Mawlid* continued among people, an official ceremony was out of question. However, after 1989, during the prime ministry of Özal, the birth of Muhammad started to be celebrated as the Holy Birth Week by the Presidency of Religious Affairs and the Turkish Religion Foundation. The aim of the week was defined as: "To let the religious reflection go beyond the mosque" and "to spread the love for the Prophet Muhammad." This way the celebrations started to be institutionalized at a state level. In 1994, it was decided that the Holy Birth Week, which was being celebrated according to the lunar calendar, should be celebrated according to the Gregorian one, the official national calendar. While people continued to celebrate *Mawlid* according to the lunar calendar, another celebration occasion around April 20 was created by the state.

During the JDP rule, the scope of this institutionalization widened. What provoked this widening was, ironically, the need to answer some laicist demands. During the first years of the JDP, some activities organized during the Holy Birth Week caused severe discussions, and the issue became very problematic. Most of the celebrations were coinciding with the National Sovereignty and Children's Day, which was interpreted, by the laicist nationalists, as a move against national values. The armed forces, in its declaration in April 2007, pointed out a related religious drama performance at a primary state school as an example of the acts against laicism. The issue also took place in the trial of closure against the JDP prosecuted by the Constitutional Court in March 2008. In 2008, the Presidency of Religious Affairs fixed the time of the Holy Birth Week in a way that it would not coincide with the National Sovereignty and Children's Day, and the content of the celebrations were limited. The on-going criticisms led to a further standardization of the celebrations in 2010, and a regulation was published in the official newspaper. While this seemed like taking the celebrations under control, it was, in fact, institutionalization of the celebrations more and more as a state activity. At last, in 2011, the Ministry of National Education included the week in the list of "days and weeks" to celebrate. The ministry, in a notice distributed to all schools in Turkey, has clearly established a link between the moral values to be taught to children at schools, and the good personality of the prophet Muhammad, who was referred as "our master, the prophet." The notice was demanding the schools to organize activities celebrating the week.

With the Holy Birth Week, an institutionalized and nationalized religious commemoration day had been involved among the national rituals serving the reproduction and reshaping of national identity. These examples, as well as similar ones, has not only strengthened the JDP's place in the national field, but also defined the destiny of Islam as a symbolic capital in Turkish national identity. In a compatible way with its conservative democrat positioning, Islam, in the JDP's discourses, has become the match of the "national" and the "vernacular" situated against the "foreign" and the "elite."

Here it is important to point out that the content of "people," "national," or the "vernacular" is always ambiguous in anti-elitist populist discourses such as this. The JDP case is not an exception. "People" or "nation" is an obscure entity to be defined, working as an identity-founding and, at the same time, "othering" tool.[36] So far, the JDP has promoted its neoliberal politics as "the nation's progress": its foreign policy approach aims to create an impact area in the Middle East and Africa as "helping countries with whom the nation has cultural commonalities"; its educational policies look to strengthen Imam Hatip schools (Turkey's Religious Vocational School) as "defending the nation's schools"; and showing the privileged place Sunni Islam has in state policies as liberating "the nation's religion." Accordingly, any opposition against these policies or similar ones have been accused of being "against the nation." Turkey witnessed many examples of this approach, particularly after the 2011 General Elections, where the JDP won 49.8 percent of the votes.[37] For example, activists in the Gezi Park Protests or academics supporting Kurdish politics have been substantially accused, even criminalized, of betrayal to the nation's values. Each time a practice has been legitimized or delegitimized as compatible or contradictory to nation's values, not only the nation but also its values, including religiosity, have been defined. As a result, the early Republic's "laicity as loyalty to the state" has started to leave its place to "religiosity as loyalty to the state"; on one hand, it gives power to Islamic culture in the national field, while on the other hand, in a way, it is limiting it once more with the national vision of the state.[38]

July 15, 2016 was the ultimate example of the Islamization of nationalization and, at the same time, the nationalization of Islam in Turkey. On that day, Turkey witnessed a coup d'état attempt by a clique in the army. The state declared that the religious Gülen movement, which started to be referred as the Fethullahist Terror Organization (FETÖ) after the event, was responsible for the attempt. It is beyond the limits of this work to discuss the details of this failed coup. However, how religion was used to mobilize citizens, particularly the JDP electorate, against the attempt is critical for the issue addressed in this work. During the night of the attempt, when the government officials called citizens to go out and fight against it, the mosques started broadcasting extra *selahs* and calls for prayer throughout Turkey that continued almost through the night. In the following days, citizens continued to gather in various areas to avoid a possible second attempt. The mosques and imams were effective also in this mobilization. These gatherings ended with a big meeting in Yenikapı organized by the Presidency. The meeting was named The Democracy and Martyr's Rally. Millions of people attended the Rally with Turkish flags that were once used by laicist Republicans to protest pro-Islamist governments. Even Atatürk posters were present in the meeting area. The motto used during the "democracy watches" and the Rally was, "We the nation shall never let Turkey be manipulated by coup plotters and terrorists." Although representatives of some other parties participated in the gatherings and the rally, the great majority of the participants were the JDP voters. The Democracy and Martyr's Rally was a symbolic threshold, ending the first phase of the JDP rule and opening to a new one. The phase, when ended, was marked by the claim for the ownership of the nation-state through the adoption of its symbols and an Islamic redefinition of them. The phase that was opened has been continuing to be about the securing of this ownership. This was also a crossroad in the dialectic of Turkish nation-building; it can be proposed that the July 15 incident strengthened the national-belonging feelings in the JDP party electorate. The effects of the incident on other electorates in context of national-belonging deserve further research.

A FEW CONCLUDING WORDS ON THE LAST ELECTIONS

On June 24, 2018, Presidential and Parliamentary elections were held in Turkey. Erdoğan was reelected as president in the first round, getting 52.6 percent of the votes. In the parliamentary elections, the electoral alliance, which Erdoğan's party (the People's Alliance; *Cumhur İttifakı*) was a part of, got 53.7 percent of the votes. On the other side, the Nation Alliance (*Millet İttifakı*), led by the RPP, got 33.9 percent, and the Peoples' Democratic Party (PDP) got 11.7 percent of the votes.[39]

These elections were highly significant in Turkish history in many ways. First of all, the country completed its shift to a new governmental system with these elections. The shift had started with the referendum in 2007 where the election procedure of the president changed and the president began being elected directly by the people. This was a step from the parliamentary system to semi-presidency. In fact, this change had taken place as the JDP's response to the crisis it faced when it nominated Gül as candidate for presidency. Ten years later, on April 16, 2017, Turkey officially passed to presidential system with another referendum. Finally, with the 2018 elections, the change accepted in the referendum was put into practice. There are still debates going on about the new system since it grants the president too much power and lacks adequate checks-and-balances mechanisms. Putting these debates aside in the limits of this paper, what I want to point out here is rather the symbolic meaning of this shift. The JDP had long defined itself as the rescuer and the re-founder of Turkey. And while July 15 concretized the rescuer role, the shift to a new governmental system now symbolizes the re-founder role, consolidating the JDP's and its electorate's share in the nation-building process and the definition of national identity.

This election was also important for the course of the Turkish history with its election alliances. First, both alliances had names referring to their claim to represent the whole nation. This points out how the nation-building process is still very alive in Turkey. On the other hand, these alliances reflected also an alteration in the traditional cleavage of Turkish politics. The JDP formed a coalition with a Turkish nationalist and an Islamist-Turkish nationalist party underlining its nationalist march. However, the RPP formed a coalition with a nationalist party (the GP); a center-right party (the new DP), which is the successor of its old rival the DP; and an Islamist party (the FP), which is the current successor of Turkey's first Islamic party. The parties declared that they formed this alliance on the basis that all were against the proposed presidential system and they wished to strengthen the separation of powers within the state. Accordingly, there was much less reference to either Islam or laicity in the discourses of both parties during this pre-election period. This is a promising development for Turkish politics because it is an example where social and political problems such as the quest for democracy have succeeded to outweigh identity politics.

The last but not least point is about the PDP, the only party who succeeded to enter the parliamentary without being a part of an alliance. The PDP is the successor of a series of parties that represented Kurdish politics in Turkey; however, the party had decided, before the elections in 2015, to extend its electoral base, adopting a more moderate discourse and shifting its focus from Kurds to all minorities. The last two elections showed that the party has been successful in its new orientation. The Kurdish politics in Turkey and the positioning of the PDP is completely another topic of research and analysis. However, considering its new orientation and particularly its unofficial collaboration with the other opposition parties in the last pre-election period, it is important to add as a final note that there is much more to discuss in the context of the dialectics of Turkish nation-building.

NOTES

1. Pierre Bourdieu, *Practical Reason: On the Theory of Action* (Stanford, CA: Stanford University Press, 1998); Pierre Bourdieu and Loïc J. D. Wacquant, *An Invitation to Reflexive Sociology* (Cambridge: Polity Press, 1996).

2. İsmail Kara, *Din ile Modernleşme Arasında: Çağdaş Türk Düşüncesinin Meseleleri* (İstanbul: Dergah Yayınları, 2014).

3. İlber Ortaylı, *İmparatorluğun En Uzun Yüzyılı* (İstanbul: Alkım Yayınevi, 2001); İlber Ortaylı, *Avrupa ve Biz* (Ankara: Turhan Kitabevi, 2007).

4. Çağlar Keyder, *Türkiye'de Devlet ve Sınıflar* (İstanbul: İletişim Yayınları, 2005).

5. Şerif Mardin, *Jön Türklerin Siyasi Fikirleri: 1895–1908* (İstanbul: İletişim Yayınları, 2006).

6. Tanıl Bora, *Türk Sağının Üç Hâli: Milliyetçilik, Muhafazakârlık, İslamcılık* (İstanbul: Birikim Yayınları, 2012).

7. For an inspiring work on the relationship between inferiority complex and nationalism see Partha Chatterjee *The Nation and Its Fragments: Colonial and Postcolonial Histories,* (Princeton, NJ: Princeton University Press, 1993).

8. Pierre Bourdieu, *Practical Reason.*

9. Steve Bruce, *Politics and Religion* (Cambridge: Polity Press, 2003).

10. Büke Koyuncu, *"Benim Milletim..."* *AK Parti İktidarı, Din ve Ulusal Kimlik* (İstanbul: İletişim, 2014); Büke Koyuncu, "AK Parti: Devlete Sadakat Olarak Laiklikten Devlete Sadakat Olarak Dindarlığa," in *Kimlik ve Din*, edited by Abdullah Özbolat and Mustafa Macit (Adana: Karahan Kitabevi, 2016).

11. Baskın Oran, "Azınlıklar," www.baskınoran.com; Mesut Yeğen, *Müstakbel Türk'ten Sözde Vatandaşa* (İstanbul: İletişim Yayınları, 2006).

12. Büke Koyuncu, *"Benim Milletim..."*.

13. Şerif Mardin, "Center-Periphery Relations: A Key to Turkish Politics?" *Deadalus* 102, no. 1 (1973): 169–90; Emin Baki Adas, "The Making of Entrepreneurial Islam and the Islamic Spirit of Capitalism," *Journal for Cultural Research* 10, no. 2 (2006): 113-137; Mehmet Altan, *Kent Dindarlığı* (İstanbul: Timaş Yayınları, 2010).

14. Yüksel Taşkın, *Anti-Komünizmden Küreselleşme Karşıtlığına Milliyetçi Muhafazakâr Entelijansiya* (İstanbul: İletişim Yayınları, 2013); Çağlar Keyder, *Türkiye'de Devlet ve Sınıflar*, (İstanbul: İletişim Yayınları, 2005); Nilüfer Narlı, "The Tension between the Center and Peripheral Economy and the Rise of a Counter Business Elite in Turkey," *Islam en Turquie, Les Annales de L'Autre Islam* no. 6 (1999): 50–72.

15. Pierre Bourdieu, *Practical Reason*; Pierre Bourdieu and Loïc J. D. Wacquant, *An Invitation to Reflexive Sociology*.

16. Büke Koyuncu, *"Benim Milletim . . ."*.

17. Ibid.

18. Fulya Atacan, "Explaining Religious Politics at the Crossroad: AKP-SP," *Turkish Studies* 6, no. 2 (2005): 187–89; Haldun Gülalp, "Political Islam in Turkey: The Rise and Fall of the Refah Party," *The Muslim World* 89, no. 1 (1999): 22–41.

19. Ibid.

20. Selin Çağlayan, *Müslüman Kardeşler'den Yeni Osmanlılar'a İslamcılık* (Ankara: İmge Kitabevi Yayınları, 2011).

21. Şebnem Gümüşçü, "Economic Liberalization, Devout Bourgeoisie and Change in Political Islam: Comparing Turkey and Egypt," *EUI Working Papers, RSCAS* 19 (2008); Korkut Boratav, *Türkiye İktisat Tarihi 1908–2005* (Ankara: İmge Kitabevi, 2006); Alev Çınar, *Modernity, Islam and Secularism in Turkey: Bodies Places and Time* (Minneapolis: University of Minnesota Press, 2005).

22. Haldun Gülalp, *Kimlikler Siyaseti: Türkiye'de Siyasal İslamın Temelleri* (İstanbul: Metis Yayınları, 2003); Büke Koyuncu, *"Benim Milletim..."*.

23. www.secim-sonuclari.com/1995 (October 2, 2018).

24. M. Hakan Yavuz, *Islamic Political Identity in Turkey* (New York: Oxford University Press, 2003); Büke Koyuncu, *"Benim Milletim..."*.

25. Mücahit, Bilici, "İslam'ın Bronzlaşan Yüzü," In *İslamın Yeni Kamusal Yüzleri ve Kamusal Alan Üzerine Bir Atölye Çalışması*, edited by Nilüfer Göle (Istanbul: Metis Yayınları, 2000).

26. Yalçın Akdoğan, *Muhafazakâr Demokrasi* (İstanbul: Şehir Yayınları, 2000); Yalçın Akdoğan, *AK Parti ve Muhafazakâr Demokrasi* (İstanbul: Alfa Yayınları, 2004).

27. Yüksel Taşkın, *Anti-Komünizmden Küreselleşme Karşıtlığına Milliyetçi Muhafazakâr Entelijansiya* (İstanbul: İletişim Yayınları, 2013).

28. Büke Koyuncu, *"Benim Milletim…"*.
29. "Genelkurmay Hükümetin Emrinde," *Sabah*, April 28, 2007.
30. "Film Afişi Gibi Tepki İlanı," *Milliyet*, June 10, 2007.
31. Ibid.
32. "'Milletin Adamları' Kartpostal Oldu," *Yeni Şafak*, July 31, 2007.
33. www.secim-sonuclari.com/2007, accessed October 2, 2018.
34. "Erdoğan: Uzlaşma Yüzde Yüzle Sağlanmaz", *Hürriyet*, (October 2, 2007).
35. For further details about these two examples and other related ones please, see Büke Koyuncu, *"Benim Milletim…"*.
36. Paul Taggart, *Popülizm* (İstanbul: İstanbul Bilgi Üniversitesi Yayınları, 2004).
37. secim.haberler.com/2011, accessed October 2, 2018.
38. Büke Koyuncu, *"Benim Milletim…"*.
39. secim.haberler.com, accessed October 2, 2018.

RESOURCES

Adas, E. Baki. "The Making of Entrepreneurial Islam and the Islamic Spirit of Capitalism." *Journal for Cultural Research* 19, no. 2 (2006): 113–37.
Akdoğan, Yalçın. *Muhafazakâr Demokrasi*. İstanbul: Şehir Yayınları, 2000.
———. *AK Parti ve Muhafazakâr Demokrasi*. İstanbul: Alfa Yayınları, 2004.
Altan, Mehmet. *Kent Dindarlığı*. İstanbul: Timaş Yayınları, 2010.
Atacan, Fulya. "Explaining Religious Politics at the Crossroad: AKP-SP." *Turkish Studies* 6, no. 2 (2005): 187–89.
Bilici, Mücahit. "İslam'ın Bronzlaşan Yüzü." In İslamın Yeni Kamusal Yüzleri ve Kamusal Alan Üzerine Bir Atölye Çalışması, edited by Nilüfer Göle. İstanbul: Metis Yayınları, 2000.
Bora, Tanıl. *Türk Sağının Üç Hâli: Milliyetçilik, Muhafazakârlık, İslamcılık*. İstanbul: Birikim Yayınları, 2012.
Boratav, Korkut. *Türkiye İktisat Tarihi 1908–2005*. Ankara: İmge Kitabevi, 2006.
Bourdieu, Pierre. *Practical Reason: On the Theory of Action*. Stanford, CA: Stanford University Press, 1998.
Bourdieu, Pierre, and Loïc J. D. Wacquant. *An Invitation to Reflexive Sociology*. Cambridge: Polity Press, 1996.
Bruce, Steve. *Politics and Religion*. Cambridge: Polity Press, 2003.
Çağlayan, Selin. *Müslüman Kardeşler'den Yeni Osmanlılar'a İslamcılık*. Ankara: İmge Kitabevi Yayınları, 2011.
Çınar, Alev. *Modernity, Islam and Secularism in Turkey: Bodies Places and Time*. Minneapolis: University of Minnesota Press, 2005.
Gülalp, Haldun. "Political Islam in Turkey: The Rise and Fall of the Refah Party." *The Muslim World* 89, no. 1 (1999): 22–41.
———. *Kimlikler Siyaseti: Türkiye'de Siyasal İslamın Temelleri*. İstanbul: Metis Yayınları, 2003.
Gümüşçü, Şebnem. "Economic Liberalization, Devout Bourgeoisie and Change in Political Islam: Comparing Turkey and Egypt." *EUI Working Papers, RSCAS 19* (2008).

Keyder, Çağlar. "The Dilemma of Cultural Identity on the Margin of Europe." *Review (Fernand Braudel Center)* 16, no. 1 (1993): 19–33.

———. *Türkiye'de Devlet ve Sınıflar*. İstanbul: İletişim Yayınları, 2005.

Koyuncu, Büke. *"Benim Milletim…" AK Parti İktidarı, Din ve Ulusal Kimlik*. İstanbul: İletişim, 2014.

———. "AK Parti: Devlete Sadakat Olarak Laiklikten Devlete Sadakat Olarak Dindarlığa." In *Kimlik ve Din*, edited by Abdullah Özbolat and Mustafa Macit. Adana: Karahan Kitabevi, 2016.

Mardin, Şerif. "Center-Periphery Relations: A Key to Turkish Politics?" *Deadalus* 102, no. 1 (1973): 169–90.

———. *Jön Türklerin Siyasi Fikirleri: 1895–1908*. İstanbul: İletişim Yayınları, 2006.

Narlı, Nilüfer. "The Tension between the Center and Peripheral Economy and the Rise of a Counter Business Elite in Turkey." *Islam en Turquie, Les Annales de L'Autre Islam* 6 (1999): 50–72.

Oran, Baskın. "Azınlıklar." www.baskınoran.com. Accessed November 1, 2012.

Ortaylı, İlber. *İmparatorluğun En Uzun Yüzyılı*. İstanbul: Alkım Yayınevi, 2001.

———. *Avrupa ve Biz*. Ankara: Turhan Kitabevi, 2007.

Taggart, Paul. *Popülizm*. İstanbul: İstanbul Bilgi Üniversitesi Yayınları, 2004.

Taşkın, Yüksel. *Anti-Komünizmden Küreselleşme Karşıtlığına Milliyetçi Muhafazakâr Entelijansiya*. İstanbul: İletişim Yayınları, 2013.

Yavuz, M. Hakan. *Islamic Political Identity in Turkey*. New York: Oxford University Press, 2003.

Yeğen, Mesut. *Müstakbel Türk'ten Sözde Vatandaşa*. İstanbul: İletişim Yayınları, 2006.

Chapter Three

Nation-Building and the Religion-State Relations in Turkey: The Presidency of Religious Affairs

Ali Yaman

When we look at studies[1] dealing with the Ottoman Empire and with the Turkish Republic, the former's heir from various angles, it appears that they both attach significance to the role of religion. In this regard, it is often discussed how those governing the state view religion as a domain subordinate to the state not only in the Ottoman days but also during the Republican era. Turkish nationalism, which developed in the late Ottoman era, has long been intertwined with religion (Islam) and even with sect (Sunni Hanafism). Thus, the state religious policy in Turkey can be expressed as a model of Turkish-Sunni synthesis subordinate to the state. This model has always been under political influence, so religious policy has varied greatly, and the position of the Presidency of Religious Affairs, which has grown stronger since its establishment, has taken shape accordingly.

It is clear that nation-building based on a Turkish identity with a religious dimension is a complicated process stretching from the Ottoman days to the Republican era. Defining the dominant elements in the Ottoman Empire through Islam first gave way to the mention of the Turkish nation along with Islam, and then a stage was reached in the Republican era where the nation was expressed with a religious attribute, the Muslim Turkish nation. Thus, Turkishness ceased to be one of the many pieces making up the Islamic millet/ummah in which many nations, such as Turks, Arabs, and Albanians, existed. In the words of Şerif Mardin, ". . . the subjects of a multiethnic, cosmopolitan empire were being transformed into the citizens of a republic determining the fundamentals of genuine Turkishness and embracing them,"[2] The fact that this transformation was accompanied by devastating wars and land losses during the dissolution of a great empire and, eventually, a nation-state shaped through Turkishness was founded led to the birth of certain ethnic and religious sensitivities among the ruling elite.

It is without a doubt that the Turkish nation-building style rests on the Ottoman legacy.[3] To see this better, it will be essential to look into how the religion-state relations have taken course over the centuries in the Empire, how Turkish nationalism developed following the strengthening of different nationalisms, and the Ottoman attempts at modernization that took place until their collapse. These modernization efforts manifest themselves clearly in various legal and institutional arrangements introduced with the foundation of the Republic. The Ottoman legacy and this modernization history constitute an important reference point to understand the process that led to the establishment of the Presidency of Religious Affairs. Therefore, it is first necessary to touch in general terms upon Ottoman Islam and how the religion–state–society relations have evolved.

The study will focus on the question of what kind of a role the Presidency of Religious Affairs has played in the nation-building process since the Turkish Republic was founded. In doing so, it will first review the Ottoman Islamic legacy, which the Turkish Republic has inherited, and indicate how Turkish nationalism developed in parallel with the dissolution of the Ottoman Empire. It will then address the legal, administrative, and institutional structure of the Presidency of Religious Affairs, founded by the Turkish Republic to manage the religious domain, and analyze the function the organization performs and the politics of religion that is based on a single sect. The Justice and Development Party (JDP) era, during which the Presidency of Religious Affairs has grown more powerful in every aspect and has become better able to involve in the nation-building task, will be dealt with in a separate chapter, and the organization's role and functions will also be set forth therein.

ISLAM IN THE OTTOMANS FROM POPULAR ISLAM TO THE ISLAM OF THE MEDRESE

It seems plausible to argue that as the Ottoman central state gained strength over the course of history, beginning with the foundation of the Empire, a trend to move from folk Islam to Medrese Islam, or in other words, a propensity to transition from a religious scene where folk *babas* were influential to a religious scene where the state *ulema* were influential came about. Ahmet Yaşar Ocak mentions four main sources producing Islamic jurisprudence in the Ottomans, which are: the state, the ulema, circles of mystics, and the people.[4] While certain interactions occurred between folk Islam and mysticism, on the one hand, and between madrasa Islam and mysticism, on the other, folk Islam and madrasa Islam always remained distant to each other and represented different dispositions. Contrary to folk Islam, which had a potential to stand up against state authority and mobilize masses, madrasa Islam made part of the state machinery, acted in line with state policy, and served the function of legitimizing the state's ruling authority in the eyes of the people from a religious perspective.

To put it in general terms, it is a well-known fact that socioreligious formations such as Ahiism and Babaiism and colonizing border ghazis and Turkmen babas holding titles, such as *abdal, ghazi, ahi,* and *alp,* were influential beginning from the foundation of the Ottoman Empire.[5] As the Ottoman state moved from being a principality with a less bureaucratic structure to an Empire with a more sophisticated bureaucratic organization, however, a religious bureaucracy emerged within the state and increasingly became one of its inseparable administrative parts. Thus, while folk Islam and mystic orders were more influential during the foundation era, madrasa, the representative of Sunni Islam, broadened its authority from the fifteenth century onwards.[6] Behind the Ottoman bureaucracy, defined as a "sultan-bureaucracy" by Kemal Karpat, ". . . were religious elites belonging to the established brand of Islam who provided the arguments required to legitimize state authority and ensure the obedience of the people . . ."[7]

Therefore, the religious domain, which had a more autonomous outlook in the foundation years of the Empire when the centrist power of the state was still weak, increasingly came under state control. Mystic sheikhs and folk babas, such as Sheikh Edebali, who is both the respected father-in-law of Osman Ghazi (1299–1324), the founder of the Ottoman dynasty, and a member of the Vefaiye order, and Geyikli Baba,[8] revered dearly by Osman Ghazi's son, Orhan Ghazi, lost their influence as the Ottoman state became more centralized in time. This was not only because the *ilmiye* class, the official religious bureaucracy led by the Sheikh-ul-Islam, gained power within the Ottoman administrative structure over time, but also due to the part played by the institutionalization and domestication of Ottoman mystical groups, as pointed out by Derin Terzioğlu.[9] Besides, it was not possible for tekke Islam to compete with madrasa, which had a place in the state bureaucratic structure and performed educational, religious, and legal functions. In addition, madrasa teachers and ulema working in courts started getting paid as civil servants in the sixteenth century.[10] While the Ottoman state kept religion under control with both its tekkes and ulema, the Sheikh-ul-Islam and the religious bureaucracy, in turn, looked for ways to strengthen their positions within the state machinery. Just as the sultan controlled all domains and refused to share his power with any other authority, the Sheikh-ul-Islam and the religious bureaucracy denied other actors, such as religious orders, a share in the power they derived through religion. Thus, the ulema, somewhat representing the state and madrasa, generally had a negative opinion of tekke Islam, represented by religious orders, save for a few exceptions.[11]

The tekke organization, which, even though it did not have a place in the state machinery, enjoyed financial and administrative autonomy, began to lose that autonomy in the nineteenth century. As the state grew weaker, religious orders received their share from the state's efforts to strengthen its central authority again. While certain tekke foundations were linked to Evkaf-ı Humayun and an obligation to notify the Sheikh-ul-Islam of sheikh service appointments was introduced in 1812, Meclis-i Meşayih was established under the Sheikh-ul-Islam, consisting of members from different orders, and tekkes were brought under madrasa control in 1866.[12] These regulations were followed by another regulation concerning Meclis-i Meşayih, dated 1915–1916.[13] Again, in 1916, the Sheikh-ul-Islam lost his place as a member of the government, and his office came under the Ministry of Justice, his capacity to manage foundations was revoked, and the management of madrasas was linked to the Ministry of Education.[14]

Thus, madrasa and tekke Islam were now both under state control. However, it was only possible to exist in this domain within the boundaries of Sunni Hanafism, the official sect. While all four schools allowed by Ottoman Sunni jurisprudence (*fiqh*), which are Hanafi, Maliki, Shafi'i, and Hanbali, were recognized, Hanafism enjoyed favoritism. According to Donald Quatert, ". . . while the ulema of Damascus adhered to the Shafi'i, Hanafi, and Hanbali schools of jurisprudence in 1650, nearly all were Hanafi in 1785. . . ."[15] Although it is possible to find abuses and anti-state attitudes by order sheikhs throughout the Ottoman history, only Bektashism was officially banned, in 1826. It appears that in the aftermath of that incident, Bektashis were removed from public office.[16] This is in line with the general character of the Ottoman official ideology. Opposition to the Ottoman official ideology and to the Ottoman system was judged with a strict Sunni understanding.[17]

There are many reasons why Sunnism, which the Republic inherited from the Ottomans, almost reached the status of an official religion, both internal and external. Kudret Emiroğlu rightly summarizes this process as follows: ". . . As the Ottomans ceased to be a tribal beylik and turned into a state and empire, they became alien to the Turkmen bodies, with whom they had shared the same faith. Therefore, from the common faith world of the foundation years were born Anatolian Alevism and Ottoman Sunnism. . . ."[18] The Sunni understanding embraced by the Sultan and the state bureaucracy only consolidated further when the caliphate passed over to the Ottomans in the sixteenth century and when the Safavids adopted Shi'a Islam. Challenges to Ottoman authority, on the other hand, were violently suppressed, whether they were Sunni, Shi'a, or from another Islamic sect. Ottoman rulers attached special importance to the battle on non-Sunni Islam, particularly Qizilbash

Alevism, which was followed by wide popular masses in Anatolia and the Balkans, the heart of the Ottoman state. Various methods were employed to make Sunnism the state's official religious understanding. As Mardin put it, the imposition of Sunni Islam,[19] the surveillance of Shi'a Islam, the expulsion of heterodox communities, and the efforts to create a religious elite subject to state control and an education system under the control of that elite were all intended for this aim.[20]

It seems sensible to include the Sunni schools of jurisprudence other than Hanafism in this obedient Sunnism framework as well, especially Shafi'ism. It can be argued that Hanafism and Shafi'ism,[21] which are both among the four schools of jurisprudence allowed by Sunni Islam and that constituted two major parts of the Sunni population in Asia Minor and its immediate vicinities from the Ottoman days to the Republican era, maintained a common understanding compliant to the state until the Republican era. Since the Republic's nation-state model had Turkishness as its axis, Shafi'ism was excluded from statist Sunnism due to its dominant Kurdish/Zaza character and could not sustain the status it had enjoyed in the Ottoman days. Undoubtedly, the fact that the new nation-state rested on Turkishness played a great part in this.

The Ottoman state first expanded towards the Balkans with a moderate Islamic understanding, even absorbing Christianity in various forms, but as the Quranic Islam approach gained the upper hand beginning during the rule of Mehmed II and the Ottomans engaged in a statist Hanafi-Shafi'i alliance following the Ottoman-Safevid conflict, they maintained a Sunni religious understanding expecting compliance to the Ottoman state. While a Sunni religious figure, community, or order could also face intervention, the Qizilbash communities were ostracized altogether regardless of their ethnicity from the sixteenth century on. Bektashism played an effective role in the expansion of the Ottoman Empire, especially in the Balkans, and received protection from the state until 1826, after which date, however, it met extensive hostile propaganda and was outlawed.

It should be remembered that the perception of the state was a matter of sacred faith itself just like the Islamic religion. The state, which was embodied in the person of the sultan, could only control and direct the ulema, representing Islam, because the survival of the sacred state was considered above everything else. The continuation of the state was only possible by the maintenance of "the order of the world."[22] This made the state the primary and ultimate authority in every domain, including Islam. Ocak describes this as "the identification of state and religion" and formulates it in the following words: "In the Ottoman state, everything is for the state. Religion, too, is for the state."[23]

As the head of the Ottoman ulema, the Sheikh-ul-Islam performed the role of regulating and controlling the religious domain, a potential threat to the state due to its influence on the people. In the words of Esra Yakut, "...The Sheikh-ul-Islam, the highest office in the Ottoman central organization, whose duty was to issue fatwa, assumed the role of leader of the ilmiye class, monitored affairs relating to religious courts, education in madrasas and madrasa students and acted as the sultan's proxy on such matters beginning in the sixteenth century. . . . "[24] Both before and during the Ottoman Empire, many movements, such as the Babai revolt, the Revolt of Sheikh Bedreddin, and the Şahkulu rebellion, were encountered in which religion played a part and that were led by a religious figure. For this reason, the Ottoman administration viewed the religious domain as a threat to the state and, therefore, formed a wide bureaucratic religious institutionalization having administrative, legal, and educational capacities, led by the Sheikh-ul-Islam, in an effort to bring the religious domain under state control in time.[25] This bureaucratic apparatus lacked autonomy, and its staff, from the Sheikh-ul-Islam to the lowest-rank officer, were civil servants whose pay, service appointment, dismissal, and fatwas[26] were all subject in every aspect to the command of politics—that is, the sultan.[27] Many Sheikh-ul-Islams were dismissed, sent on exile, or executed for a number of reasons such as old age, complaints, not being on good terms with the grand vizier, slander, and involvement in political affairs.[28] As stated by Madeline Zılfı, "The Sheikh-ul-Islam was the voice of sharia, and the sultan was subject to the terms of sharia, but it was still the sultan who appointed or dismissed the Sheikh-ul-Islam. . . ."[29] When the Ministry of Justice and the Ministry of Education were founded with the Tanzimat to deal, respectively, with legal and educational affairs, the office of the Sheikh-ul-Islam found its scope of authority narrowed down and restricted to the religious domain, but it had a seat in *Heyet-i Vükela*, that is, the Council of Ministers. Between 1920 and 1923, when the new Republic was to be founded yet, this office was taken over by a minister called Şer'iye ve Evkaf Vekili, the Minister of Sharia and Foundations, from İcra Vekilleri Heyeti, the Council of Ministers.[30]

To sum up, the main function of the Ottoman institution of the Sheikh-ul-Islam and the religious bureaucracy thereunder is to ensure the legitimacy of political decisions from a religious perspective. Some relevant examples are as follows: the issuance of a fatwa when Selim I or Yavuz Sultan Selim asks the ulema for a fatwa regarding whether a battle on the Qizilbash Alevis in Anatolia is permissible;[31] the issuance of a fatwa by the Sheikh-ul-Islam upon the request of Mahmud II to elicit popular consent for the Ottomans to receive military assistance from Russia against Egypt;[32] the approval by a fatwa of the Sheikh-ul-Islam of the decision made by the Senate (*Meclis-i Ayan*) and the Chamber of Deputies (*Meclis-i Mebusan*) under the name the General National Assembly (*Meclis-i Umumi-i Milli*) to dethrone Abdulhamid II.[33]

FROM THE OTTOMAN NATION TO THE TURKISH NATION

While the transition from an empire to a nation-state might appear to have taken place rapidly, behind it was the tragic geographical and mental ruptures that occurred in the Ottoman territory in the nineteenth century. As a response to the emerging nationalism, the Ottomans first turned to Ottomanism, aimed at keeping Muslims and non-Muslims together, in an effort to transform the Empire's subjects into citizens. When it turned out that the disengagement of non-Muslims could not be prevented, however, the Ottomans took to the idea of Islamic unity. This proved not to be the remedy either, and the spread of nationalism among Muslims could not be avoided.[34] The various salvation formulas that were given a try in the late Ottoman era eventually gave in to Turkish nationalism. Islam bore great importance in Ottoman society, but due to the growing influence of nationalism, it was far from ensuring unity in society on its own. In this regard, Jean-François Bayart's point that the nation-state was born out of the empire, not the nation, but the main carrier of that transition was Islam, is quite well-placed.[35] Thus, it is possible to observe the overlapping and contradicting aspects of Turkishness and Islam in all debates that surrounded language and religion throughout the Turkish Republican history.[36]

It is well-known that the founding elements of the Ottomans and their dynasty had Turkish origins.[37] On the other hand, as the Empire expanded towards the Balkans in the fourteenth and fifteenth centuries and towards the east in the sixteenth century, it seems to have acquired a cosmopolitan face not only in terms of the ethnic/religious diversity of its geography but also regarding the ethnic/religious diversity among its administrative ranks. While the Turkish communities, which made up one of the Empire's dominant nations, did not hold a privileged place in the eyes of the emerging high culture or urban Ottoman elites or before law, it was still possible to talk about a Muslim/non-Muslim distinction in the Ottoman millet system. As stated by Hugh Poulton, ". . . The first requirement for high office in the Ottoman Empire was to be Muslim, and the second was to speak Ottoman Turkish. Ethnicity was not a factor by itself, and many grand viziers and high-rank officers came from Albanian, Muslim, Slavic, or other Ottoman Muslim populations. . . ."[38] In addition, Turkishness, which rests on Turkish nationalism and that has been praised throughout Turkey's Republican history, could take on a pejorative meaning in the Ottoman days.[39] As has partly been explained above, however, the process that the Empire was going through at the time left the ruling elite no choice other than to submit to Turkish nationalism. As the Balkan nations left the Empire, the ratio of Muslims rose, and Islam became more highlighted along with Ottomanism. The idea that the survival of the Empire could be through Turkishness gained greater force, however, when other Muslim communities, such as Arabs, began leaving the Empire as well. As rightly conveyed by Reşat Kasaba, the increasing political challenges, military defeats, and economic hardships in the late nineteenth century oriented the Ottoman ruling elite to the idea that ". . . it was only through defining a homogenous and cohesive community that they could maintain their existence, which they believed to be synonymous with the survival of the state and the land. . . ."[40] The founding fathers of the Republic, led by Mustafa Kemal Pasha, began revealing their intentions concerning the religious domain more clearly as the regime consolidated itself. Those who had asked the leaders of religious orders for their assistance during the war were the same cadres who enacted the legislation banning religious orders in 1925.

The founders of the Republic, who were raised in the late Ottoman era and witnessed the dramatic destruction of that great empire, appear to have taken the process of modernization that began in the Ottoman days further and placed it in a direction with Turkishness and Turkish nationalism rather than Islam as its axis. That was the product of the developments in the late Ottoman era. According to them, it was clear that the nation-state founded under the name "The Republic of Turkey" could not have a foundation with religious principles. The head of the Istanbul government, who was also the caliph, was a prisoner in Istanbul. The article that "sovereignty belongs to the people without condition," the first article accepted by the Assembly in Ankara, which involved many religious representatives, dated to January 20, 1920, bears importance. This article shows the latest phase of Ottoman modernization at the time and the national character of the new Republic clearly. Turning to a new political system in which worldly power was separated from sultanic rule, the Assembly of Ankara engaged in the task of founding the Turkish nation-state through a series of operations.[41] This construct of a nation-state was to establish the Directorate of Religious Affairs, subjecting a model of religious organization based on the regulation and control of the religious domain by the state, which became increasingly highlighted in the late Ottoman era, to the will of the nation and its parliament instead of to the authority of the sultan.

STATE MANAGEMENT OF ISLAM IN THE TURKISH REPUBLIC: THE PRESIDENCY OF RELIGIOUS AFFAIRS

As I argued in a previous study,[42] the Presidency of Religious Affairs was established and developed as an invention of the "secular" Republic to handle the issue of religion in Turkey. According to Karpat, the Presidency of Religious Affairs can be regarded to be the contemporary counterpart of the Ottoman institutions of *Meshihat* and the Sheikh-ul-Islam.[43] It can be observed clearly in the activities relating directly or indirectly to the issue of religion during the early years of the Republic that the question of reform and modernization in the Islamic religion occupied the minds of the founding cadres and that they saw a need to take radical steps in that regard. The Presidency of Religious Affairs is one of the most important among such steps and should be evaluated in light of a number of other relevant developments. This part will cover the process of the legal, administrative, and institutional formation of that organization.

If we take a look at the historical process, Pasha and his friends seem to have advanced step by step towards their objective. The founding cadres, who had made efforts to take advantage of religious figures and institutions in the years of the National Liberation War, began implementing their own designs, intended to narrow down the role of religion and the religious bureaucracy in social life, as the regime consolidated its power. The Republican regime inherited from the Ottomans a large religious bureaucracy with influence in the domains of education and religion and a social order in which hundreds of tekkes and the different orders thereunder reigned. During the National Liberation War, the social influence of religious orders was sought, and Pasha wrote strong order sheiks letters asking for support. He paid a visit to the Haci Bektash tekke and appointed Abdulhalim Efendi, the sheikh of the Mevlana dargah in Konya, as one of the deputy speakers of the parliament, and Cemaleddin Efendi,[44] the leader of the Haci Bektash dargah, as another. He also paid a visit to the tomb of Hacı Bayram-ı Veli in Ankara during the opening of the Grand National Assembly in 1920.[45] After he attended the noon prayer in the Haci Bayram Mosque that day, the flag of Hacı Bayram-ı Veli was taken to the Assembly premise and was erected above the speaker's stand. According to Bernard Lewis, ". . . one fifth of the first Grand National Assembly were members of the religious profession, and some of them, both from the ulema and from the religious orders, played an important role in the Kemalist movement."[46] This way it became apparent that the founders of the Republic were aware of the influence religion had enjoyed on society for centuries and that they were prepared to make use of the power of religious orders and of the religious sentiments of the people where they saw fit. As the Republican regime gained force, they tried to change the old religious structure and create a more controllable religious domain. One example of this is the gradual strategy followed by Pasha in his efforts to abolish the Ottoman sultanate and the caliphate. He did not target the sultanate and the caliphate both at once. He made a speech in the National Assembly on November 1, 1922, where he expressed a need to separate the sultanate and the caliphate and the absolute need to abolish the sultanate. The following day, the legislation outlawing the sultanate was declared to the world.[47] The abolition of the sultanate was followed by the declaration of the Republic, the abolition of the caliphate, and the adoption of the Constitution of 1924, all of which were developments that bear significance with regard to the religion-state relations in the new Republic.

When all these regulations are evaluated as a whole, they can be viewed as practices intended to keep the religious domain in the service of the state and under its control, beginning from the early days of the Republic. In this regard, it is striking that following the foundation of the Republic, Pasha and the founding cadres introduced various reforms in the legal, educational, and social domains that complemented one another. The following are some of the important developments that took place concerning religious affairs: the abolition of the caliphate; the transformation of the Ministry of Sharia and the Foundations (Şeriye ve Evkaf Vekaleti) into a general directorate; and the passing of the Law on the Unification of Education (*Tevhid-i Tedrisat*).

What is relevant to our discussion here is the establishment of the Presidency of Religious Affairs on March 3, 1924, which constitutes the "sharia" part of the Ministry of Sharia and the Foundations. The Ministry of Sharia and the Foundations was abolished, and in its place were established the Presidency of Religious Affairs (*Diyanet İşleri Reisliği*; later *Diyanet İşleri Başkanlığı*) and the Directorate General of Foundations (*Evkaf Umum Müdürlüğü*, later *Vakıflar Genel Müdürlüğü*) under the Office of the Prime Minister. The area of duty of the Presidency of Religious Affairs was defined in Legislation No. 429 on March 3, 1924, as "carrying out affairs relating to the Islamic faith and its places of worship and managing religious institutions." The responsibility to manage all mosques (*masjids*) in the country and their staff, as well as tekkes and *zaviyes* and their staff, was given to the Presidency.

This development was followed by the abolition of tekkes and *zaviyes* a year later. Prior to this, on August 30, 1925, however, Pasha made a speech in Kastamonu against religious orders and tekkes, and he stated, "O gentlemen and o nation, you must know, and know well, that the Republic of Turkey cannot be the land of sheikhs, dervishes, disciples, and laymen. The straightest, the truest order is the order of civilization."[48] That speech was followed by a Cabinet decision providing for the closure of tekkes, *zaviyes*, and sacred tombs a few days later on September 2, 1925, and Legislation No. 677 on November 30, 1925, officially outlawed religious orders and tekkes.[49] Thus, with the closing down of tekkes and *zaviyes*, the duties relating to them were omitted from the sphere of responsibility of the Presidency of Religious Affairs. During the opening of the Ankara School of Law on November 5, 1925,

Pasha indicated that the new Republic would rest on the unity of "the nation" (*ulus*), using the following words: "The nation believes that the common bond it needs to preserve its existence is membership to the Turkish nation, not centuries-old religious or sectarian bonds."[50] This statement was another sign that the new nation-state would be based on loyalty to the nation-state rather than religious or sectarian bonds. It was followed by a number of reforms intended to empower the nation-state and weaken the influence of religion.

Later on, the Swiss civil code was adopted, and the link between sharia law and criminal law was broken in 1926, the constitutional article mentioning Islam as the state religion was annulled in 1928, and the transition from the Arabic script to the Latin script took place in 1928.[51] These changes bore important consequences with regard to the religious domain. The budget bill of 1927 allocated the Presidency of Religious Affairs 7,172 staff positions and introduced various administrative regulations. The budget bill of 1931 transferred the management of all mosques and their staff to the General Directorate of Foundations, and thus the Directorate of Religious Institutions (*Dini Müesseseler Müdürlüğü*) and the Directorate of Supplies (*Levazım Müdürlüğü*) were passed over to the General Directorate of Foundations with all their staff, including 4,081 "charity servants" (*hayrat hademesi*) and twenty-six preachers. Legislation No. 2800 on June 22, 1935, on the Organization and Obligations of the Presidency of Religious Affairs is the first organizational legal document of the Presidency. The Bill No. 5634 of April 29, 1950, changed the name of the Presidency from *Diyanet İşleri Reisliği* to *Diyanet İşleri Başkanlığı,* and the management of mosques and their staff positions, which had been transferred to the General Directorate of Foundations, were returned to the Presidency of Religious Affairs. The Presidency of Religious Affairs first received a place in the general state administration with the Constitution of 1960, which stated that its duty was to perform the functions specified in the special bill. Legislation No. 633 of August 15, 1965, on the Establishment and Duties of the Presidency of Religious Affairs expanded the Presidency's area of operation. Some amendments to Legislation No. 633 were introduced by Legislation No. 1982 of March 26, 1976, but they were later annulled by the Constitutional Court on December 18, 1979. The Constitution of 1982 involves the following provision on the Presidency of Religious Affairs: "The Presidency of Religious Affairs, which makes part of the general state administration, performs the functions specified in the special bill, remaining outside all political opinions and ways of thinking and aiming at national solidarity and integration, in line with the principle of secularism." The major novelty introduced thereby is the assignment of a "national solidarity and integration" task to an institution, the main function of which is to offer religious services. The Presidency of Religious Affairs, which already performed such a task in conformity with state policy even though it was not in the Constitution, was explicitly charged by the post-military coup Constitution with a solidarity and integration task. This can be interpreted to mean that the state wanted the Presidency of Religious Affairs to make a greater contribution to the nation-building project. The Presidency was reorganized later by Decree No. 190 of December 14, 1983. With each JDP government since 2002, the status of the Presidency of Religious Affairs within the general state administration has been promoted further, its area of operation has been broadened, and its staff number has been increased. In line with the conservative Islamist politics of the government over this period, the position of religion and, thus, the Presidency in the nation-building process has attained greater importance. Therefore, the JDP-era developments need to be addressed separately later.

RELIGION AND THE PRESIDENCY OF RELIGIOUS AFFAIRS AS POWERFUL INSTRUMENTS OF THE NATION-STATE

The Presidency of Religious Affairs, whose legal, administrative, and structural transformation over the course of history we have tried to summarize earlier in this chapter, has served as one of the most important instruments in the Turkish Republic's project of creating an ethnically and religiously homogenous nation. As Mardin put it, "The Republican state achieved to keep religion under control through the Presidency of Religious Affairs, truly an institution of the Republic."[52] The developments that took place during the dissolution of the Empire and all remedies the Ottomans resorted to in order to keep the disintegrating Empire together ultimately led to a Turkish nationalism intertwined with Sunni Hanafism. Efforts were made, using all means of the state, to spread the Sunni Hanafi religious understanding among popular masses, the state's official ideology from the Ottoman days to the Republic. Since the Ottoman Empire to the present day, alternative religious understandings were not allowed to emerge or to exist alongside the Sunni understanding. In this framework, many ethnic and religious communities that were not Sunni in the past had to adopt the Sunni understanding over the course of time.[53] As can be inferred from the fatwas of the Sheikh-ul-Islams and other official documents, this has been implemented as a state policy since the Ottoman times to the Republican era and played a prominent part in the Turkish nation-building process.[54] It should be remembered at this point that not only Religious Affairs employees, such as imams and preachers are public personnel on the state payroll, but at the same time, the mosque is a kind of government office. Religious services are under state control and are run by the Presidency of Religious Affairs on behalf of the state. It is significant that this institution has preserved its importance during the period of every government from the foundation of the Republic to the present day, be it secular, Islamic, or from a different pole. Every ruling party has had different important justifications for the need for this organization.[55] As observed by İştar Gözaydın, the importance of the Presidency of Religious Affairs "in shaping and reproducing religiosity in Turkey"[56] is evident.

Just as the office of the Sheikh-ul-Islam in the Ottoman state was subject to politics like the rest of the entire bureaucratic apparatus of the sultan, the Presidency of Religious Affairs has been an institution subject to politics, including while the decision to create it was being made. In the words of Feroz Ahmad, "The Kemalists did not introduce the principle of the separation of religion and state but a brand of Islam controlled by the state. They intended to use Islam in such a way that the Presidency of Religious Affairs would legitimize their revolution and their reform program whenever necessary."[57] While the religious bureaucracy assumed duties and liabilities for the survival of the Ottoman Empire in the past, the Presidency of Religious Affairs is under the command of the ruling power and operates in the construction of the nation-state of a new, "secular" regime—that is, the Republic. As pointed out by Bayart, the Presidency of Religious Affairs has brought religious services and religious training under its control and has thus suppressed all kinds of challenges to the ideology of the Republic.[58] This way, it has been possible to preclude any opposition likely to emerge among the people, particularly concerning the modernizing changes introduced by the Republic.

The Presidency of Religious Affairs is a wide organizational network that can reach out to the remotest villages with its 150,000 staff members. Considering that there is a mosque even in villages with no school, it is evident what an important function Religious Affairs staff, such as imams, preachers, and Quran instructors, serve by making the state's religious understanding accessible to the remotest places. The local chaplain, himself a villager, has been an inseparable part of the village for centuries. The teacher, on the other hand, has remained a person sent on a mission by the Republic, an outsider in the local community. Marcel Bazin puts this as follows: "Another prominent figure in the village is the *hodja* or the sheikh (the chaplain who is one of the villagers himself). The Kemalist Republic sends a key third person to the village, and this person is the teacher. This uninvited guest from outside the village, however, most often remains outside the local community."[59] The Republican administration outlawed religious orders, brought religious places such as mosques, tekkes, and dargahs under its control, and narrowed down the informal religious domain drastically through its official courses and educational institutions, which became more widespread in the course of time. On the other hand, the chaplain who takes part as a public officer in such a broad network of mosques has been able to serve important functions as an efficient propaganda tool as well, and the state has acquired an opportunity to convey its imperatives to the remotest places through him. This way, the support of religion was obtained in getting the people to embrace different aspects of the nation-building project.

It seems that the Presidency of Religious Affairs is under state control, with its staff subject to service appointment and its activities dependent on political decisions, and that it is used as an efficient and plain instrument not only in spreading the official understanding of religion but also in making political decisions accessible to society. The efforts of the Presidency of Religious Affairs from its establishment to the present day to spread and legitimize actions by the ruling power are clear. Its wide organizational network and the prestigious place of religion in society render the Presidency of Religious Affairs important from this perspective. The appointment and dismissal of the President of Religious Affairs depends entirely on the ruling party.[60] In this regard, politicians and the General Staff have often interfered in the work of the Presidency of Religious Affairs throughout the history of Turkey.[61]

Many Presidents of Religious Affairs were dismissed, resigned, or were forced to retire in the past. To see this better, it is sufficient to look at how the directors over the JDP era since 2002 were appointed and how they left office: Mehmet Nuri Yılmaz, the fifteenth President of Religious Affairs, was appointed in 1992 and resigned in 2003; Ali Bardakoğlu, the sixteenth President of Religious Affairs, was appointed in 2003 and resigned in 2010; Mehmet Görmez, the seventeenth President of Religious Affairs, was appointed in 2010 and resigned in 2017; and Ali Erbaş, the eighteenth President of Religious Affairs, was appointed in 2017 and is currently in office.

It is possible to observe traces of political influence in the work of the Presidency of Religious Affairs and in many statements made by its officials. The President of Religious Affairs, or other high-rank Religious Affairs officials, often releases statements in line with state policies. The impact of the ruling power can also be seen clearly in the organization's official communications. It is well-known that the use of the Western-style hat was encouraged in the early years of the Republican regime. The Presidency of Religious Affairs sent offices of the mufti communications to encourage the Western-style hat. In 1926, a letter was sent to offices of the mufti informing that wearing the hat during prayer was fine,[62] and another letter was sent demanding all mosque participants to wear the hat during prayer.[63] Let us turn to more recent examples. We have noted previously that since the Ottoman times, the state, which wanted to hold a monopoly in the religious domain, kept their distance from religion, and especially the ilmiye class and its head, the Sheikh-ul-Islam, generally displayed a negative approach towards religious orders. The same holds true for the Republican era. It is well-known that the Presidency of Religious Affairs keeps a distant approach to religious orders and communities in its publications and statements and intends to control religious orders and communal formations within the principle of regulating the religious domain, a principle that it views as one of its legal obligations.[64] In the process following the unsuccessful coup attempt by former Religious Affairs staff member Fethullah Gülen, who transformed his community into a terrorist organization, the Presidency of Religious Affairs organized a meeting with the representatives of various religious orders and communities under the name *The Communities and Orders Meeting*.[65] The representatives of religious orders and communities invited to attend the meeting were sent by the Presidency of Religious Affairs various principles to follow to comply with the framework drawn by the state.[66] The denial of status to places of worship other than the mosque is also part of state policy. Although it is not a secret that Alevis attend the *cemevi*, not the mosque, Religious Affairs officials persistently defend this practice in conformity with state policy. In this regard, it is sufficient to take a look at the statements made by the current director in this direction. While it is a well-established fact that Alevis have traditionally not attended the mosque for centuries, the President of Religious Affairs has released a statement reiterating the official opinion that "the mosque is the place of worship of both the Sunnis and the Alevis."[67] The JDP government is also known to support participation banking, sometimes called Islamic banking. Not only has participation banking been promoted by the state, but at the same time, the largest state bank has opened a participation banking unit. Officials of the Presidency of Religious Affairs have made statements in favor of participation banking to conform with the stance of the ruling power.[68] In addition, the collection of skins from animal sacrifices, which is significant economically, has always ignited debate in Turkey, and this issue is handled in accordance with decisions by the political organ. Religious communities, orders, scholars, and, albeit not explicitly, the circles of the Presidency of Religious Affairs, which was already being given a share, were uneasy with the official policy to allocate skins from animal sacrifices to the Turkish Aeronautical Association. A communication dated November 11, 1945, to the Office of the Mufti in Konya requested that "preachers and orators make calls to the public to donate skins and intestines from their animal sacrifices to the Turkish Aeronautical Association."[69] A news article from 1998 reads: "The Presidency of Religious Affairs has decided to donate to the Turkish Aeronautical Association the 10 percent share it receives from animal skins collected by the Foundation of Religious Affairs."[70] A legal amendment in 2013 abolished the Turkish Aeronautical Association's monopoly on skins from animal sacrifices.[71]

Power/regime changes and mentality changes immediately reflect on the work of the Presidency of Religious Affairs, and the institution of politics tries to legitimize such changes in the eyes of the general population through religion. For instance, in a communication to offices of the mufti, dated January 1, 1923,[72] preachers and orators were asked to make public that Abdulmecid had been elected caliph to replace Vahideddin. This way, the fact that an office that claims to be the leader of not only Ottoman Muslims but all Muslims around the world is under government control is made known to all citizens. In another letter sent to offices of the mufti on March 7, 1924,[73] religious staff was instructed to pray for the Republic and the nation, not for the Caliph (the Ottoman sultan), in their mosque speeches. This is because the caliphate, for which the Sheikh-ul-Islam and the religious bureaucracy had prayed for centuries from the time of Yavuz Sultan Selim, was abolished, and in its place was founded the Republican rule in the name of the nation. Thus, religious staff must now pray and have the people pray for the new ruling power and in the way desired by the new ruling power. Similarly, a letter sent to offices of the mufti, dated March 1, 1927, requests that old-edition mawlid books involving a prayer for the Ottoman sultan to be collected and new mawlid books be prepared and published.[74] In addition, the contents of religious books and sermons were kept under control.[75] Following the replacement of the Arabic script with the Latin script, efforts were made to spread the new regime's language policy.[76] It is also striking that after the decision to recite the Islamic call to prayer in the Turkish language was adopted, legal action was taken against those who failed to abide by it.[77] As can be seen from all these examples, the Presidency of Religious Affairs performs important services in the nation-building process as the Republic's most powerful instrument on society. The examples described here show that different policies that come with different governments immediately reflect on the work of the Presidency of Religious Affairs.

THE SINGLE-SECT POLICY OF THE NATION-STATE AND THE PRESIDENCY OF RELIGIOUS AFFAIRS

The previous chapter uses various exemplary incidents to give an account of how religion is a state institution instrumentalized by the nation-building project in Turkey. We will now try to examine how the sectarian structure inherited from the Ottomans has been maintained and how the Presidency of

Religious Affairs has employed a single-sect approach to creating a homogenous nation-state since the foundation of Turkey.

While it operates using an enormous budget financed by all taxpayers, the Presidency of Religious Affairs offers services for the Sunni citizens only; tries to define Alevism through the lens of Sunnism and assimilate the former into the latter; and functions with its staff, publications, and work as the most important instrument of the state policy based on a single sect. A general agreement exists among researchers on the sectarian role of the Presidency of Religious Affairs in the nation-state building task. Ocak says, "On the other hand, while no explicit reference to Sunnism or Alevism was made when Ataturk personally ordered the establishment of the Presidency of Religious Affairs in the Republican era, it has been evident from the term in office of the first President of Religious Affairs and from the first official publications of the organization to the present day that the Presidency has been structured according to Sunni Hanafism,"[78] and Mardin argues that the Presidency of Religious Affairs represents and promotes the Sunni Hanafi faith.[79] The expressions "followers of the Islamic sects opposed to the Sunni Muslim faith"[80] and "followers of the sects opposed to the Sunni Muslims"[81] are such as to demonstrate the discriminatory and single-sect character of the Presidency of Religious Affairs based on an "us vs. them" mentality.

Governments, ruling parties, Religious Affairs circles, religious scholars, and the Sunni community tend to deny and generally defend the Presidency's sectarian role.[82] The argument by former President of Religious Affairs, Professor Ali Bardakoğlu, that the Presidency of Religious Affairs was never a Sunni organization, did not pursue any policy to spread Sunnism, and offered government service at an equal distance to all citizens,[83] and the statement by Kara that "since its establishment to this day, it has never released a publication against the Alevis or Alevism, save for some indirect anti-esoteric remarks. . . ."[84] are products of the same efforts to conceal sectarianism. Despite this defensive approach and their assessment of Islam from the Sunni perspective only, some religious scholars and Religious Affairs staff members feel obliged to acknowledge indirectly that some aspects of the Presidency of Religious Affairs are discriminatory against Alevism. For instance, while School of Religion faculty member Sönmez Kutlu says, "Not only could Alevism and Bektashism not find room in khutbas, preaches, or religious publications until the late 1980s, but at the same time, almost no serious publication relating to any of these was made by the Presidency,"[85] former Religious Affairs chief inspector Abdülkadir Sezgin admits the existence of defamations against the Alevis using the following words: "The vilifications that started in 1826 were carried on by the state, mosques, schools, and madrasas, and the Turkish intelligentsia earned heroic achievements in this smear campaign. This is a big disgrace for us all. I continue to be ashamed of it as a religious staff member, as an intellectual, as a scientist."[86]

The entire historical process reveals the function performed by the Presidency of Religious Affairs as the most important tool in the state project of building a monosectarian nation. The Presidency of Religious Affairs, which operates in a contradictory manner, both under the principle of secularism and with a monosectarian understanding, has a constitutional status. We shall first try to expose through the relevant legislation and then through its structure, functioning, and work how the Presidency of Religious Affairs implements the state's sectarian policy.

According to Article 136 of the Constitution of 1982, "The Presidency of Religious Affairs, which makes part of the general state administration, performs the functions specified in the special bill, remaining outside all political opinions and ways of thinking and aiming at national solidarity and integration, in line with the principle of secularism." Thus, this constitution, a product of the regime following the military coup of September 12, 1980, places on the institution the objectives to handle religious affairs in line with "secularism" and to ensure solidarity and integration whenever necessary. The functions specified in the bill are a reference to the Legislation on the Organization and Obligations of the Presidency of Religious Affairs, which regulates the organization of the Presidency of Religious Affairs. Its Article 1, entitled "the duty," is: "The Presidency of Religious Affairs has been founded under the Office of the Prime Minister in order to conduct affairs relating to the beliefs and the rules of worship and morality of the Islamic religion, to illuminate society regarding religion, and to manage places of worship."[87] Evidently, not only is it not possible for the High Committee on Religious Affairs—which is the highest decision-making and advisory body under the Presidency and that rests on Sunni Islam judging from its staff members and the state religious policies—to remain impartial while performing some of its many duties such as following religious publications in the country and abroad, assessing them, setting forth the principles for counter-publication, and preparing reports on the textbooks, syllabi, and programs of religious courses, but at the same, this situation seriously harms the principle of secularism.[88] It runs contrary to secularism that while many constitutional articles emphasize it,[89] there exists an institution based on Sunni Islam that is financed from the general budget formed by all the taxpayers' money. In other words, it is not clear how the Presidency of Religious Affairs, which has been founded, according to its special bill, "in order to conduct affairs relating to the beliefs and the rules of worship and morality of the Islamic religion, to illuminate society regarding religion, and to manage places of worship" can perform its functions ". . . in line with the principle of secularism. . . ."

as provided for by Article 136. Another problem is that since it is grounded in the Sunni understanding of Islam, it fails to offer public service impartial even to different members of the Islamic religion. The existence of the Presidency of Religious Affairs and its activities explicitly contravene Article 10 of the Constitution, entitled "Equality before Law," and Article 24, entitled "Freedom of Religion and Conscience."

The fact that the Republic has, since its foundation, been grounded in secularism, a model based on the separation of state and religion, while it has also taken various steps to form an ethnically and religiously homogenous order is proof of pseudo-secularism and constitutes a contradictory situation, which has come to pass as ordinary in Turkey. This is summarized by Öktem as follows: "There is not an exact separation of state and religion in Turkey. This is most clearly seen in the fact that the Presidency of Religious Affairs operates under the roof of the state. The Presidency of Religious Affairs organizes the official religious ideology of the state." Politicians and Religious Affairs officials see it necessary regarding their personal interests that religious services and training based only on Sunni Islam are publically financed and are imposed on society in various forms, and they defend this situation, arguing that Religious Affairs is "above all sects." Article 10 of the Constitution says, "Everyone is equal before law without distinction as to language, race, color, sex, political opinion, philosophical belief, religion and sect, or any such grounds. No privilege shall be granted to any individual, family, group, or class. State organs and administrative authorities are obliged to act in compliance with the principle of equality before law in all their proceedings," and it is a clear violation of the principle of equality before law that the Presidency of Religious Affairs, a state institution operating with a budget financed by all taxpayers' money, offers Sunni Islam services, and imposes them on other citizens in various forms. The motive underlying such practices in which the Presidency of Religious Affairs assumes the greatest part is the state's single-sect policy.

It can be argued that the religious policies in the Republican era have acquired a traditional character. The administrators and staff members of the Presidency of Religious Affairs from the bottom to the top ranks since the foundation of the Republic to the present day have come from families belonging to the Sunni community and are persons who have received education at Sunni madrasas, Quranic courses, imam-hatip (imam and orator) schools, high Islamic institutes, or schools of religion. In this framework, if the biographies[90] of and statements by the Directors since the foundation of the republic including the present one are analyzed, it can be seen that they have worked for the promotion of a single sect—that is, the understanding of Islam imposed by the state, which they have been trained in. In this regard, it is sufficient to take a look at the publications by the Presidency of Religious Affairs and statements by the organization and its staff. Ahmet Hamdi Akseki, the second President of Religious Affairs, who was also the deputy of Rifat Börekçi, the first President of Religious Affairs of the secular Republic, did not refrain from making statements that can be evaluated as hate speech against the non-Sunni Islamic schools of belief. In a foreword he penned for a book published by the Presidency of Religious Affairs, he describes Alevis, Qizilbashes, Bektashis, and many other groups as heretic and "demonic-souled" and ends with the following remark: "Protecting our nation against deception by these demonic-souled people is essential. We will do our best to add many more to our publications that aim to fulfill this duty. Guidance and assistance come from God."[91] The publication of the work, entitled *Sahih-i Buhari Muhtasarı Tecrid-i Sarih*, the most important source of *hadith* in Sunni Islam, is also a product of the single-sect understanding.[92] A communication sent by the Presidency of Religious Affairs to offices of the mufti on October 10, 1953, quotes the book İman ve İslam Rehberi by Preacher of Maraş: "Since they have no book, animals slaughtered by Alevis and Qizilbashes are not halal."[93] Another book released by the Presidency of Religious Affairs talks about "the ignorance of the Alevis" and argues that they call Ali by the name God and their faith is close to the Christian doctrine of trinity.[94] Another Religious Affairs publication authored by a professor of religion denigrates religious orders uses derogatory language and anonymously targets Alevism, saying "they hold religious ceremonies with alcohol, dance, and music, as in a primitive religion."[95] Examples abound and show the mentality based on a single sect promoted by the state through religious education and services.

Another consequence of the sectarian policies is the installation of the Sunni understanding in various forms. The state institution responsible from the field of religion—a field revolving around places of worship—is the Presidency of Religious Affairs. The mosque, which is the only officially recognized place of worship of Islam and is financially supported by the state, is supervised by the Presidency of Religious Affairs. Thus, being the only officially recognized place of worship, the mosque is promoted through many instruments, including the law. This leads to many problematic situations from forced state construction of mosques in non-Sunni villages to the construction of a mosque being put forth as a prerequisite for the provision of other public services, such as road construction. In some villages, while there is an imam assigned by the Presidency, there is no mosque participation.[96] In many others, while there is a mosque built, there is neither an imam nor a mosque-goer. As a result of the centuries-old sectarian policies, a great many villages have become Sunni or present themselves as such. Since the nation-building project has been carried out through Sunnism using all coercive means, it is quite understandable why many non-Sunni citizens choose to present themselves as such. This manifests itself particularly in neighborhood relations and at the workplace. In an effort to be known as Sunni Muslim, people often deny their religious, sectarian, and ethnic roots. They attend the Friday prayer, get up at night even though they do not fast, send their children to Quran study, and tell their children to conceal their Alevi identity.[97]

The state policy not to recognize the *cemevi* as a place of worship while there are thousands of *cemevis* operating around the nation is legitimized by the help of the Presidency of Religious Affairs. Similarly, the formation of a state institution to offer religious services for the Alevis is highly contested. It appears that differing from the type of pious Muslim portrayed by the Presidency of Religious Affairs is often evaluated and highlighted as a negative attribute not only by the state but also by the Presidency of Religious Affairs itself. Former President of Religious Affairs Ali Bardakoğlu legitimizes the existence of a Sunni Presidency of Religious Affairs through a discourse of Republican gains and unity and peace[98]: "Bardakoğlu noted that the proposals to establish an Alevi Presidency of Religious Affairs alongside the current one ran contrary to the Republican gains and might harm unity and peace."[99] In addition, the Presidency of Religious Affairs tries to eliminate debates as to the recognition of the *cemevi*, saying, "the *cemevi* cannot be accepted as an alternative to the mosque," and resorting to a theme of unity.[100] This strategy has been pursued since Bardakoğlu's term in office. In an interview, Erbaş, the current director, repeats the official opinion, which former directors had frequently voiced, and says, "Our brothers can engage in a friendly chat at the *cemevi*. They can perform the daily prayer (*namaz*) there if they like to. But the Muslim place of worship is the mosque. The mosque belongs to the Sunnis and the Alevis both."[101] It should be added here that the Presidents of Religious Affairs who preceded Prof. Mehmet Görmez did not pay visits to *cemevis* as a result of the sectarian policy at their time. In 2011, Görmez became the first President of Religious Affairs to pay a visit to a *cemevi* in the history of the Turkish Republic.[102] As can be inferred from the exclusionist policy against the *cemevi*, the state uses the Presidency of Religious Affairs to promote the mosque as the only place of worship and encourage Sunni religious practices such as fasting during Ramadan and the daily prayer so that a homogenous nation can be created.

THE JDP ERA, THE PRESIDENCY OF RELIGIOUS AFFAIRS, AND NATION-BUILDING

While it is well-known that the Presidency of Religious Affairs has sustained a growth trend in every aspect since the foundation of the Republic to this day, the developments in the JDP era render it necessary to address this era separately. It can be seen clearly from its concrete actions that as an Islamist conservative party[103] with a religious electorate, the JDP has made efforts to widen the religious domain, raising fundamental criticisms of the Turkish-type secularism, unlike the ruling parties that preceded it. The most important of such concrete actions include the spread of imam-hatip schools and Schools of Religion; the introduction of optional courses on religion along a compulsory course on religious culture and ethics in school curricula; the increase in the number of religious culture and ethics teachers; and the strengthening of the Presidency of Religious Affairs in every aspect. This seems in line with the pious Sunni nature of the ruling cadres and voters of the JDP, a party pursuing conservative Islamist politics,[104] and it consolidates the party's conservative base. The staff members of the Presidency of Religious Affairs and the other, educational institutions mentioned above mainly come from among the party's voters.[105]

All party programs from the 58th government (2002)—the first JDP government—to the 65th government (2016) seem to involve promises regarding the freedom of religion and conscience, religious services, and religious education.[106] Similarly, the party's 2023 Political Vision highlights religious sensitivities.[107] The 60th government program offers extensive room for the Presidency of Religious Affairs and states the support given to the organization in clear terms: "Dear Members of the Parliament, our government views religious services as an important field with regard to the survival of our moral and intangible values and the provision of our national solidarity and unity. During our term in office, all kinds of support have been granted for religious services to be conducted effectively. . . ."[108] In addition, the promises articulated before the recent presidential and parliamentary elections of 2018 include the foundation of an Academy of Religious Affairs that aims to provide Religious Affairs staff professional and vocational training. The same election declaration expresses the goal to offer services concerning the educational needs of the children of citizens abroad in collaboration with the Turkey Maarif Foundation.[109] The desire to establish an Academy of Religious Affairs as an addition to the existing imam-hatip schools and Schools of Religion is an advanced step in shaping society through Religious Affairs.

During the course of this legal and administrative transformation process, which we have tried to summarize in this chapter, the place of the Presidency of Religious Affairs within the state protocol, its areas of work, its budget, and its number of staff have all gradually increased. The amendments of 2010 raised the Presidency of Religious Affairs from the degree of general directorate to undersecretary and are expressed on the Presidency's official website as follows: "The existing structure of the Presidency was designated by the Law 6002, published on 01.07.2010 [July 1, 2010], which made a wide range of changes in the Law 633. The Law in point provided many significant gains for the Presidency. The Presidency, hierarchically, was raised from the degree of general directorate to undersecretary, in addition to two perpetual boards, fourteen service units being nine of them as at the level of general directorate, were constituted. . . ."[110] Furthermore, a number of debates on the place of the Presidency of Religious Affairs within the state protocol took place over the JDP era. Former Vice Prime Minister Bülent Arınç stated that the President of Religious Affairs was in the top five ranks within the protocol in Atatürk's time, and President Erdoğan expressed that while he was still prime minister, the place of the President of Religious Affairs was to be raised.[111] Moreover, when the official car purchased for former President of Religious Affairs Görmez ignited controversy, and he stopped using the car, Erdoğan ordered for the allocation of another car for the President. Most recently, with the transition to the presidential government system within the constitutional and administrative structure following the elections of January 24, 2018, the Decree No. 703 of July 2, 2018 made the Presidency of Religious Affairs one of the few important institutions that fall directly under the Office of the President rather than under the Office of the Prime Minister.[112] While a new protocol list has not been made,[113] it can be inferred from press news that the new state protocol list is likely to introduce new regulations and will place the Presidency of Religious Affairs higher.[114]

Owing specially to the "generous" resources granted during the JDP rule, the Presidency of Religious Affairs has turned into an enormous bureaucratic organization that conducts state religious policies by engaging in a number of areas ranging from foreign operations to national television and radio channels to the Turkish Foundation of Religious Affairs, which it manages using state resources, to educational services to healthcare. Recently, the Turkish Association of Religious Affairs has obtained a permit to launch a television channel as an addition to the state channel *TRT Diyanet TV*.

Also during the JDP era, the construction of many new mosques in the country and abroad was undertaken. In one of his statements, the President of Religious Affairs said, "No neighborhood should remain without a mosque in any of our cities." As of 2017, the number of mosques affiliated with the Presidency of Religious Affairs exceeds the total number of schools in the country, having reached 90,000.[115] Although it is one of the state institutions with the largest budget and the highest number of staff, Presidents of Religious Affairs and Religious Affairs employees have always expressed their discontent with the place of Religious Affairs within the state protocol and their desire to extend beyond the religious domain. Religious Affairs executives know very well the state's intentions to control the religious domain and to shape the nation through Religious Affairs and thus its need for Religious Affairs, and they have always endeavored to further their influence within the state bureaucracy. It seems that owing to the JDP's base and their dispositions, such demands can be articulated with relative ease. For instance, the farewell speech of former President of Religious Affairs Görmez to the Religious Affairs staff is significant: "The distance between the place of our Presidency of Religious Affairs in the heart of our dear nation and its place within the state bureaucracy must definitely be reconsidered. . . . It is imperative to decide in absolute terms whether this rooted organization is merely a bureaucratic institution or an institution representing the ilmiye and managing and guiding our spiritual life."[116]

During the JDP era, the institution has been strengthened in every aspect except autonomy. It is possible to see from its budget, resources, and work how the Presidency of Religious Affairs, which is the major state institution in the religious domain, played the lead role in the nation-building project based on Sunnism. For instance, the current organizational structure of the Presidency of Religious Affairs has been set forth by the Law No. 6002 of July 1, 2010, bringing amendments to the Law No. 633. It has raised the organization from the degree of general directorate to undersecretary, introduced new administrative regulations, and permitted non-religious services, such as television and radio channels.[117] The organizational structure the central organization of the Presidency of Religious Affairs consists of a president and five deputy presidents and involves advisory, regulatory, and auxiliary units in addition to main service units, such as the Presidency of the High Committee of Religious Affairs, the Presidency of the Committee of Quranic Study and Recitation, the Presidency of the Internal Inspection Unit, the Presidency of the Committee of Guidance and Supervision, the General Directorate of Religious Services, the General Directorate of Educational Services, the General Directorate of the Pilgrimage and Umrah, the General Directorate of Religious Publications, the General Directorate of External Relations, the General Directorate of Human Resources, the General Directorate of Managerial Services, and the Presidency for Strategy Development. The provincial organization of the Presidency of Religious Affairs consists of provincial and district offices of the mufti and directorates of educational centers. The Presidency, which has created a wide organizational and service network abroad, has been organized in the form of Undersecretaries of Religious Services within the embassies and in the form of Offices of the Attaché of Religious Services within the general consulates. We should add to these the Directorate of Legal, Press, and Public Relations and the Office of the Chief of Cabinet.[118] The Presidency of Religious Affairs also has connections in various areas with many organizations abroad, such as the Turkish–Islamic

Union for Religious Affairs,[119] the umbrella organization of 896 associations in Germany, and the Turkish–Islamic Union for Cultural and Social Solidarity in Austria.[120]

The annual reports, the last issue of which was released in 2017, provide important data on the budget, staff, and activities of the Presidency of Religious Affairs. The total budget spent in 2017 was 7,246,972,684 Turkish lira (TL). Of its 109,332 staff members, the largest groups are made up by 62,923 imam-hatip school employees, 19,299 Quran instructors, and 11,755 muezzins and mosque caretakers. According to the Presidency of Religious Affairs, which has duties relating to the pilgrimage,[121] 81,712 citizens went on pilgrimage. Eighty-two books were published with a total number of 8,975,664 copies, of which 237,842 were distributed for free within the country and abroad, and the Religious Affairs calendar was published in 2,644,400 copies. Many programs were produced for the television channel *Diyanet TV*. The budget is not spent entirely on the construction and renewal of mosques, offices of the mufti, and education centers in Turkey, but at the same time, for instance, many projects are currently in progress in Kirgizstan, Albania, Macedonia, Sierra Leone, and Gambia, and 112 mosques are under renewal in the city of al-Bab in Syria in collaboration with the Turkish Foundation of Religious Affairs.[122]

If we take a comparative look at the past years regarding staff and budget, the number of staff ranged from around 74,000 between 1989 and 2004[123] to 121,845 in 2013, and following the dismissals relating to the FETÖ investigations,[124] that number fell to 109,332 in 2017. This overall rise in the number of staff clearly demonstrates the importance the JDP government attaches to the Presidency of Religious Affairs.[125] The real increase in the Religious Affairs budget over the JDP era is visible in figures. The Religious Affairs budget experienced a 176 percent increase in the year 2012 as compared to the year 2002, and this is above the education, healthcare, and culture spending amounts in ratio.[126]

The developments that occurred following the unsuccessful coup attempt by the FETÖ strongly reveal the role of Religious Affairs in the national-building process. As part of the fight on the FETÖ, thousands of Religious Affairs staff members were dismissed, and a comprehensive action plan was put into place by the Presidency. In this framework, an extensive memorandum was issued. The ten-page memorandum regarding the events of July 15, 2016, which was sent by the Presidency of Religious Affairs to the Offices of the Governor on September 2, 2016, a detailed list of rules for Religious Affairs staff to abide by on the issue of the FETÖ was offered.[127] The anniversary of the day the coup attempt took place was declared by the JDP government as the 15th of July Democracy and National Unity Day, and many public institutions, including Religious Affairs, planned a series of activities in this regard. The circular dated 2018 concerning the 15th of July Democracy and National Unity Day states the importance of transforming the July 15 spirit into a common awareness in children and the nation and declares that a campaign by the name "We Recite the Quran For Our Martyrs" was launched. Also, a complete reading of the Quran was to be undertaken at least once in every mosque until July 15. According to the circular, the program included a Quran recitation feast in central mosques before the Friday prayer on July 13 for the souls of the martyrs; Quranic recitations in other mosques; and the reading of a Friday preaching concerning July 15 in all mosques around the country. Moreover, orders were given to organize a special program commemorating the martyrs under the themes of patriotic love and national unity and solidarity with the participation of summer-term Quran course instructors, students, and parents; to conduct in penal institutions and in temporary accommodation centers conferences entitled "What Happened on the 15th of July?" with their content to be determined by offices of the mufti; to pray for the souls of the martyrs in meetings organized by administrative chiefs with popular participation; and to pay visits to the martyrs' cemeteries and to the martyrs and veterans and their families under committees led by muftis. This comprehensive circular also included a plan to conduct "seminars on the fight against terrorist organizations abusing religion" and public conferences entitled "The 15th of July and Our Religious Security" in forty-one designated provinces during the month of July.[128] Thus, it appears that the Presidency of Religious Affairs extends beyond the religious domain and assumes duties relating to state security.

With the JDP coming to power, the Presidency of Religious Affairs, TIKA (the Turkish Cooperation and Coordination Agency), YTB (the Presidency for Turks Abroad and Related Communities),[129] the Yunus Emre Institutes, and, until the FETÖ coup attempt, the Gulenist schools all engaged in an unprecedented collaboration to support the project of Turkish Islam abroad, particularly in countries where Turkish and related communities and large Turkish worker populations live. The emphasis "Turks living abroad," which began to have a place in party programs beginning with the 59th program, has been widened over the years to include kin and related communities. This finds expression in the 65th JDP government program, the last before the presidential regime, as follows: "We will promote the improvement of the capacity of religious services abroad, extend their outreach to the whole society and the NGOs representing it [the whole society], and introduce a policy of local assignment."[130] Thus, the foreign operations of the Presidency of Religious Affairs have gradually grown regarding budget and staff and enhanced the organization's place in Turkish foreign policy. The main understanding underlying the foreign operations is in line with Turkey's nation-building project. The operations carried out by religious attachés and staff abroad, who are Religious Affairs employees or religious scholars, in collaboration with non-governmental organizations (NGOs) based there, are part of Turkey's foreign diplomatic missions. While religious services offered in Macedonia, Bulgaria, and Greece[131] in the Balkans are especially well-received by the Sunni communities and establish stronger bonds with those communities, the Alevi-Bektashi communities feel discriminated against, and thus they distance themselves away from Turkey. Similarly, the close political and religious bonds with the Sunnis in Iraq and Syria[132] are considered as the product of Turkey's sectarian approach by the Alevi Turkmen communities living in those countries, which, as a result, sometimes grow away from Turkey and turn to Shi'a Islam. While the sectarian approach followed by Turkey, both domestically and abroad, which the Presidency of Religious Affairs assumes a part in, consolidates the Sunni populations around the JDP government's nationalist and religious-based policies, the Alevi Turks living in Turkey and abroad believe that Turkey maintains the sectarian understanding inherited from the Ottomans under different forms, and they express unease.

In conclusion, over the JDP era, religious education has been promoted regarding the numbers of schools, courses, and teachers; the Presidency of Religious Affairs has intensified its religious services domestically and abroad; and the organization's role in the creation of a nation consisting of acceptable citizens desired by the state has been broadened. As an institution that not only provides religious services for a particular sect but also assumes the function to ensure national unity and solidarity, the Presidency of Religious Affairs has been supported with regard to its budget, staff, and activities during the JDP era more than ever before.

CONCLUSION

It appears that the Presidency of Religious Affairs occupies a central place in the nation-building project of the Republic of Turkey. The country's religious policy was formed taking into account the positions held by the institution of the Sheikh-ul-Islam, which was part of the Ottoman state tradition and that evolved over time, and by the religious orders vis-à-vis the state and society. The Islamic domain in the Ottoman Empire rested on a balance in which the ulema, implementing the official religious understanding and legitimizing state policy in the eyes of the people from a religious perspective, and the religious orders close to folk Islam existed within a certain distribution of power. As the centralist state gradually grew stronger, efforts were made to restrain religious orders, which could potentially pose a threat to the state, and to make the ulema as loyal servants of the Ottoman state more active in the religious domain. Even though the ulema's power in the legal, administrative, and educational domains was narrowed down and almost became restricted to the religious domain in the late Ottoman era, the Republic, nevertheless, inherited a legacy in which religion mattered to a great extent. In this regard, the institution of the Sheikh-ul-Islam as the leader of the ulema and the transformation of the religion-state and religion-society relations over the course of history constituted an important source of reference for the founders of the Republic. Thus, the Presidency of Religious Affairs, which was created taking the Ottoman legacy and the Ottoman religion–state–society relations into account, assumes the function to legitimize important components of the new nation-state model, such as the nation and the parliament today. The nationalisms that emerged in the late Ottoman era seem to have compelled the Ottoman ruling elite to Turkism. Therefore, the new, post-imperial regime had to rest on a Turkish nation made up by ethnically and religiously homogenous citizens. In this new model, the legacies of Turkishness and Sunni Hanafism drew the framework of the official ideology concerning educational and religious policies as the two indispensable foundations of the new state organization. The Presidency of Religious Affairs has the widest organizational network among Turkey's state institutions, and since it enjoys the capacity to regulate and control the religious domain on behalf of the state, it has played a great part in getting political decisions embraced by society.

In an effort to bring the religious domain entirely under control, the Republican administration first banned all religious orders and then founded the Presidency of Religious Affairs. By holding the monopoly to inform society on Islam and the use of religion, it sought to preclude potential dissent concerning the new state's religious reforms. It acted cautiously in doing so, however, and it appears that the social influence of religious orders was used in the National Liberation War, and religious figures were esteemed highly in the first Assembly, but as the regime grew strong, the regulation of the religious domain was transferred to the Presidency of Religious Affairs. It is possible to argue that the Presidency of Religious Affairs is not an autonomous religious organization but a government institution subordinate to the state from every angle and that it is open to government intervention under any ruling party. In this framework, considering the exercise of control on the content of khutbas by a certain body and the place of the institution and its staff within the general state administration, it is evident that offices of the mufti, Quranic courses, and mosques each function as a public office. Since the early years of the Republic to the present day, the directives of the political authority were put into place not only concerning the religious domain but also in getting its actions embraced by the general population. Examples of the most striking of such directives include the use of the Western-style hat, the collection of skins from animal sacrifices, and the circular letters regarding July 15.

This institution and its domain of activity have constantly grown since its establishment, and in breach of the principles of "secularism" and "equality before law" in the Constitution, it has remained based on the state ideology, Sunni Hanafism. It has maintained the official distant policy towards religious orders and undertook work and publications in line with assimilationist policies such as denial, otherization, and sectarianism against the Alevis. Due to the central role of the state in the nation-building process and its power to hold a monopoly in the religious domain, the Presidency of Religious Affairs is financed publicly, but it offers services only for one sect and only in the officially recognized places of worship. Citizenship is not adequate by itself to receive the state's religious services and it is necessary to fall under the national and religious/sectarian framework it has drawn. The state pursues the same service policies abroad, and its many institutions conduct their work relying on this national and religious/sectarian framework in collaboration with the Presidency of Religious Affairs. Such activities cause a sectarian-based service approach to be sustained through the Presidency of Religious Affairs outside the country as well. For instance, in collaboration with NGOs such as the Turkish-Islamic Union for Religious Affairs in Europe and the Turkish-Islamic Union for Cultural and Social Solidarity in Austria, the Presidency of Religious Affairs spreads the state's religious understanding and works to transform the communities that fall outside it or denies them service.

It can be argued that the Presidency of Religious Affairs has been supported regarding its budget, staff number, and foreign outreach over the JDP rule since 2002 much more than ever before. Statistical data reveals this clearly. The Religious Affairs annual budget falls short even though it exceeds those of many ministries, and the organization often requests additional budget.[133] Moreover, the JDP government has handled the issue of the promotion of the Presidency's place within the protocol, which has become, following the transition to the Presidential government system, one of the few institutions that fall directly under the Office of the President. If the scope of Religious Affairs foreign operations over the JDP era is considered, the organization appears to have turned into an important actor in foreign policy. Turkey's efforts to become the leader of the Sunni world in the Middle East, which became more apparent with the Syrian Civil War, can be regarded to be in line with the work of the Presidency of Religious Affairs in the Balkans and elsewhere as well.

In the light of all these developments, the Presidency of Religious Affairs has been the state's most important instrument in raising "acceptable citizens" as part of the Republican nation-building project. Thus, its budget resources and the scope of its domestic and foreign operations have constantly been broadened. It is possible to contend that the Presidency of Religious Affairs will preserve this position in the immediate future.

NOTES

1. Erik Jan Zürcher, *Osmanlı İmparatorluğu'ndan Atatürk Cumhuriyeti'ne Bir Ulusun İnşası* (Istanbul: Akılçelen Kitabevi, 2015), 428; Bernard Lewis, *Modern Türkiye'nin Doğuşu*, 5th edition (Ankara: Türk Tarih Kurumu Yayınları, 1993), 11–17, 397.

2. Şerif Mardin, *Türkiye, İslam ve Sekülarizm, Makaleler 5* (Istanbul: İletişim Yayınları, 2012), 109.

3. Çağlar Keyder puts this as follows: "Most who analyze the Turkish case agree that there exists a continuity between the Ottoman modernizers and the founders of the Republic of Turkey. . . ." Çağlar Keyder, "1990'larda Türkiye'de Modernleşmenin Doğrultusu," in *Türkiye'de Modernleşme ve Ulusal Kimlik* 2nd edition, edited by Reşat Kasaba and Sibel Bozdoğan (İstanbul: Tarih Vakfı Yayınları, 1999), 31. See also on Turkish modernization. Niyazi Berkes, *Türkiye'de Çağdaşlaşma* 16th edition (İstanbul: Yapı Kredi Yayınları, 2002).

4. Ahmet Yaşar Ocak, "Osmanlı İmparatorluğu ve İslam (Problematik bir yaklaşım denemesi)," in *XIII. Türk Tarih Kongresi, Ankara, 4–8 September 1999, Kongreye Sunulan Bildiriler* vol. 3 (Ankara: Türk Tarih Kurumu Yayınları, 2002), 5.

5. Ömer Lütfi Barkan, "Osmanlı İmparatorluğunda Bir İskan ve Kolonizasyon Metodu Olarak Vakıflar ve Temlikler I, İstila Devirlerinin Kolonizatör Türk Dervişleri ve Zaviyeler," *Vakıflar Dergisi* 2 (1942): 279–67; Yusuf Halaçoğlu, *XIV-XVII. Yüzyıllarda Osmanlılarda Devlet Teşkilatı ve Sosyal Yapı* (Ankara: TTK Yayınları, 2014), 149–50; Davut Dursun, *Yönetim-Din İlişkileri Açısından Osmanlı Devletinde Siyaset ve Din* (Istanbul: İşaret Yayınları, 1989), 103.

6. Dursun, *Yönetim-Din İlişkileri*, 25.

7. Kemal Karpat, *Osmanlı'dan Günümüze Elitler ve Din* (Istanbul: Timaş Yayınları, 2009), 154.

8. Aşık Paşazade, *Osmanoğullarının Tarihi, Tevârîh-i Âl-i Osmân*, edited by K. Yavuz and M. A. Y. Saraç (Istanbul: Gökkubbe Yayınları, 2007), 251, 254.

9. Derin Terzioğlu, "Devlet İnşası ve Mezhepleşme Çağında Sufiler," in *Osmanlı Dünyası*, edited by C. Woodhead, translated by G. Ç. Güven (Istanbul: Alfa Basım Yayım Dağıtım, 2018), 133.

10. Madeline C. Zılfı, "Osmanlı Uleması," in *Türkiye Tarihi 1603–1839, Geç Osmanlı İmparatorluğu* vol.3, translated by F. Aytuna, (Istanbul: Kitap Yayınevi, 2010), 256.

11. Mustafa Kara, *Dini Hayat, Sanat açısından Tekkeler ve Zaviyeler* (Istanbul: Dergah Yayınevi, 2010), 91.

12. Mustafa Kara, *Metinlerle Günümüz Tasavvuf Hareketleri* (Istanbul: Dergah Yayınevi, 2010), 30; Rüya Kılıç, *Osmanlı'dan Cumhuriyete Sufi Geleneğin Taşıyıcıları* (Istanbul: Dergah Yayınları, 2009), 84.

13. Kılıç, *Osmanlı'dan Cumhuriyete*, 85.

14. Kudret Emiroğlu. *Kısa Osmanlı – Türkiye Tarihi, Padişahlık kültürü ve Demokrasi Ülküsü* (Istanbul: İletişim Yayınları, 2015), 310.

15. Donald Quataert, *Osmanlı İmparatorluğu 1700-1922*, 3rd edition, translated by A. Berktay (Istanbul: İletişim Yayınları, 2004), 162.

16. Fahri Maden, *Bektaşi Tekkelerinin Kapatılması (1826) ve Bektaşiliğin Yasaklı Yılları* (Ankara: TTK Yayınları, 2013), 210.

17. Ahmet Yaşar Ocak, *Osmanlı Toplumunda Zındıklar ve Mülhidler (15–17. Yüzyıllar)*, 2nd edition (Istanbul: Tarih Vakfı Yurt Yayınları, 1999), 104.

18. Emiroğlu, *Kısa Osmanlı*, 35.

19. As an example of the measures by Yavuz against Shi'a Islam following the Battle of Chaldiran (August 23, 1514), it is meaningful that the immigrant population expulled from the Caucasus were settled in Kemaliye (Eğin), Erzincan, and were given the meat business of the palace for subsistence. See. Sahir Kozikoğlu, *Eğin (Tarih, Edebiyat, Folklor, Ekonomi)*, 1968, quoted by Zeki Arıkan, "Eğin Kasabasının Tarihsel Gelişimi," *OTAM (Osmanlı Tarihi Araştırma ve Uygulama Merkezi Dergisi)* no 12, (2001): 8.

20. Şerif Mardin. *Türkiye'de Din ve Siyaset (Makaleler / 3)* 2nd edition, (Istanbul: İletişim Yayınları, 1992), 41.

21. This alliance, which began in the run-up to the Battle of Chaldiran, especially against the Anatolian Qizilbash Turkmens supporting Shah Ismail, continued in its aftermath and can be seen as a turning point in this regard.

22. Kılıç, *Osmanlı'dan Cumhuriyete*, 82–83.

23. Ocak, *Osmanlı Toplumunda*, 73.

24. Esra Yakut, *Şeyhülislamlık, Yenileşme Döneminde Devlet ve Din* (Istanbul: Kitap Yayınevi, 2005), 14.

25. The reforms in the field of education in the late Ottoman era restrained the religious bureaucracy's power not only in the field of education but also within the entire bureaucratic structure. In addition to the many reforms put into place during the Tanzimat era to break its power, Abulhamid II tried to academize and professionalize bureaucracy. Jean-François Bayart, *Cumhuriyetçi İslam, Ankara, Tahran, Dakar*, translated by E. Atuk (Istanbul: İletişim Yayınları, 2015), 199; Mardin, *Türkiye'de Din ve Siyaset*, 41, 45.

26. Ocak, *Osmanlı Toplumunda*, 104.

27. For instance, if the *Sheikh-ul-Islam Letters to the Sultan and the Sultanic Wills* (1845–1878) are analyzed, it is clear that the religious domain entirely depends on the sultan. On the appointment of religious staff to different regions and offices, their promotion, and their de-promotion; on who will be religious staff and their pay, etc., the sultan is the sole authority. See. İlhami Yurdakul, Şeyhülislam Arzları ve Padişah İradeleri (1845–*1878)* (Ankara: Türkiye Bilimler Akademisi, 2017), 59, 68, 77.

28. Yusuf Halaçoğlu, *XIV-XVII. Yüzyıllarda Osmanlılarda Devlet Teşkilatı ve Sosyal Yapı,* 155; The weak position of the Sheikh-ul-Islam vis-à-vis the political organ is evident. One of many examples that relate to this is that Abdulhamid II first sends Sheikh-ul-Islam Hasan Hayrullah Efendi to exile and then to prison. See. Kemal Karpat, *Osmanlı'dan Günümüze,* 166.

29. Zılfı, *Osmanlı Uleması,* 260.

30. *Diyanet İşleri Başkanlığı Teşkilat Tarihçesi (1924–1987),* edited by N. Aytürk, Y. Çelik, and E. Şahinarslan (Ankara: T.C. Başbakanlık Diyanet İşleri Başkanlığı APK Dairesi Başkanlığı, 1987), 7.

31. Müneccimbaşı Ahmet Dede, *Müneccimbaşı Tarihi* vol: 2, (Istanbul: Tercüman 1001 Temel Eser, n.d.), 456.

32. Feroz Ahmad, *Bir Kimlik Peşinde Türkiye,* 5th edition, translated by S. C. Karadeli (İstanbul: İstanbul Bilgi Üniversitesi Yayınları, 2014), 32.

33. Ibid., 57.

34. İlter Turan, "Türkiye'de Din Ve Siyasal Kültür," in *Batı Düşüncesinde İslam,* edited by R. Tapper (Istanbul: Sarmal Yayınevi, 1991), 46–47.

35. Bayart, *Cumhuriyetçi İslam,* 46.

36. This can be seen very clearly in the debates surrounding the transition to the Latin alphabet under the nation-state model and the importance of the use of the Turkish language; the promotion of the Arabic script in religious education and services, particularly in Quranic courses; the language of the Islamic call to prayer; the imam-hatip schools; Religious Affairs; and the relations between religious orders and politics. On the other hand, these endless debates are insolvable and will continue to exist as an inseparable part of the problematic Ottoman–Republican continuity.

37. Karpat, *Osmanlı'dan Günümüze,* 46.

38. Hugh Poulton, *Silindir Şapka, Bozkurt ve Hilal* (Istanbul: Sarmal Yayınevi, 1999), 57.

39. E.g., see, Peter Alford Andrews (Ed.). *Ethnic Groups in the Republic of Turkey* (Wiesbaden: Dr. Ludwig Reichert Verlag, 1989), 41; Emiroğlu, Kısa Osmanlı – Türkiye Tarihi, Padişahlık kültürü ve Demokrasi Ülküsü, 37.

40. Reşat Kasaba, "Eski ile Yeni Arasında Kemalizm ve Modernizm," in *Türkiye'de Modernleşme ve Ulusal Kimlik,* 2nd edition, edited by Sibel Bozdoğan and Reşat Kasaba (Istanbul: Tarih Vakfı Yayınları, 1999), 23.

41. Mardin, *Türkiye'de Din ve Siyaset,* 66.

42. Ali Yaman, "Laik Cumhuriyetin Türkiye'de Din Sorununa Yönelik Bir İcadı Olarak Diyanet İşleri Reisliği/Başkanlığı," in *Sur İçinde Bir Yaşam Toktamış Ateş'e Armağan* (Istanbul: Bilgi Üniversitesi Yayınları, 2014), 293–308.

43. Karpat, *Osmanlı'dan Günümüze Elitler ve Din,* 214.

44. Mustafa Kara, *Metinlerle Günümüz Tasavvuf Hareketleri* (Istanbul: Dergah Yayınevi, 2010), 83; Enver Behnan Şapolyo, *Mezhepler ve Tarikatlar Tarihi,* 2nd edition (Istanbul: Elif Kitabevi, 2004), 372.

45. Füruzan Hüsrev Tökin, *İslam Tarikatleri* (Istanbul: M. Sıralar Matbaası, n.d.), 44.

46. Lewis, *Modern Türkiye'nin Doğuşu,* 398.

47. Toktamış Ateş. *Türk Devrim Tarihi* (Istanbul: Filiz Kitabevi, 1989), 311–12.

48. https://www.diyanet.gov.tr/tr-TR/Kurumsal/Detay/1, accessed March 26, 2018.

49. Kılıç, *Osmanlı'dan Cumhuriyete*, 92.

50. Ateş, *Türk Devrim Tarihi*, 337.

51. Mardin, *Türkiye'de Din ve Siyaset*, 67.

52. Mardin, *Türkiye'de İslam ve Sekülarizm*, 69.

53. E.g., see, Arsen Yarman, "Eğin (Agn) Ermenileri—I," *Kebikeç* 37 (2014): 284–85.

54. See, Ahmet Refik, *Onaltıncı Asırda Rafızilik ve Bektaşilik* (Istanbul: Muallim Ahmet Halit Kitaphanesi, 1932); Murat Alandağlı, "Kızılbaşlara dair iki rapor: 19. Yüzyılın Son Çeyreğinde Osmanlı İdarecilerinin Gözüyle Kızılbaşlar," in *Kızılbaşlık Alevilik Bektaşilik, Tarih-Kimlik-İnanç-Ritüel* (Istanbul: İletişim Yayınları, 2015), 227–44; former Prime Minister Şemsettin Günaltay, too, sees Alevism as a disease in line with the Ottoman sectarian tradition and does not refrain from proposing Sunnization through opening schools. M. Şemseddin Günaltay, *Türk İslam Mecmuası* II, no 89 (Aralık 1947): 11.

55. See, for different perspectives on Diyanet, Neslihan Cevik, *Muslimism in Turkey and Beyond: Religion in the Modern World* (London and New York: Palgrave Macmillan, 2016), 76–79.

56. İştar Gözaydın, *Diyanet Türkiye Cumhuriyeti'nde Dinin Tanzimi* (Istanbul: İletişim Yayınları, 2009), 243.

57. Ahmad, *Bir Kimlik Peşinde Türkiye*, 90.

58. Bayart, *Cumhuriyetçi İslam*, 224.

59. Marcel Bazin, "Köylerin Açılması," in *Türkler, Doğu ve Batı, İslam ve Laiklik* 2nd edition, edited by Stephane Yerasimos, translated by T. Keşoğlu (Istanbul: Doruk Yayınevi, 2006), 81.

60. https://www.yenisafak.com/hayat/diyanetin-aci-tarihi-2474830, accessed July 20, 2018. While the conservative press back against the presidents of Religious Affairs, except Mehmet Nuri Yılmaz, and generally criticize the ruling parties, they somehow do not remember the fact that this institution and its presidents are obliged to act under the direction of the political organ.

61. See also. İsmail Kara, "Türkiye'de Laiklik Uygulamaları Açısından Diyanet İşleri Başkanlığı," in *Devlet ve Din İlişkileri—Farklı Modeller, Konseptler ve Tecrübeler* (Istanbul: Konrad Adenauer Vakfı Yayınları, n.d.,), 100–1.

62. January 5, 1926, "Namaz esnasında şapka giymenin mahzuru olmadığına dair genelge sureti," Location No: 051… 2 13 22 (2), *the Catalogue of the Presidency of Religious Affairs* (Ankara: the Directorate General of State Archives at the Office of the Prime Minister of the Republic of Turkey, the Department of Republican Archives, 1998), 25.

63. "Camilerde bütün cemaatin namaz kılarken şapka giymeleri suretiyle yeknesaklığı temin etmeleri", Location No: 051… 13 115 5 (1), *the Catalogue of the Presidency of Religious Affairs* (Ankara: the Directorate General of State Archives at the Office of the Prime Minister of the Republic of Turkey, the Department of Republican Archives, 1998), 169.

64. The book *Müslümanlık,* authored by Professor of Religion Yusuf Ziya Yörükan and published by the Presidency of Religious Affairs (Ankara: Diyanet İşleri Başkanlığı Yayınları, 1961), denigrates religious orders. One of the most important arguments of those who argue for the existence or necessity of the Presidency of Religious Affairs is that a religious life that is not under the control of the Presidency of Religious Affairs would lead to an environment of chaos among different communities and orders.

65. "Diyanet 30 tarikatlarla görüştü: 'Cemaatler ve Tarikatlar Buluşması' düzenleyecek", *CNN Turk,* https://www.cnnturk.com/turkiye/diyanet-30-tarikatlarla-gorustu-cemaatler-ve-tarikatlar-bulusmasi-duzenleyecek, accessed July 20, 2018.

66. "Diyanet İşleri'nden tarikatlara 5 ilke," *Yeni Şafak,* https://www.yenisafak.com/gundem/diyanet-islerinden-tarikatlara-5-ilke-2591729, accessed July 20, 2018.

67. *Cumhuriyet Daily,* http://www.cumhuriyet.com.tr/haber/turkiye/941553/Diyanet_isleri_Baskani_Erbas__Camiler_hem_sunni_hem_Alevi_nin_ibadet_yeridir.html, accessed July 20, 2018.

68. "Diyanet'ten katılım bankacılığını teşvik," *NTV,* https://www.ntv.com.tr/turkiye/diyanetten-katilim-bankalarina-tavsiye,ZraMHHsuU0eZ1O8FF0k6WQ?_ref=infinite, accessed July 20, 2018.

69. November 7, 1945, "Kurban deri ve barsaklarını Türk Hava Kurumu'na vermeleri hususunda vaiz ve hatiplerin halka duyuruda bulunmaları," Location No: 051… 12 103 65 (1), *the Catalogue of the Presidency of Religious Affairs* (Ankara: the Directorate General of State Archives at the Office of the Prime Minister of the Republic of Turkey, the Department of Republican Archives, 1998), 135.

70. *Zaman Daily,* March 24, 1988, cited in İsmail Kara, *Cumhuriyet Türkiyesi'nde Bir Mesele Olarak İslam I,* 4th edition (Istanbul: Dergah Yayınları, 2010), 135.

71. "Kurban Derisi Toplamada Artık tek Yetkili THK Değil," *Hürriyet,* September 23, 2013.

72. January 1, 1923, Location No: 051… 2 4 3 (3), *the Catalogue of the Presidency of Religious Affairs* (Ankara: the Directorate General of State Archives at the Office of the Prime Minister of the Republic of Turkey, the Department of Republican Archives, 1998), 10.

73. March 7, 1924, "Halifenin durumu ve halifelik makamının kaldırılması dolayısıyla hutbelerde millet ve cumhuriyetin selamet ve saadetine dair dua edilmesi," Location. No: 051… 2 1 30 (1), *the Catalogue of the Presidency of Religious Affairs* (Ankara: the Directorate General of State Archives at the Office of the Prime Minister of the Republic of Turkey, the Department of Republican Archives, 1998), 10.

74. March 1, 1927, "Sultanlara dua kısmı bulunan eski baskı mevlid kitaplarının toplattırılarak zemin ve zamana uygun mevlid kitabı hazırlattırılması," Location No: 051… 2 6 20 (1), *the Catalogue of the Presidency of Religious Affairs* (Ankara: the Directorate General of State Archives at the Office of the Prime Minister of the Republic of Turkey, the Department of Republican Archives, 1998), 15.

75. July 24, 1942, "Kadrolu dersiam ve vaizlerce itikat ve ibadetlere dair veya islam dinini müdafaa maksadıyla yazılacak eserlerin, basılmadan evvel tetkik edilmesi için Diyanet'e gönderilmesi," Location No: 051… 4 36 14 (1); July 24, 1942 "Adliye mesleğinde bulunanları müstesna, bütün dersiam ve vaizlerin vaaz özetlerini

Diyanet'e gönderilmek üzere müftülüklere vermeleri," Location No: 051... 4 36 16 (1), *the Catalogue of the Presidency of Religious Affairs* (Ankara: the Directorate General of State Archives at the Office of the Prime Minister of the Republic of Turkey, the Department of Republican Archives, 1998), 56.

76. November 14, 1934, "Yazışmalarda elden geldiği kadar öztürkçe kullanılması," Location No: 051... 12 101 13 (1), *the Catalogue of the Presidency of Religious Affairs* (Ankara: the Directorate General of State Archives at the Office of the Prime Minister of the Republic of Turkey, the Department of Republican Archives, 1998), 125.

77. June 28, 1945, "Arapça ezan okuyan Mehmet İyibildiren hakkında yapılan işlem," Location No: 051... 12 102 4 (1), *the Catalogue of the Presidency of Religious Affairs* (Ankara: the Directorate General of State Archives at the Office of the Prime Minister of the Republic of Turkey, the Department of Republican Archives, 1998), 133.

78. Ahmet Yaşar Ocak, "AKP'nin Açılımı Alevileri Dönüştürme Amacı Gütmemeli," *Anlayış* (January 2009): 59–60.

79. Mardin, *Türkiye'de İslam ve Sekülarizm*, 69.

80. April 13, 1959, "Hülasa: Alevilerin cenaze namazlarının kılınması hk," Location No: 051 V33 0000 4 33 7, *the Catalogue of the Presidency of Religious Affairs* (Ankara: the Directorate General of State Archives at the Office of the Prime Minister of the Republic of Turkey, the Department of Republican Archives, 1998).

81. October 10, 1953, "Maraş Vaizi Zekeriya Güvenen hk," Location No: 051.4.37.12, *the Catalogue of the Presidency of Religious Affairs* (Ankara: the Directorate General of State Archives at the Office of the Prime Minister of the Republic of Turkey, the Department of Republican Archives, 1998).

82. A research paper by TESEV on Imam-Hatip Schools and the Presidency of Religious Affairs states that "*most pious Sunnis in Turkey including religious staff, Religious Affairs executives and mosque-goers are clearly in a very backward position with regard to recognizing the Alevi identity and respecting its demands...*" and indicates how the religious domain influences society negatively through the promotion of a single-sect approach. İrfan Bozan, *Devlet ile Toplum arasında: Bir Okul: İmam Hatip Liseleri... Bir Kurum: Diyanet İşleri Başkanlığı...* (Istanbul: TESEV Yayınları, 2007), 88.

83. "Diyanet İşleri Başkanı: Diyanet Sünni bir Kuruluş Değildir," https://www.memurlar.net/haber/16910/diyanet-isleri-baskani-diyanet-sunni-bir-kurulus-degildir.html, accessed July 20, 2018.

84. Kara, *Cumhuriyet Türkiyesi'nde Bir Mesele Olarak İslam I*, 99.

85. Sönmez Kutlu, "Diyanet İşleri Başkanlığı ve İslamiçi Dini Gruplarla (Mezhep ve Tarikatlar) İlişkileri," *Dini Araştırmalar* 12, no. 33 (January–April 2009): 113.

86. Abdülkadir Sezgin, *Türkiye'de Alevîlik-Bektaşilik* (Conference held on June 12, 1998 at the Office of the Director of the Ottoman Archives in Istanbul with the consent of the Office of the Prime Minister), restricted, (Ankara: the Directorate General of State Archives at the Office of the Prime Minister of the Republic of Turkey, the Department of the Ottoman Archives, Publication No: 38, n.d.,), 48.

87. http://www.mevzuat.gov.tr/MevzuatMetin/1.5.633.pdf, accessed July 20, 2018.

88. Berke Özenç, *Avrupa İnsan Hakları Sözleşmesi ve İnanç Özgürlüğü* (Istanbul: Kitap Yayınevi, 2006), 130–31.

89. Many parts of the Constitution, including its introduction (Article 2, Article 13, Article 14, Article 68, Article 81, Article 103, Article 136, Article 174, and provisional Article 2), draw attention to the secular Republic and secularism. Similarly, Article 136 involves the Presidency of Religious Affairs and draws a link between the organization and the principle of secularism. https://www.tbmm.gov.tr/anayasa/anayasa_2018.pdf, accessed July 21, 2018.

90. https://www.diyanet.gov.tr/tr-TR/Kisi/Baskanlar//3/diyanet-isleri-baskanlari, accessed July 20, 2018.

91. Ahmet Hamdi Akseki, "Gizli Tarikatlar Nasıl Başladı?", in *Bâtınilerin ve Karmatîlerin İçyüzü*, edited by Muhammed Hammadi, translated by İ. H. Erzen (Ankara, Diyanet İşleri Başkanlığı Yayınları, 1948), 12–13. The same article previously appeared in the Sunni Islamist journal *Sebilürreşad* (*Sebilürreşad Dergisi* , nos. 24 and 25).

92. Bozan, *Devlet ile Toplum Arasında*, 52.

93. Letter by the Presidency of Religious Affairs to the Offices of the Mufti dated October 10, 1953, the Directorate General of State Archives, the Republican Archives, Location No: 051 V37 4 3712.

94. M. Zerrin Akgün, *İlim Bakımından İslamiyet* (Ankara: Diyanet İşleri Başkanlığı Yayınları, 1955), 43, note 1.

95. Yusuf Ziya Yörükan, *Müslümanlık,* 2nd edition (Ankara: Diyanet İşleri Başkanlığı Yayınları, 1961), 154–55.

96. "Alevi Köyünde Yalnız bir İmam," *Radikal*, October 17, 2010, http://www.radikal.com.tr/turkiye/alevi-koyunde-yalniz-bir-imam-1024083/, accessed July 22, 2018); "Alevi Türbesi Cami Oldu," *Cumhuriyet*, July 17, 2014, http://www.cumhuriyet.com.tr/haber/turkiye/95719/Alevi_turbesi_cami_oldu.html, accessed July 22, 2018.

97. White gives the account of a similar example. Jenny White, *Müslüman Milliyetçiliği ve Yeni Türkler,* translated by F. Güllüpınar and C. Taştan (Istanbul: İletişim Yayınları, 2013), 99.

98. One of the functions of the Presidency of Religious Affairs that helps the organization reach out to society directly is the Khutbah. The 1998 Khutbah *They Want To Break My Nation Into Pieces* and the 2011 Khutbah *Unity and Solidarity* can be given as examples. *Sosyo-Ekonomik Politikalar Bağlamında Diyanet İşleri Başkanlığı, Kamuoyunun Diyanet'e Bakışı Tartışmalar ve Öneriler* (Istanbul: Helsinki Yurttaşlar Derneği, 2014), 36.

99. "Alevi Diyanet'i olmaz," *Milliyet*, December 14, 2007, http://www.milliyet.com.tr/2007/12/14/guncel/gun05.html.

100. "Cemevi Diyanet'in Kırmızı Çizgisidir," *Milliyet*, http://www.milliyet.com.tr/cemevi-diyanet-in-kirmizi-siyaset-2172767/, accessed July 30, 2018.

101. "Diyanet İşleri Başkanı Ali Erbaş: Fetva Soranlara Yazılı Cevap Verilecek," *Karar*, http://www.karar.com/hayat-haberleri/son-dakika-diyanet-isleri-baskani-ali-erbas-fetva-soranlara-yazili-cevap-verilecek-782879, accessed July 30, 2018.

102. "Diyanet İşleri Başkanı'ndan Cemevi'ne Ziyaret," *Habertürk,* https://www. haberturk.com/gundem/haber/634694-diyanet-isleri-baskanindan-cemevine-ziyaret, accessed July 21, 2018.

103. As Cevik stated, JDP is a "'moderate' Islamic political party" and "the JDP, here, is seen as the main agent of religious change." Cevik, *Muslimism in Turkey and Beyond,* 18.

104. The fact that one of the JDP's election campaign songs is called "Haydi Bismillah" (*In the Name of God Now!*) is one of the many examples that point to its different nature from other parties. https://www.akparti.org.tr/site/dosyalar#!/1-kasim-2015-secim-beyannamesi-brosurleri (Accessed 21.07.2018)

105. According to a field survey, confidence in and satisfaction with the Presidency of Religious Affairs are highest among the JDP voters. *Sosyo-Ekonomik Politikalar Bağlamında,* 86–90.

106. For the JDP programs, see. https://www.akparti.org.tr/site/dosya/66517, accessed July 21, 2018.

107. https://www.akparti.org.tr/site/akparti/2023-siyasi-vizyon, accessed July 21, 2018.

108. https://www.akparti.org.tr/site/dosya/66517, accessed July 21, 2018.

109. https://www.bbc.com/turkce/haberler-turkiye-44396024, accessed August 9, 2018; https://www.ntv.com.tr/turkiye/iste-ak-partinin-secim-beyannamesi,az78klPr MkOkXstD9izr4A, accessed August 9, 2018.

110. https://diyanet.gov.tr/en-US/Institutional/Detail//1/establishment-and-a-brief-history, accessed August 9, 2018.

111. It is stated that President Abdullah Gül did not ratify the decision to raise the place of the Presidency of Religious Affairs within the protocol. http://www. cumhuriyet.com.tr/haber/turkiye/289679/Diyanet_e_protokol_ayari.html, accessed July 21, 2018.

112. http://www.internethaber.com/cumhurbaskanligi-hukumet-sistemi-yeni-baskanliklar-mitin-adi-degisti-foto-galerisi-1886514.htm?page=4, accessed July 18, 2018.

113. The President of Religious Affairs has the fifty-third place on the protocol list, entitled *The Capital City Protocol List Approved by Mr. President,* which is currently found on the official website of the Governorship of Ankara. http://www. ankara.gov.tr/kurumlar/ankara.gov.tr/ankara2017/dosyalar/2018/BaskentProtokol-Listesi.pdf.

114. http://www.milliyet.com.tr/protokol-listesi-degisecek-siyaset-2704304/.

115. https://www.cnnturk.com/turkiye/diyanete-bagli-cami-sayisi-2017de-90-bine-ulasti.

116. https://www.cnnturk.com/son-dakika-diyanet-isleri-baskanligindan-ayrilan-mehmet-gormez-veda-ediyor, accessed July 20, 2018.

117. https://www.diyanet.gov.tr/tr-TR/Kurumsal/Detay/1, accessed May 26, 2018.

118. https://www.diyanet.gov.tr/tr-TR/Kurumsal/TeskilatSemasi/4, accessed July 20, 2018.

119. http://www.ditib.de/index.php?id=&lang=en, accessed July 20, 2018.

120. https://www.atib.at/tr/irtibat/kuenye/, accessed July 26, 2018.

121. See on the pilgrimage, Kemalettin Taş, *Türk Halkının Gözüyle Diyanet* (Istanbul: İz Yayıncılık, 2002), 96-97.

122. The 2017 Annual Report, http://www2.diyanet.gov.tr/StratejiGelistirme/Faaliyet/2017%20Y%C4%B1l%C4%B1%20Faaliyet%20Raporu.pdf, accessed July 22, 2018.

123. İrfan Bozan, *Devlet ile Toplum Arasında*, 64.

124. Fethullah Gülen, the leader of Gülen community, has been well respected in the right-wing sectors as a preacher and ex-personel of Directory of Religious Affairs. After the July 15, 2016 coup attempt, both he and organization known as FETÖ were named as a terror organization in Turkey.

125. http://stratejigelistirme.diyanet.gov.tr/sayfa/57/istatistikler (Accessed 21.07.2018)

126. *Sosyo-Ekonomik Politikalar Bağlamında*, 22–25.

127. https://Istanbul.diyanet.gov.tr/esenler/Sayfalar/contentdetail.aspx?MenuCategory=Kurumsal&contentid=91 (Accessed 21.07.2018)

128. https://www.diyanet.gov.tr/tr-tr/Kurumsal/Detay/11737/diyanetten-15-temmuza-ozel-hazirlik, accessed July 20, 2018.

129. The 61st Government Program states that YTB (the Presidency for Turks Abroad and Related Communities) will be given a more active role.

130. https://www.akparti.org.tr/site/dosya/66517, accessed August 22, 2018.

131. The efforts to Sunnize Osmanlı Harabati Baba (Sersem Ali Baba), the Bektashi tekke located in the city of Tetovo in Macedonia since the sixteenth century, with the cooperation of the Presidency of Religious Affairs and other Turkish institutions and the region's radical Sunni groups draw strong reaction from the Alevi-Bektashi communities. In my visit to the location in 2009, Bektashi Baba Abdulmuttalip Derviş talked to me about the issue in detail. During my visit to Bulgaria, I also found out that the Alevis of Bulgaria were disturbed that Turkey was building mosques in the Alevi villages as a response to the construction of *cemevis* by the Shi'a. Following the reaction of the Alevis concerning the Sunnizing approach towards the Alevi community adhering to the Seyyid Ali Sultan Dergah in the vicinity of the village of Ruşenler, a minority among the Turks of Greece, the annual wrestling event of Seçek Yaylası, which had been organized by the Turkish community jointly for centuries, separated into two different events. I had the opportunity to observe this firsthand from August 3–5, 2018.

132. In my interviews with Kakaid and Shabaks living in Iraq, as well as with prominent figures among the Turkmens living in Syria and their religious men, the fact that the religious policy pursued by Turkey has led to Shi'ization was expressed with various examples.

133. http://www.cumhuriyet.com.tr/haber/turkiye/1050208/Diyanet__ek_butce_istedi_.html; https://www.sozcu.com.tr/2015/gundem/diyanet-ek-butce-istedi-911679/, accessed July 21, 2018.

RESOURCES

Ahmad, Feroz. *Bir Kimlik Peşinde Türkiye*, 5th edition. Translated by S. C. Karadeli. İstanbul: İstanbul Bilgi Üniversitesi Yayınları, 2014.

Ahmet, Refik. *Onaltıncı Asırda Rafızilik ve Bektaşilik.* İstanbul: Muallim Ahmet Halit Kitaphanesi, 1932.

Akgün, M. Zerrin. *İlim Bakımından İslamiyet.* Ankara: Diyanet İşleri Başkanlığı Yayınları, 1955.

Akseki, Ahmet Hamdi. "Gizli Tarikatlar Nasıl Başladı?" In *Bâtınilerin ve Karmatîlerin İçyüzü*, Edited by Muhammed Hammadi. Translated by İ. H. Erzen, 12–13. Ankara, Diyanet İşleri Başkanlığı Yayınları, 1948.

Alandağlı, Murat. "Kızılbaşlara dair iki rapor: 19. Yüzyılın Son Çeyreğinde Osmanlı İdarecilerinin Gözüyle Kızılbaşlar." In *Kızılbaşlık Alevilik Bektaşilik, Tarih-Kimlik-İnanç-Ritüel.* İstanbul: İletişim Yayınları, 2015, 227–44.

"Alevi Diyanet'i olmaz." *Milliyet*, December 14, 2007. http://www.milliyet.com. tr/2007/12/14/guncel/gun05.html.

"Alevi köyünde yalnız bir imam." *Radikal.* October 17, 2010. Accessed July 22, 2018. http://www.radikal.com.tr/turkiye/alevi-koyunde-yalniz-bir-imam-1024083/.

"Alevi türbesi cami oldu." *Cumhuriyet.* July 17, 2014. Accessed July 22, 2018. http:// www.cumhuriyet.com.tr/haber/turkiye/95719/Alevi_turbesi_cami_oldu.html.

Andrews, Peter Alford, ed. *Ethnic Groups in the Republic of Turkey.* Wiesbaden: Dr. Ludwig Reichert Verlag, 1989.

Arıkan, Zeki. "Eğin Kasabasının Tarihsel Gelişimi." *OTAM (Osmanlı Tarihi Araştırma ve Uygulama Merkezi Dergisi)* no 12, (2001): 1–64.

Aşık, Paşazade. *Osmanoğullarının Tarihi, Tevârîh-i Âl-i Osmân.* Edited by K. Yavuz and M. A. Y. Saraç. İstanbul: Gökkubbe Yayınları, 2007.

Ateş, Toktamış. *Türk Devrim Tarihi.* İstanbul: Filiz Kitabevi, 1989.

Barkan, Ömer Lütfi. "Osmanlı İmparatorluğunda Bir İskan ve Kolonizasyon Metodu Olarak Vakıflar ve Temlikler I, İstila Devirlerinin Kolonizatör Türk Dervişleri ve Zaviyeler." *Vakıflar Dergisi* no. 2 (1942): 279–367.

Bayart, Jean-François. *Cumhuriyetçi İslam, Ankara, Tahran, Dakar.* Translated by E. Atuk. İstanbul: İletişim Yayınları, 2015.

Bazin, Marcel. "Köylerin Açılması." In *Türkler, Doğu ve Batı, İslam ve Laiklik* 2nd edition, edited by Stephane Yerasimos, 79–95. Translated by T. Keşoğlu. İstanbul: Doruk Yayınevi, 2006.

Berkes, Niyazi. *Türkiye'de Çağdaşlaşma* 16th edition. İstanbul: Yapı Kredi Yayınları, 2002.

Bozan, İrfan. *Devlet ile Toplum Arasında, Bir okul: İmam Hatip Liseleri. . . . Bir Kurum: Diyanet İşleri Başkanlığı.* İstanbul: TESEV Yayınları, 2007.

"Cemevi Diyanet'in kırmızı çizgisidir." *Milliyet.* Accessed July 30, 2018. http:// www.milliyet.com.tr/cemevi-diyanet-in-kirmizi-siyaset-2172767/.

Cevik, Neslihan. *Muslimism in Turkey and Beyond: Religion in the Modern World.* (London and New York: Palgrave Macmillan, 2016.

"Diyanet İşleri Başkanı Ali Erbaş: Fetva Soranlara Yazılı Cevap Verilecek." *Karar.* Accessed July 30, 2018. http://www.karar.com/hayat-haberleri/son-dakika-diyanet-isleri-baskani-ali-erbas-fetva-soranlara-yazili-cevap-verilecek-782879.

"Diyanet İşleri Başkanı: Diyanet Sünni bir Kuruluş Değildir." Accessed July 20, 2018. https://www.memurlar.net/haber/16910/diyanet-isleri-baskani-diyanet-sunni-bir-kurulus-degildir.html.

"Diyanet İşleri Başkanı'ndan Cemevi'ne Ziyaret." *Habertürk.* Accessed July 21, 2018. https://www.haberturk.com/gundem/haber/634694-diyanet-isleri-baskanin-dan-cemevine-ziyaret.

Diyanet İşleri Başkanlığı Teşkilat Tarihçesi (1924–1987), edited by N. Aytürk, Y. Çelik, and E. Şahinarslan. Ankara: T. C. Başbakanlık Diyanet İşleri Başkanlığı APK Dairesi Başkanlığı, 1987.

"Diyanet İşleri'nden Tarikatlara 5 Ilke." *Yeni Şafak.* Accessed July 20, 2018. https://www.yenisafak.com/gundem/diyanet-islerinden-tarikatlara-5-ilke-2591729.

"Diyanet 30 Tarikatlarla Görüştü: 'Cemaatler ve Tarikatlar Buluşması' Düzen-leyecek." *CNN Turk.* Accessed July 20, 2018. https://www.cnnturk.com/turkiye/diyanet-30-tarikatlarla-gorustu-cemaatler-ve-tarikatlar-bulusmasi-duzenleyecek.

"Diyanet'ten Katılım Bankacılığını Teşvik." *NTV.* Accessed July 20, 2018. https://www.ntv.com.tr/turkiye/diyanetten-katilim-bankalarina-tavsiye,ZraMHHsuU0eZ1O8FF0k6WQ?_ref=infinite.

Dursun, Davut. *Yönetim-Din İlişkileri Açısından Osmanlı Devletinde Siyaset ve Din.* Istanbul: İşaret Yayınları, 1989.

Emiroğlu, Kudret. *Kısa Osmanlı—Türkiye Tarihi, Padişahlık kültürü ve Demokrasi Ülküsü.* Istanbul: İletişim Yayınları, 2015.

Gözaydın, İştar. *Diyanet Türkiye Cumhuriyeti'nde Dinin Tanzimi.* Istanbul: İletişim Yayınları, 2009.

Günaltay, M. Şemseddin. *Türk İslam Mecmuası* 2, no 89 (Aralık 1947): 11.

Halaçoğlu, Yusuf. *XIV-XVII. Yüzyıllarda Osmanlılarda Devlet Teşkilatı ve Sosyal Yapı.* Ankara: TTK Yayınları. 2014.

Kara, İsmail. "Türkiye'de Laiklik Uygulamaları Açısından Diyanet İşleri Başkanlığı." In *Devlet ve Din İlişkileri—Farklı Modeller, Konseptler ve Tecrübeler.* Istanbul: Konrad Adenauer Vakfı Yayınları, n.d., 87–106.

Kara, Mustafa. *Dini Hayat, Sanat açısından Tekkeler ve Zaviyeler.* Istanbul: Dargah Yayınevi, 2010.

———. *Metinlerle Günümüz Tasavvuf Hareketleri.* Istanbul: Dargah Yayınevi, 2010.

Karpat, Kemal. *Osmanlı'dan Günümüze Elitler ve Din.* Istanbul: Timaş Yayınları. 2009.

Kasaba, Reşat. "Eski ile Yeni Arasında Kemalizm ve Modernizm." In *Türkiye'de Modernleşme ve Ulusal Kimlik* 2nd edition, edited by Sibel Bozdoğan and Reşat Kasaba, 12–28. Istanbul: Tarih Vakfı Yayınları, 1999.

Keyder, Çağlar. "1990'larda Türkiye'de Modernleşmenin Doğrultusu." In *Türkiye'de Modernleşme ve Ulusal Kimlik* 2nd edition, Edited by Reşat Kasaba and Sibel Bozdoğan, 29-42. Istanbul: Tarih Vakfı Yayınları, 1999.

Kılıç, Rüya. *Osmanlı'dan Cumhuriyete Sufi Geleneğin Taşıyıcıları.* Istanbul: Dargah Yayınları, 2009.

"Kurban Derisi Toplamada Artık Tek Yetkili THK Değil." *Hürriyet.* September 23, 2013.

Kutlu, Sönmez. "Diyanet İşleri Başkanlığı ve İslamiçi Dini Gruplarla (Mezhep ve Tarikatlar) İlişkileri." *Dini Araştırmalar* 12, no. 33 (January–April 2009): 107–27.

Lewis, Bernard. *Modern Türkiye'nin Doğuşu* 5th edition. Ankara: Türk Tarih Kurumu Yayınları, 1993.

Maden, Fahri. *Bektaşi Tekkelerinin Kapatılması (1826) ve Bektaşiliğin Yasaklı Yılları.* Ankara: Türk Tarih Kurumu Yayınları, 2013.

Mardin, Şerif. *Türkiye'de Din ve Siyaset (Makaleler / 3)* 2nd edition, Istanbul: İletişim Yayınları, 1992.

———. *Türkiye, İslam ve Sekülarizm, Makaleler 5.* Istanbul: İletişim Yayınları, 2011.

Müneccimbaşı, Ahmet Dede. *Müneccimbaşı Tarihi* vol. 2. Istanbul: Tercüman 1001 Temel Eser, n.d.

Ocak, Ahmet Yaşar. *Osmanlı Toplumunda Zındıklar ve Mülhidler (15-17. Yüzyıllar)*, 2nd edition. Istanbul: Tarih Vakfı Yurt Yayınları, 2002.

———. "Osmanlı İmparatorluğu ve İslam (Problematik bir yaklaşım denemesi)." In *XIII. Türk Tarih Kongresi, Ankara, 4–8 September 1999, Kongreye Sunulan Bildiriler* vol. 3, 1-21. Ankara: Türk Tarih Kurumu Yayınları, 2002.

———. "AKP'nin Açılımı Alevileri Dönüştürme Amacı Gütmemeli." *Anlayış* (January 2009): 59–60.

Özenç, Berke. *Avrupa İnsan Hakları Sözleşmesi ve İnanç Özgürlüğü.* Istanbul: Kitap Yayınevi, 2006.

Poulton, Hugh. *Silindir Şapka, Bozkurt ve Hilal.* Istanbul: Sarmal Yayınevi, 1999.

Quataert, Donald. *Osmanlı İmparatorluğu 1700–1922* 3rd edition. Translated by A. Berktay. Istanbul: İletişim Yayınları, 2004.

Sezgin, Abdülkadir. *Türkiye'de Alevîlik-Bektaşilik* (Conference held on June 12, 1998 at the Office of the Director of the Ottoman Archives in Istanbul with the consent of the Office of the Prime Minister), Restricted, (Ankara: the Directorate General of State Archives at the Office of the Prime Minister of the Republic of Turkey, the Department of the Ottoman Archives, Publication No: 38, n.d.,)

Sosyo-Ekonomik Politikalar Bağlamında Diyanet İşleri Başkanlığı, Kamuoyunun Diyanet'e Bakışı Tartışmalar ve Öneriler. Istanbul: Helsinki Yurttaşlar Derneği, 2014.

Şapolyo, Enver Behnan. *Mezhepler ve Tarikatlar Tarihi* 2nd edition. Istanbul: Elif Kitabevi, 2004.

Taş, Kemalettin. *Türk Halkının Gözüyle Diyanet.* Istanbul: İz Yayıncılık, 2002.

Terzioğlu, Derin. "Devlet İnşası ve Mezhepleşme Çağında Sufiler." In *Osmanlı Dünyası*, edited by C. Woodhead, 124-141. Translated by G. Ç. Güven. Istanbul: Alfa Basım Yayım Dağıtım, 2018.

The 2017 Annual Report. Accessed July 22, 2018. http://www2.diyanet.gov.tr/StratejiGelistirme/Faaliyet/2017%20Y%C4%B1l%C4%B1%20Faaliyet%20Raporu.pdf.

Tökin, Füruzan Hüsrev. *İslam Tarikatleri.* Istanbul: M. Sıralar Matbaası, n.d.

Turan, İlter. "Türkiye'de Din Ve Siyasal Kültür." In *Batı Düşüncesinde İslam*, edited by R. Tapper, 39–69. Istanbul: Sarmal Yayınevi, 1991.

White, Jenny. *Müslüman Milliyetçiliği ve Yeni Türkler.* Translated by F. Güllüpınar and C. Taştan. Istanbul: İletişim Yayınları, 2013.

110   *Ali Yaman*

Yakut, Esra. *Şeyhülislamlık, Yenileşme Döneminde Devlet ve Din.* İstanbul: Kitap Yayınevi, 2005.

Yaman, Ali. "Laik Cumhuriyetin Türkiye'de Din Sorununa Yönelik Bir İcadı Olarak Diyanet İşleri Reisliği/Başkanlığı." In *Sur İçinde Bir Yaşam Toktamış Ateş'e Armağan*, 293–308. İstanbul: Bilgi Üniversitesi Yayınları, 2014.

Yarman, Arsen. "Eğin (Agn) Ermenileri—I." *Kebikeç* 37 (2014): 261–92.

Yörükan, Yusuf Ziya. *Müslümanlık* 2nd edition. Ankara: Diyanet İşleri Başkanlığı Yayınları, 1961.

Yurdakul, İlhami. *Şeyhülislam Arzları ve Padişah İradeleri (1845–1878).* Ankara: Türkiye Bilimler Akademisi, 2017.

Zılfı, Madeline C. "Osmanlı Uleması." In *Türkiye Tarihi 1603–1839, Geç Osmanlı İmparatorluğu* vol. 3, 255–74. Translated by F. Aytuna. İstanbul: Kitap Yayınevi, 2011.

Zürcher, Erik Jan. *Osmanlı İmparatorluğu'ndan Atatürk Cumhuriyeti'ne Bir Ulusun İnşası.* İstanbul: Akılçelen Kitabevi, 2015.

Chapter Four

Laiklik and Nation-Building: How State–Religion–Society Relations Changed in Turkey under the Justice and Development Party

Edgar Şar

"Nation-building," in its broadest sense, aims at creating a sufficient amount of commonality of interests, goals, and preferences among the members of a "nation" so that they feel like a part of it and wish to live together.[1]To that end, nation-building requires the creation and promotion of a common "national" identity for the unification of all people within the state.

Nevertheless, national identity is usually not constructed with the participation of diverse social sections, but on the very contrary, it often becomes an arena of struggle among them.[2] Particularly in the contexts where there is not a sufficient degree of elite consensus on subjective perceptions of history and politics, the fundamental beliefs and values, the foci of identification and loyalty, and the political knowledge and expectations,[3] there might well be "a continuous struggle within the society over the ability to define who 'we' are as a nation."[4] The social sections that become so dominant as to capture state power can be expected to embark on nation-building by means of social engineering to terminate the continuous struggle over national identity[5] by creating a majority.[6] However, this strife is unlikely to end permanently and might even escalate if the process of nation-building is based on identity-based polarization and homogenization without paying any attention to the diversity within the society.[7]

Turkey sets quite a good example, where there has been a political polarization between different definitions of "who we are" and "who we want to be" as a nation. Although the struggle over the national identity is sometimes oversimplified and reduced to oppositional state–society relationship, whereby the state is constantly repressing the society,[8] the identitarian, and partly ideological, conflict within the society and its capacity to shape the process of nation-building should by no means be underestimated. In these conflicts, whether between the state and the society or within the society

111

itself, religion has always had a special place. The establishment of Turkey as a "secular" Republic did not change the fact that Islam looms large in the definition and representation of the Turkish nation. Therefore, state–religion–society relations and the Turkish model of secularism, or *laiklik*,[9] that manages these relations have been developed in tandem with the process of nation-building throughout the Republican era.

Laiklik and state–religion–society relations are also significant to understand the "New Turkey" under the Justice and Development Party (JDP) and its leader, President Recep Tayyip Erdoğan. A wide array of scholars who have dealt with Turkey's transformation under Erdoğan seems to agree that Turkey has almost "reinvented" itself over the past decade.[10] It is also obvious that this reinvention has been followed by a new process of nation-building modeled on Islamist-conservative values, whereby the JDP's objective was to generate and preserve its majority within the society. According to the well-known narrative based on the "Old Turkey vs. New Turkey" that dominates the relevant literature, the new process of nation-building under the JDP represents the downfall of the omnipotent Kemalist regime based on the repression of the society by ultra-laicist means. While this narrative based on Kemalist–Islamist dichotomy may give an idea about how JDP started to change Turkey as it consolidated its grip on power, it would be over-simplistic to argue that the omnipotent Kemalist state project has been flawlessly imposed on a reluctant society for almost eighty years and that the JDP started to change everything in Turkey when it came to power in 2002. Therefore, analyzing Turkish political history by means of such dichotomies would not allow us to profoundly grasp the transformation of Turkish political life in the 2000s and the conditions that paved the way for it. Nor does it provide a right perspective to explain how *laiklik*—as one of the core principles of the nation-building process during the early Republican era—has transformed over time and what consequences this transformation had in contemporary Turkey.

JDP's incumbency is a turning point in Turkish political history in many respects. Nevertheless, to understand how *laiklik* and state–religion–society relations changed with the JDP-launched project of nation-building, one should look beyond the JDP era and clarify "what was there before." According to the aforementioned narrative based on the "Old Turkey vs. New Turkey," *laiklik,* as a solid, anti-religious state ideology, was persistently and oppressively implemented until JDP consolidated its grip on the state and "moderated" the state–religion–society relations. Here, too, this narrative is fallacious. In fact, as I elaborately discuss in the following paragraphs, *laiklik* has never been a properly defined principle but, on the very contrary, proved to be vulnerable to political developments throughout the entire Republican era. Therefore, in this chapter, I will also deal with how *laiklik* was before the JDP to clearly set forth how it was changed by the JDP by addressing the following questions: How were state–religion–society relations and *laiklik* projected in the early Republican era? How did they shift following the transition to multi-party democracy? How does the role of Islam change in the national identity? What consequences did these changes bring about leading into the 2000s?

Although there is more than one turning point in the political history of *laiklik* in Turkey, JDP's coming to power in 2002 as a conservative Islamist party led to an unprecedented debate on *laiklik* and, thus, is paid special attention. In the early years of the JDP era, many hoped that by embracing secular politics and liberal values, the JDP would have helped develop a softer and more democratic version of *laiklik*. Nevertheless, as it consolidates its power in the state institutions, the JDP and its leader Erdoğan embarked on a new process of nation-building, where the state-favored interpretation of Islam plays a much more definitive role. In this context, this study argues that the way *laiklik* was debated during the 2002–2010 period led to what I call the collapse of *laiklik,* which eventually paved the way for the process of "desecularization of the state," which I indicate the incumbent JDP embarked on in tandem with its nation-building project modeled on a conservative and Islamist *Weltanschauung.*

A SHORT HISTORY OF *LAIKLIK* (1924–2002): A PRINCIPLE OF ALL SEASONS?

To understand how *laiklik* changed during the JDP's incumbency, we should first reveal what it was like before. *Laiklik* has been a constitutionally defined characteristic of the state since 1937, which became unamendable in 1961 and has remained so since then. Having remained constitutionally unchanged over the decades, *laiklik* may well be expected to be a deep-rooted state principle with a set of steady political values and goals that all governments in the Republican era would endorse despite ideological differences. This is, however, far from reality. During the entire Republican era, state–religion–society relations have constantly changed in accordance with the shifting political landscape.[11] Governments pursued almost antipodal policies towards religion for the sake of short-term political goals and used the guise of *laiklik* to legitimize them. Therefore, *laiklik* is more a principle of all seasons than a consistently preserved or gradually evolved state principle.

The abolition of the caliphate in 1924 is generally taken as the beginning of the history of *laiklik* in Turkey. By abolishing the caliphate, the state did not only give up its "legitimate" authority over the Islamic *umma* at the cost of being accused of rejecting Islam and being *kafir*,[12] but also it clearly set forth that the identity of the new Turkish *nation* was no longer to be defined within the so-called Islamo-Ottoman context.[13] Nevertheless, Islam, as "the primary social identity maker," was the only element that could unite Turk-ish-, Arabic-, Kurdic-, Circassian-, Albanian-, Bosnian-, and Laz-speaking populations and, thus, was one of the first issues to be addressed by the na-tionalist cadres that founded the Republic of Turkey.[14] Therefore, despite the abolition of the caliphate, the state was not willing to relinquish its oversight and control over religion, and they instead founded a new office, the Director-ate of Religious Affairs (*Diyanet*). The *Diyanet* was authorized to administer the mosques, religious lodges, and so on and to hire and fire *imams* and other mosque staff and to oversee the *muftis*.[15]

Following the abolition of the caliphate, the constitutional secularization of the state continued with the removal of Islam as the official religion from the Constitution in 1928, and it was finally complete with the introduction of *laiklik* as a constitutional characteristic of the state in 1937. Furthermore, throughout the 1920s and 1930s, many reforms were made for the seculariza-tion of the Turkish legal and educational systems. However significant these were at that time, *laiklik* could not be institutionalized in a way that would ensure a gradual development of separation between state and religion. Ac-cording to Kemal Karpat, *laiklik* was not a sophisticated but rather a comple-mentary element in the ideology of the founder Republican People's Party (RPP). Underpinned and redefined by *laiklik*, nationalism was freed from the Islamo-Ottoman content.[16] However, religion never lost its position as a key symbol in Turkish national identity at the grassroots level,[17] which is the main reason why the Republican regime adopted an understanding of *laiklik* that sustained its predecessor regimes' (the Hamidian and the Committee of Union and Progress) quest of controlling and instrumentalizing the religion rather than separating it from the state.[18] Therefore, despite the constitutional-ization of *laiklik*, on the one hand, the state extended its control over religion by marginalizing any religious interpretation other than the official one,[19] and on the other hand, religion was used in the nation-building at the expense of causing systematic exclusion as in the examples of assimilation of Alevis and the law on wealth tax applied particularly to non-Muslims. Hence, in practice, *laiklik* fell short to encompass notions of civic citizenship that guarantee an inclusive and pluralistic polity.[20]

The post-World War II period marked a new era for Turkish democracy. The establishment of multi-party democracy, in 1946, brought about a much wider freedom of expression for various movements of thought.[21] In the meantime, the onset of competitive politics that arose from the foundation of a new party, the Democrat Party (DP), somewhat enforced the ruling RPP to pay more attention to the masses' expectations, at the cost of revising its policies of *laiklik* that had hitherto been consistently implemented.[22] In the 7th Congress of RPP that was held in November 1947, it was widely voiced that conventional *laiklik* policies that had marginalized Islam throughout the single-party era had to be softened, and religion got to be the cement of the society.[23] As a matter of fact, certain policies of *laiklik* were remarkably softened thereafter.[24] The first-ever emphasis upon the "freedom of conscience" in the government program, the reintroduction of religious education in public schools, the opening of imam-hatip schools, and the opening of *türbes* to visit and state-led facilitation for *haj* are the most outstanding developments of this softening process. In the 1946–1950 period, religion and, thus, policies of *laiklik* apparently became a means of electioneering and have remained so since then.

The interest-based clientelistic relationship between politics and religion took root in Turkey throughout the 1950s. Particularly early on in the decade, the ruling Democrat Party (DP) developed considerably affirmative relations with the conservative sections of the society, including Islamist communities, by restoring the *ezan* in Arabic, abolishing the ban over the activities of *tekkes* and *tarikats,* and extending the scope of the previously introduced religious education—turning it into compulsory in public schools and increasing the number of imam-hatip schools. As Ioannis N. Grigoriadis underlines, "The social engineering projects focusing on the marginalization of religion were no longer on the agenda."[25] These affirmative relations went so far as to form election alliances with some popular *tarikats* that survived state assaults throughout the single-party era and managed to organize significant networks of social support and influence, such as *Nurcus*.[26] Taken altogether, the DP is generally identified with the "revival of Islam" through which its place in the public sphere was rehabilitated[27] and Islamization gathered pace at the social level in the 1950s.[28]As Grigoriadis puts it:

> Islam was no more seen as the reason for the decline of the Ottoman Empire and the failure of the Turkish nation to keep up with political, economic, military, and intellectual developments in the West; it was increasingly seen as a source of social solidarity and substantial element of Turkish national identity.[29]

When compared with the single-party era of the 1930s and 1940s, the bi-party politics of the 1950s marked serious differences regarding state–religion–society relations. The instrumentalization of religion for political purposes that had begun during the last RPP government (1946–1950) under Prime Minister Şemsettin Günaltay continued at full speed during the 1950s.[30]

The military junta that ousted the DP government and Prime Minister Adnan Menderes on May 27, 1960, was very critical of the state–religion–society relations developed by the DP throughout the 1950s. However, as opposed to the expectations, the leaders of the military junta did not pursue militant laicist policies. Despite elite debates that questioned its compatibility with *laiklik*, the *Diyanet* was not abolished, but instead, it became a constitutional institution to engage in religious activities in favor of the state.[31] Thus, the state's quest to further control religion remained despite the relatively liberal atmosphere that came out of the 1961 Constitution.

Moreover, the instrumentalization of religion by the state gained a new dimension during the 1960s. Particularly, when the conservative right was in power, the religion was used as an ideological counterforce against growing socialism. The Islamic communities that had previously been banned and, benefiting from the freedom of organization envisaged by the new Constitution, took to the stage as associations and interest groups supported the conservative right.[32] Given the fact that the Islamic movement was increasingly gaining strength and taking root in the society, religion got politicized and became an even more important instrument for the state. In the late 1960s, the Islamists got their own party for the first time that came to power in 1973 as the smaller coalition partner of the RPP and, later, as one of the partners of National Front coalitions. The existence of an Islamist party in the governments made itself evident, particularly in educational policies. Both the number of imam-hatip schools and their students marked a huge increase throughout the 1970s.[33] "In the meantime, the state-led and funded religious schools were bearing fruit in terms of recruitment into state cadres. The graduates were not only religious functionaries but received places in universities and state bureaucracy."[34]

Under the conditions of political pluralism condoned by the 1961 Constitution, more and more people and groups became a part of "centrifugal forces," such as socialism and Kurdish nationalism in the 1970s. It was not unexpected that the state resorted to Islam as a key "centripetal force" in defining the Turkishness.[35] The instrumentalization of religion by the state had never been as intensive as it was in the 1980s. Beyond an ideological counterforce, religion became the central instrument in the hand of the state to pursue comprehensive social engineering. "Turkish-Islamic Synthesis" was promoted as the official state ideology, and all other alternatives were presented as a threat to Turkish national culture.[36] The expansion of the *Diyanet* and imam-hatip schools and the introduction of mandatory religious classes in public schools are some of the prominent implementations of the military junta in the early 1980s. In spite of the state-led Islamization, the military junta never abandoned *laiklik* and always uttered that what was done was done for the sake of *laiklik*.[37] Deniz Kandiyoti calls this "the transmogrification" of *laiklik* and contends that it aimed at further legitimizing the Turkish-Islamic Synthesis and outlawing all other alternatives, including the Islamic ones, to put forward *laiklik* as the preferred narrative.[38] In other words, both Islam and *laiklik* were welcomed by the state, as far as state's version of these were promoted.[39]

Following the departure of Kenan Evren, Turgut Özal's Motherland Party adopted a more pragmatic approach in state–religion–society relations. The coup-sponsored conservatization of politics and society led to a further rise of political Islam in Turkey. It was Necmettin Erbakan's Welfare Party (RP) that benefited from the transformation in the 1990s, and he managed to come to power, in 1996, as a senior partner of a coalition government. For the military, that was the initiator of this process with the 1980 coup, the unprecedentedly rising role of Islam in state and society was an unintended consequence, and it grew increasingly concerned about this process, of which it already had lost the control. The military intervened again in politics through a "soft coup" on February 28, 1997, which broke with "a pattern of state-Islam relations that allowed for negotiation and compromise between Turkey's political Islamists and the establishment."[40] The abolition of secondary imam-hatip schools, the introduction of an eight-year mandatory schooling system, and the de facto ban on headscarves at public universities are some of the prominent measures that were taken during the February 28 Process. On the other hand, mandatory religious classes introduced by the military junta in the early 1980s remained intact in all schools, which indicate that the military was still supporting that the state controlled and, if necessary, instrumentalized religion in line with the "Turkish-Islamic Synthesis."[41]

This short history of *laiklik* shows how it has become a "principle for all seasons" that was constantly used to legitimize the state–religion–society relations organized by the establishment of the day. The fact that *laiklik* has constantly been used as an instrument of legitimacy without having a set of consistent principles creates confusion about how the state has approached religion in Turkey. In the following section, I approach critically the existing narratives of *laiklik* to find out which one could account for its historical background throughout the Republican era.

CONFLICTING NARRATIVES: WHAT KIND OF PRINCIPLE IS *LAIKLIK*?

As I indicated in the previous section, state–religion–society relations in the Republican era have been politically inconsistent and interest-driven, and therefore, they make it difficult to make a coherent narrative on *laiklik*. Is there any defining characteristic of state–religion–society relations in Turkey despite the inconsistencies? What kind of a state–religion–society relation does *laiklik* envisage?

Two contradictory narratives seem to dominate the literature. The first one, which for Kandiyoti achieved the stature of a "master narrative,"[42] provides a reading of history, where the state, as a modern and secular one, has conventionally been hostile to religion, while the Turkish society and culture are mainly religious.[43] According to Hakan Yavuz, for example, "modern Turkey, like a transgendered body with the soul of one gender in the body of another, is in constant tension… The soul of white Turkey and its Kemalist identity is in constant pain with the national body politic of Turkey."[44] In other words, the implementation of *laiklik* brought about an oppositional state–society relationship, where the values of the modern secular state are at odds with those of the larger society. This conflict spilled over even into the realm of habitus, cultural codes, and lifestyles[45] and, thus, makes the public sphere a contested zone between the modern *laiklik* state and the religious/conservative society. Ahmet Kuru, for instance, maintains that *laiklik*, in the form of what he calls "assertive secularism," always tried to remove religion from the public, privatize it, and confine it to the individual conscience, whereas the passive secularists, including the Muslim-conservative JDP, wanted to protect the freedom of conscience while avoiding to favor a particular religion.[46]

The other narrative provides an alternative reading of history full of observations that clearly diverge from those of the "master narrative." It calls into question the secular vocation of *laiklik*, arguing that through the implementation of *laiklik*, the Turkish state has controlled and also promoted Islam.[47] According to Andrew Davison, for instance, the Turkish state has never approached religion as a completely private matter and, thus, religion and state have never been entirely separate. The state, on the very contrary, has established its own version of Islam by institutionally supporting, financing, and promulgating it.[48] Murat Somer, too, draws attention to the incompatibility of these claims with the "master narrative," maintaining that "the state cannot simultaneously oppress/privatize and establish/promote religion."[49] Kuru and Alfred Stepan, whose main argument is that *laiklik* systematically excludes religion from the public sphere, claim that this argument is not incompatible with but complementary for Davison's argument that the state has established and publicly promoted Islam through its understanding of *laiklik*.[50] Somer opposes it, saying "I cannot see how this is possible" and continues:

> Whether or not Turkish state removes, or tries to remove, religion from the public realm is an empirically testable claim. This can be done for example by counting changes in the number of mosques, identifying state involvement in

their construction, and observing other religion-related state practices in public realms such as education, social policy, public security, national defense, and regulation of the public sphere.[51]

In fact, the short history of *laiklik*, too, evidently shows that religion has constantly been controlled and instrumentalized by the state for political purposes.[52] However different the ways to do it were throughout the 1923–2002 period, there is a significant common trait concerning the state's approach to the religion, which can be summarized in two points. First, given the way the state instrumentalized religion throughout the Republican era, it is impossible to maintain, as the accounts based on a binary opposition between secular state and religious society do, that "the rise of Islamic actors owes its momentum exclusively, or even primarily, to dynamics emanating from the grassroots of society while the state remained secular."[53] The Turkish state's actions, particularly during the late 1940s, 1950s, and 1980s, portray an "integrationist and symbiotic relationship" between state and religion where the state is the controlling and dominant party.[54] Second, if we understand secularism as a political principle that is supposed to separate religious affairs from those of the state, the secular credentials of the *laiklik* appear fairly thin. As a matter of fact, "Turkish nationhood and claims of national belonging were never divorced from being Muslim and Sunni,"[55] and Islam has constantly been promoted for nation-building, public morality, and bolstering state legitimacy.[56]

THE CONTEXT OF THE *LAIKLIK* IN THE 2000S

In the aftermath of the February 28 Process, the military that had already intensified its tutelage over politics publicly launched a campaign against *irtica* (reaction). Having been classified as a threat to national security, this military-led campaign against *irtica* had several results that would have an impact on the political climate of the next period. Among these are the closure of the previously governing Welfare Party, removal of many military officers and bureaucrats from their posts due to their alleged Islamic lifestyle, and the ban on headscarves at all educational institutions.

It was mainly the consequences of the February 28 Process and the military tutelage over politics that kept *laiklik* at the top of the national political agenda as Turkey was entering the new millennium. The three-party coalition government called an early election and scheduled it on November 3, 2002. In the course of the election campaigns, a newly founded political party attracted more notice than any other new formation that came out before the snap elections: the Justice and Development Party (JDP). The reason for that attraction was not only that the new party appeared to be, by far, in the lead in most of the opinion polls but also that the party openly distinguished itself from *Milli Görüş* (National View), the Islamist ideology of its predecessors, by declaring itself as a "conservative democratic party," which, unlike its predecessors, did not have a categorical antagonism to the Western values and *laiklik*.

JDP's decision to abandon the traditional ideology of its prominent founders and to accept and remain within the system was undoubtedly related to the fate of the WP, which had been banned during the February 28 Process. During the November 3 elections, JDP came in first and won by an overwhelming majority in the parliament. The main reason behind JDP's preference to remain within the system was not to relinquish its right to use the means of power, decision-making mechanisms, and its overwhelming majority in the parliament. "Acting and keeping itself within the system, JDP could consolidate its power to challenge the system and be its 'changer' or even its 'annihilator.'"[57] Nevertheless, in its first term, the JDP was far from an anti-system party, but on the contrary, it challenged the military tutelage over politics through certain legislation, emphasizing the importance of political inclusion, democracy, and freedom of conscience. Among those was the reform package of 2003 that aimed at the demilitarization of the system for the adaptation to the European Union (EU) norms being the most remarkable.

Despite the JDP's victory in the November 3 elections that enabled it to form a single-party government, the military tried to keep its political power and made sure that the February 28 Process continued. In that context, the concerns about *laiklik* arising from the ideological background of JDP's prominent leaders were predominantly voiced by the top generals and high court judges as well as President Ahmet Necdet Sezer, who himself was a former chief justice of the Constitutional Court. For them, *laiklik* is not merely a political principle that denotes to the separation between state and religious affairs but is a "philosophy of life" that refers to the separation of all worldly affairs from religion.[58] Being defined as such, *laiklik* was apparently not a political principle that is to guarantee basic rights and freedoms but, on the very contrary, a comprehensive doctrine that is superior to them. Meanwhile, the JDP took a remarkably accommodationist stance on *laiklik*, obviously considering that it was the Achilles' heel of the former political parties of *Milli Görüş*. According to the JDP's "conservative democratic" approach, religion is a social phenomenon in the first place and, thus, deserves to have proper relations with politics.[59] In this context, the function of *laiklik* is to enable the state to treat all beliefs in an egalitarian way and to create a pluralist environment where religious differences can coexist.[60] Hence, "*laiklik* is the guarantee of religious freedom, as it is understood in all stable democracies."[61] Consequently, defining *laiklik* as compatible with conservative democracy that it officially held, the JDP wanted to show that it was possible to relate religion to politics in a "pluralist and democratic" basis.[62]

THE STRIFE BETWEEN THE STATE AND
THE JDP (2002–2008): THE COLLAPSE OF *LAIKLIK*

During the early 2000s, a clash started between these two diverging under-standings of *laiklik*: on one side was the comprehensive *laiklik* advocated by the state, namely the President, the military, and the judiciary, and on the other hand was what can be called "political" *laiklik* that was asserted by the top JDP officials and liberals.[63] Within that period, what happened between these different approaches was not a sophisticated deliberation that would result in a democratic, pluralist, and inclusionary conclusion but rather a clash based on "my version is more the true meaning of *laiklik*" claims. I think that the reason for the lack of a fruitful intellectual and public deliberation on "what should *laiklik* be for?" is twofold.[64] First, the supporters of comprehen-sive *laiklik* never believed that JDP had given up *Milli Görüş* or was genuine in its remarks on *laiklik* and never trusted it in the sense that the JDP had an anti-secularist "hidden agenda." As a matter of fact, President Sezer, with his veto power, the military, with their public remarks and "e-coup" on April 27, 2007, and the judiciary, with the closure case, were openly at war with JDP. Second, the liberal-looking discourse of political *laiklik* that JDP developed by emphasizing freedom of conscience was never supported with concrete actions. JDP has never been as effective for the rights of Alevis and non-Muslims as it has been for the headscarf ban and the educational restrictions on imam-hatip students, which had been the most significant problems of its own social base. More importantly, the JDP has mainly preserved the status quo with regard to the *Diyanet* and obligatory religious instruction in public schools and, thus, failed to extend its emancipatory activism to encompass all individuals and groups in Turkey.[65]

As a result, the polemical discussions on "the true meaning of *laiklik*" not only failed to lead to a broad-based debate on how *laiklik* had to be rethought so that freedom of conscience and equality could go beyond rhetoric and be realized in practice, but it also made *laiklik* a source of confusion and ten-sion. This source of confusion came about because neither the supporters of comprehensive *laiklik* nor those of "political" *laiklik* could produce a consis-tency between their discourses and actions. Although both parties justify their standpoints by referring to freedom and equality, their practices were either clearly anti-democratic or fell short to be consistent with their discourses.

Even more importantly, it became a source of tension because the more comprehensive secularists emphasizing JDP's "insincerity" about *laiklik* resorted to anti-democratic ways to undermine it, the more *laiklik* became a social fault line that deepened the polarization between the JDP's social base and those in opposition. Meanwhile, *laiklik* started to be increasingly considered as ideology reminiscent of military tutelage, and thus, those voicing their concerns about it were labeled as anti-democrats. This process resulted in the collapse of *laiklik*,[66] whereby desecularization was almost considered as a precondition for democratization.[67]

NATION-BUILDING UNDER JDP: DESECULARIZATION OF THE STATE (2008–2018)

I have so far underlined that *laiklik* is a "principle of all seasons" that is not based on a principled separation between state and religion. In that sense, with its ends, institutions and law, and policies that allow for the control and instrumentalization of religion, Turkey has never been a truly secular, or *laik*, polity. Nevertheless, following the collapse of *laiklik* and the power consolidation of the JDP government, the state has moved relentlessly away from *laiklik*, becoming less secular even in respects that it had been previously secular.[68] In this respect, the process of desecularization of state is carried out in tandem with the process of nation-building, both of which takes place to the extent that the state takes on a comprehensive outlook through its self-understanding and policies and tries to implant a comprehensive doctrine or worldview on the society, usually by using social engineering methods.

To analyze the process of desecularization of state, I use Rajeev Bhargava's "three orders of connection" and argue that the state apparently exceeded the limits of connection with religion for a secular state and de-secularized itself at the levels of ends, institutions, and law and policies.[69]

Ends

Ends of state are made up almost purely by written and spoken discourses, and thus, their analysis always includes the risk of being too idealistic or mere speculation and not reflecting what is indeed going on. To take a related and familiar example, Turkey has constitutionally called itself a *laik* state, namely, a state that separates religion from its affairs. However, as I have shown in previous sections, this was hardly the case throughout the entire Republican era. For this reason, reach valid conclusions regarding the transformation of ends, it is important to examine also the concrete actions—such as adoption of new laws, policies, and institutions—that this transformation concomitantly brings about. Within this context, the analysis of ends is helpful for at least two reasons. First, ends reflect short- and long-term goals and objectives of a state and thus demonstrate whether this set-up will be followed by a process of continuity or change. In fact, a process of change mostly begins with a change in the level of discourse, which gives an idea about the route of that change. In that respect, ends loom large for the process of nation-building too. Second, a change in ends not only sets forth a new set of goals and objectives but also designates how to achieve them and prepares the ground to do so. Therefore, when analyzed in tandem with the subsequent actions, ends can reveal much more than a mere discourse could about a process of change.

Taking all these into account, a scrutiny of ends of state gives an idea about, if not completely explains, the story of change during the JDP rule. In terms of ends, the first remarkable change took place with regard to Welt-anschauung. In the earlier period of its rule as a party that claimed itself to be the representative of the victimized and excluded masses, the JDP emphasized that the social diversity is under the guarantee of universal values, human rights, and freedoms and the state should recognize and not intervene on it.[70] Here, the JDP explicitly criticizes state's resort to social engineering techniques in dealing with the groups that it claims to represent, particularly during the February 28 Process, and refers to democracy, human rights, and universal values as the guarantee of social diversity as well as the solution of that problem. In the later stages of its rule, however, the emphasis on universal values gradually decreased and was ultimately replaced by the reference to "our ancient values" *(kadim değerlerimiz)*, which the restoration or the building of *Yeni Türkiye* (New Turkey) was to be based on.[71] In Ahmet Davutoğlu's terms, a former Minister of Foreign Affairs and Prime Minister who is also known as the originator of this discourse, it is clear that these concepts point out some kind of discontent about how Turkey's identity was constructed in the period of modernity and nationalization, and restoration of "ancient civilization's values"[72] aims at building a new identity and, thus, transforming the society.[73] In this regard, the following quotation from Aziz Babuşçu, then head of JDP's Istanbul Organization and now JDP Istanbul MP, indicates this new process of nation-building:

> Those who were somehow our partners over the past ten years, say liberals, will not be able to be our partner in ten years to come. . . . No matter if they put up with it or not, next ten years will make up the "building period" and the building period will not be as they would like it to be. Our government has accomplished much in ten years, yet all these accomplishments may easily be ruled out, unless

they are written in state's institutional memory, for which AK Party [JDP] must remain in power for a longer period.[74]

As this quotation clearly puts forward, the concepts of "building," "restoration," and "ancient values" that underlie the new discourses clearly point to a new process of nation-building, which requires, as I will elaborate herein, the use of social engineering techniques.

The remarkable change in Weltanschauung, which reshaped the state's stance in its relations with the society, brought about an expected change in the role of religion in state–society relations. As I mentioned at the beginning of this chapter, the JDP took a considerably accommodationist stance towards *laiklik*, interpreting it as a quality of state that guarantees equal treatment towards all religions and beliefs.[75] Although party and government officials have mostly preserved this interpretation of *laiklik* so far,[76] a set of new ends were adopted that charge the state with religious-moral "missions."[77] These missions, which are mainly concerned with education, youth, and children, are to be accomplished to realize the greater societal imagination.[78] Education of children and youth comprise a greater part of the new ends of state. In 2002, the JDP declared that its education policy would be designed so as to raise a generation that is free in thought and conscience.[79] Later, however, the ends of education became radically comprehensive at the level of discourse. In 2014, the envisioned aim of education was declared to be for "a youth that is moral and faithful to its past and values."[80] Moreover, President Erdoğan made a number of statements where he refers to education as a crucial means to reach the imaginary society, and for this purpose, education should be "radically reconstructed."[81] He said more than once that it was part of the government's objectives to raise not atheists but "devout generations"[82] and that the education system should offer a particular lifestyle to students from preschool onwards.[83]

Institutions

The absence of a church-like religious institution and a clerical class "equipped with holy abilities to speak on behalf of God and religion"[84] in Islam was generally used by states as a source of legitimacy to engage in religious affairs. In the Turkish case, as a matter of fact, although the foundation of the Directorate of Religious Affairs *(Diyanet)* is attributed to the state's response to the social need for the provision of religious services,[85] it is a fact that the state aimed at keeping religion under its control by this means. Hence, as far as Turkey is concerned, the state never fully disconnected itself from religion at the institutional level, and *Diyanet* has always been the key actor in state's engagement in religious affairs throughout the Republican era.

A supervisory engagement of state in the provision of religious services by public or private entities does not necessarily contradict with *laiklik*.[86] However, in the case of *Diyanet*, there are at least two features that are, by definition, exclusionary. First, *Diyanet*'s function is beyond providing religious services and includes the enlightenment of society about Islam, which makes it an administrative tool to propagate and inculcate official view about religion and Islam.[87] Second, despite being financed by tax money as a governmental institution, *Diyanet* is providing services exclusively for Sunni Muslims in Turkey. In other words, Alevis, non-Muslims, and non-believers are neither represented in the only legal religious institution of the country that they are equal citizens of nor able to claim any kind of tax exemption for financing an exclusively Sunni institution.

Moreover, being the only legal religious institution that is constitutionally charged with seeking national unity and solidarity,[88] *Diyanet* is a source of homogenizing and monist power that all Turkish governments have made use of in various forms in line with power relations and conjunctural developments.[89] That is to say that independent of the JDP's policies, the way that *Diyanet* is organized has been one of the conventional flaws of the *laiklik* in Turkey. However, during the JDP era, the *Diyanet* further expanded, which enlarged the scope of its exclusionary practices, contributing to the process of desecularization of state at the institutional level. This expansion can be analyzed in two respects: field of activity and budget.

To begin with, *Diyanet* significantly expanded regarding its field of activity in the 2000s and especially after 2010. Even before this expansion, in fact, *Diyanet* was never merely an organization to provide religious services but always had certain political and sociological functions. However, with the revision of its law on organization in 2010, *Diyanet* became a much more influential governmental institution that had an important position in the network of political and social relations.[90] In other words, *Diyanet*'s activities spilled out of the mosques and spread into new fields both at home and abroad. As for at home, the expansion of its working field led *Diyanet* to become an instrument of social engineering in the hands of the government, particularly in the field of social policy.[91] This is evident in the deepening cooperation between *Diyanet* and several national ministries:

- *Diyanet*'s cooperation protocol with the Ministry of Family and Social Policies in 2011 enlarged the scope of its activities regarding woman and family and aimed at "protecting and strengthening family structure and values to hand down to the next generations and raising awareness over the problems that threaten the family and its members within society." In 2013, likewise, the ministry signed a protocol with the Turkiye Diyanet Foundation, which aimed at organizing joint meetings with several institutions to enlighten the family on psychological, economic, cultural, and religious matters in line with religious values. Herewith, *Diyanet* became a part of the policy-making and implementation process on contemporary social policy issues such as gender equality, violence against women, family, and upbringing of children.[92]

- *Diyanet*'s cooperation protocol with the Ministry of Youth and Sports on "values education" dated February 26, 2015, aims at "contributing to youth's spiritual development," "providing the demanding students with instruction on religion and values," and "organizing *umrah* trips for the spiritual development of the youth."[93]

- *Diyanet*'s cooperation protocol with the Ministry of Health, which was dated January 1, 2015, aims at providing "faith-based moral motivation" for the demanding sick and their acquaintances in the public hospitals.[94]

- *Diyanet*'s cooperation protocol with the Ministry of Justice, which was dated February 10, 2011, aims at improving the moral and religious emotions of the arrested and convicted people to contribute to their process of decarceration.[95]

The expansion of *Diyanet*'s field of activity is evident in its international activities as well. In fact, *Diyanet*'s work abroad is nothing new and can be traced back to the 1970s, when it started to provide growing Turkish immigrant communities in Europe with religious services. A special department to conduct foreign affairs within the *Diyanet* was established in 1983, and it has been organized in various European countries since then.[96] Nevertheless, with the new organizational law introduced in 2010, *Diyanet* started focusing more on its international activities.[97] These activities are carried out by *Diyanet*'s foreign organizations and the Turkiye Diyanet Foundation and include providing humanitarian aid for victimized Muslims around the world, building mosques around the world, providing religious education for Turkish and foreigner Muslims both abroad and in Turkey, printing and handing out the Qur'an, opening up schools abroad, organizing conferences, panels, symposiums, and so on. Like in its activities at the national level, *Diyanet*'s international activities that have a transnational target group, also aim at providing "healthy information" regarding Islam. However, given the fact that it is a governmental institution, *Diyanet*'s activities abroad can hardly be thought separately from the Turkish government's foreign policy plans and objectives. As a matter of fact, the rising international activism of the *Diyanet* has gone hand in hand with the civilizational discourse that dominated the JDP's foreign policy since 2010. Therefore, being a governmental institution that affirms Turkish official ideology and values regarding Islam, *Diyanet*'s activism abroad can be considered as a means of cultural imperialism to achieve foreign policy goals of the Turkish government.[98]

The second aspect that illustrates *Diyanet*'s expansion in the 2000s, though partially only, is concerned with its budget. Having remarkably expanded so far, the *Diyanet*, with its branches overseas that serve the Turkish diasporas, nowadays commands the second largest budget among the institutions within Turkish bureaucracy.[99] In her profound analysis of *Diyanet*'s budget, Nil Mutluer points out the fact that a considerable part of *Diyanet*'s activities, particularly those introduced after 2010, have been carried out by the Turkiye Diyanet Foundation, whose budget and personnel data is not open to the public. Given the fact that *Diyanet*'s official budget, which is a part of the governmental budget, has been subject to remarkable changes over decades in line with economic and political conjuncture, Mutluer underlines, and analyzing the Turkiye Diyanet Foundation's budget would help reveal much more regarding *Diyanet*'s recent expansion.[100]

Nevertheless, *Diyanet*'s budget analysis is solely illustrative enough to mark its distinguished expansion that started in the 2000s. In this regard, I will refer to two data analyses. The first one is about the real budget amounts of *Diyanet*. The 2000s marked the biggest real increases in *Diyanet*'s budget throughout the entire Republican era. The real increase, in 2012 with respect to 2002, is 176 percent.[101] The second one is concerned with a comparison between the budget increases of *Diyanet* and the amounts appropriated for other policy areas, such as education, health, and transport, each of which has its own ministry to be responsible for. The budget increase of *Diyanet* overweighed that of other important budget items, such as health, education, and culture and tourism, in the 2002–2012 period. In 2002, for instance, *Diyanet*'s budget was 5.5 percent of the education budget and 6.29 percent of the health budget, whereas in 2012, these ratios became 7.56 percent and 8.82 percent, respectively. Moreover, as Mutluer rightfully underlines, given the wide range of activities that the Turkiye Diyanet Foundation carries out, the increase in the budget for *Diyanet*-overseen activities is probably much more remarkable than it seems with the available data.[102]

Law and Policies

Desecularization of state at the level of laws and policies is evident in many social policy areas, such as education, family, woman, youth, and so on. In each of these, the government has been recently pursuing conspicuously homogenizing and exclusionary policies that reflect a particular ideological Weltanschauung and aims at designing the society accordingly. Knowing that each process of desecularization that these policy areas have been through is a subject broad enough to be dealt with by separate theses, I would like to focus exclusively on educational policies owing to two main factors. First, being one of the widest policy areas, education touches on each social policy area specified above and, thus, the government's approach while forming and pursuing educational policies is usually reflective of its approach to other social policy areas. Therefore, analyzing educational policies enables to draw indicative and valid conclusions regarding the desecularizing stance of the state while enacting law and policies. Second, particularly in Turkish political history, education has always been the first policy area to be reorganized whenever there was a change in the dominant official ideology. To implant and indoctrinate the official ideology over the younger generations, social engineering techniques used by the state are usually manifested first through educational policies.[103]

In Turkey, the 2000s inherited some substantial problems regarding the management and content of education, most of which were the legacy of the coup d'état of 1980 and the February 28 Process. Among these were the most notable ones, including compulsory religious instruction in public schools, the headscarf ban at universities, and the limitations on imam-hatip students to enter universities. The JDP governments' officials have constantly voiced their objection to the legacies of these coups but took a conspicuously selective stance in abandoning and reversing the policies of these legacies. As a matter of fact, whilst the problematic laws and policies regarding the freedoms of headscarfed students and women and imam-hatip students were eventually resolved, other problems of the educational system that created exclusions for Alevis, non-Muslims, other minorities, non-believers, and so on remained not only unresolved but also clearly worsened.[104] It is possible to argue that the worsening of educational policies, regarding both management and content, points out to the process of desecularization of the state at the level of law and policies. In what follows, I would like to provide some empirical data that explicitly reveals this process.

To begin with, management of education is an important element of inclusive education. For the educational system to be inclusive, managerial elements such as legislation, policy-formation, and implementation should also be inclusive, participatory, and non-discriminatory.[105] In Turkey, however, the period between 2010 and 2016 witnessed a clear regress in the inclusiveness of educational management in at least two ways. First, the Turkish educational systems underwent a substantial revision in 2012, and the processes of policy formation and legislation were harshly criticized as not being inclusive and participatory. In fact, the bill of the "4+4+4 Educational System," as it is publicly known, was neither developed in a participatory way nor discussed sufficiently by the public. Even throughout the legislation process, where public discussion mechanisms by means of parliamentary commissions and sub-commissions of civil society representatives are procedurally definite, there was only limited public debate, and eventually, the bill remained nearly unrevised after all feedback had been given by the stakeholders.[106] The report of the Education Reform Initiative (ERG) draws attention to the fact that the bill was apparently not based on a preplanned governmental program either. The bill was released to the public after the 2011 election was won by the JDP, and JDP did not mention in its election declarations about such a substantial change to the educational system. The bill was based merely on the advice of the National Educational Council, which is the highest advisory council for the National Ministry of Education and is responsible for examining the educational system to improve its quality and for taking advisory decisions. In this regard, the bill may be taken to have certain legitimacy given the existence of representatives and stakeholders in the council. However, this reveals a further problem regarding the composition of the council. In 2010, with a substantial by-law change, the ratio of ministry-appointed members of the council increased from 60 to 75 percent. The ERG report puts forward that with this change the contribution of the council to the supposedly participatory formation of educational policies is open to discussion.[107] Moreover, despite all of the problems regarding its composition and non-transparent membership appointments, in its 19th summit in 2014, the council brought forth quite substantial propositions, such as the abolition of mixed education and the intensification of religious education in public schools. The decisions concerning the substantial elements of education could be publicly debated, but only after they become definite. This is a structural problem for the inclusive and participatory management of education.[108]

Another development about the management of education that threatens both state impartiality and inclusiveness of education is the increasing engagement of a set of foundations, all publicly known to have particular religious identities that are close to that of the JDP, with the management and the content of public education. According to the available data, the Ministry of National Education signed twenty-two protocols regarding religious education with certain foundations. These include TÜRGEV, Ensar Foundation, Hizmet Foundation, İlim Yayma Cemiyeti, and Şuurlu Öğretmenler Derneği.[109] I find it substantially problematic that these foundations engage with public education for at least two reasons. First, as I underlined earlier, these foundations declare themselves to affirm particular comprehensive doctrines in their missions and visions that include elements such as "spiritual dynamics," "ethical development," "jihadist consciousness," and "spreading of the truth."[110] Thereby, engagement of these foundations with regular national education activities would certainly point out the involvement of such thick and comprehensive elements in public education, which undoubtedly destroy the prospects of inclusive education. Secondly, the protocols that the ministry or the directorates of national education signed with these foundations mostly involve certain objectives and purposes, particularly regarding the content of education, which, from a legal perspective, directly fall into the area of responsibility of the ministry itself, and this makes sense, given the fact that inclusion of public education can better be guaranteed by public institutions than private foundations with particular Weltanschauung. Arguably, due to legal concerns, the JDP government has been recently working on a bill on the establishment of a new state-mandated foundation called Maarif Vakfı,[111] which is supposed to take over the activities of the Ministry of National Education abroad and train its own instructors. According to the bill passed on June 17, 2016, the board of trustees will have seven permanent members, appointed by the president and three appointed by the council of ministers, and an amount of one million Turkish liras (TL) will be transferred to the foundation from the budget of the Ministry of National Education. The opposition parties severely objected the bill drawing attention to the risks of a foundation that is managerially dependent on the governing party's leaders taking over a part of national ministry's tasks and budget for the inclusiveness of education and impartiality of state.[112]

The second element of inclusive education is the content of education. For the educational system to be inclusive, the content of education should meet the criteria of neutrality and objectivity and must not include any discriminatory element. So far, the curriculum of Turkish public education has been profoundly handled by a number of academic works as well as various reports regarding the content of education. Due to the limitations of space, I can neither refer to all of these works nor provide a new examination of the entire curriculum, but owing to its prevalent place in the debates on *laiklik,* I would rather focus on the issue of religious instruction and its content in public education.

Religious instruction in public schools has been a constitutional provision since 1982. From the perspective of inclusive education, religious instruction in Turkish public schools (the course "Religious Culture and Ethics") has two substantial problems. First, it is among the compulsory courses of the curriculum, and an exemption is possible merely for non-Muslim pupils and based on declaration. Nevertheless, reports of some minority communities reveal that there have been some cases where non-Muslim pupils' parents faced either bureaucratic or practical difficulties in using their right of exemption.[113] Second, being a "religious course" on a particular interpretation of Sunni Islam rather than a "course on religions," the curriculum of the compulsory "Religious Culture and Ethics" is monist, exclusionary, and propagandist. The imposition of Sunni religious instruction to the Alevis, non-Muslims, or non-believers has long been discussed in public, and this problem became a matter of judicial cases several times. Turkish administrative courts gave contradictory rulings on the issue. Whereas provincial administrative courts of Sakarya and Sivas found the curriculum of the course one-dimensional and exclusionary for Alevis, the provincial administrative court of Ankara found it acceptable and "supra-sectarian," and the Council of State approved its ruling.[114] The issue was brought before the European Court of Human Rights (ECHR) in 2007 and 2014. In 2007, the ECHR ruled that the course of "Religious Culture and Ethics" seeks to infuse a specific religious interpretation and thus is against the criteria of neutrality and objectivity as required by the law of human rights.[115] The court also drew attention to the inexistence of a non-discriminatory exemption mechanism. Following this ruling, the curriculum of the course "Religious Culture and Ethics" was revised twice. However, as Mine Yıldırım reveals, despite some positive changes, the curriculum still maintains its characteristics of being a religious education of Sunni Islam[116] and is thus against the Toledo Guiding Principles on Teaching about Religions and Beliefs in Public Schools.[117] As a matter of fact, in 2014, the ECHR almost repeated its ruling regarding the compulsory religious instruction in Turkey, drawing attention to the need for a neutral and pluralist content for the course.[118]

In fact, the courses regarding religion and belief offered in public education are directly related to human rights, particularly in the context of freedom of thought and conscience. As ECHR rulings also reveal, Turkey has done very little to make the religious education compatible with human rights. Within the context of the European Convention of Human Rights, the courses on religion and belief should be not compulsory but optional, and the content has to be neutral and egalitarian. Furthermore, the right of exemption should be performed without having to declare one's belief and granted to all.[119] Nevertheless, while problems regarding the compulsory "Religious Culture and Ethics" course are still unresolved, a new set of elective courses regarding religion and belief—"Qur'an," "The Life of Prophet Mohammed," and "Religious Basics"—was introduced with the adoption of 4+4+4 Educational System. The fact that these courses are elective courses does not mean that they are totally compatible with freedom of thought and conscience, but without the state taking certain measures, these elective courses can turn into a mechanism of declaration of belief and pressure.[120] The ERG report draws attention to the fact that parents or pupils might feel obliged to elect these courses to avoid any probable discrimination and exclusion.[121] Besides, the report reveals that several non-Muslim and Alevi pupils had to elect these courses due to practical inadequacies in public schools across Turkey.[122] Therefore, the state must guarantee that these elective courses do not become de facto compulsory courses by offering a sufficient number of alternative courses. Furthermore, the state should be neutral, take a pluralist stand, and respect diversity in deciding what courses to offer as well as their content, financing, and implementation.

CONCLUSION

The most apparent indication for the fact that the JDP under President Erdoğan embarked on a new nation-building process is that the national and state identity in Turkey looks somehow very different today, both from inside and outside, then it was a decade ago. As I emphasized earlier in this chapter, the national identity is an area of constant struggle over the ability to define "who we are as a nation," and having "conquered"[123] the state, the JDP managed to remain the winner of this struggle throughout its sixteen-year incumbency.

Religion has always been central to the national and state identity throughout the Republican era. During the early Republican period, *laiklik* was of critical importance for the building of the "Turkish nation." Although the founding cadres of the Republic tried to marginalize, or at least minimize, the role of Islam in the newly built national identity, the Islamic identity was almost the only element that could unite different populations that were supposed to make up the nation. Religion has never lost its significance at the grassroots level, and the newly founded Republic preferred to establish a sort of state–religion–society relationship, whereby it keeps religion under control rather than completely separate its affairs from those of religion. Therefore, *laiklik* could not be properly institutionalized as the separation between religious and state affairs. Separation remained very limited to certain social areas.

With the introduction of multi-party politics, religion became a political instrument in the hands of the governments and political parties. Particularly in the 1980s, the Turkish-Islamic Synthesis became the official ideology, through which the state managed to remarkably transform the society by using social engineering techniques. This social transformation paved the way for the Islamists to become prominent in the divided political arena of the 1990s and dominant in the 2000s.

When it came to power in 2002, the JDP had to face the entire state: the military, the judiciary, and the bureaucracy. It took a long time and many struggles for the JDP to conquer the state from them and form its own military, judiciary, and bureaucracy. It had to make and end alliances to remain in power. The fact that in the early years in power the JDP was mainly confronted by the state that was formed during the February 28 Process created a perception based on an urban legend that the state had always been ultra-laicist and Kemalist in Turkey, which prevailed all the way through the Republican era until the JDP came to power and did away with it. This narrative neglects the transformations that the state has been through during the entire Republican era. As a matter of fact, without the Turkish-Islamic Synthesis becoming the official ideology as of the early 1980s, Islamists would never have been so powerful in the first place.

As a result of the fight between the state and the JDP, *laiklik* became more vulnerable than ever. As I repeatedly underlined, *laiklik* was not based on a proper but a partial or selective separation between state and religious affairs. The battle between the JDP and the state was a critical juncture, when the flawed understanding of *laiklik* could have been fixed with the idea of a state that guarantees freedom of conscience and equality rather than controls and instrumentalizes the religion. As the idea that political Islam can coexist with democracy and freedom flourished, and the concepts such as "Muslim democracy" and "moderate Islam" were widely raised by academic circles, Turkey, under the JDP, consolidated its profile as the exemplary model for other countries with Muslim majority populations before the international community. Undoubtedly, as a political movement that had suffered much from state-led exclusion during the February 28 Process, the JDP's democratic and liberal discourse in the early 2000s was found credible by secular liberals at home as well as by the international community.[124] Those who expected Turkey to become a model of liberal "Muslim democracy" ruled by conservative Muslims who embraced pluralist values ruled out the possibility that the JDP would instrumentalize state power to do social engineering and impose its own comprehensive doctrine over the entire society when it consolidates its power. Nevertheless, the JDP was apparently not eager to relinquish its "right" to benefit from having conquered the state, and many intellectuals who could initiate a fruitful debate on how to fix *laiklik* relentlessly sided with the JDP without properly questioning its intentions. Therefore, the *laiklik* collapsed, and the JDP finally had the adequate power to embark on a new process of nation-building and to redefine "who we are as a nation." The new nation-building was put into effect with a relentless process of desecularization of the state and a corresponding project of social engineering.

If we consider the building of Turkish national identity, of which being Turk and Sunni is an inseparable part and Turkish state's conventional institutional support and finance (of an own version) of Islam as symptoms of a "covert establishment" of Sunni Islam in disguise of *laiklik*, then we can well conclude that with the process of desecularization of the state at the level of ends, institutions, and law and policies, the establishment becomes overt, through which a particular interpretation of Sunni Islam moves beyond being a defining element of national identity and becomes the incontestable official ideology of the state at the levels of ends, institutions, and law and policies. In this respect, the new process of nation-building under the JDP should be read as a story of both continuity and change. Whereas the "sacred synthesis" of being Turkish and Sunni continues to be the definition of "Turkishness,"

134   *Edgar Şar*

due to the unprecedented process of desecularization the state has never been as far away from *laiklik* as it is today.

NOTES

1. See Alberto Alesina and Bryony Reich, "Nation-building," NBER Working Paper No. w18839 (February 2013), 2; and Joseph Zajda, "Nation-Building, Identity and Citizenship Education: Introduction," in *Nation-Building, Identity and Citizenship Education: Cross-Cultural Perspectives*, edited by Joseph Zajda, Holger Daun, and Lavrence S. Saha, 2–3 (Springer, 2009).

2. Toni Alaranta, *National and State Identity in Turkey* (London. Rowman & Littlefield, 2015), 13.

3. For Archie Brown, this is the definition of what he calls "political culture." His conception of political culture is so broad as to reflect a "common identity" through its reference to the questions of how the past is perceived from present and how the present is shaped by the past. See "Introduction," in *Political Culture and Political Change in Communist States,* edited by Archie Brown and Jack Gray, 1 (London: The Macmillan Press, 1979). Besides, the "elite consensus" is taken to be a factor of successful nation-building, without which the elements of the common national identity cannot be spread widely among the people. See Raphael Utz, "Nations, Nation-Building an Cultural Intervention: A Social Science Perspective," *Max Planck Yearbook of United Nations Law* 9 (2005: 633.

4. Alaranta, *National and State Identity in Turkey*, 15.

5. Zajda, Nation-Building, Identity and Citizenship Education: Introduction," 4.

6. See Karl W. Deutsch, "Nation-Building and National Development," in *Nation Building in Comparative Contexts,* edited by Karl W. Deutsch and William J. Foltz, 9–12 (New York: Routledge, 2017).

7. See Utz, "Nations, Nation-Building an Cultural Intervention," 641–47.

8. See Hakan Yavuz, "Cleansing Islam from the Public Sphere," *Journal of International Affairs* 54, no. 1 (2000): 21; Berna Turam, *Secular State and Religious Society: Two Forces in Play in Turkey* (New York: Palgrave Macmillan, 2012); and Ahmet T. Kuru, *Secularism and State Policies towards Religion: The United States, France and Turkey* (New York: Cambridge University Press, 2009).

9. *Laiklik* means secularism. It has its roots in French word *laïque* and is used as being synonymous for *laïcité*. The similarity between the concepts is not linguistic only. Many have compared French *laïcité* and Turkish *laiklik* in literature, generally emphasizing upon their "assertive" character and the limitations they set to the public visibility of religion. (See Kuru, Ibid.). Nevertheless, despite these linguistic and conceptual similarities with French *laïcité*, *laiklik* has been a quality of the state of Turkey, which allows it to intervene in religious affairs intensively. As İştar Gözaydın shows, this kind of understanding of *laiklik* is inherited from Turkey's territorial ancestors, the Ottoman and Byzantine Empires. See "Bizans, Osmanlı ve Cumhuriyet… Üçünde de din Devletin Kontrolünde,"January 28, 2015, retrieved from http://sosyal.

hurriyet.com.tr/yazar/ahmet-hakan_131/bizans-osmanli-ve-cumhuriyet-ucunde-de-din-devletin-kontrolunde_28065223, accessed September 24, 2018.

10. Alaranta, *National and State Identity in Turkey*, 2.

11. Murat Somer, "Is Turkish Secularism Antireligious, Reformist, Separationist, Integrationist, or Simply Undemocratic?" *Journal of Church and State* 55, no. 3 (2013: 592.

12. Niyazi Berkes, *Türkiyede Çağdaşlaşma* (Istanbul: Yapı Kredi Yayınları, 2009), 506–8.

13. Kemal Karpat, *Türk Siyasi Tarihi* (Istanbul: Timaş Yayınları, 2011), 58.

14. Ioannis N. Grigoriadis, *Instilling Religion in Greek and Turkish Nationalism: A "Sacred Synthesis"* (New York: Palgrave Macmillan, 2013), 2–3.

15. Bernard Lewis, *Modern Türkiye'nin Doğuşu* (Ankara: Arkadaş Yayınları, 2013), 557.

16. Karpat, *Türk Siyasi Tarihi*, 58–59.

17. Ibid., 58; Grigoriadis, *Instilling Religion in Greek and Turkish Nationalism*, 62–67.

18. See Haldun Gülalp, "Enlightenment by Fiat: Secularization and Democracy in Turkey," *Middle Eastern Studies* 41, no. 3, (2005): 351–72; Grigoriadis, *Instilling Religion in Greek and Turkish Nationalism*, 60–62.

19. Erik Jan Zürcher, *Modernleşen Türkiye'nin Tarihi* (İstanbul: İletişim, 2012), 277.

20. Deniz Kandiyoti, "The Travails of the Secular: Puzzle and Paradox in Turkey," *Economy and Society* 41, no. 4, (2012): 517.

21. Lewis, *Modern Türkiye'nin Doğuşu*, 563.

22. Grigoriadis, *Instilling Religion in Greek and Turkish Nationalism*, 68.

23. TBMM, Republican People's Party, 7th Party Congress, retrieved from https://www.tbmm.gov.tr/eyayin/GAZETELER/WEBKUTUPHANEDE%20BULUN AN%20DIJITAL%20KAYNAKLAR/KITAPLAR/SIYASI%20PARTI%20YAYIN LARI/197603391%20RPP%207%20NCI%20BUYUK%20KURULTAYI/ 197603391%20RPP%207%20NCI%20BUYUK%20KURULTAYI%200077_ 0138%20UCUNCU%20BIRLESIM.pdf, accessed September 24, 2018.

24. Hikmet Bila, *RPP: 1919–1999* (Istanbul: Doğan Kitap,1999), 53.

25. Grigoriadis, *Instilling Religion in Greek and Turkish Nationalism*, 68.

26. Ibid.

27. Ibid.

28. See Feroz Ahmad, *The Making of Modern Turkey* (London: Routledge, 1993).

29. Grigoriadis, *Instilling Religion in Greek and Turkish Nationalism*, 69.

30. Nilüfer Narlı, "Türkiye'de Laikliğin Konumu," *Cogito* no. 1 (1994): 27.

31. Ibid., 28.

32. Narlı, Ibid.; Grigoriadis, *Instilling Religion in Greek and Turkish Nationalism*, 69–70.

33. Kandiyoti, "The Travails of the Secular," 518.

34. Ibid., 519.

35. Grigoriadis, *Instilling Religion in Greek and Turkish Nationalism*, 70.

36. Kandiyoti, "The Travails of the Secular," 520.

37. Edgar Şar and Alphan Telek, "Rethinking Secularism as a Political Principle in the Middle East: From Negative to Positive Perception of Secularism," in *Sources of Secularism: Enlightenment and Beyond*, edited by Anna Tomaszevska and Hasse Hamalainen, 269 (Cham: Palgrave Macmillan, 2017).

38. Kandiyoti, "The Travails of the Secular," 521.

39. Şar and Telek, "Rethinking Secularism as a Political Principle in the Middle East."

40. Kandiyoti, "The Travails of the Secular," 524.

41. Grigoriadis, *Instilling Religion in Greek and Turkish Nationalism*, 78.

42. Kandiyoti, "The Travails of the Secular," 515.

43. Somer, "Is Turkish Secularism Antireligious," 585.

44. Yavuz, "Cleansing Islam from the Public Sphere."

45. Nilüfer Göle, "Secularism and Islamism in Turkey: The Making of Elites and Counter-Elites," *Middle East Journal* 51, no. 1, (1997): 46–58.

46. Kuru, *Secularism and State Policies towards Religion*, 173–77.

47. Kandiyoti, "The Travails of the Secular," 516; Somer, "Is Turkish Secularism Antireligious," 586.

48. Andrew Davison, "Turkey, a 'Secular' State? The Challenge of Description," *South Atlantic Quarterly* 102, nos. 2–3, (2003): 340–41.

49. Somer, "Is Turkish Secularism Antireligious," 587.

50. Ahmet T. Kuru and Alfred Stephan, "Introduction," *Democracy, Islam and Secularism in Turkey (Religion, Culture and Public Life)*, edited by Ahmet Kuru and Alfred Stephan, 6 (New York: Columbia University Press, 2012).

51. Somer, "Is Turkish Secularism Antireligious."

52. During the single-party era, namely from 1925, when Atatürk consolidated his power in the state, until 1946, the "control" aspect was apparently much more visible than the "instrumentalization." After 1946, however, both instrumentalization and control became evident in state–religion–society relations and even during the 1960 and 1980 coups, when *laiklik* was "radically" defended, these relations remained intact.

53. Kandiyoti, "The Travails of the Secular," 519.

54. Somer, "Is Turkish Secularism Antireligious," 588.

55. Kandiyoti, "The Travails of the Secular," 516–17.

56. Somer, "Is Turkish Secularism Antireligious," 587.

57. Gérard Groc, "AKP, Türkiye'deki Laikliğin Derdi mi Dostu mu?" in *Tartışılan Laiklik: Fransa ve Türkiye'de İlkeler ve Algılamalar*, edited by Samim Akgönül, 43–44 (Istanbul: Bilgi Üniversitesi Yayınları, 2011).

58. Turkish Constitutional Court, Ruling No: 1998/1.

59. Yalçın Akdoğan, *Muhafazakar Demokrasi* (Ankara: AK Parti Yayınları, 2003), 100.

60. Ibid., 97.

61. Ibid., 95.

62. Groc, "AKP, Türkiye'deki Laikliğin Derdi mi Dostu mu?" 51.

63. Ahmet Kuru's distinction between "assertive secularism" and "passive secularism" may also be of use to signify the mentioned divergence (2011). However, I

do not prefer to use the concept based on this distinction due to two reasons. First, as I showed in the previous chapter, the history of *laiklik* in Turkey cannot be merely explained by two types of approaches. It is rather the dominant political landscape and actors' interests that have been the driving force in the formation and pursuit of state policies. Second, in Kuru's terms it is predominantly whether the state allows or bans religions to be publicly visible, what differentiates between passive and assertive secularism. In my comprehensive, political distinction, however, it is mainly equality and inclusion that makes two concepts different from one another, which I believe much more openly asserts the difference between two types of secularisms.

64. Şar and Telek, "Rethinking Secularism as a Political Principle in the Middle East," 276.

65. Ibid.

66. Groc, "AKP, Türkiye'deki Laikliğin Derdi mi Dostu mu?" 45.

67. See Şar and Telek, "Rethinking Secularism as a Political Principle in the Middle East," 276–77.

68. The question of whether a state is secular or not cannot usually be answered with a simple yes/no answer. Avoiding an in-depth theoretical discussion on what is secularism and assuming that it, one way or another, necessitates a sort of separation between religious affairs and those of state. A state with the totality of public institutions may display qualities that are secular and comprehensive, and this is, at any point in time, an empirical question that can be elucidated only through empirical analysis of various pivotal institutions and policies as well as broader ends under which they are formed. For an in-depth theoretical discussion on what is secularism, see Şar and Telek, "Rethinking Secularism as a Political Principle in the Middle East," 247–53.

69. Rajeev Bhargava uses "three orders of connection" to distinguish between "secular states" and "religion-centered states," each having its own distinct versions. In this regard, Bhargava also distinguishes between various types of secular states; namely, amoral and value-based secular states as well as states that are committed to "disconnection," "one-sided exclusion," or "principled distance" (2011, 96–99). Referring to the concept of principled distance, which is an integral element of contextual secularism, his favorite model of state–religion relations, Bhargava asserts that a secular state does not have to "make a fetish" of the third-order disconnection, which is to say that abiding by certain *principles* a secular state may connect itself with religion through some laws and policies (105). Nevertheless, I prefer to look at all three orders of connection in my analysis of desecularization of state in order to show that the connection between state and religion overreached the limits set by secularism as a political principle, also at the level of law and policies, which causes a dangerous regress in state's capacity to take diversity as a fact. See Rajeev Bhargava, "Rehabilitating Secularism," in *Rethinking Secularism*, edited by Craig Calhoun, Mark Juergensmeyer, and Jonathan Van Antwerpen, 96–105 (New York: Oxford University Press, 2011).

70. See Akdoğan, *Muhafazakar Demokrasi*; AKP (2002). "2002 Genel Seçimleri Seçim Beyannamesi," retrieved from http://www.JDParti.org.tr/upload/documents/2002-beyanname.pdf, accessed September 24, 2018.

71. "İşte Erdoğan'ın Vizyon Belgesi," July 15, 2014, *CNNTurk*, http://www.cnnturk.com/fotogaleri/turkiye/iste-erdoganin-vizyon-belgesi?page=1, accessed September 24, 2018.

72. Turkish Ministry of Foreign Affairs (TMFA). (2013). "Dışişleri Bakanı Ahmet Davutoğlu'nun Diyarbakır Dicle Üniversitesi'nde Verdiği 'Büyük Restorasyon: Kadimden Küreselleşmeye Yeni Siyaset Anlayışımız' Konulu Konferans. 15 Mart 2013, Diyarbakır," http://www.mfa.gov.tr/disisleri-bakani-ahmet-davutoglu_nun-diyarbakir-dicle-universitesinde-verdigi-_buyuk-restorasyon_-kadim_den-kuresellesmeye-yeni.tr.mfa, accessed September 24, 2018.
Nebi Miş and Ali Aslan, "Erdoğan Siyaseti ve Kurucu Cumhurbaşkanı Vizyonu," *Seta Analiz* no. 19, September 2014.

73. Şar and Telek, "Rethinking Secularism as a Political Principle in the Middle East," 283.

74. "Babuşçu: Gelecek 10 yıl Liberaller Gibi Eski Paydaşlarımızın Arzuladığı Gibi Olmayacak," *T24*, April 1, 2013, http://t24.com.tr/haber/babuscu-onumuzdeki-10-yil-liberaller-gibi-eski-paydaslarimizin-kabullenecegi-gibi-olmayacak,226892, accessed September 24, 2018.

75. Ibid.

76. After what I earlier called "the collapse of *laiklik,*" secularism has never become again a daily matter of discussion like in the early 2000s, but it was discussed twice during the 2010–2016 period. First, in his "Arab Spring tour" in 2011, Prime Minister Erdoğan called on three uprising-hit Arab states—Egypt, Tunisia, and Libya—to adopt secular government, saying "a secular state is the one that treats all religious groups equally, including Muslim, Christian, Jewish, and atheist people." See "Erdoğan Calls for a Secular Egypt," *Egypt Independent,* September 13, 2011, retrieved from http://www.egyptindependent.com/news/erdogan-calls-secular-egypt, accessed September 24, 2018; and second, in 2016 the Speaker of Turkish Parliament, İsmail Kahraman, suggested the removal of secularism in the new Constitution, and Erdoğan disagreed with him, emphasizing the state's equal distance from all religions, which is guaranteed by secularism. See "President Erdoğan Defends Secularism After Remarks by Parliament Speaker," *Hurriyet Daily News,* May 11, 2016, retrieved from http://www.hurriyetdailynews.com/president-erdogan-defends-secularism-after-remarks-by-parliament-speaker.aspx?pageID=238&nID=98392&NewsCatID=338, accessed September 24, 2018.

77. "İşte Erdoğan'ın Vizyon Belgesi", 15.07.2014, *CNNTurk,* Retrieved from http://www.cnnturk.com/fotogaleri/turkiye/iste-erdoganin-vizyon-belgesi?page=1 (accessed September 24, 2018)

78. Şar and Telek, "Rethinking Secularism as a Political Principle in the Middle East."

79. See JDP, Ibid.

80. "İşte Erdoğan'ın Vizyon Belgesi," *CNNTurk*, September 15, 2014, http://www.cnnturk.com/fotogaleri/turkiye/iste-erdoganin-vizyon-belgesi?page=1, accessed September 24, 2018.

81. "Erdoğan Eğitimi Yeniden İnşa Etmekten, Radikal Adımlar Atmaktan Bahsetti," *Diken,* March 26, 2016, http://www.diken.com.tr/erdogan-egitimde-radikal-kararlar-atmaktan-bahsetti/, accessed September 24, 2018.

82. "Dindar Gençlik Yetiştireceğiz," Diken, February 2, 2012, http://www.hurriyet.com.tr/dindar-genclik-yetistirecegiz-19825231; and "Erdoğan Hedefine Bağlılık Bildirdi: Dindar Nesil Yetiştireceğiz," *Diken,* February 27, 2016, http://www.diken.com.tr/erdogan-sozunden-vazgecmedi-hedefimiz-dindar-nesil-yetistirmek/, accessed September 24, 2018.

83. "Erdoğan Eğitim Şurası'nda konuştu: Anaokulundan başlayarak yeni bir yaşam tarzı...", 02.12.2014, *Hurriyet,* retrieved from http://www.hurriyet.com.tr/erdogan-egitim-s-rasinda-konustu-anaokulundan-baslayarak-yeni-bir-hayat-tarzi-27691352 and "Evlatlarımız değerlerimiz çerçevesinde hazırlanan çizgi filmleri izlemeli", 19.06.2015, *Posta,* retrieved from http://www.posta.com.tr/siyaset/HaberDetay/-Evlatlarimiz-degerlerimiz-cercevesinde-hazirlanan-cizgi-filmleri-izlemeli-.htm?ArticleID=287637, accessed September 24, 2018.

84. Ali Bardakoğlu, *Religion and Society: New Perspectives from Turkey* (Ankara: Publications of Presidency of Religious Affairs, 2006), 11.

85. Ali Bardakoğlu, "The Evasive Crescent: The Role of Religion in Politics," in *Turkish Policy Quarterly* (İstanbul: ARI Movement, 2004), 368.

86. İştar Gözaydın, "Management of Religion in Turkey: The Diyanet and Beyond," in *Freedom of Religion and Belief in Turkey,* edited by Özgür Heval Çınar and Mine Yıldırım, 13 (Cambridge: Cambridge Scholars Publishing, 2014).

87. Ibid.

88. Turkish Constitution Article Nr.136.

89. Nil Mutluer, "Yapısal, Sosyal ve Ekonomi Politik Yönleriyle Diyanet İşleri Başkanlığı," in *Sosyo-Ekonomik Politikalar Bağlamında Diyanet İşleri Başkanlığı: Kamuoyunun Diyanet'e Bakışı, Tartışmalar ve Öneriler* (Istanbul: Helsinki Yurttaşlar Derneği, 2014), 3–5.

90. Ibid., 8, 64.

91. Şar and Telek, "Rethinking Secularism as a Political Principle in the Middle East," 284.

92. Turkish Ministry of Family and Social Policies, "Aile ve Sosyal Politikalar Bakanlığı ile Diyanet İşleri Başkanlığı Arasında İşbirliği Protokolü,", October 26, 2011; Turkish Ministry of Family and Social Policies, *Kadına Yönelik Şiddetle Mücadele Eylem Planı 2012–2015* (Ankara); Turkish Ministry of Family and Social Policies, "Aile ve Sosyal Politikalar Bakanlığı ile Türkiye Diyanet Vakfı Arasında İşbirliği Protokolü," May 29, 2013.

93. Turkish Ministry of Youth and Sports, "Gençlik ve Spor Bakanlığı ile Diyanet İşleri Başkanlığı Arasında Değerler Eğitimi İşbirliği Protokolü İmzalandı," GSB, February 26, 2015, http://www.gsb.gov.tr/HaberDetaylari/1/33369/genclik-ve-spor-bakanligi-ile-diyanet-isleri-baskanligi-degerler-egitimi-isbirligi-protokolu-imzalandi.aspx, accessed September 24, 2018.

94. Turkish Ministry of Health, "Hastanelerde Manevi Destek Sunmaya Yönelik İşbirliği Protokolü İmzalandı," January 7, 2015, http://saglik.gov.tr/SaglikTurizmi/belge/1-39351/hastanelerde-manevi-destek-sunmaya-yonelik-isbirligi-pr-.html, accessed September 24, 2018.

95. Turkish Ministry of Justice, "Adalet Bakanlığı ile Diyanet İşleri Başkanlığı Arasında Tutuklu ve Hükümlülerin Dini ve Ahlaki Gelişimlerini Sağlamaya Yönelik Protokol," February 10, 2011.

140 Edgar Şar

96. David Lepeska, "Turkey Casts the Diyanet," *Foreign Affairs*, May 17, 2015, https://www.foreignaffairs.com/articles/turkey/2015-05-17/turkey-casts-diyanet, accessed September 24, 2018.

97. Mutluer, "Yapısal, Sosyal ve Ekonomi Politik," 8

98. Gözaydın, "Management of Religion in Turkey"; and Kadri Gürsel, "Yeni Türkiye'nin Kültür Emperyalizmi Aygıtı: Diyanet," *Al Monitor*, March 11, 2015, March 11.

99. See İştar Gözaydın, *Türkiye Cumhuriyeti'nde Dinin Tanzimi* (İstanbul: İletişim, 2009).

100. Mutluer, "Yapısal, Sosyal ve Ekonomi Politik," 18.

101. Mutluer, "Yapısal, Sosyal ve Ekonomi Politik," 22.

102. Mutluer, "Yapısal, Sosyal ve Ekonomi Politik," 26.

103. Şar and Telek, "Rethinking Secularism as a Political Principle in the Middle East," 285.

104. Ibid.

105. UNESCO, "Inclusive Education: The Way of the Future," *International Conference on Education*. Conference in Geneva, July 18, 2008, http://www.ibe.unesco.org/fileadmin/user_upload/Policy_Dialogue/48th_ICE/CONFINTED_48-3_English.pdf, accessed September 24, 2018.

106. Education Reform Initiative, *Eğitim İzleme Raporu 2011*, 39–41. http://www.egitimreformugirisimi.org/sites/www.egitimreformugirisimi.org/files/EIR20 11.19.12.12.WEB_.pdf, accessed September 24, 2018.

107. Ibid., 41.

108. Education Reform Initiative, *Eğitim İzleme Raporu 2014–15*, 29–30. http://www.egitimreformugirisimi.org/sites/www.egitimreformugirisimi.org/files/EIR2014_04.09.15.WEB.pdf, accessed September 24, 2018.

109. "Bakanlık Devre Dışı, Eğitimin Dümeni Dinci Vakıflarda," *Birgün*, June 3, 2015.

110. See "Ensar Vakfı,"http://www.ensar.org/ensar-vakfi_W26.html; "Niçin ÖĞ-DER Şuurlu Öğretmenler Derneği," http://www.ogder.org/tr/genel.asp?islem=incele&id=82; and "Hizmet Vakfı Tarihçesi," http://www.hizmetvakfi.org/tarihce, all accessed September 24, 2018.

111. *Maarif* has an Arabic origin and means "education" in Ottoman-Turkish. The preference of this word to the much more widely used and known *milli eğitim* (national education) has been also publicly discussed and attributed to the will of imposing particular values by means of public education.

112. "Maarif Vakfı Yeni Bir Cemaat Yapılanması," *Birgün*, June 13, 2016, http://www.birgun.net/haber-detay/bakanlik-devre-disi-egitimin-dumeni-dinci-vaki-flarda-114522.html, accessed September 24, 2018.

113. Protestan Kiliseler Derneği, "Protestan Kiliseler Derneği 2014 Raporu," http://www.esithaklar.org/protestan-kiliseler-dernegi-2014-raporu/, accessed September 24, 2018.

114. Education Reform Initiative, *Eğitim İzleme Raporu 2010*, 81–82, http://www.egitimreformugirisimi.org/sites/www.egitimreformugirisimi.org/files/EIR2010_izleme%20raporu.pdf, accessed September 24, 2018.

115. European Court of Human Rights, *Hasan and Zeynep Cengiz v. Turkey* 1448/04.

116. See Mine Yıldırım, *DKAB 2011–2012 Program Değerlendirmesi,* Eğitim Reformu Girişimi, http://inancozgurlugugirisimi.org/kaynaklar/erg-dkab-2011-2012-program-degerlendirmesi/, accessed September 24, 2018.

117. Toledo Principles aim at providing a guide about how to perform the education about religions and beliefs based on respect for growing religious diversity and human rights and emphasizes upon an inclusionary, non-doctrinal, and neutral curriculum (OSCE, 2007).

118. European Court of Human Rights, *Mansur Yalçın and others v. Turkey* 21163/11.

119. Education Reform Initiative, *Eğitim İzleme Raporu 2014–15,* 83, http://www.egitimreformugirisimi.org/sites/www.egitimreformugirisimi.org/files/EIR2014_04.09.15.WEB.pdf, accessed September 24, 2018.

120. Şar and Telek, "Rethinking Secularism as a Political Principle in the Middle East," 286.

121. Education Reform Initiative, *Eğitim İzleme Raporu 2012,* 104, http://www.egitimreformugirisimi.org/sites/www.egitimreformugirisimi.org/files/ERG-EIR2012-egitim-izleme-raporu-2012-(12.09.2013).pdf, accessed September 24, 2018.

122. Ibid.

123. See Murat Somer, "Conquering versus Democratizing the State: Political Islamists and Fourth Wave Democratization in Turkey and Tunisia," *Democratization* 24, no. 6 (2017): 1025–30; and Alaranta, *National and State Identity in Turkey,* 19.

124. "Interview: We misread AKP and Erdoğan, Legitimized Crude Power Grab," *Hurriyet Daily News*, August, 29, 2015, http://www.hurriyetdailynews.com/interview-west-misread-JDP-and-erdogan-legitimized-crude-power-grab.aspx?pageID=238&nid=87678, accessed September 24, 2018.

RESOURCES

Ahmad, Feroz. *The Making of Modern Turkey.* London and New York: Routledge, 1993.

AKP. "2002 Genel Seçimleri Seçim Beyannamesi." http://www.JDParti.org.tr/upload/documents/2002-beyanname.pdf.

Akdoğan, Yalçın. *Muhafazakar Demokrasi.* Ankara: AK Parti Yayınları, 2003.

Alaranta, Toni. *National and State Identity in Turkey.* London: Rowman & Littlefield, 2015.

Alesinai, Alberto, and Reich, Bryony. "Nation-building." NBER Working Paper No. w18839, February 2013.

"Babuşçu: Gelecek 10 yıl Liberaller Gibi Eski Paydaşlarımızın Arzuladığı Gibi Olmayacak." *T24.* April 1, 2013. http://t24.com.tr/haber/babuscu-onumuzdeki-10-yil-liberaller-gibi-eski-paydaslarimizin-kabullenecegi-gibi-olmayacak,226892.

"Bakanlık Devre Dışı, Eğitimin Dümeni Dinci Vakıflarda." *Birgün*. June 3, 2015. http://www.birgun.net/haber-detay/bakanlik-devre-disi-egitimin-dumeni-dinci-vakiflarda-114522.html.

Bardakoğlu, Ali. "The Evasive Crescent: The Role of Religion in Politics." *Turkish Policy Quarterly*. İstanbul: ARI Movement, 2004.

———. *Religion and Society: New Perspectives from Turkey*, Ankara: Publications of Presidency of Religious Affairs, 2006.

Berkes, Niyazi. *Türkiye'de Çağdaşlaşma.* Istanbul: Yapı Kredi Yayınları, 2009.

Bhargava, Rajeev. "Rehabilitating Secularism." In *Rethinking Secularism*, edited by Calhoun, Juergensmeyer, and Van Antwerpen, 92–113. New York: Oxford University Press, 2011.

Bila, Hikmet. *RPP: 1919–1999.* Istanbul: Doğan Kitap, 1999.

"Bizans, Osmanlı ve Cumhuriyet… Üçünde de Din Devletin Kontrolünde." *Hurriyet.* January 28, 2015. http://sosyal.hurriyet.com.tr/yazar/ahmet-hakan_131/bizans-osmanli-ve-cumhuriyet-ucunde-de-din-devletin-kontrolunde_28065223.

Brown, Archie. "Introduction." In *Political Culture and Political Change in Communist States,* edited by Archie Brown and Jack Gray, 1–24. London: The Macmillan Press, 1979.

Davison, Andrew. "Turkey, a 'Secular' State? The Challenge of Description." *South Atlantic Quarterly* 102, nos. 2–3 (2003): 333–50.

Deutsch, Karl W. "Nation-Building and National Development." In *Nation Building in Comparative Contexts,* edited by Karl W. Deutsch and William J. Foltz, 1–16. New York: Routledge, 2017.

"Dindar Gençlik Yetiştireceğiz." *Hurriyet.* February 2, 2012. http://www.hurriyet.com.tr/dindar-genclik-yetistirecegiz-19825231.

Education Reform Initiative (ERG). *Eğitim İzleme Raporu 2010.* http://www.egitimreformugirisimi.org/sites/www.egitimreformugirisimi.org/files/EIR2010_izleme%20raporu.pdf.

———. *Eğitim İzleme Raporu 2011.* http://www.egitimreformugirisimi.org/sites/www.egitimreformugirisimi.org/files/EIR2011.19.12.12.WEB_.pdf.

———. *Eğitim İzleme Raporu 2012.* http://www.egitimreformugirisimi.org/sites/www.egitimreformugirisimi.org/files/ERG-EIR2012-egitim-izleme-raporu-2012-(12.09.2013).pdf.

———. *Eğitim İzleme Raporu 2014–15.* http://www.egitimreformugirisimi.org/sites/www.egitimreformugirisimi.org/files/EIR2014_04.09.15.WEB.pdf.

"Ensar Vakfı." http://www.ensar.org/ensar-vakfi_W26.html.

"Erdoğan Calls for a Secular Egypt." *Egypt Independent.* September 13, 2011. http://www.egyptindependent.com/news/erdogan-calls-secular-egypt.

"Erdoğan Eğitim Şurası'nda Konuştu: Anaokulundan Başlayarak Yeni Bir Yaşam Tarzı…" *Hurriyet.* December 2, 2014. http://www.hurriyet.com.tr/erdogan-egitim-s-rasinda-konustu-anaokulundan-baslayarak-yeni-bir-hayat-tarzi-27691352.

"Erdoğan Eğitimi Yeniden İnşa Etmekten, Radikal Adımlar Atmaktan Bahsetti." *Diken.* March 26, 2016. http://www.diken.com.tr/erdogan-egitimde-radikal-kararlar-atmaktan-bahsetti/.

"Erdoğan Hedefine Bağlılık Bildirdi: Dindar Nesil Yetiştireceğiz." *Diken.* February 27, 2016. http://www.diken.com.tr/erdogan-sozunden-vazgecmedi-hedefimiz-dindar-nesil-yetistirmek/.

European Court of Human Rights (ECHR), *Hasan and Zeynep Cengiz v. Turkey* 1448/04.

———. *Mansur Yalçın and others v. Turkey* 21163/11.

"Evlatlarımız Değerlerimiz Çerçevesinde Hazırlanan Çizgi Filmleri İzlemeli." *Posta.* June 19, 2015. http://www.posta.com.tr/siyaset/HaberDetay/-Evlatlarimiz-degerlerimiz-cercevesinde-hazirlanan-cizgi-filmleri-izlemeli-.htm?ArticleID=287637.

Göle, Nilüfer. "Secularism and Islamism in Turkey: The Making of Elites and Counter-Elites." *Middle East Journal* 51, no. 1 (1997): 46–58.

Gözaydın, İştar. *Diyanet: Türkiye Cumhuriyeti'nde Dinin Tanzimi.* İstanbul: İletişim, 2009.

———. "Management of Religion in Turkey: The Diyanet and Beyond." In *Freedom of Religion and Belief in Turkey*, edited by Özgür Heval Çınar and Mine Yıldırım, 10–35. Cambridge Scholars Publishing, 2014.

Grigoriadis, Ioannis N. *Instilling Religion in Greek and Turkish Nationalism: A "Sacred Synthesis."* New York: Palgrave Macmillan, 2013.

Groc, Gerard. "AKP, Türkiye'deki Laikliğin Derdi mi Dostu mu?" In *Tartışılan Laiklik: Fransa ve Türkiye'de İlkeler ve Algılamalar*, edited by Samim Akgönül, 41–62. Istanbul: Bilgi Üniversitesi Yayınları, 2011.

Gülalp, Haldun. "Enlightenment by Fiat: Secularization and Democracy in Turkey." *Middle Eastern Studies* 41, no. 3 (2005): 352–72.

Gürsel, Kadri. "Yeni Türkiye'nin Kültür Emperyalizmi Aygıtı: Diyanet." *Al Monitor.* March 11, 2015.

"Hizmet Vakfı Tarihçesi." http://www.hizmetvakfi.org/tarihce.

"Interview: We Misread AKP and Erdoğan, Legitimized Crude Power Grab." *Hurriyet Daily News.* August, 29, 2015. http://www.hurriyetdailynews.com/interview-west-misread-akp-and-erdogan-legitimized-crude-power-grab.aspx?pageID=238&nid=87678.

"İşte Erdoğan'ın Vizyon Belgesi." *CNNTurk.* July 15, 2014. http://www.cnnturk.com/fotogaleri/turkiye/iste-erdoganin-vizyon-belgesi?page=1.

Kandiyoti, Deniz. "The Travails of the Secular: Puzzle and Paradox in Turkey." *Economy and Society* 41, no. 4 (2012): 513–31.

Karpat, Kemal. *Türk Siyasi Tarihi.* Istanbul: Timaş Yayınları, 2011.

Kuru, Ahmet. *Secularism and State Policies towards Religion: United States, France and Turkey.* New York: Cambridge University Press, 2009.

Kuru, Ahmet, and Alfred Stephan. "Introduction." In *Democracy, Islam and Secularism in Turkey (Religion, Culture and Public Life)*, edited by Ahmet Kuru and Alfred Stephan, 1–11. New York: Columbia University Press, 2012.

Lepeska, David. "Turkey Casts the Diyanet." *Foreign Affairs.* May 17, 2015. https://www.foreignaffairs.com/articles/turkey/2015-05-17/turkey-casts-diyanet.

Lewis, Bernard. *Modern Türkiye'nin Doğuşu.* Ankara: Arkadaş Yayınları, 2013.

"Maarif Vakfı yeni bir cemaat yapılanması." *Birgün.* Jun 13, 2016, June 13.

Miş, Nebi, and Aslan, Ali. "Erdoğan Siyaseti ve Kurucu Cumhurbaşkanı Vizyonu." *Seta Analiz*, no. 19 (September 2014).

Mutluer, Nil. "Yapısal, Sosyal ve Ekonomi Politik Yönleriyle Diyanet İşleri Başkanlığı." In *Sosyo-Ekonomik Politikalar Bağlamında Diyanet İşleri Başkanlığı: Kamuoyunun Diyanet'e Bakışı, Tartışmalar ve Öneriler*. Istanbul: Helsinki Yurttaşlar Derneği, 2014.

Narlı, Nilüfer. "Türkiye'de Laikliğin Konumu." *Cogito* no. 1 (1994, 2014): 23–31.

"Niçin ÖĞ-DER Şuurlu Öğretmenler Derneği." http://www.ogder.org/tr/genel. asp?islem=incele&id=82.

OSCE, *Toledo Guiding Principles on Teaching about Religions and Beliefs in Public Schools*, 2007.

"President Erdoğan Defends Secularism after Remarks by Parliament Speaker." May 11, 2016. http://www.hurriyetdailynews.com/president-erdogan-defends-secularism-after-remarks-by-parliament speaker.aspx?pageID=238&nID=98392& NewsCatID=338.

Protestan Kiliseler Derneği. "Protestan Kiliseler Derneği 2014 Raporu." http://www. esithaklar.org/protestan-kiliseler-dernegi-2014-raporu/.

Şar, Edgar, and Alphan Telek. "Rethinking Secularism as a Political Principle in the Middle East: From Negative to Positive Perception of Secularism." In *Sources of Secularism: Enlightenment and Beyond*, edited by Anna Tomaszevska and Hasse Hamalainen, 245–93. Cham: Palgrave Macmillan, 2017.

Somer, Murat. "Conquering versus Democratizing the State: Political Islamists and Fourth Wave Democratization in Turkey and Tunisia." *Democratization* 24, no. 6: 1025–43, doi: 10.1080/13510347.2016.1259216.

———. "Is Turkish Secularism Antireligious, Reformist, Separationist, Integrationist, or Simply Undemocratic?" *Journal of Church and State* 55, no. 3 (2013): 585–97; doi: 10.1093/jcs/cst052.

TBMM, Republican People's Party, 7th Party Congress. https://www.tbmm.gov. tr/eyayin/GAZETELER/WEB/KUTUPHANEDE%20BULUNAN%20DIJIT AL%20KAYNAKLAR/KITAPLAR/SIYASI%20PARTI%20YAYINLARI/ 197603391%20RPP%207%20NCI%20BUYUK%20KURULTAYI/ 197603391%20RPP%207%20NCI%20BUYUK%20KURULTAYI%200077_ 0138%20UCUNCU%20BIRLESIM.pdf.

Turam, Berna. *Secular State and Religious Society: Two Forces in Play in Turkey*. New York: Palgrave Macmillan, 2012.

Turkish Constitutional Court (TCC). Ruling No: 1998/1, 1998.

Turkish Ministry of Family and Social Policies (TMFSP). "Aile ve Sosyal Politikalar Bakanlığı ile Diyanet İşleri Başkanlığı Arasında İşbirliği Protokolü." October 26, 2011.

———. *Kadına Yönelik Şiddetle Mücadele Eylem Planı 2012–2015*, Ankara.

———. "Aile ve Sosyal Politikalar Bakanlığı ile Türkiye Diyanet Vakfı Arasında İşbirliği Protokolü", May 29, 2013.

Turkish Ministry of Foreign Affairs (TMFA). 2013. "Dışişleri Bakanı Ahmet Davutoğlu'nun Diyarbakır Dicle Üniversitesi'nde Verdiği 'Büyük Restorasyon: Kadimden Küreselleşmeye Yeni Siyaset Anlayışımız' Konulu Konferans. 15 Mart

2013, Diyarbakır." http://www.mfa.gov.tr/disisleri-bakani-ahmet-davutoglu_nundiyarbakir-dicle-universitesinde-verdigi-_buyuk-restorasyon_-kadim_den-kuresellesmeye-yeni.tr.mfa.

Turkish Ministry of Health (TMH). "Hastanelerde Manevi Destek Sunmaya Yönelik İşbirliği Protokolü İmzalandı." January 7, 2015. http://saglik.gov.tr/SaglikTurizmi/belge/1-39351/hastanelerde-manevi-destek-sunmaya-yonelik-isbirligi-pr-.html.

Turkish Ministry of Justice (TMJ). "Adalet Bakanlığı ile Diyanet İşleri Başkanlığı Arasında Tutuklu ve Hükümlülerin Dini ve Ahlaki Gelişimlerini Sağlamaya Yönelik Protokol." February 10, 2011.

Turkish Ministry of Youth and Sports (TMYS). "Gençlik ve Spor Bakanlığı ile Diyanet İşleri Başkanlığı Arasında Değerler Eğitimi İşbirliği Protokolü İmzalandı." February 26, 2015. http://www.gsb.gov.tr/HaberDetaylari/1/33369/genclik-ve-spor-bakanligi-ile-diyanet-isleri-baskanligi-degerler-egitimi-isbirligi-protokolu-imzalandi.aspx.

UNESCO. "Inclusive Education: The Way of the Future." *International Conference on Education.* Conference in Geneva, July 18, 2008. http://www.ibe.unesco.org/fileadmin/user_upload/Policy_Dialogue/48th_ICE/CONFINTED_48-3_English.pdf.

Utz, Raphael. "Nations, Nation-Building and Cultural Intervention: A Social Science Perspective." *Max Planck Yearbook of United Nations Law* 9 (2005): 615–47.

Yavuz, Hakan. "Cleansing Islam from the Public Sphere." *Journal of International Affairs* 54, no. 1, 2000.

Yıldırım, Mine. *DKAB 2011–2012 Program Değerlendirmesi.* Eğitimde Reformu Girişimi, 2012. http://inancozgurlugugirisimi.org/kaynaklar/erg-dkab-2011-2012-program-degerlendirmesi/.

Zajda, Joseph. "Nation-Building, Identity and Citizenship Education: Introduction." In *Nation-Building, Identity and Citizenship Education: Cross-Cultural Perspectives*, edited by Joseph Zajda, Holger Daun, and Lavrence S. Saha, 1–11. New York: Springer, 2009.

Zürcher, Erik Jan. *Modernleşen Türkiye'nin Tarihi.* Istanbul: İletişim Yayınları, 2012.

Chapter Five

Nation-Building and Gender Regime in Turkey

Senem Kurt Topuz

The focus of this chapter is to analyze the nation-building process that started in Turkey with the proclamation of the Republic. It also covers the 1980s and Justice and Development Party (JDP) period after 2000 and aims to scrutinize women's status, position, and their missions and roles during the process of nationalization. Therefore, the basic aim of this study is to uncover how nation-building processes in Turkey, covering different periods, affected and shaped the gender regime in the country. In other words, it is to analyze women's status, roles, and missions assigned to them during the nation-building processes in Turkey. It has to be stated here that this study is based on the modernist approach among the theories that aim to explain the concepts of nation and nationalism. Within this context, this study is based on the claim of the modernist approach that nations are historically built and invent imaginary communities and structures. In addition, another theory of this study, which aims to reveal the relation between the process of nationalization and gender regime, is dependent upon imagining the nation as male. What is specifically tried to be emphasized in this study, according to this claim, is that women are excluded from the process of nation-creation and from the founding ideologies of the nation-state and its founding positions or that their inclusion into this ideology and positions are limited by men. However, it has to be emphasized at this point that countries that went through different nation-state processes assigned different missions and roles to women. In this study, Turkey is considered as one of the countries within the category that both aims to modernize and fight against colonization according to Jill Vickers' study.[1] In such countries, women could be involved in the national project within the limits drawn by men. Therefore, this study, which tries to be based upon both the modernist approach and the claim of imagining the nation as male, focuses on the effects of these theories' manifestations on the process of nation-building in Turkey and on the effects of this process on the gender regime.

There are three basic sections in this study. The first section essentially discusses the era from the early Republic period (1920–1935) and covering the early modernization period (1870–1935) to the 1980s. In the second section, nation-building within the process from the 1980s to the 2000s and women's position and roles within this building are studied. The third section discusses the new national discourse that has been tried to be created by the New Turkey slogan of the JDP terms, women's position and status within this discourse, and the new identity that woman created. In the conclusion, nationalization dynamics in Turkey and the effects of these dynamics on the gender regime are reviewed by making a general evaluation from these three periods.

THEORETICAL BACKGROUND: IMAGINING THE NATION AS MALE

A modernist approach, which is one of the theories trying to explain the nation and nationalism terms, both of which are modern concepts,[2] claims that nations are historically built structures.[3] From this point, it can be asserted that Ernest Gellner, Eric Hobsbawm, and Benedict Anderson's views are full of detailed information regarding the process of nation-building.[4] According to Gellner, what creates nations is the ideology of nationalism.[5] Nations are invented as a result of the effect of the ideology of nationalism. In other words, what forms a nation is not self-consciousness existing within a community that shares the desire and belief to be a part of the same nation, but it is actually a process of building. Anderson, on the other hand, envisions a nation as an imaginary community, a political society that is a union and partnership of a human group who does not know or has an awareness of each other and defines the nation as fiction or delusion rather than a construction.[6] In addition, a nation that is an imaginary community, in Anderson's view, is also a limited unit, and the protector of the nation is the sovereign state. A nation is limited because it gains its existence through its *difference* from other communities. In other words, a nation has no desire or claim to include all people because the nation (however or whatever the actual inequalities or exploitation relations might exist within its structure) is designed, in essence, as a horizontal and deep companionship, brotherhood, and solidarity.[7] However, at this point, it has to be emphasized that feminist studies[8] examining the process of nation-building from the angle of gender construction claim that the nation is not based on the brotherhood, companionship, and solidarity of all people but rather on the brotherhood and solidarity among men. Within this context, according to McClintock, nation or national unity emphasizes the unity among men that reflects institutionalized gender discrimination, not the unity of all people who create the nation.[9] Therefore, it is also claimed that "homeland" (*la patrie*) is the basic ground that refers to unity, equal share, and solidarity and which bears the same responsibility among men[10] and that heroic warrior men are symbolized as the builder and protector of the nation and the homeland.[11] The most significant emphasis made by this image of warrior men, without a doubt, is the implication that men hold the real power that defines the nation,[12] and therefore, state power and effective political power will remain masculine.[13]

At this point, it should not be wrong to assert that the nation, as a constructed or created reality, is a reflection of masculine imagination. The theory of a nation as a masculine imagination, in essence, is focused on how women are excluded from the creation of the nation and from the building of ideologies and positions or that their contribution to the ideology and positions are limited by men. Within the context of the theory of a nation as a masculine imagination, it is claimed that the only sphere where women are not excluded from or limited by men while building the nation and nation-state is in the "symbolic sphere."[14] In this sense, putting national values on the concepts of language and the homeland as a "mother tongue" or "motherland" or embodying national symbols with a woman's body are reflections of symbolic significance given to women during the process of nation-building.[15]

Nira Yuval-Davis and Floya Anthias state, in their study titled *Woman-Nation-State,* that women and men contribute to the process of nation-building with different tasks and representations. According to the authors, women contribute to the nation-building process on five different levels. First, one is contributing to the nation-building process as the ones who secure the nation's genes; in other words, who are the biological producers of the new nation? The second level deals with the agents who help to draw cultural boundaries of the nation against other nations; in other words, as the reproducers of boundaries of the ethnic and cultural groups. The third level is as ones who are the teachers, conveyors, and ideological reproducers of genuine culture that provides the nation with identity. The fourth one is as symbols that are placed in the center of the ideological discourse used in the transformation and reproduction of ethnic and national categories distinguishing national differences and in nation-building. The last level is as the contributors to the national struggles (e.g., national, economic, political, and military). According to Yuval-Davis and Anthias, women are called upon to the nation-building processes to realize the roles attributed to them and fulfill the tasks. Besides, it has never been the case that is desired or accepted that women carry out equal and/or same tasks with men for other responsibilities and representations.[16] Therefore, differentiation in tasks and representations between men and women during the nation-building process shows us how gender roles play a constitutive part in the process.

At this point, it has to be stated that it is not a coincidence that nation in nation-building is described as a family and that nation is a family where women and men play their natural roles and where the man is the head of the family.[17] Thus, the principal role of the man is being the head of the family and who is the founder, protector, and the strong one, and the woman's role is being the mother, who biologically reproduces. It has to be stated, by referring to Mervat Hatem, that defining the nation through family and kinship relations causes the woman's position and function in the society to be symbolized as "motherhood" and being a man's "wife."[18] According to Rubina Saigol, women's participation in the nation-building or their entrance visa to the nation-state is related to their being a mother.[19] Therefore, motherhood attributed to woman is a primary responsibility for the protection and continuity of the homeland that can never be neglected. Thus, women protect the home, not the nation, and they create a feminine domestic sphere against the fictive masculine world created by men. Building the nation is designed by men, and women only prepare the backdrop.[20] Simone de Beauvoir explains this situation as where the woman is left behind because of her biological motherhood task she bears, and that she is the guardian of what is "internal," and since a man goes "outside," he develops himself as "homo faber" and is allowed to sovereign the world.[21]

According to Hobsbawm, one of the significant aspects of nation-building is to create certain traditions regarding the human community forming that nation and to constantly reproduce those traditions.[22] Without a doubt, a women's role and responsibility in this creation and reproduction process are more primary than men's. In other words, women's responsibility in building and reproducing the cultural sphere is more explicit because figures that are symbolized as the conveyor of the cultural traditions through generations during the process of nation-building have always been women.[23] Therefore, a woman faces representation burden as she is the indication of differentiation of a nation from other nations; in other words, she is the national symbol. This representation also causes the woman to be symbolized as the bearer of the honor and chastity of the family and nation or national family because the woman holds a position that differentiates a nation from the others with her appearance, her behaviors, and her status as well as attitudes both in public and private spheres. Thus, it justifies especially masculine state's domination on women because woman's honor and chastity pave the way for state's or man's intervention in woman's subjectivity and spontaneity.[24]

According to Najmabadi, honor is "a concept that is tightly coupled with nation's being man and homeland's being woman".[25] Thus, the homeland is built like a female figure both which man's desire is directed to and which man protects and owns. As a natural result of it, the concept of nation that is fictionalized as lover and mother transformed the concept of woman and gave birth to new womanhood and manhood. Thus, the nation-state as a men's community responsible for protection of the "female homeland" has been increasingly masculinized on the symbolic level, and the state has gained the role of "protective male" more and more as the nation has been entirely categorized as woman-protected.[26]

However, at this point, Vickers's study titled "Gendering the Hyphen: Gender Dimensions of Modern Nation-State Formation in Euro-American and Anti- and Post-Colonial Contexts" on understanding the role of women from different countries played in nation-building and their status afterwards should be mentioned because Vickers underlined that countries that went through different nation-building processes assigned different tasks and roles to women.[27] Vickers determined that communities that fought against the colonial oppression to build a nation-state—in other words, communities that were outright colonies—lived under the sovereignty of colonial powers, and they fought for their independence that entitled women to equal civil rights with men. Finland and Norway nation-states can be given as examples. Women in those two countries took part in the center of the fight for independence and contributed to nation-building together with men right from the beginning.[28]

However, Vickers stated that women are honored through their motherhood roles within the family and that they are defined by their motherhood roles rather than as citizens when "failed, late, or incomplete" nation-state processes, such as Germany and Italy, are considered. In the same study, Vickers also looked at the nation-building processes of countries that wished to modernize on the one hand and those that fought against colonialism on the other. He stated that women were included in the nation-building process as the symbol and defender of modernism in the public sphere and the conveyor and pursuer of the tradition at home in these countries (e.g., India). In such countries, women could be included in the national project within the limited areas determined by men.[29]

For Partha Chatterjee, to be able to complete the nationalization process fully and entirely in such countries, it is necessary to benefit from the physical techniques of the West on the one hand and to protect and empower the genuine moral essence of the national culture on the other.[30] In this context, woman and home appear as the genuine moral essence of the national culture. Similarly, Serpil Sancar states that women in Turkey, just as women in India, were included in the nation-building process as the symbol and defender of modernism in the public sphere and the conveyor and pursuer of the tradition at home.[31] Therefore, in this study, following Sancar, in the analysis of the relation between the process of nationalization in Turkey and the gender regime, Turkey is taken as one of the countries that both aims to modernize on one hand and to fight against colonialism on the other.

NATION-BUILDING IN TURKEY AND WOMAN

Early Modernization Period

It is not wrong to claim that the nation-building process in Turkey is closely related to modernity,[32] and therefore, this process took place within the center of the desire to modernize on the one hand and the fight against colonialism on the other. Within this context, the roots of Turkish modernization can be traced back to Westernization movements started during the Ottoman Empire times; in other words, to the second half of the nineteenth century.[33] Sancar finds it suitable to call the period of Turkish modernization that lasted from the middle of the nineteenth century to the middle of the twentieth century the "early modernization" period (1870–1935) and explained the dynamics of the early modernization process through Republican modernization by linking those with Tanzimat reforms and Constitutionalism movements.[34]

According to Sancar, founder elites of the early modernization period determined the modernization and nationalization dynamics generally within the context of such issues as an ideal society, modern family, strong state, and modern female-male relations by emphasizing national culture, contemporary civilization, and human nature. Sancar also states that the most significant mediation of the narratives fictionalized on these issues was women. In other words, the topic of these narratives was women and family relations in the center of which women were placed.[35]

If we look at the status of women in social life in the Ottoman Empire during the seventeenth century, when the Empire experienced an economic crisis, and when the public sphere started to be shaped from the center of the Empire, it is claimed that women of the "ruling class" and "wealthy group" contributed significantly to the public life and even to the construction of social complexes, *madrasas*, and mosques.[36] It can be said that this situation arose from women's taking part in social life and lasted until the proclamation of the First Constitution (*Birinci Meşrutiyet*, 1876). During this period (from seventeenth century to the First Constitution in 1876), the state's reaction to women's socialization or to women's movements was two-phased. The first phase was the banning phase. Within this context, royal decrees were published that dealt with women's clothing and explained in detail how women were to behave on the street and at the market. These decrees not only regulated how women should behave but also included restrictions about how they should not behave. The second reaction of the state to women's existence in social life emerged as placing importance on women's education as from the first quarter of the nineteenth century.[37]

It is seen that women were involved in social life especially with the mission of becoming a "social actor" during the period from the First Constitution (1876) to the proclamation of the Republic (1923).[38] During this period, attitude of the state towards women was generally "protective and encouraging" by standing by women. It can be claimed that, during this time frame, especially with Abdulhamid II in rule and the Union and Progress government, there was placed special importance on the issue of woman and steps (such as forming a battalion of women in the army) were taken to pave the way for women to take part in social life.[39] As Ayşe Durakbaşa also states that matters such as placing special importance on women's education and protecting and encouraging women during this historical period could be related to the troubling feeling of being underdeveloped that was in the minds of the modernization group or to the desire to be a part of the civilized world.[40]

Indeed, during the process that started with the imperial edict of Gulhane (*Tanzimat Fermanı*, 1839) and continued with the proclamation of the First (1876) and Second Constitutions (İkinci Meşrutiyet, 1908), the basic emphasis was on the ideal of modernization and alleviating the troubling feeling of being underdeveloped. At this point, it can be stated that the same emphasis affected the proclamation of the Republic, and within this context, the issue of women was dealt with a modern mindset. In other words, within the framework of a modernization mindset, woman was determined as the symbol or indication of the society being underdeveloped and dealt with as a "problem" that needed to be solved to free the society from being underdeveloped,[41] as Nilüfer Göle points out that "the modernization project in Turkey shows equivalence between the liberation of women and development of the nation."[42]

Therefore, it can be claimed that women being chosen as the focal point of a society's underdevelopment and being the symbol of modernization are neither new nor unique to Turkey because women, as Fatmagül Berktay states, have been generally used as a means or an indication of representations of meanings that do not really "define" them and that they do not "choose," no matter what the context is.[43] For example, with the social transformation emerging after the proclamation of the Republic, young girls in shorts, school uniforms, or military uniforms carrying flags at parades or women in gowns dancing in ballrooms are imprinted in people's minds as the most significant symbols of the modernism of the newly founded Republic.[44]

At this point, it should be stated that every new state sets the goal of building a new nation, a new state structure, and a new man. In this context, political elites—in other words, founders—of the newly founded Turkish Republic wanted to establish a collective social structure regarding culture and class to build a strong state. With that goal in mind, they tried to have a new man whose cultural ties had been broken thanks to the cultural revolution actualized only by the state itself.[45] When this building of a new man is considered from the viewpoint of genders, it can be claimed that a new image of a woman who has sealed off her femininity emerged with the proclamation of the Republic. This new female image matches, to a large extent, the image of a social female because, as mentioned above, founders of the Republic supported women's contribution to the social life to actualize the Republic's modernization ideal and to gain a modern state image. The status and place of women in public life were one of the indications of the contemporary civilization, and within this context, "modern woman was, before anything else, a social woman."[46]

From Early Republic Period to the 1980s

The most distinct feature of the female image that was tried to be created during the early Republic period (1920–1935)[47] was addressing a woman as she was sealed off her gender; in other words, as if she was genderless. Women who were symbolized as genderless during the early Republic period were seen as being the most significant soldiers serving to build a modern, Western, civilized nation, and of this modernization process, they were coded as a "national cause" or "civilization war." In this process, what was expected both from men and women was abandoning their own sense of self for the sake of the nation and homeland with a strong feeling of patriotism and uniting for the "national development" by setting aside all their personal expectations and desires.[48] In this context, accepting that "women and men who share the same national responsibilities and goals are equal as the nation's people" turned into women's existence alongside men in social life.[49] Therefore, it is not incorrect to state that women's existence in public life was seen as a means to deliver national development and their public visibility was not "a means to create a personal consciousness for themselves."[50]

At this point, Chatterjee's statement that the "middle-class family should be looked at in order to understand the anti-colonial nation-building" provides a very useful analysis with which to scrutinize the role of women in the process of nation-building during the early Republic period in Turkey. Since, according to Chatterjee, it is seen that women contributed actively to the nation-building project, which was carried out while trying to modernize on the one hand and fighting against colonialism on the other, by starting modern families.[51] According to Sancar, women during the early periods of Turkish modernization were involved in the nation-building process, called a "national cause," as mentioned earlier, through "family-focused moderniza-tion actualized together with institutional and ideological dimensions." In this context, the modern Turkish family that was attempted to be built during the process of modernization was the middle-class family that would be the role model of the modern city life for the newly built nation. It can be claimed that the modern Turkish family in this process was a "means of modernization" as a founding element of the nation to be included in the nation-building. Hence, modern womanhood is a fiction actualized through educating and raising women, and women in this process are the actors who take the responsibility of fulfilling the state's goal of creating modern families.[52] Akşit explains this with the concept of "silence of girls." According to Akşit, raising women as housewives and that being their contribution to nation-building caused women to be invisible in public life and that further created the assumption in women that they contributed to nation-building not because it was a social responsibility and citizenship duty but because it was "a service to the na-tion," and this mission was maintained quietly.[53]

Actually, during the war of independence to build a new state, the role of men was being a strong and protective warrior while the role of women was to support the fighting men in any way possible. In other words, women were not the ones who build, but instead, they were the ones who support; they are the ones who do not have primary roles or duties but secondary ones. There-fore, as a result of the differentiation in roles, it is not plausible or realistic to expect both genders to be included in the same duties and representations.[54]

In this context, roles and duties expected from women were "to contribute to the building of a modern society by building modern families, homes, children, and a modern daily life alongside men but in different forms." The modern Turkish woman in this process was educated and taught according to the cause; they were created as "a collective subject" who would exist for her family and nation not as "selfish" or who would follow her personal choices, pleasures, and desires;[55] and they were made to see and accept themselves this way.

Therefore, while differentiating the roles and duties attributed to men and women during the level of building a nation-state of Turkish modernization, a gender regime was shaped where women were responsible for social and cultural tasks while men were responsible for politics. Thus, the equivalence of the social and cultural tasks given to women in working life would be oc-cupations such teaching and nursing that would comply with motherhood and being a housewife. At this point, it is plausible to state that the Republic's policy of creating a modern woman and family excluded women (and if not excluded, then instead silenced or made them secondary) regarding the political area and government by creating social roles and public statuses unique to women and created "female areas" for women.[56]

Indeed, it is seen that the issue of women being the subject of political rights as voters or electives did not exist in the 1921 or 1924 Constitutions, and women not taking part in the first-term political decision-making mechanisms was not considered a problem. In other words, it is understood that discourse indicating that the Republic made "a women's revolution"[57] does not mean giving equal political rights to women or of women taking part in the government.[58] Therefore, Yaprak Zihnioğlu defines the Republic as a "women's revolution without women" and states that founders did not see women as the nation's creators, equal citizens (in the context of de facto equality), or political decision-makers.[59]

However, through time, when the Republic started to settle and became rooted, women's participation in political life on the symbolic level became possible. When the time came, entitling women with political rights was put on the agenda, and President Mustafa Kemal Atatürk himself emphasized the timing. In Atatürk's words: "We founded the Republic, while it completes its tenth year, all the requirements of the democracy should be put into practice as the occasion arises. Recognizing women's rights will be one of them."[60] Therefore, decisions of the executive units, political elites are of primary for women to access political rights rather than women's demands. It is the masculine political power that entitles women to political rights. It should also be stated here that recognizing women's rights was used to indicate that the newly founded nation-state had broken all ties with the Ottoman Empire; in other words, it was a means to symbolize new a nation-state for the executive units. Opposite to the Ottoman Empire—in de jure sense—women's being equal citizens legally has been the distinctive feature of the Republic.[61]

Therefore, it has been believed that women were given—in other words, granted—political rights by the state without a fight or demand. This common belief provided a reason to limit the role of women who worked alongside men in the political arena and caused women to be described as "contributing but quiet and decent woman."[62] Another significant emphasis in this narrative is that a woman should not neglect her motherhood and family responsibilities even if she participates in the political arena because the common belief of the era was that the major responsibility of a woman is being a mother.[63]

When the role of woman in the society outside the political area during the first years of the Republic is considered, it is seen that the view of a woman was never to create "a working woman" by putting off her traditional roles of motherhood and being a housewife. Some women gained more publicity in the building of the nation-state compared to others. However, these "other women," who were greater in number, were involved in the modernization process as modern housewives who started modern families while elite women had professions and jobs.[64]

What was expected from women in a professional working life was to serve the national cause that was modernizing the country. The mission of women was to appear as individuals who had professions and to reflect a modern model in public. According to Durakbaşa, the first-generation women of the Republic embraced the ideology of the Republic sincerely and became successful women in their professions with a sound sense of duty in accordance with the mission laid on them by the Republic.[65] However, it should be stated that these women did not represent all women and that they were a group of advantageous women. The difference between these women and the rest of the women in the society was that they were seen as "the respected symbols of the Republic" in service of the state, not as women who took part in the bureaucracy of the newly founded state together with men. These symbolic women were included in the new "middle-class elite" composed of educated groups such as teachers, public officers, and bureaucrats created by the Republic. However, a sharp distinction between rural women and educated elite women was caused that was institutionalized as a result of the structure of Turkish society and described as the status stratification among women.[66]

In addition, it was necessary to isolate a woman from her gender in the public sphere on the one hand and to get her to embrace her role of being a mother to her family and to the society as a whole on the other in this new state order that enabled women's public visibility and her participation in social life.[67] Thus, woman's honor and chastity could be protected and woman would embrace the methods of protecting her honor and chastity. According to Deniz Kandiyoti, a "woman officer's graceful suit and open face that shadow her femininity and highlight her genderless identity" could give the message that "she is sexually unattainable."[68] In this context, the message a woman sent to society through her clothes, behaviors, and attitudes was the image of a genderless, honorable, and chaste modern Turkish woman.

According to Sancar,[69] it can be seen how the new society was born with a reconciliation: "Providing the right to not to cover oneself but also not banning to cover, enacting monogamy but also not objecting religious marriage ceremony (on the condition that it would take place together with the official one), and enacting the comprehensive right for women to divorce, directing women's rights of education and having occupations suitable for women, and not approving equal political participation at all." Therefore, this reconciliation was one of the concrete indications of the Republic being a revolution for women's rights without women.

However, it should be stated here that distinct "women's rights discourse" (even though it was "women's rights without women") of the early Republic period covering the years between 1920 and 1935 faded during the chaos of World War II.[70] After that, the issue of the woman reemerged in another form during the period between 1945 and 1965. Sancar defined this period as "the period of conservative modernization."[71]

In this period, there was a consensus between the Republicans and Conservatives on the limits of women's freedom, duties attributed to family and women, and how these duties would be actualized by women within which limitations and with what ideological legitimization. The concrete evidence of this consensus on women, in 1965, was the transformation of women from public to "private" as being a families' "unconditional, emotional effort" provider. In this context, "being a modern Turkish woman required being a mother and a wife primarily, fulfilling religious responsibilities to a certain extent, going for feminine occupations beneficial for the society such as nursing and teaching, and staying within the boundaries drawn by the rules of honor–chastity. As opposed to woman, man was represented as one who existed with his desires and whose conflicts with his desires would never spoil modernism, survival of the state, sexual morality, and family."[72]

The end of the conservative modernization period that pacified woman, isolated her from her gender, and expected the woman to actualize the duties assigned to her within the clear boundaries set by the male mind and male power was reached when emerging criticism and innovation policy arrived in Turkey after the worldwide spread of 1960s radicalism.[73]

Actually, when the period from the 1960s to the 1980s is examined, the 1960s and 1970s are the years when there was a trigger regarding women's movements during the conjuncture after World War II. However, according to Suna Kili, women who participated in the movement in line with the ideologies under the 1960s and 1970s ideological atmosphere defended the superiority of their ideology they believed in rather than their rights.[74] However, Şirin Tekeli states that there was an atmosphere where the concepts such as inequality and exploitation became the basic concepts in political discourse in the 1970s and that women were given an active role in this environment.[75] Women, who started to realize that they formed "a gender group" who were not treated equally even though they were claimed to be equal under the law, accepted socialism as a savior, seeing it as the only solution to overcome the problems stemming from women putting forth a double effort by working both at home and also working under the leadership of women workers. Moreover, women were invited to the class struggle where they would fight with men shoulder to shoulder for their freedom.[76]

Therefore, it can be claimed here that women's movements in Turkey were affected by the intellectual and ideological world of the leftist creeds developed after 1968; however, it should be stated that the real acceleration of the feminist movement in Turkey coincides with the period after the military coup on September 12, 1980.[77] Ömer Çaha described the feminist movement in Turkey after 1980 as "the phase of woman's search for identity" and stated that this phase was the reflection of effort of women and their objective to search for their identity by lifting said identity to a level where they are the subject. According to Çaha, the first reaction of the state to this new movement was "watching and staying on alert."[78]

The 1980s and After

It can be said that women's movements in the 1980s emerged with the military regime.[79] After the military coup on September 12, 1980, active policy in Turkey ended, and all the political parties were closed by suppressing political movements. In this context, politics was isolated naturally from the public sphere, and the military banned all political actions in order to hold political power in their hands.[80] However, this oppression caused a "paradoxical" environment for the women's movements in Turkey because, after the 1980 coup and the period following, women in Turkey had the opportunity to start talking in their defense and for their interest.[81] Betül Karagöz states that this paradoxical environment was supported by the neoliberal and individualistic discourse of 1980s feminism and it found a living space for itself within the initiative to establish a new order triggered by the economic crisis.[82] Moreover, the necessity to re-identify the society together with the need of the regime to have the public support of the dominant class enabled a state-supported feminism movement to emerge.[83] Arat associated the reason why the women's movement could make itself heard and increased in this oppressive environment was that "women groups had not been cared about or the Kemalist tradition legitimized the women issue."[84] During the period when the army banned all political activities and ended active civil politics in order to hold the power, women's right defenders and women groups were not considered as a threat, which is thanks in part to the discrimination between the political sphere and the public sphere. In addition, the actions of the women's movement and organizations therein were not accepted as a political movement or political opposition. These factors all enabled the women's movement to be heard during this otherwise oppressive period.

However, whatever the underlying reasons or agreements might be and however it emerged, after the 1980 military coup, it can be said that a women's movement emerged in Turkey. Women brought up, expressed, and discussed issues they faced caused only by being a woman. The movement moved forward and left a significant mark on the social mobilization progression in 1980s. However, it should also be stated that the movement did not spread across society and become socialized during those years.[85]

The first emphasis standing out regarding the women's movements during this period is that it was independent from the state and was self-emerged.[86] Çaha compares the class and cultural structure of women who joined the feminist movement in this period to leftist organizations.[87,88] According to Çaha, most of these women "belonged to middle class, were urbanite, educated, professional, and intellectual."[89] Moreover, according to Arat, these women were composed of small groups sometimes gathered around a certain media and sometimes a certain identity or individual authors, artists, and journalists.[90] Aksu Bora states that the most distinct characteristic of these women is that they were well-educated and that they could follow literature in Western languages.[91] Thus, they discovered feminism through Western resources thanks to knowing a foreign language and being able to follow foreign literature that enabled them to understand the problems they were experiencing and the inequalities they were facing. This discovery made them realize that new feminist approaches were on the rise in the West, and it led them to focus on filling in the gap in the local feminist literature by translations.[92] Thus, patriarchal patterns existing in the society were starting to be questioned with a collective effort, and the main objective emerged of questioning the problems women faced just because they were a woman and as seeking solutions to those problems. Naturally, different ideologies were expressed regarding this objective.[93] However, from the broadest point of view, the objective during this period was "to raise women's consciousness, form concepts of sexism, decode it in the society, and provide solutions."[94,95] Çaha claims that the most radical discourse of the period came from these groups thanks to women starting to question patriarchal patterns and inequalities they faced with a common effort as they tried to reach their objectives in the 1980s. According to him, "feminist groups that rejected all the existing institutions in Turkish culture actually opened up a new page in Turkey. They not only criticized the existing policy regarding women but also the family accepted as the basis for social solidarity in Turkish culture and the patriarchal system claimed to be the source of family-related values."[96] Actually, it can be accepted as natural for women in this period to question the patriarchal structure comprehensively through family and family-related values. In other words, it is understandable to start questioning from family and family values. As Ayşe Kadıoğlu states, after the proclamation of the Republic, issues regarding women were generally based on and discussed through the understanding of women as "the objects of major social projects" and "members of the family unit," not as individuals.[97] Therefore, women starting to question the patriarchal structure due to problems and inequalities they faced as an individual and as a woman formed the first primary area.

However, Çaha states that women who could be considered as feminist in 1980s not only questioned or criticized the patriarchal structure but also acted on it. According to him, feminist women of the 1980s burned bridges between the official and traditional structures completely as they started to question the family institution and their position within the family because family was accepted as "the miniature of the Turkish society," according to the Republic's official policy since the proclamation of the Republic.[98]

Thus, designed as a collective subject and defined by her roles and responsibilities within the family, women started to question society's general values and the nation-building process of the newly founded state, starting with the proclamation of the Republic together with questioning the family institution in the 1980s. Actually, as Arat states, the women's movement of the 1980s found its place in the intersection of the local and universal plane.[99] In other words, the women's movement during this period set off from the local plane and tried to reach universal borders and universal values such as equality and freedom being determined as basic objectives. Without a doubt, a local struggle was fought depending on personal experiences on the local plane to actualize these universal objectives.

Therefore, it was made possible to question the patriarchal system and male dominance and to include the problems that seemed to belong to the private sphere into the public sphere. Another tendency that marked the 1980s period appeared at this point. In this period, the attempt to redefine gender perception and roles and woman's identity designed through male dominance was tried to be actualized through the redefinition and the questioning of ideological, ethnic, national, and religious frameworks.[100]

However, it has to be stated here that the feminist movement in 1980s was shaped not only by two main veins established by socialist and liberal feminists but also by radical, ethnic, Islamist, and cultural feminist trends. At this point, it can be claimed, as a result of a general evaluation, that women of this period, based on the aforementioned frameworks, headed for new pursuits, went through questioning their old identities, and were excited about a new formation (though, without doubt, it is not realistic to think that different movements and trends are one and the same).[101]

However, it does not seem that this positive movement, both on a discursive level and on the organizational level, seen among women regarding women's rights and gender roles and state's not showing any negative attitude towards this movement changed the social conditions women were experiencing in this period or the perception of woman in the society. Thus,

Tekeli's assertion that "women in Turkey in [the] 1980s still suffered in all classes of the society; in other words, women were still subjected to patriarchal pressure and judgments" is quite significant.[102] Although there was a momentum regarding women's rights during the period continuing since the 1980s, "the belief that woman is someone weak who should obey the male dominance and who is incapable of surviving on her own is still a very common value judgment"[103] stands very clearly as a social reality.

According to Sancar, the period of 1985–1995 during which this momentum emerged was a quite poor period regarding social movements seeking freedom and equality. Poorness of this period stems from the fact that freedom and equality demands could not find a "de facto" reaction. That, without a doubt, was valid for the feminist movements and the feminist organizations developed by finding a "niche" during the period of heavy political prohibitions of resulting from the coup, and the military regime could not get the chance of developing simultaneously with the rising democratization and liberation movement until the 2000s.[104] In other words, the feminist movement in the 1980s paradoxically seems to have a positive momentum or significance, which was caused by the fact that women's organizations or women's movements were not considered as a political opposition movement during the period after 1980. However, it is hard to say that it has been a democratization or liberalization movement on the social level during the process from the 1980s to the 2000s. Therefore, this situation pacified women's organizations and the movement like all the other groups that sought equality and freedom in the society. Thus, women's increasing "questioning, criticizing, opposing" attitude, compared to the early Republic and conservative modernization periods (even if it was on the discourse level), did not gain tangibility, or the concrete achievements, if they were gained, were generally weak and they could not create any effective results in the revision of women's social status and gender roles.

2000s and After: Justice and Development Party Period (JDP)

The Justice and Development Party (JDP) is a conservative democrat party that came into power by winning the 2002 elections held after an economic crisis that took place in 2001.[105] While defining and positioning itself on the political spectrum, the JDP emphasized that it comes from political Islamic traditions and embraces the liberal democratic principles in its program and basics.[106] In this context, the JDP claimed to embrace the liberal democratic principles while following the Islamic tradition materialized this identification with, in its own words, "a conservative democrat" ideology. The most distinct sign of this materialization is that the JDP built and registered itself

on the concepts "local/authentic/Muslim" while defining other political positions and parties as identified by the adjectives "Western/elite/secular."[107]
The party that gained the position of the ruling party by winning the
elections held in 2002 pursued this position through to today. However, it
attracts attention that the JDP transformed perceptibly in its discourse and
actions with its third term that started in 2011. The most distinct sign of this
transformation is the discourse of "New Turkey," as stated by Elçin Aktoprak. Aktoprak defines this discourse as renovating the state's backbone on
the one hand and as nation-building on the other and examines this building
process and policy within the context of post-colonial nationalism. Aktoprak
explains the reason why he examines the new nation-building process of the
JDP through post-colonial nationalism as that the JDP and the population
supporting the JDP defines the JDP as a national independence movement: "It
is seen that even though the colonial 'other' is coded generally as the Western
civilization; Kemalism, Kemalist regime, and elites are accepted as the main
colonial offender as the representatives of the West specifically in Turkey."[108]
However, at this point, it should be emphasized that the most distinct points
of this transformation, which should be evaluated through the discourse of a
new nation-building process, are political and cultural spheres by means of
prioritizing the economic sphere.[109]

It is clear that the basic dynamics of the new nation-building process that
has gained momentum since 2011 is designed through conservatism. As a
conservative democrat party, the JDP built on the concepts of "locality, authenticity, and Muslimism" that overlap more with the desire and dynamic
of conservatization, especially in the political and cultural areas most evident
since 2011. Metin Yeğenoğlu and Simten Coşar explain why this conservative
transformation, which tried to be actualized through new nation-building process, is aimed at the political and cultural areas rather than the economic one
through "neoliberal economic policy" the JDP is pursuing since its foundation. As a matter of fact, embracing a discourse that is liberal in the economic
sphere but conservative in the cultural one, especially in "the preservation of
cultural features of Turkishness," is one of the most concrete indications of
the neoliberalization process (designed on nationalist and religious patterns
in Turkey) that includes the JDP like all the other governments in the period
after 1980.[110] According to Aktoprak, the word "development" in the JDP's
name refers to the unbreakable connection between the JDP and the capitalism and neoliberal policy in the economic area.[111] As stated by Yükselbaba,
the JDP defines itself as the protector of Islamic values by positioning itself
against the Western/elite/secular values and, in this context, what forms the
basis of the Islamic values the JDP holds onto is neoliberal economic policy
such as deregulation and privatization.[112]

At this point, it can be claimed that Islam is an effective reference to create a new nation aimed to be built through New Turkey discourse when the relation between religion and Islam and the JDP is looked at because the New Turkey discourse is, as stated previously, focused not only on the idea of renovating the backbone of the state but also on building a new nation, and religion and Islam are a significant point of emphasis in building just such a new nation.[113] However, according to Ülkü Doğanay, the JDP is not using religion as a reference only to renovate the backbone of the state or to realize the dream of building a new nation. The JDP takes religion as a reference point while trying to solve the existing or potential tensions between religion and politics, religion and state, tradition and modernism, and relations between the state, society, and the individual. In other words, the JDP assigns religion not only the role of determining political life but also the role "to associate a human-centered politics with the ethical values of a religious life."[114] Thus, the JDP sets forth its difference from previous political formations and governments by "transforming the definition of an Islamic-centered national identity into an ideology"[115] for the first time. According to Aktoprak, the JDP is building the new nation that it aims with a religious nationalism. Here, religious nationalism is the process of placing the religion into the center of the national identity because religion in religious nationalism is the most significant sign and value of cultural difference and, naturally, of "cultural heritage" created by religious narratives and symbols.[116] In addition, according to Cenk Saraçoğlu, the emphasis on religion and other conservative values such as family and tradition is a means for the JDP to use "when problems such as poverty, inequality, and unemployment stemming from the neoliberal policy" that the JDP has implemented since the year it came to power to "start to threaten the social order and the individual."[117]

Therefore, while the JDP actualizes transformation in the cultural and political areas aimed in the nation-building process by "harmonizing neoliberalism with religion, tradition, and family so that they can coexist"[118] on the one hand, it also ensures the sustainability of the neoliberal economic policy on the other. However, at this point, what is significant for us is that we should not miss the fact that femininity is especially included in the new building process during the JDP era within the context of emphasis put on religion, tradition, and family. A new model of womanhood and family has been designed particularly since 2011 when the discourse of New Turkey was actualized and this design has been tried to be reinforced through a conservative ideology blended with neoliberal economic policy.

JDP, FAMILY, AND WOMAN

According to Sancar, the JDP governments that started to rule in 2002 brought about a new era and momentum regarding the women's movement.[119] Here, it is a clear fact that the JDP, as a conservative party, implemented some legal reforms to protect women's human rights. Especially during its first (2002–2007) and second (2007–2011) terms, the JDP made significant regulations regarding democracy, human rights, and being a state of law as a result of the effects of the liberal understanding it embraces and implements in its policies and actually within the context of becoming a member of the EU. Without a doubt, the subject of some of these regulations was women and, therefore, that affected women's social status in a positive way on the legal level. In these two time periods, during which a number of regulations were made regarding women's rights and gender equality, some insurances were guaranteed for women both within the family and at work and precautions were increased to protect women from physical or psychological abuse.[120] However, the effects of these legal precautions taken and regulations made on the everyday lives of women are open to question. In other words, it can be claimed that these legal reforms implemented during the first two terms do not quite match with the JDP's active policies presented regarding women because the active policies of the JDP during these two periods were generally to pursue women's traditional roles.[121] Therefore, it seems that there is a discrepancy between the legal reforms and regulations implemented, specifically regarding women and its active policies towards women stemming from the liberal democratic values claimed to be embraced and the conservative ideology of the JDP.

This discrepancy started to disappear during the JDP's third term between the years 2011 and 2015 as the JDP embraced a more conservative policy regarding women because the relations with the EU entered a regression period starting in 2011 and has continued since then to bring about a transformation in the JDP policies regarding women from conservative democracy to absolute conservatism.[122]

At this point, looking at the status of woman in conservatism would provide a more sound basis for understanding the JDP's policies regarding women. Before all, woman in conservatism was designed through an ethical understanding built on tradition, family, and an ideal society objective and placed according to gender perceptions, basically. Roles attributed to a woman according to this ethical understanding are outcomes of natural discrimination between genders. Women, for conservatives, who start off from the reality that biology is accepted as fate in some ways is a being who is suitable to stay in the background in the society compared to men and to play a "domestic" role because of their physical and anatomic structure.[123] Thus, a woman who is suitable to play a domestic role is defined, generally, as a mother, wife, daughter, and/or sister within the family institution and crowned with a role of one who transfers and reproduces tradition. Here, it seems very usual to draw a parallel line between conservatism and patriarchal perception and thought.[124]

Besides, Yeğenoğlu and Coşar explain the JDP's women or gender policies through "neoliberal religious/conservative patriarchy" in their study. The essence of this definition is based on two basic understandings.[125] As it will be discussed in more detail in the following section, the first one is including women into the labor market within the context of the neoliberal-conservative patriarchy, and the second one is organizing this inclusion in a way that women would not ignore their responsibilities for their families. In essence, the concept of neoliberal religious/conservative patriarchy describes the JDP's gender policy that is based upon the alliance between neoliberalism and conservatism. What is tried to be conveyed with this concept is that conservatism, blended with national and religion-based discourse and applications by the JDP during its each and every term, should be dealt with neoliberal policies. Without a doubt, it shows that the JDP takes steps in line with neoliberal policies while preserving its conservative discourse regarding women's rights.[126] That is reflected by the JDP's policies regarding women, especially during its first two terms, such as the increase in the number of females in the parliament; mandating municipalities that have a population of more than 50,000 to open up shelters for women; founding the Turkish Grand National Assembly Commission for Women–Men Equality of Opportunity. On the other side, there has been a discourse that encourages women to have at least three children, discussions that suggest abortion is murder, and debates that propose that divorce should be prevented.[127] Of course, neoliberal economic policies also have a determining effect on the JDP's gender policies. Especially increasing an active labor force through the increase in population and, therefore, obtaining a cheap labor force, which cannot be achieved by ignoring women or worsening their legal status. Within this process, women would be employed if they could keep up with flexible market conditions as required by neoliberal policies. That is, they would be more visible in the labor force in new working structures named, such as part-time jobs, temporary term jobs, and limited-time jobs provided by private employment agencies as well as working from home. On the other hand, they would fulfill the requirements of their roles within the family as a mother/wife. According to Şenel, this neoliberal conservative patriarchy that forms the background of the JDP's policies, especially regarding women, puts more weight on the shoulders of women (by increasing their responsibilities within the family) while it seems to improve the lives of women (by such qualities as enabling women to take part in the labor market and to be perceived as economically free individuals).[128] This is because, within the context of the JDP's new nation, the concept of family is "consecrated among the triangle of state–homeland–culture," and this concept effectively defined new gender policies and especially the new definition of womanhood. It should be stated here that "family and woman are considered almost as organic pieces of a puzzle" in the JDP's gender paradigm. In this framework, it is expressed in the JDP's 2023 Vision document that the "JDP considers family as the biggest dynamo so that New Turkey of 2023 is composed of individuals whose physical and emotional states are protected and whose ethical and basic values are sound. In this direction, a 'social awareness' environment will be created so that all the elements of the society will protect the concept of family."[129]

According to Gülay Toksöz, not including the word "woman" (despite all the efforts and initiatives of women's organizations) in the name of the Ministry of Family and Social Policies, which replaced the State Ministry of Woman and Family in 2011, is a concrete sign of the transition to the discourse regarding the importance of women for the continuity of the family and of bringing the family to the forefront.[130] Indeed, discourse regarding "woman's importance for the strength and continuity of the family" accelerated dealing with a woman not as an individual but through her passive identity constrained within the family as a reflection of the patriarchal social structure and, thus, it went through a new understanding where the status of women, within the JDP's conservative framework, was shaped by family, society, and the state.[131]

It should be stated here that a strong family discourse is very important for the JDP, and the family has significant functions as an institution because, in conservative thought, the family is the first institution where social values and norms are familiarized with and where the individual starts to get socialized. Traditional structure, religious norms, authority relations, and the collective will are all realized and actively experienced in-person thanks to this institution.[132] Moreover, family relations cannot be reduced only to "the function of reproducing the species." Family surrounds a number of activity areas from politics to the economy like a net and, as mentioned previously, family is a founding element of collectivism.[133]

When we look at the issue from the perspective of Turkish history, it can be seen that defining woman primarily through the family and her "mother" identity have remained the same (especially in regards to the right-wing political line) throughout the years. When the political powers wish, especially, to reshape the social order, to actualize a new state backbone, or to realize the dream of a new nation, it is seen that they interfere with the family and population and suggest an ideal family vision according to the values and priorities of the government.[134,135]

As stated by Ferhunde Özbay, this ideal family is defined sometimes as a "modern family" or "national family," sometimes even as a "happy family," and sometimes, as currently, as a "sacred family."[136] A modern or national family was the vision of an ideal family of the early Republic period. In that family model, giving birth to children was accepted as a service to the country and having a number of children was to be encouraged. In addition, members of the modern family are described by both Western and nationalist characteristics. A "happy family" is, on the other hand, a Western-looking nuclear family. Happiness is the quality of life, and having a certain number of children so that families can raise them well is suggested and encouraged by family planning clinics and mother and children healthcare centers. Therefore, the quality of the family and the wealth of the state will increase.

However, the "sacred family, today's ideal family vision, is different both from [the] modern and happy family. There is no discussion over whether [a] sacred family should be a nuclear family or an extended family; however, the most significant emphasis is on respect and to protect family elders. In this family, women should give birth to children and take a selfless motherhood role. There is no objection against women being educated, but they are expected and wanted to be submissive to their husbands."[137]

However, according to Özbay, a sacred family is not a retransformation to the traditional extended family. Sometimes, traditional life norms before capitalism are referred to through a sacred family that is inspired by the Islamic perspective; however, it does not ignore the fact that a sacred family is a new family vision that emerged with the JDP.[138]

At this point, with its sacred family/strong family discourse, the JDP emphasizes the contradiction in the failing family structure of the West on the one hand and offers a primary means of solution to all the socioeconomic and political problems that the country faces or will potentially face with "strong Turkish family" emphasis on the other. In this context, thanks to the references to family, the JDP both forms the basis for the political identity it tries to create and makes concrete and physical changes that are to be actualized, especially through social policies and social state mechanisms that are easy to be legitimized on the discourse level.[139] Therefore, "family" for the JDP is both a metaphor used as a reference for the JDP's design of an ideal nation based on organic harmony and a means to eradicate the socioeconomic and social unrest created by neoliberalism.[140]

As stated many times before in this section, the JDP carries traces of conservatism on the cultural and political spheres while showing a harmony with neoliberal economic policies in the economy. In this context, the needs of JDP conservatism and the neoliberal economy require empowerment of the family, not women.[141]The reason is that neoliberal social security systems are generally determined by two rationales. The first one is the differentiating rationale. It defines women through the emphasis on their caregiver and motherhood identities and imprisons them within these definitions. The second one is liberal equality rationale. It is based on the equality among genderless, abstract individuals. In countries where social state implementations are generally limited and social security mechanisms and social policies are determined within the framework of neoliberal perspective, women are generally constrained within these two rationales. As a result, as also happens in Turkey, "women either are forced to be confined in the caregiver–mother identity or pushed towards the illusion of genderless abstract individuals by ignoring unreturned house chores."[142] In this context, thanks to the discourse of the sacred family myth, responsibilities regarding children, the elderly, and patient care that should be realized by the social state are put on the shoulders of the family; that is, it is put on the shoulders of women and sustainability of poverty is ensured by extended family ties.[143] Indeed, there is a social consensus in Turkey that family and woman's labor within the family regarding the elderly and patient and disabled care are essential. While encouraging women to have more children to increase the youth population, the JDP does not consider the elderly or patient and disabled care as a public responsibility, and women's labor at home in care services are accepted as data.[144] Moreover, there is another advantage for the government as women are busy with care services at home. That is relieving the labor market. Holding women primarily responsible for care services at home somewhat decreases male unemployment as it makes women step aside from the working population that is already too crowded.[145] Women in the labor market are expected to keep up with the flexible market conditions as demanded by neoliberal policies in Turkey like throughout the world, and at the same time, they are expected to fulfill their roles as mother/wife at home.[146] It has to be emphasized here that both Ninth and Tenth Plans' and National Employment Strategy's (2014–2023) basic feature of flexible working structures are proposed as the miraculous solution that will increase women's participation into the labor market. A flexible working structure is miraculous for women, according to the JDP, because women can reconcile work and family lives thanks to it. In other words, women's participation in the labor market is made possible without ignoring the requirements of gender-based division of labor.[147]

To conclude, it is not wrong to claim that although significant legal regulations have been made during the time the JDP has been in power to improve women's social roles and statuses, these steps are limited to the desire of the conservative ideology that perceives women only within the context of motherhood and family.[148] It is indeed true that discourses on women of the right-wing and conservative political parties that played a part in Turkish politics in previous years, parallel to party ideologies, prioritize women's "wife" and "mother" identities more in the private areas and deal with women in the public area within the traditional roles of women without leaving out the "working woman" image.[149] Thus, the JDP defines the identity of woman with a discourse that prioritizes the social status of women reflecting traditional structure by emphasizing that "woman is the central element of both social life and the family, our children, and youth building the future."[150] Within this context, it is clear that the JDP does not consider a woman as a citizen who has equal rights with a man under the law, as an individual has equal rights with a man in the labor market, and a family member who equally shares the responsibilities of family and children with men and has an equal right in decision-making within the family. From a general perspective, the JDP defines a woman within the triangle of "mother–wife–housewife" and confines her within it.[151]

It has to be emphasized here that sexism that surfaces in the JDP's discourse and its policies and legal regulations regarding gender equality during its continuous, sixteen-year government reign cannot be separated from the state's discourse. Such an approach would be a deficit and faulty. However, women in the early Republic period were considered as the carrier of the family and the nation and the biological reproducer of the nation. Therefore, it is more appropriate to consider the JDP's gender policies as a part of the state's tradition. However, it is also crucial to differentiate the JDP's policies in regards to women from other terms and to evaluate the women issue within the context of the JDP's own original structure. Here, the most significant point of reference for the JDP, which differentiates the JDP from particularly early Republic period and other previous terms before the JDP, is the model of womanhood and family that has been tried to be formed through the New Turkey discourse and actualized especially since 2011. This model tries to be based upon a conservative ideology blended with neoliberal economic policies. As stated before, the JDP has traces of conservatism in cultural and political areas but shows a compatible side with its neoliberal economic policies. Thus, the JDP's conservatism and the needs of the neoliberal economy should be maintained in coordination. This obligation directly affects and determines the JDP's gender policies. The "neoliberal religious/conservative patriarchy" term used by Yeğenoğlu and Coşar that summarizes the JDP's women policies and its approach to gender issue sums up the position of women in the JDP's policies. Within this context, neoliberal-conservative patriarchy primarily aims to include women into the labor market. However, this inclusion should be designed in such a way that women would not ignore their responsibilities within the family. Therefore, the combination of the JDP's conservatism and neoliberal economic policies (as discussed in detail previously) try to include women into the labor market while still holding them responsible for their mission within the family.

CONCLUSION

This chapter titled "Nation-Building in Turkey and Gender Regime" tries to explain the relation between building a nation and the gender regime through the argument of "envisioning the nation as male" because including the nation-building process together with the gender regime into the analysis—in other words, trying to study nation-building through gender regime—would take us to the argument of envisioning the nation as male. In this context, the basic issue that was tried to be emphasized in this study that deals with nation as a reality built up is that women are excluded from the nation-building and from the founding ideologies and positions of the nation-state or are limited by men. Yuval-Davis and Anthias, who put forth the dimensions of this limitation, clearly state that women take part in the process of nation-building as biological producers (e.g., through women's function and mission of childbearing), as means (e.g., as determiners of cultural boundaries), as reproducers (e.g., as the teachers, carriers, and ideological reproducers of culture), as symbols (e.g., as symbols of national differences), and as supplementary for all kinds of national struggle.[152]

Moreover, another significant point of emphasis to see the relation between nation-building and gender regime is envisioning the nation as a family. Besides, the inclusion of women into the nation-building processes as biologic producers of the nation in the first stage is important to understand the relation between the nation and the family. In this context, as mentioned before, for women to enter the nation-building process or the nation-state is related to their role as a mother.

However, it should not be ignored that there are different countries that present examples of women's inclusion into different nation-building processes. If we leave other countries in Vickers' study aside and deal with the issue from the context of Turkey,[153] we can, first of all, claim that the nation-building process in Turkey has been shaped by the desire to modernize on the one hand and by the struggle carried out against colonization on the other. The most distinct feature of such a building process is the necessity to both benefit from the West's physical techniques and protect and strengthen the unique moral core of the national culture. At this point, the greatest mission of women is to be the symbol and defender of modernism in the public sphere and the carrier and supporter of the tradition at home. Therefore, women could take part in such building processes within the limited areas determined by men. The boundaries of these limits are drawn through "family" in such building processes. In other words, women participated in the nation-building project actively by starting modern families. In this context, women were involved in the nation-building process in the early stages of Turkish modernization through family-based modernism that was realized by institutional and ideological dimensions. Family, according to Republican modernism, is both the area where social relations are organized and the image and strategic object of social relations. Within this context, the major mission and role of a woman is defined by being a mother and a wife. A Turkish woman who is a mother and a wife making an unconditional emotional effort and having female occupations and working within the boundaries of honor–chastity rules if working.

To summarize, after the proclamation of the Republic, issues regarding women were generally focused on and discussed through the understanding that women were the object of major social projects and members of the family unit, not individuals. Although this was severely criticized and questioned by women in the 1980s, it is seen that women in Turkey in the 1980s were still suppressed in all social classes; in other words, they were still subject to patriarchal pressure and prejudice. It is possible to state that perspectives and perceptions towards women have not changed much when we look at the JDP terms that came to power in Turkey in 2002 and claims to have a goal to build a new nation through New Turkey discourse and afterward. Although there were some legal reforms realized during the first and second terms of the JDP to protect the human rights of women, it could be said that there was a transformation from conservative democracy to absolute conservatism in regards to women's policies during the Party's third term that covers the years between 2011 and 2015. At this point, within the context of the JDP's new nation, emphasis made on the significance of women for the strength and continuity of the family shows us that women are dealt with their passive identity constricted within the family as a reflection of the patriarchal social structure rather than as an individual.

As a result, it can be claimed that not much has changed in Turkey within the context of the nation-building processes as of the periods examined in sections starting from the proclamation of the Republic. It can be stated that women's subordination, being excluded from the nation-building processes except the symbolic areas, being positioned generally outside the public sphere through their role as "a mother" and "a wife," and being defined by a collective identity rather than as an individual are the reflections of the male state and a state policy independent from the government essence with gender inequality and sexism.[154]

However, it will be useful to conclude this chapter by making a general comparison of the differences and similarities between the historical periods. As stated previously, gender policies cannot be separated from the state's discourse neither in the early Republic period (1920–1935) nor from the 1980s to the 2000s and finally to the JDP terms. However, it does not mean that it is not necessary to point out periodic differences or similarities.[155] First, when we look at the early Republic period, it is seen that this period is called a women's revolution. It can be claimed that freedoms brought to women by the rights provided with the Civil Law in 1926 regarding modern family life and public visibility were the cause during the Republic period for such a women's revolution. In this period, the state made a number of significant reforms that improved women's status under the law, such as education reform that entitled women with equal education rights, reform that banned polygamy, and reform that granted women with the right of succession. However, it should be stated that the position of women did not improve in daily life as much as it was stated in reforms. The way for the women to be included in public life was to have a genderless identity, even to assume a male identity to some extent. Thus, women were expected to appear in public life with a genderless identity; in addition, they were expected both to adopt and carry the Republican ideology and to raise patriotic children as a mother of their own children and the nation. It could be said that this common perception was dominant until the end of the 1980s. Despite the momentum in the feminist movement during the period after 1980, the general image of women was designed around the roles of being a mother and a wife. In the 1990s, women were predominantly defined as equal individuals under the law. Moreover, it was also emphasized that roles of women as a mother and a wife would not prevent them from participating in the public life. This assumption suggests that being a mother or a housewife is a free choice for women. The most significant result caused by this assumption was pushing women into homes; that is, pushing them into private lives and ignoring their problems. When we look at the gender policies of the JDP governments after the 2000s, it is seen that the JDP has both taken steps in line with neoliberal policies (especially in regards to the rights of women) and carried on its conservative discourse regarding women's issues. Therefore, it is important to emphasize that the JDP's approach is summarized in its concept of neoliberal religious/conservative patriarchy and determines its gender policies is the most significant point where the JDP terms differentiate from both the early Republic period and the period from the 1980s to the 2000s. However, it is also necessary to state that, rather than their individual identities or through human rights discourse, women have been approached as a part of the collective entity through their roles as mothers and wives within the family and have been defined by these roles during the JDP terms as in the previous political periods.

NOTES

1. Jill Vickers, "Gendering the Hyphen: Gender Dimensions of Modern Nation-State Formation in Euro-American and Anti-And Post-Colonial Contexts," in *Gendering the Nation-state: Canadian and Comparative Perspectives*, edited by Yasmeen Abu-Laban, 21–45 (Vancouver: UBC Press, 2008).

2. There are three basic theories trying to explain the nation and nationalism terms. These can be defined as primordialist, modernist, and ethno-symbolist approaches; see Umut Özkırımlı, *Milliyetçilik Kuramları Eleştirel Bir Bakış* (Ankara: Doğu Batı Yayınları, 2009). As the modernist approach is the basic reference theory for this study, the other two arguments are not discussed; thus, this study directly starts with the modernist approach.

3. Eric J. Hobsbawm, *Nations and Nationalism since 1780: Programme, Myth, Reality* (Cambridge: Cambridge University Press, 2012).

4. Umut Özkırımlı, *Milliyetçilik Kuramları Eleştirel Bir Bakış* (Ankara: Doğu Batı Yayınları, 2009).

5. Ernest Gellner, *Nations and Nationalism* (New York: Cornell University Press, 2009).

6. Benedict Anderson, *Imagined Communities: Reflections on the Origin and Spread of Nationalism* (London: Verso, 1991).

7. Ibid.

8. Tamar Mayer, "Gender Ironies of Nationalism: Seting the Stage," in *Gender Ironies of Nationalism: Soring the Nation*, edited by T. Mayer, 1–22 (London: Routledge, 2000); A. McClintock, "Family Feuds: Gender, Nationalism and the Family," *Feminist Review* 44 (1993): 61–80; and Lois A. West, *Feminist Nationalism* (London: Routledge, 1997).

9. McClintock, "Family Feuds."

10. West, *Feminist Nationalism.*

11. Mayer, "Gender Ironies."

12. Ibid.

13. V. Spike Peterson, "Gendered Nationalism," *Peace Review, Special Issue on Nationalism and Ethnic Conflict* 6, no. 1 (1994): 77–84.

14. Carol Delaney, *The Seed and the Soil: Gender and Cosmology in Turkish Village Society* (Berkeley, CA: University of California Press, 1991); Karima Omar, "National Symbolism in Constructions Of Gender: Transformed Symbols in Post-Conflict States,"*Seton Hall Journal of Diplomacy and International Relations* (2004):49–67; and Partha Chatterjee, *The Nationalist Resolution of the Women's Question* (Calcutta: Centre for Studies in Social Sciences, 1987).

15. Omar, "National Symbolism."

16. Nira Yuval-Davis, and Floya Anthias, *Woman-Nation-State* (London: Palgrave Macmillan, 1989).

17. J. Nagel, "Masculinity and Nationalism: Gender and Sexuality in the Making of Nations," *Ethnic and National Studies* 21, no. 2 (1998): 242–69.

18. Mervat Hatem, "Secularist and Islamist Discourses on Modernity in Egypt and the Evolution of the Postcolonial Nation-State," in *Islam, Gender and Social Change,*

edited by Y. Y. Haddad and J. L. Esposito, 85–99 (New York: Oxford University Press, 1998).

19. Rubina Saigol, "Militarization, Nation and Gender: Women's Bodies as Arenas of Violent Conflict," in *Deconstructing Sexuality in the Middle East: Challenges and Discourses*, edited by P. Ilkkaracan, 107–20 (Aldershot: Ashgate, 2008).

20. George Mosse, *Nationalism and Sexuality: Respectability and Abnormal Sexuality in Modem Europe* (New York: Howard Fertig, 1997).

21. Simone de Beauvoir, *Kadın "İkinci Cins" Genç Kızlık Çağı*, translated by B. Onaran (İstanbul: Payel Yayınları, 1993).

22. Hobsbawm, *Nations and Nationalism.*

23. Nira Yuval-Davis, *Gender and Nation* (London: Sage Publications, 1997).

24. Ibid.

25. Afsaneh Najmabadi, "The Erotic Vatan [Homeland] as Beloved and Mother: To Love, to Possess, and to Protect,"*Comparative Studies in Society and History* 39, no. 3 (1997): 442–67.

26. Ibid.

27. Vickers, "Gendering the Hyphen."

28. Ibid.

29. Ibid.

30. Chatterjee, *The Nationalist Resolution.*

31. Serpil Sancar, *Türk Modernleşmesinin Cinsiyeti Erkekler Devlet Kadınlar Aile Kurar* (İstanbul: İletişim Yayınları,2014).

32. Şerif Mardin, *Türkiye'de Toplum ve Siyaset* (İstanbul: İletişim Yayınları, 1995).

33. Sibel Bozdoğan, *Modernizm ve Ulusun İnşası: Erken Cumhuriyet Türkiye'sinde Mimari Kültür* (İstanbul: Metis Yayınları, 2002).

34. Sancar, *Türk Modernleşmesinin Cinsiyeti*

35. Ibid.

36. Ömer Çaha,"Türkiye'de Kadın Hareketi Tarihi: Değişen Bir Şey Var mı?" in *The History of Women Movement in Turkey (Kadın Bienali Ekinlikleri Çerçevesinde Türkiye'de Kadın ve Sivil Toplum)* (İstanbul, 2001).

37. Ibid.

38. Ibid.

39. Ibid.

40. Ayşe Durakbaşa, "Cumhuriyet Döneminde Kemalist Kadın Kimliğinin Oluşumu," *Tarih ve Toplum* 51 (1988): 167–71.

41. Durakbaşa, "Cumhuriyet Döneminde Kemalist Kadın."

42. Nilüfer Göle, "Modernleşme Bağlamında İslami Kimlik Arayışı," in *Türkiye'de Modernleşme ve Ulusal Kimlik*, edited by S. Bozdoğan and R. Kasaba, 70–81 (İstanbul: Tarih Vakfı Yurt Yayınları, 1999).

43. Fatmagül Berktay, *Kadın Olmak Yaşamak Yazmak* (İstanbul: Pencere Yayınları, 1998).

44. Deniz Kandiyoti, "Modernin Cinsiyeti: Türk Modernleşmesi Araştırmalarında Eksik Boyutlar," *Türkiye'de Modernleşme ve Ulusal Kimlik*, edited by S. Bozdoğan and R. Kasaba, 99–117 (İstanbul: Tarih Vakfı Yurt Yayınları, 1999).

176   *Senem Kurt Topuz*

45. Faik Gür, "Atatürk Heykelleri ve Türkiye'de Resmi Tarihin Görsellesmesi," *Toplum ve Bilim* 90 (2001): 147–66.
46. Durakbaşa, "Cumhuriyet Döneminde Kemalist Kadın."
47. This dating is taken from Sancar, *Türk Modernleşmesinin Cinsiyeti.*
48. Berktay, *Kadın Olmak.*
49. Durakbaşa, "Cumhuriyet Döneminde Kemalist Kadın."
50. Berktay, *Kadın Olmak.*
51. Partha Chatterjee, *Nationalist Thought and the Colonial World: A Derivative Discourse* (Minneapolis, MN: University of Minnesota Press, 1993).
52. Sancar, *Türk Modernleşmesinin Cinsiyeti.*
53. Elif Ekin Akşit, *Kızların Sessizliği: Kız Enstitülerinin Uzun Tarihi* (İstanbul: İletişim Yayınları, 2005).
54. Sancar, *Türk Modernleşmesinin Cinsiyeti.*
55. Ibid.
56. Ibdi.
57. According to Sancar (2014), what led to the interpretation of the Republic as women's revolution was the freedom and public visibility provided to women by the Civil Law enacted in 1926 that regulated modern family life. According to Tekeli (1995), the status of women improved greatly compared to the Ottoman era. The state made a number of very significant reforms for women. Developments such as the Civil Law enacted in 1926, education reform that provided women with equal education rights, and the right to vote and be elected paved the way for the women in Turkey to gain equal citizenship rights. Having an official law—instead of Shi'a law, which allows polygamy, prohibits divorce, withholds woman's inheritance rights, and limits even basic rights—improved women's legal status. See Yeşim Arat, "Türkiye'de Modernleşme Projesi ve Kadınlar," in *Türkiye'de Modernleşme ve Ulusal Kimlik*, edited by S. Bozdoğan and R. Kasaba, 82–98 (İstanbul: Tarih Vakfı Yurt Yayınları, 1999).
58. Sancar, *Türk Modernleşmesinin Cinsiyeti.*
59. Yaprak Zihnioğlu, *Kadınsız İnkılap Nezihe Muhittin, Kadınlar Halk Fırkası, Türk Kadınlar Birliği* (İstanbul: Metis Yayınevi, 2003).
60. Arat, "Türkiye'de Modernleşme Projesi."
61. Berktay, *Kadın Olmak,* 4.
62. Sancar, *Türk Modernleşmesinin Cinsiyeti.*
63. Hande Gülen, "Kemalist Modernleşme'de Aile, Ulus, Kadın ve Kadın Yolu/ Türk Kadın Yolu (1925–1927) Dergileri," *Mimar Sinan Güzel Sanatlar Üniversitesi Sosyal Bilimler Enstitüsü Dergisi* 12 (2015): 152–64.
64. Arat, "Türkiye'de Modernleşme Projesi."
65. Durakbaşa, "Cumhuriyet Döneminde Kemalist Kadın."
66. Ayşe Durakbaşa, *Halide Edib Türk Modernleşmesi ve Feminizm* (İstanbul: İletişim Yayınları, 2007).
67. Berktay, *Kadın Olmak,* 3.
68. Kandiyoti, "Modernin Cinsiyeti."
69. Sancar, *Türk Modernleşmesinin Cinsiyeti.*
70. Ibid.

71. Ibid.

72. Ibid.

73. Ibid.

74. Suna Kili, "Modernleşme ve Kadın," in *Türkiye'de Kadın Olmak*, edited by N. Arat, 9–20 (İstanbul: Say Yayınları, 1996).

75. Şirin Tekeli, "1980'ler Türkiye'sinde Kadınlar," in *1980'ler Türkiye'sinde Kadın Bakış Açısından Kadınlar*, edited by Ş. Tekeli, 7–37 (İstanbul: İletişim, 1993).

76. Tekeli, "1980'ler Türkiye'sinde Kadınlar."

77. Serpil Sancar, *Türkiye'de Kadın Hareketinin Politiği: Tarihsel Bağlam, Politik Gündem ve Özgünlükler* (İstanbul: Koç Üniversitesi Yayını, 2011). http:// kasaum.ankara.edu.tr/files/2013/09/Serpil-Sancar-T%C3%BCrkiye%E2%80%99de-Kad%C4%B1n-Hareketinin-Politi%C4%9Fi.pdf, accessed February 15, 2018.

78. Çaha, *Türkiye'de Kadın Hareketi Tarihi*.

79. Betül Karagöz, "Türkiye'de 1980 Sonrası Kadın Hareketinin Siyasal Temelleri ve İkinci Dalga Uğrağı," *Memleket Siyaset Yönetim* 3, no. 7 (2008): 168–90.

80. Şirin Tekeli, "80'lerde Türkiye›de Kadınların Kurtuluşu Hareketinin Gelişmesi," *Birikim Dergisi* 3 (1989): 34–41.

81. Ibid.

82. Karagöz, "Türkiye'de 1980 Sonrası Kadın."

83. Here, what is meant by "state support" is not to emphasize that the direction and development dynamics of the feminist movement was directly determined and assigned by the state but that, as Çaha (2001) states, the first reaction of the state towards the feminist movements in this period was to watch and stay on alert rather than being proscriptive and oppressive.

84. Yeşim Arat, "1980'ler Türkiye'sinde Kadın Hareketi: Liberal Kemalizmin Radikal Uzantısı," *Toplum ve Bilim* 53 (1991): 7–19.

85. Karagöz, "Türkiye'de 1980 Sonrası Kadın."

86. Arat, "1980'ler Türkiye'sinde Kadın Hareketi."

87. Ömer Çaha, *Sivil Kadın: Türkiye'de Sivil Toplum ve Kadın*, (İstanbul: Vadi Yayınları, 2010).

88. However, Çaha's comparison does not change the fact that the women's movement in this period developed independently from the leftist movement, state, and authorities. According to Tekeli (1995), women raised in leftist organizations came together and formed reading groups, sort of increased-consciousness groups in this period. What they learned from their experience in the leftist organizations was that the leftist movement under the male hegemony did not offer a solution to gender inequality, and they sought the source of gender inequality through class struggle. Therefore, basically, "male leaders' ideological hegemony" was questioned during this period.

89. Çaha, *Sivil Kadın*.

90. Arat, "1980'ler Türkiye'sinde Kadın Hareketi."

91. Aksu Bora, *Feminizm Kendi Arasında* (İstanbul: Ayizi Yayınları, 2011).

92. Ibid.

93. Arat, "1980'ler Türkiye'sinde Kadın Hareketi"; Bora, *Feminizm Kendi Arasında*.

94. According to Sancar (2011), development of small-scale, face-to-face interactions based on raising consciousness women's groups were not considered as political, and thus, they were not banned or directly oppressed.

95. Serpil Çakır, "Feminizm: Ataerkil İktidarın Eleştirisi," in *Modern Siyasal İdeolojiler*, edited by Birsen Örs, 412–75 (İstanbul: Bilgi Üniversitesi Yayınları, 2007).

96. Çaha, *Sivil Kadın*.

97. Ayşe Kadıoğlu, "Cinselliğin İnkârı: Büyük Toplumsal Projelerin Nesnesi Olarak Türk Kadınları," in *75 Yılda Kadınlar ve Erkekler*, edited by A. Berktay Hacımirzaoğlu (İstanbul: Türkiye İş Bankası, İstanbul Menkul Kıymetler Borsası, Tarih Vakfı Yayını, 1998).

98. Çaha, *Sivil Kadın*

99. Yeşim Arat, "Women's Studies in Turkey From Kemalizm to Feminizm," *New Perspectives on Turkey* 9 (1993): 119–35.

100. Karagöz, "Türkiye'de 1980 Sonrası Kadın."

101. Çaha, *Sivil Kadın*.

102. Tekeli, "80'lerde Türkiye'de Kadınların Kurtuluşu."

103. Ibid.

104. Serpil Sancar, *Türkiye'de Kadın Hareketinin Politiği*.

105. Evren Haspolat, "Kadın, Anne, Yurttaş Ana Akım Siyasal Partilerin Seçim Bildirgelerinde Kadın Algısı:1 Kasım 2015 Genel Seçimleri Örneği," *Toplum ve Demokrasi* 9 (2015): 73–107.

106. Simten Coşar and Metin Yeğenoğlu, "New Ground for Patriarchy in Turkey? Gender Policy in the Age of AKP," *South European Society and Politics* 16, no. 4(2011): 555–73.

107. Onur Yıldız, *Siyasal İslam, Neoliberalizm ve Yeni Sağ: AKP Üzerine, Siyasal Bir Gözden Geçirme* (2010), http://www.halkevleri.org.tr/diger/siyasal-islam-neoliberalizm-ve-yeni-sag-akp-uzerine-siyasal-bir-gozden-gecirme-onur-yildiz-0, accessed March 9, 2018.

108. Elçin Aktoprak, "Postkolonyal Bir 'Dava' Olarak Yeni Türkiye'nin Yeni Ulusu," *Ankara Üniversitesi SBF Dergisi* 71, no. 1 (2016):1–32.

109. Burcu Şenel,"Biz Büyük Bir Aileyiz: Türkiye'de Devlet Söyleminde Makbul Kadınlık ve Aile," *Mülkiye Dergisi* 41, no. 2 (2017): 31–69.

110. Metin Yeğenoğlu and Simten Coşar, "AKP ve Toplumsal Cinsiyet Meselesi: Neoliberalizm ve Patriyarka Arasında Mekik Dokumak. İktidarın Şiddeti: AKP'li Yıllar," in *Neoliberalizm ve İslamcı Politikalar*, edited by S. Coşar and G. Yücesan-Özdemir, 158–81 (İstanbul: Metis Yayınları, 2014).

111. Aktoprak, "Postkolonyal Bir 'Dava.'"

112. Ülker Yükselbaba, "AKP'nin Kadına Yönelik Söylem ve Politikaları: Neo-Liberalizm, Ilımlı İslam ve Kadın," *Kadın/Woman 2000* 14, no. 2 (2013): 67–92.

113. Aktoprak, "Postkolonyal Bir 'Dava.'"

114. Ülkü Doğanay, "AKP'nin Demokrasi Söylemi ve Muhafazakârlık: Muhafazakâr Demokrasiye Eleştirel Bir Bakış,"*Ankara Üniversitesi SBF Dergisi* 62, no. 1 (2007): 65–88.

115. Aktoprak, "Postkolonyal Bir 'Dava.'"

116. Ibid.

117. Cenk Saraçoğlu, "Türkiye Sağı, AKP ve Kürt Meselesi," in *Türk Sağı–Mitler, Fetişler, Düşman İmgeleri*, edited by İ. Ö. Kerestecioğlu and G. G. Öztan, 243–82 (İstanbul: İletişim Yayınları,2014).

118. Haspolat, "Kadın, Anne, Yurttaş."

119. Sancar, *Türkiye'de Kadın Hareketinin Politiği*.

120. Nezahat Altuntaş and Yahya Demirkanoğlu, "Adalet Ve Kalkınma Partisi'nin Kadına İlişkin Söylem ve Politikalarına Bakış: Muhafazakâr Demokratlıktan Muhafazakârlığa Doğru Evrilişin İzdüşümleri," *Akademik Yaklaşımlar Dergisi* 8, no. 1 (2017): 65–96.

121. Meltem Yılmaz Şener, "Kadını Anne Olarak Güçlendirmek? AKP'nin Sosyal Politika ve Toplumsal Cinsiyet Yaklaşımını Şartlı Nakit Transferleri (ŞNT) Üzerinden Okumak," *Kadın/Woman 2000* 17, no. 1 (2016): 31–49.

122. Altuntaş and Demirkanoğlu, "Adalet Ve Kalkınma Partisi'nin."

123. Andrew Heywood, *Political Ideologies: An Introduction* (London: Palgrave Macmillan, 2012).

124. A. Baran Dural, "Muhafazakârlığın Tarihsel Gelişimi ve Muhafazakâr Söylem," *Muhafazakâr Düşünce Dergisi* 1 (2004): 121–33.

125. Yeğenoğlu and Coşar, "AKP ve Toplumsal Cinsiyet Meselesi."

126. That is the most significant point that differentiates JDP governments from previous political terms.

127. See Şenel,"Biz Büyük Bir Aileyiz."

128. Ibid.

129. Aktoprak, "Postkolonyal Bir 'Dava.'"

130. Gülay Toksöz, "Transition from 'Woman' to 'Family': An Analysis of AKP Era Employment Policies from a Gender Perspective," *Journal für Entwicklungspolitik* XXXII 1, no. 2 (2016): 64–83.

131. Altuntaş and Demirkanoğlu, "Adalet Ve Kalkınma Partisi'nin."

132. M. Zeki Duman, "Aile Kurumu Üzerine Tarihsel Bir Okuma Girişimi ve Muhafazakâr İdeolojinin Aileye Bakışı," *İnsan Ve Toplum Bilimleri Araştırmaları Dergisi* 1, no. 4 (2012): 19–51.

133. Aksu Bora, "Aile: En Güçlü İşsizlik Sigortası," in *Boşuna mı okuduk? Türkiye'de Beyaz Yakalı İşsizliği*, edited by T. Bora, A. Bora, N. Erdoğan, and İ. Üstün, 181–201 (İstanbul: İletişim Yayınları, 2012).

134. Ferhunde Özbay, *Dünden Bugüne Aile, Kent ve Nüfus* (İstanbul: İletişim Yayınları, 2015).

135. It is necessary, at this point, to underline the fact that confining women through family within a private area is not unique only to conservatism (Bostan Ünsal, 2013). According to Haspolat (2015), the JDP's positioning of the family as a nuclear unit within the organic society and in the vision of the nation is actually a general characteristic of the right-wing political line according to the history of Turkey.

136. Ferhunde Özbay, "Demografik Dönüşüm Sürecinde İktidar," in *Başka Bir Aile Anlayışı Mümkün Mü?*, edited by N. Boztekin, 106–11 (İstanbul: Görsel Dizayn Ofset, 2014).

137. Ibid.

138. Ibid.
139. Berna Yazıcı, "The Return to the Family: Welfare, State, and Politics of the Family in Turkey," *Anthropological Quarterly* 85, no. 1 (2012): 103–40.
140. Saraçoğlu, "Türkiye Sağı."
141. İnci Özkan Kerestecioğlu, "Mahremiyetin Fethi: İdeal Aile Kurgularından İdeal Aile Politikalarına," in *Başka Bir Aile Anlayışı Mümkün Mü?*, edited by N. Boztekin, 10–21 (İstanbul: Görsel Dizayn Ofset, 2014).
142. A. Dericioğulları Ergun, "Sosyal Güvenlik Reformunun Öteki Yüzü: Kadınların Eşitliği (!)," *Toplum ve Demokrasi* 2, no. 4 (2008): 211–18.
143. Kerestecioğlu, "Mahremiyetin Fethi."
144. Toksöz, "Transition from 'Woman' to 'Family.'"
145. Özbay, "Demografik Dönüşüm Sürecinde İktidar."
146. Şenel, "Biz Büyük Bir Aileyiz."
147. Toksöz, "Transition from 'Woman' to 'Family.'"
148. Sancar, *Türkiye'de Kadın Hareketinin Politiği.*
149. Banu Terkan, "Siyasi Partilerin Kadına İlişkin Söylem ve Politikaları: AKP ve CHP Örneği," *Selçuk İletişim Dergisi* 6, no. 2 (2010): 116–36.
150. Deniz Akın, "Siyasal Reklamlarda Kadın Söylemi ve Kadın İmgeleri: 2011 Genel Seçimleri örneğinde AKP ve CHP Televizyon Siyasal Reklamları Üzerine Bir İnceleme," İletişim Kuram ve Araştırma Dergisi 41 (2015): 277–89.
151. Evren Haspolat, "Kadın, Anne, Yurttaş,"
152. Yuval-Davis and Anthias, *Woman-Nation-State.*
153. Vickers, "Gendering the Hyphen."
154. Şenel, "Biz Büyük Bir Aileyiz."
155. See Yeğenoğlu and Coşar, "AKP ve Toplumsal Cinsiyet Meselesi."

RESOURCES

Anderson, Benedict. *Imagined Communities: Reflections on the Origin and Spread of Nationalism.* London: Verso, 1991.
Akın, Deniz. "Siyasal Reklamlarda Kadın Söylemi ve Kadın İmgeleri: 2011 Genel Seçimleri örneğinde AKP ve CHP Televizyon Siyasal Reklamları Üzerine Bir İnceleme." İletişim Kuram ve Araştırma Dergisi 41 (2015): 277–89.
Akşit, Elif Ekin. *Kızların Sessizliği: Kız Enstitülerinin Uzun Tarihi.* İstanbul: İletişim Yayınları, 2005.
Aktoprak, Elçin. "Postkolonyal Bir Dava Olarak Yeni Türkiye'nin Yeni Ulusu." *Ankara Üniversitesi SBF Dergisi* 71, no. 1 (2016): 1–32.
Altuntaş, Nezahat, and Yahya Demirkanoğlu. "Adalet Ve Kalkınma Partisi'nin Kadına İlişkin Söylem ve Politikalarına Bakış: Muhafazakâr Demokratlıktan Muhafazakârlığa Doğru Evrilişin İzdüşümleri." *Akademik Yaklaşımlar Dergisi* 8, no. 1 (2017): 65–96.
Arat, Yeşim. "Türkiye'de Modernleşme Projesi ve Kadınlar." In *Türkiye'de Modernleşme ve Ulusal Kimlik*, edited by S. Bozdoğan and R. Kasaba, 82–98. İstanbul: Tarih Vakfı Yurt Yayınları, 1999.

―――. "1980'ler Türkiye'sinde Kadın Hareketi: Liberal Kemalizmin Radikal Uzantısı." *Toplum ve Bilim* 53 (1991): 7–19.

―――. "Women's Studies in Turkey From Kemalizm to Feminizm." *New Perspectives on Turkey* 9 (1993): 119–35.

Beauvoir, Simone de. *Kadın "İkinci Cins" Genç Kızlık Çağı.* Translated by B. Onaran. İstanbul: Payel Yayınları, 1993.

Berktay, Fatmagül. *Kadın Olmak Yaşamak Yazmak.* İstanbul: Pencere Yayınları, 1998.

Bora, Aksu. "Aile: En Güçlü İşsizlik Sigortası." In *Boşuna mı okuduk? Türkiye'de Beyaz Yakalı İşsizliği,* edited by T. Bora, A. Bora, N. Erdoğan, and İ. Üstün, 181–201. İstanbul: İletişim Yayınları, 2012.

―――. *Feminizm Kendi Arasında.* İstanbul: Ayizi Yayınları, 2011.

Bostan Ünsal, Fatma., "Müslüman Kadınlar 'İdeal Aile'yi Nasıl Tanımlıyor, Nasıl Sorguluyor?" In *Başka Bir Aile Anlayışı Mümkün Mü?*, edited by N. Boztekin, 22–25. İstanbul: Görsel Dizayn Ofset, 2014.

Bozdoğan, Sibel. *Modernizm ve Ulusun İnşası: Erken Cumhuriyet Türkiye'sinde Mimari Kültür.* İstanbul: Metis Yayınları, 2002.

Chatterjee, Partha. *Nationalist Thought and the Colonial World: A Derivative Discourse.* USA: University of Minnesota Press, 1993.

―――. *The Nationalist Resolution of the Women's Question.* Calcutta: Centre for Studies in Social Sciences, 1987.

Coşar, Simten, and Yeğenoğlu Metin. "New Ground for Patriarchy in Turkey? Gender Policy in the Age of AKP." *South European Society and Politics* 16, no. 4(2011): 555–73.

Çaha, Ömer. "Türkiye'de Kadın Hareketi Tarihi: Değişen Bir Şey Var mı?" In *The History of Women Movement in Turkey* (Kadın Bienali Ekinlikleri Çerçevesinde Türkiye'de Kadın ve Sivil Toplum). İstanbul, 2001.

―――. *Sivil Kadın: Türkiye'de Sivil Toplum ve Kadın.* İstanbul: Vadi Yayınları, 2010.

Çakır, Serpil. "Feminizm: Ataerkil İktidarın Eleştirisi." In *Modern Siyasal İdeolojiler,* edited by Birsen Örs, 412–75. İstanbul: Bilgi Üniversitesi Yayınları, 2007.

Delaney, Carol. *The Seed and the Soil: Gender and Cosmology in Turkish Village Society.* Berkeley, CA: University of California Press, 1991.

Dericioğulları Ergun, Ayşe. "Sosyal Güvenlik Reformunun Öteki Yüzü: Kadınların Eşitliği (!)." *Toplum ve Demokrasi* 2, no. 4 (2008): 211–18.

Doğanay, Ülkü. "AKP'nin Demokrasi Söylemi ve Muhafazakârlık: Muhafazakâr Demokrasiye Eleştirel Bir Bakış."*Ankara Üniversitesi SBF Dergisi* 62, no. 1 (2007): 65–88.

Durakbaşa, Ayşe. "Cumhuriyet Döneminde Kemalist Kadın Kimliğinin Oluşumu." *Tarih ve Toplum* 51 (1988): 167–71.

―――. *Halide Edib Türk Modernleşmesi ve Feminizm.* İstanbul: İletişim Yayınları, 2007.

Duman, M. Zeki. "Aile Kurumu Üzerine Tarihsel Bir Okuma Girişimi ve Muhafazakâr İdeolojinin Aileye Bakışı." *İnsan Ve Toplum Bilimleri Araştırmaları Dergisi* 1, no. 4 (2012): 19–51.

182   Senem Kurt Topuz

Dural, A. Baran. "Muhafazakârlığın Tarihsel Gelişimi ve Muhafazakâr Söylem." *Muhafazakâr Düşünce Dergisi* 1 (2004): 121–33.

Gellner, Ernest. *Nations and Nationalism.* New York: Cornell University Press, 2009.

Göle, Nilüfer. "Modernleşme Bağlamında İslami Kimlik Arayışı." In *Türkiye'de Modernleşme ve Ulusal Kimlik,* edited by S. Bozdoğan and R. Kasaba, 70–81. İstanbul: Tarih Vakfı Yurt Yayınları, 1999.

Gülen, Hande. "Kemalist Modernleşme'de Aile, Ulus, Kadın ve Kadın Yolu/ Türk Kadın Yolu (1925–1927) Dergileri." *Mimar Sinan Güzel Sanatlar Üniversitesi Sosyal Bilimler Enstitüsü Dergisi* 12 (2015): 152–64.

Gür, Faik. "Atatürk Heykelleri ve Türkiye'de Resmi Tarihin Görselleşmesi." *Toplum ve Bilim* 90 (2001): 147–66.

Haspolat, Evren. "Kadın, Anne, Yurttaş Ana Akım Siyasal Partilerin Seçim Bildirgelerinde Kadın Algısı:1 Kasım 2015 Genel Seçimleri Örneği." *Toplum ve Demokrasi* 9 (2015): 73–107.

Hatem, Mervat. "Secularist and Islamist Discourses on Modernity in Egypt and the Evolution of the Postcolonial Nation-State." In *Islam, Gender and Social Change,* edited by Y. Y. Haddad and J. L. Esposito. New York: Oxford University Press, 1998.

Heywood, Andrew. *Political Ideologies: An Introduction.* London: Palgrave Macmillan, 2012.

Hobsbawm, Eric J. *Nations and Nationalism since 1780: Programme, Myth, Reality.* London: Cambridge University Press, 2012.

Kadıoğlu, Ayşe. "Cinselliğin İnkârı: Büyük Toplumsal Projelerin Nesnesi Olarak Türk Kadınları." In *75 Yılda Kadınlar ve Erkekler,* edited by A. Berktay Hacımirzaoğlu. İstanbul: Türkiye İş Bankası, İstanbul Menkul Kıymetler Borsası, Tarih Vakfı Yayını, 1998.

Kandiyoti, Deniz. "Modernin Cinsiyeti: Türk Modernleşmesi Araştırmalarında Eksik Boyutlar." In *Türkiye'de Modernleşme ve Ulusal Kimlik,* edited by S. Bozdoğan and R. Kasaba, 99–117, İstanbul: Tarih Vakfı Yurt Yayınları, 1999.

Karagöz, Betül. "Türkiye'de 1980 Sonrası Kadın Hareketinin Siyasal Temelleri ve İkinci Dalga Uğrağı." *Memleket Siyaset Yönetim* 3, no. 7 (2008): 168–90.

Kerestecioğlu, İnci Özkan. "Mahremiyetin Fethi: İdeal Aile Kurgularından İdeal Aile Politikalarına." In *Başka Bir Aile Anlayışı Mümkün Mü?,* edited by N. Boztekin, 20–21. İstanbul: Görsel Dizayn Ofset, 2014.

Kili, Suna. "Modernleşme ve Kadın." In *Türkiye'de Kadın Olmak,* edited by N. Arat, 9–20. İstanbul: Say Yayınları, 1996.

Şerif, Mardin. *Türkiye'de Toplum ve Siyaset.* İstanbul: İletişim Yayınları, 1995.

Mayer, Tamar. "Gender Ironies of Nationalism: Seting the Stage." In *Gender Ironies of Nationalism: Soring the Nation,* edited by T. Mayer, 1–22. London: Routledge, 2000.

McClintock, Anne. "Family Feuds: Gender, Nationalism and the Family." *Feminist Review* 44 (1993): 61–80.

Mosse, George. *Nationalism and Sexuality: Respectability and Abnormal Sexuality in Modem Europe.* New York: Howard Fertig, 1997.

Najmabadi, Afsaneh. "The Erotic Vatan [Homeland] as Beloved and Mother: To Love, to Possess, and To Protect." *Comparative Studies in Society and History* 39, no. 3 (1997): 442–67.

Nagel, Joane. "Masculinity and Nationalism: Gender and Sexuality in the Making of Nations." *Ethnic and National Studies* 21, no. 2 (1998): 242–69.

Omar, Karima. "National Symbolism in Constructions Of Gender: Transformed Symbols in Post-Conflict States." *Seton Hall Journal of Diplomacy and International Relations* (2004): 49–67.

Özbay, Ferhunde. *Dünden Bugüne Aile, Kent ve Nüfus*. İstanbul: İletişim Yayınları, 2015.

———. "Demografik Dönüşüm Sürecinde İktidar." In *Başka Bir Aile Anlayışı Mümkün Mü?*, edited by N. Boztekin, 106–11, İstanbul: Görsel Dizayn Ofset, 2014.

Özkırımlı, Umut. *Milliyetçilik Kuramları Eleştirel Bir Bakış*. Ankara: Doğu Batı Yayınları, 2009.

Peterson, V. Spike. "Gendered Nationalism." *Peace Review, Special Issue on Nationalism And Ethnic Conflict* 6, no. 1 (1994): 77–84.

Saigol, Rubina. "Militarization, Nation and Gender: Women's Bodies as Arenas of Violent Conflict." In *Deconstructing Sexuality in the Middle East: Challenges and Discourses*, edited by P. Ilkkaracan. Aldershot: Ashgate, 2008.

Sancar, Serpil. *Türkiye'de Kadın Hareketinin Politiği: Tarihsel Bağlam, Politik Gündem ve Özgünlükler*. İstanbul: Koç Üniversitesi Yayını, 2011. http://kasaum.ankara.edu.tr/files/2013/09/Serpil-Sancar-T%C3%BCrkiye%E2%80%99de-Kad%C4%B1n-Hareketinin-Politi%C4%9Fi.pdf, accessed February 15, 2018.

———. *Türk Modernleşmesinin Cinsiyeti Erkekler Devlet Kadınlar Aile Kurar*. İstanbul: İletişim Yayınları, 2014.

Saraçoğlu, Cenk. "Türkiye Sağı, AKP ve Kürt Meselesi." In *Türk Sağı-Mitler, Fetişler, Düşman İmgeleri*, edited by İ. Ö. Kerestecioğlu and G. G. Öztan, 243–82, İstanbul: İletişim Yayınları, 2014.

Şenel, Burcu. "Biz Büyük Bir Aileyiz: Türkiye'de Devlet Söyleminde Makbul Kadınlık ve Aile." *Mülkiye Dergisi* 41, no. 2 (2017): 31–69.

Tekeli, Şirin. "80'lerde Türkiye'de Kadınların Kurtuluşu Hareketinin Gelişmesi." *Birikim Dergisi* 3 (1989): 34–41.

———. "1980'ler Türkiye'sinde Kadınlar." In *1980'ler Türkiye'sinde Kadın Bakış Açısından Kadınlar*, edited by Ş. Tekeli, 7–37. İstanbul: İletişim, 1993.

———. "Introduction: Women in Turkey in the 1980s." In *Women in Modern Turkish Society: A Reader*, edited by Ş. Tekeli, 1–24. London: Zed Books, 1995.

Terkan, Banu. "Siyasi Partilerin Kadına İlişkin Söylem ve Politikaları: AKP ve CHP Örneği." *Selçuk İletişim Dergisi* 6, no. 2 (2010): 116–36.

Toksöz, Gülay. "Transition from 'Woman' to 'Family': An Analysis of AKP Era Employment Policies from a Gender Perspective." *Journal für Entwicklungspolitik* XXXII 1, no. 2 (2016): 64–83.

Vickers, Jill. "Gendering the Hyphen: Gender Dimensions of Modern Nation-State Formation in Euro-American and Anti- and Post-Colonial Contexts." In *Gendering the Nation-State Canadian and Comparative Perspectives*, edited by Yasmeen Abu-Laban, 21–45. Vancouver: UBC Press, 2008.

West, Lois A. *Feminist Nationalism*. London: Routledge, 1997.

Yazıcı, Berna. "The Return to the Family: Welfare, State, and Politics of the Family in Turkey." *Anthropological Quarterly* 85, no. 1 (2012): 103–40.

Yeğenoğlu, Metin, and Simten Coşar. "AKP ve Toplumsal Cinsiyet Meselesi: Neoliberalizm ve Patriyarka Arasında Mekik Dokumak." In *İktidarın Şiddeti: AKP'li Yıllar, Neoliberalizm ve İslamcı Politikalar*, edited by S. Coşar and G. Yücesan-Özdemir, 158–81, İstanbul: Metis Yayınları, 2014.

Yıldız, Onur. *Siyasal İslam, Neoliberalizm ve Yeni Sağ: AKP Üzerine, Siyasal Bir Gözden Geçirme.* 2010. http://www.halkevleri.org.tr/diger/siyasal-islam-neoliberalizm-ve-yeni-sag-akp-uzerine-siyasal-bir-gozden-gecirme-onur-yildiz-0, accessed March 9, 2018.

Yılmaz Şener, Meltem. "Kadını Anne Olarak Güçlendirmek? AKP'nin Sosyal Politika ve Toplumsal Cinsiyet Yaklaşımını Şartlı Nakit Transferleri (ŞNT) Üzerinden Okumak." *Kadın/Woman 2000* 17, no. 1 (2016): 31–49.

Yuval-Davis, Nira. *Gender and Nation*. London: Sage Publications, 1997.

Yuval-Davis, Nira, and Floya Anthias. *Woman-Nation-State*. London: Palgrave Macmillan, 1989.

Yükselbaba, Ülker. "AKP'nin Kadına Yönelik Söylem ve Politikaları: Neo- Liberalizm, Ilımlı İslam ve Kadın." *Kadın/Woman 2000* 14, no. 2 (2013): 67–92.

Zihnioğlu, Yaprak. *Kadınsız İnkılap Nezihe Muhittin, Kadınlar Halk Fırkası, Türk Kadınlar Birliği*. İstanbul: Metis Yayınevi 2003.

Chapter Six

Why Afet İnan Had to Measure Skulls

Béatrice Hendrich

THE REPUBLICAN WOMAN:
EDUCATED, OBEDIENT, AND WHITE

Afet İnan, the so-called adopted daughter of Mustafa Kemal Atatürk, was a history teacher and, in her later life, a kind of cultural ambassador for Turkey, giving lectures and publishing works on Turkish history and the emancipation of the Turkish woman. Her most spectacular work, however, was her anthropometric fieldwork in 1937–1938: Throughout Turkey, the bodily measurements of 64,000 people were taken and turned into statistics on the color of people's hair, eyes, and skin and, most importantly, on the form of their skulls. From the data gathered, İnan concluded that Turkey is inhabited by the Turkish race, which is not "yellow" or "mongoloid" but "white" and "short-skulled, brachycephalic." This conclusion became the measurable foundation for the Turkish History Thesis, which was developed in the 1930s, and also decisively formed and propagated by İnan as board member of the Turkish History Society. The racist approach to Turkish national identity was officially ousted during the Second World War, when the effects of racism became gruesomely visible, and Turkey increasingly oriented its foreign policy towards the victorious countries.

This chapter touches upon various topics that have been increasingly attracting the attention of scholars of the Humanities since the monopoly of the Kemalist narrative on the history and the society of the Turkish Republic slowly started to dissolve in the late 1980s. These topics are, to name the most important ones in the given framework, historiography,[1] gender history,[2] the masculine military state,[3] and, very recently, the history of (nationalist) racism of Turkey.[4] What I aim at in this chapter is to connect these perspectives, focusing on the case of Afet İnan and her career in the Kemalist state as the main proponent of a Turkish Historiography based on anthropometrical statistics. I ask why the duty of propagating a racist history thesis, based on racist physical anthropology, had to be carried out by a woman. Is there any significant relationship between its main architect being a woman and the vehemence of its implementation?

This chapter approaches this question in two main steps: first, I introduce the general outline of physical anthropology, its history, and the place of the "Turkish Race" in early European anthropology. I then proceed to examine İnan's biography and her career as a scientist for the Turkish cause, with her anthropometric fieldwork as its peak. Second, I question the relation between Turkish state feminism and the masculine military state. If we consider the Turkish state as fundamentally masculine and militant, what is the place of "the women of the republic," and how does it connect to the work of İnan as well as the military activities of Atatürk's other famous adopted daughter, Sabiha Gökçen?

AFET İNAN'S ANTHROPOMETRY

The History of Anthropometry

"Anthropometry is a simple, reliable method for quantifying body size and proportions by measuring body length, width, circumference (C), and skinfold thickness (SF)."[5] From this short definition, it becomes clear that anthropometry is a method, a tool, that serves endless aims without being intrinsically good or bad—very similar to a good, sharp knife. As a method, it includes a broad range of applications and sub-methods: from the automotive industry to nutrition science, from bone grafting to increasing occupational safety. It can help in the aggregation of data about people, data that may be used, for example, to help cure diseases, but it is at the same time prone to pseudoscientific imaginations and ideological (mis)use. The history of anthropometry is, at the same time, a history of science in the service of racism, racist action, and justification for the same. This holds particularly true for the measuring of the skull—craniometrics—but also for a variety of other "arguments" such as the "meaning" of skin and hair color or the construction of "human races" based on some prehistoric skeletons.

In the Turkey of the 1930s, craniometrics was the centerpiece of politically inspired anthropometry, followed by considerations related to the "true" Turkish color of hair and skin. In its basic assumptions, craniometrics and anthropometry, as they were applied by İnan and others, draw on work done earlier by physical anthropologists in Europe. The first publications in the modern history of craniometrics appeared in the middle of the eighteenth century, and Johann F. Blumenbach (1752–1840) was considered one of the most significant scientists in this field. He created skull categories such as "the Caucasian" and "the Ethiopian" but emphasized the biological unity of humanity (monogeny), and he stressed that skin color "cannot constitute a species."[6] He was far more interested in the beauty and capability of humankind than in clear-cut categories of "race." In the subsequent decades and centuries, his work was often reduced to the cranial categories—which, for Blumenbach, had been examples of human varieties rather than fixed categories, and which he certainly did not use as evidence of any kind of hierarchization between the categories—and was included in the racist canon. Unlike Blumenbach, who had no intention of relating a certain skull shape to moral character or cognitive capability, the Swedish anthropologist Anders Retzius (1796–1860) stressed a relation between the form of a person's skull and the stage of his/her historic–cultural development. He made the Cranial Index a popular issue and argued that the prehistoric peoples of Europe had been "short-skulled" (brachycephalic), whereas the younger, "superior" peoples were "long-skulled" (dolichocephalic).[7] When nationalist-racist historiographies appeared on the scene, they would frequently refer to Retzius' categories to "reconstruct" population movements and the "spread of civilization" by the owners of certain skull forms.

As the literature review shows, the "Turkish skull" and the measurements of "Turks" were of particular interest to European craniometrists.[8] Some authors were interested in establishing clear-cut categories, such as the "Turk" or "Turanian" as Non-European, Non-Teutonic, and so on, while others established a chain of descent from Asia to Europe, including the "Osmanli" as a mixed race.[9] The ever-increasing number of (mutually contradictory) "categories" and the blossoming of wild interpretations demonstrate clearly that, in most cases, the "facts" followed the ideological aim. August Weisbach (1837–1914), for example, was a physician in the Austria-Hungarian army, a circumstance that offered him the opportunity to continue his studies, which he had started as a student in the bones-and-skulls collection of his university, on a great number of people, mostly soldiers from the multi-ethnic army of the Empire. He spent some time at the Austrian Imperial Hospital in Istanbul; while his hope to measure the skulls of Istanbul's multiethnic population was frustrated, he was, however, able to collect bones from the cemeteries. In his publication, Weisbach compares, in long lists and detailed text, the measurements of the "Turkish skull" with those of the skulls from peoples from the Balkans, Anatolia, and Central Asia.[10] He was sure that he had enough experience to categorize the gathered skulls according to their racial specifics.[11] In the eyes of Weisbach, two of his seventy-eight skulls turned out to be Greek, since they were dolichocephalic; the Turks were all brachycephalic, even if Weisbach had to take the pain to open up many subcategories, such as the "very high and strong brachycephalus" or "big, thinner, lower, backward, over-arching brachycephalus."[12] Or, as Emmanuel Szurek put it: "But not all brachycephalics were placed on an equal footing, with the Turks of Anatolia being more brachycephalic than those from the Balkans, and thus a sliding scale of brachycephalisation could be detected as one moved away from Europe."[13]

Anthropometrics and physical anthropology were familiar and intriguing issues to physicians and politicians in the late Ottoman Empire and Turkish Republic. The materialist intellectual Abdullah Cevdet (1869–1932), for example, stated in the 1890s "that cranial capacity signified higher intelligence and that the nation should naturally be confided to a biologically superior elite (Hanioglu 1981: 16–18)."[14] In the early Republic, physical anthropology took the form of a secular creed. The quest for the (new) national identity based its hopes on history, and history seemed to become a concrete and objective entity through the help of anthropometric findings. The key politico-academic institutions that helped to pave the way for the anthropological and historical content of that creed were the Turkish Institute for Anthropology (Türk Antropoloji Enstitüsü), founded in 1925, and the History Society, with its historic conferences in 1931 and 1937. Yet, the anthropometrical perspective on humankind's history did not go uncontested, either in Turkey or elsewhere.

ANTHROPOMETRY AS A NATIONAL PROJECT

In 1947, towards the end of Turkey's One-Party Period, İnan's Türk Halkının Antropolojik Karakterleri ve Türkiye Tarihi (Anthropological Characteristics of the Turkish People and the History of Turkey) was published, dedicated to the "precious memory of Atatürk."[15] To understand the full implications related to its publication, it is necessary to go back in history to 1925 when Mustafa Kemal Atatürk made young Afet İnan one of his most famous and zealous propagandists.

According to most sources,[16] İnan and Atatürk met for the first time in 1925 on the occasion of Atatürk's visit to the elementary school in Izmir where İnan had her first appointment as a teacher at that time. Atatürk seemed to be interested in the girl's pedigree, as both of their families came from Thessaloniki. When İnan expressed her wish to continue studying, Atatürk had her place of employment changed to Ankara, and later in the same year, he sent her to Lausanne, to the prestigious Rochemont school, where İnan obtained the full program of education for upper-class daughters, including

French and tennis lessons. Back in Istanbul, she finalized her studies at the French Dame de Sion and started teaching history.[17] In the following decade, commissioned by Atatürk, she authored or co-authored an impressive number of very influential books that count today among the classics of Kemalist historiography and state wisdom—however disputable their content may be.

Civilized Knowledge for the Citizen

İnan's first publication of that kind was a series of textbooks published from 1929 onward, which later, as a compiled version, came to be known as *Vatandaş İçin Medeni Bilgiler* (*Civilized Knowledge for the Citizen*),[18] intended for the use at *Vatani Malumat* or *Yurttaş Bilgisi* (Homeland Knowledge) classes. The series included treatises on the state, taxes, military service, and so on.[19] In their analysis of these textbooks' notion of citizenship, Pınar Bilgin and Başak İnce come to the conclusion that this notion "was a 'civic republican' one, defining citizenship within the parameters of solidarism and community. Whereas the 'liberal' definition of citizenship casts citizenship as a status involving rights accorded to citizens, the 'civic republican' definition casts it as a practice involving responsibilities to the wider society."[20] "Responsibilities to the wider society" appears to be a key formula, a handy description of İnan's own perception of her work and life. This perspective is also mirrored in Afet İnan's later endeavor to downplay her own contribution to the *Civilized Knowledge*. In a follow-up published in 1988, she states: "I see it as my responsibility to set the historical record straight. Although these books have come out under my name, they have been written based on Atatürk's ideas and criticisms and the narrative style belongs solely to him."[21]

Civilized Knowledge includes one short paragraph related to the physical appearance of "the Turk." Under the headline "The roots of the Turks and how they came into existence," the book states:

> All individuals of the Turkish nation resemble each other, even if there are some small differences. Very naturally, there are some differences of the [bodily] form. Would it be possible at all that the present children of this very numerous human community resemble each other exactly, as this community has spread from Mesopotamia and the valleys of Egypt in prehistoric times to Central Asia, Russia, Caucasus, and Anatolia, to ancient and today's Greece, Crete, and central Italy before the Romans and shortly to the shores of the Mediterranean, has come to settle down there, and has lived under the influence of all kinds of climate for thousands of years together with many different races (*cins*)?[22]

Civilized Knowledge also contains numerous pages on military service and the army. The way these issues are depicted here differs from the later approach in the 1930s. In just a few years, Ayşe Gül Altınay argues, this approach shifts in its depiction of military service from a "necessity of our time" to a "cultural/national/racial" understanding. This shift, Altınay continues, is directly related to the emergence of the Turkish History Thesis in the following years.[23] The 1930s would show an explosion of pseudoscientific "theses" glorifying the unique history, language, race, and innate soldierly character of the Turk. Intriguingly enough, İnan was also a major player in these new fields.

An Outline of Turkish History

In 1930, Atatürk assigned İnan to deliver the opening speech of the Sixth Congress of the Turkish Hearths and made her a founding member of the Turkish Hearths' Committee for the Study of the Turkish History (*Türk Ocakları Türk Tarihi Tedkik Heyeti*). The first concrete output of the committee was a 600-page volume on Turkish History, the *Türk Tarihinin Ana Hatları (An Outline of Turkish History)*.[24] The volume was hastily prepared by a team, but İnan was and still is regarded as the main author, following Atatürk's directives.

The initial History Committee turned over time into a Society and finally an Institution (*Türk Tarih Kurumu*); this was a move that was basically related to the political ousting of the Turkish Hearths by the emerging exclusive rule of the Republican People's Party (*Cumhuriyet Halk Partisi*, CHP or RPP). Although the Turkish Hearths was ousted for political reasons, many ideas of a rather biologistic character—the quest for "ethnic origins and character"[25] of the citizen—remained part of the party's and the History Society's ideology. The History Society's overall task was to create a collective history that answered the needs of the nation-building project: "What the young Republic needed at this point was a new 'myth of origins' that went beyond the now largely dispossessed Ottoman past and revealed the superiority, rootedness, and ethnic purity of the Turkish nation."[26] Consequently, the History Society created the Turkish History Thesis (*Türk Tarih Tezi*), decisively supported by İnan's specific anthropology and reinforced by the First Language Congress in 1932 and the Sun Language Theory (*Güneş Dil Teorisi*) of 1936.

While the bulky version of the *Outline of Turkish History* was printed only a hundred times for the use of the inner circle, an abridged form was published in 1931 and disseminated as a history textbook.[27] The aim of the *Outline* was stated in its introduction: "To reveal the mysteries of the Turkish genius and moral character, to demonstrate to the Turk himself his own uniqueness and power, and to explain that our national development is embedded in deep racial roots."[28]

The *Outline* was the founding document of the Turkish History Thesis. The basic idea or quest of the History Thesis, and of the Sun Language Theory as well, was that the Turks and the Turkish language were the cradle of all—at least European and Asian—later peoples, civilizations, and languages.[29] With the help of this formula, two main tasks could be achieved at once: in the European ranking of civilizations, the Turkish civilization was no longer at the bottom, far below the European civilization, but instead, it took the topmost position. Moreover, the Turks became, on the basis of "academic proof," the first and original inhabitants and owners of Anatolia, instead of being blamed for conquering foreign territory.

In the introduction of the *Outline*, a sub-chapter is dedicated to the issue of "race" (*ırk*).[30] The text is neither consistent regarding vocabulary nor convincing in its arguments. The "initial races"[31] came into being because human communities lived restricted to certain geographies, isolated from one another. Later on, as a result of migration, races disseminated to all regions of the world and intermixed, while each regional climate produced, out of these mixed races, smaller groups (*küçük zümreler*) with dominant hair and skin colors, such as the Turks, which are "in their majority"[32] white, while Africans are black, and so on. Skin color is, however, only an evanescent characteristic of living persons, not the decisive characteristic of a race. If the historian wants to unearth the past, he has to content himself with skeletons. The skeleton, and particularly the skull, keep their original form longer than any other element of the human body. Skulls are mostly either brachycephalic or dolichocephalic, and by means of these specificities, the historian can reveal the prehistoric past of humankind. The Turks are mostly brachycephalic. On the other hand, the text comes with a caveat: "We have to state that the differences between the races as we discern them today are almost meaningless from the perspective of history. While the form of the skull is an essential characteristic for the categorization of the races, it has no social meaning at all. Its reason is that the form of the skull does hardly change. But the most essential organ inside the skull, the brain, changes."[33] In the text's last paragraph, out of the blue, race is defined as a community of those who "stem from the same blood" and whose bodies resemble one another.[34]

In 1932, the First History Congress of the Turkish Republic took place. What took place in the guise of a teachers' conference was the very event through which the future of Turkish history and the historical identity of the young nation would be defined and petrified for the following decades. Racist anthropology as an auxiliary discipline of history constituted the dominant discourse, and the *Outline* was the Bible to follow. "At this significant historical juncture, race became firmly embedded in the modernizing elite's self-conceptions and began to be disseminated through scholarship, education, and popular publications."[35] İnan was the second person to speak at the event, after the Minister of National Education, Mahmut Esat [Bozkurt] (1892–1943). During her talk, titled "Prehistoric Time and the Onset of History,"[36] İnan repeated the kernel of the *Outline*, again with some inconsistency. The cradle of the Turks, she stated, was the Central Asian plateau where they had lived in isolation and turned into a race, speaking Turkish, being short-skulled, and *of white skin*. What mattered for her was not that white is the opposite of black, but that white is non-yellow.[37] Being white-not-yellow is a topos that again and again would appear in her writings; it was a rejection of the European categorization of Turks as "mongoloid" Asians.

In addition to the history teachers, some historians of the older generation, among them respected academics from the Istanbul University (*Darül-fünun*), had been invited to the Congress. Some of them attempted to question the Turkish History Thesis, particularly Fuat Köprülü and Velidi Zeki Togan, for different ideological reasons. While Togan, a Turkist stemming from Kazan, was far more interested in a greater Turkish-Asian history, Köprülü endeavored to save history from the worst ideological distortions and rejected racist anthropology as the fundament of History Studies.[38] Köprülü's criticism was repudiated so harshly by İnan and other Congress members that he had to apologize and reformulate his arguments several times on the same day, while Togan had maneuvered himself in such a difficult situation that in 1933 he was made to leave Istanbul University and Turkey.[39]

In the 1930s and 1940s, the Turkish History Thesis and the Sun Language Theory provided the dogmatic text for any related activity in science or teaching.[40] The measurable effects of these "Theses," however, lasted and polluted Turkish academia for much longer.[41]

Success and Fall of Recherches sur les caractères anthropologiques

Backed by a significant number of scholars from Europe, the Second History Congress held in 1937 reinforced the tenets of the First Congress:

> Şevket Aziz Kansu used the analysis of skulls again to convince the audience of the racial links between contemporary Turks and past civilizations. Analyzing skull remains acquired in excavations, Kansu concluded that Seljuks, a people that invaded Anatolia in the eleventh century, were Alpine Turks, and added that Anatolia already hosted proto-Turks during the Seljuk invasions, thus ensuring the eternal ownership of Anatolian territories.[42]

The honorary congress president was Eugène Pittard (1867–1962), a Swiss anthropologist and supervisor of İnan's PhD studies, who was eventually the most influential individual of his time in the field of craniometrics in Turkey. Pittard had held the chair for Anthropology in Genève since 1916. He was known for his humanistic engagement such as the establishment of the Albanian Red Cross after the First World War. His early anthropological writings were inspired by an open-minded curiosity towards "other peoples," not by racist belittlement.[43] Because of a certain tradition of the Ottoman intellectuals to migrate to Switzerland for political or academic reasons, Pittard's contact with Turkish expats dates back to 1919 or earlier.[44] They considered him a friend of the Turkish cause; he was someone who not only did not share the downgrading behavior of other Europeans towards the Turks but also seemed to provide material arguments for the historical superiority of the Turks by means of his anthropological research. Murat Ergin characterizes Pittard's somewhat shaky and contradictory behavior as the approach of someone who does not intend to critique the Orientalism of the time but "rather hoped to shift these boundaries [between East and West] with the help of racial classifications and include the Turks under the racially delineated boundaries of the 'West.'"[45] Although Pittard had not yet been invited to the First History Congress in 1932, he had been referred to continuously in the talks of his Turkish colleagues. Atatürk had studied Pittard's publications closely and, eventually, invited him for an expedition to Eastern Anatolia in 1928; this was an opportunity that was offered to only a handful of foreigners at that time since the East was still a region of (armed) resistance against the new regime. Hans-Lukas Kieser goes so far as to say that "without the interaction of Pittard and Atatürk, the Turkish History Thesis would not have come into existence" the way it did.[46] Pittard had measured the skulls of Turkish soldiers and come to the conclusion that because of the nasal index, Turks of Anatolia were racially more homogeneous than Turks of the Balkans. The hypotheses, as Pittard himself called them, that the Anatolian Turks were part of the "brachycephalic race" and that they were European and not Asian very soon became "authoritative statements" in the minds of the Turkish public.[47] The fact that, in 1924, Pittard had categorized not the Turks but the Armenians as short-skulled was completely forgotten.[48]

From 1935–1937, İnan attended Pittard's classes in Genève. In 1939, she presented her PhD thesis, entitled *Recherches sur les caractères anthropologiques des populations de la Turquie.*[49] The thesis presents the outcome of a most spectacular period of anthropological fieldwork in 1937, particularly if we consider the poor economy and infrastructure of Turkey in those years: after a pre-study on 200 women in Ankara, İnan and her teams traveled the provinces of Turkey and carried out their craniometrics and body measurements on nearly 64,000 people.[50] Each team consisted of, at minimum, a physician and a police officer; health officers and sports teachers also joined the teams. Names and locations of research are listed in the thesis. The gathered data were transferred to Ankara to the Statistical Office where another group of employees, up to forty people, made them into lists, graphics, and statistical statements.[51] Taking into account the fieldwork, the approach, and the arguments that led to the final result, one could say that İnan did what she did to prove that Turkey (Anatolia and Thrace) was inhabited by the Turkish race because a certain number of the measured objects fit the body standards that were defined as Turkish. Even the remarkable variety of eye color throughout Turkey could be explained away, since having non-dark eyes is more European than being dark-eyed, and except in the far North-Eastern region, including Erzincan, Erzurum, and Kars, the standard Turk is not a dark-eyed person,[52] and eventually, it was defined in the following way:

> The Turks are of a size a little above average. In their majority, they are macro-skeletal. To the bigger part, they are leptorhine (narrow-nosed). Usually, their eyes and hair are in the middle; often faintly pigmented. Most of these individuals belong to the white race of Europe, known according to the classification under the name *Homo Alpinus*. Maybe that there are among them also many representatives of the race called *Homo Dinaricus*.[53]

The thesis repeats and reinforces the tenets of the Turkish History Thesis; beyond that, in almost every subchapter, İnan states that, according to the data, Turks are not yellow or mongoloid and that the foreign researchers are mistaken. She also mentions, briefly, the benefits of body metrics for the sake of society[54]—an approach that is identified by Ergin as eugenics, built upon anthropometrics.[55] It has to be added that the student outpaced the master: İnan claimed the racial unity of Turkey's inhabitants, naming what she found "the Turkish race," and avoiding any hesitation or uncertainty, totally unaffected by Pittard's reluctance towards such a gung ho approach.[56]

İnan's career was completely dependent on Atatürk's expectations and decisions. The anthropometric fieldwork, however, had been carried out with the consent of the second strong man of the Republic, İsmet İnönü, who instructed the Ministries of Defense, of Education, and of Public Health to support the research.[57] For this reason, and since the interest in physical anthropology was shared by a great number of politicians, Atatürk's death in 1938 did not (immediately) negatively influence İnan's popularity or her work. It was rather the change of the global political backdrop that called into question the public legitimacy of racist concepts, namely the Second World War, which was nurtured and justified by German racism and racist "science." "The race talk of the 1930s (in Turkey) comes to a screeching halt in the second half of the 1940. ... (After 1950), the race scholars ... turned into different careers, and they appear to be silent, if not explicitly apologetic, about their previous works."[58] In 1944, the same İnönü called racist and Turanist thoughts sick and damaging, while the "Society of Turkish History withdrew its support from racializing arguments."[59]

At the beginning of this chapter, I had mentioned that İnan's PhD thesis was published in the Turkish language as late as 1947. This delay was partly caused by the difficult economic situation in Turkey during the Second World War, but more than that, it was the change of the dominant ideological orientation of the Republican People's Party. Suavi Aydın even calls the publication "a last stand" of physical anthropology.[60] Given that chauvinist and racist political activities did not cease to exist in Turkey, and that craniometrical anthropological research continues as well, it is important to keep in mind the difference between this official attitude of the ruling party in the 1940s and the concrete effect of the Turkish History Thesis and the Sun Language Theory on Turkish perception of the world. In 2016, Prime Minister Ahmet Davutoğlu launched an investigation into the fate of architect Mimar Sinan's skull, which had been studied by a group of historians from the Turkish History Society, including İnan, in 1935, and which seems to have been missing since that time.[61]

After the tide had turned against İnan, former colleagues started to ridicule her. In 1948, Halil Demircioğlu from Ankara University spent nineteen pages making fun of her "a priori" results.[62] While Demircioğlu does not question the benefits of physical anthropology as such, he gleefully displays and dissects the meager analysis of the data, criticizing specifically İnan's use of anthropology as an auxiliary discipline for history. "She thinks she makes historical studies," he derides.[63] This time, there was no Atatürk and no one else to silence the castigator. İnan wrote a lengthy defense, but this text makes it obvious how personally offended she felt by the critic, without really answering or refuting Demircioğlu's arguments.[64]

STATE FEMINISM AND THE MASCULINE STATE

İnan spent the rest of her life giving talks in Turkey and abroad and writing primarily about two issues: Atatürk and Turkish women. She did not bid farewell completely to craniometrics as, for example, her small publication on Mimar Sinan shows, wherein she once more stressed the Turkishness of his art and character, which would earlier have been proved by his skull.[65] In the same vein, in 1962 at a UNESCO conference, she once more defended the Turks' racial Westernness in the sense of their whiteness:

> As a race, Turkish people look very much like Western people. The change in their costume makes it impossible to tell Turkish women from the women of the West. Whereas in the old days their ways of dressing and living prevented women from advancing, the changes in their outlook gave them self-respect and increased the confidence which they needed to succeed.[66]

Today, İnan is remembered in Turkey as one of Atatürk's adopted daughters and as a female exemplar of Turkish emancipation and national progress. This image is nurtured by two main elements: her activities in the name of Atatürk and the Turkish Republic, as has been demonstrated in earlier sections, and her self-construction as a successful female Turk, publishing on other successful (female) Turks. My questions for the remaining parts of this chapter will be these: How is she perceived today in public discourse and in academia? How did she herself contribute to this image? And finally, and most importantly, can we establish a specific relation between her being a woman—of being a "daughter"—and her carrying out the duties she did in the way she did?

A Fighter for Women's Rights?

In Turkish public discourse, and in the majority of Turkish academic publications, İnan is hailed for being among the first female academics, a member of the Turkish History Society, and for fighting for women's rights.[67] However, she is never celebrated for being herself, or for being original, or for being an independent feminist (which indeed she never was). Telling epitaphs include "A believing woman of the republic"[68]—which includes a pun on her chosen name "İnan" in the sense of believe/belief—or "*Cumhuriyet kızı,*"[69] daughter of the Republic. These titles are congruent with the image she established herself. Based on her ample writing, including the (auto-)biography compiled by her daughter that I mentioned earlier, we see the image of a woman who took every step with purpose, always knew which direction to head, and who never questioned or had to question her own decisions. Her biographical narratives include several "forecasts" or explanations of how she shaped her fate and that of the Republic.

A first example is a very intriguing kind of self-documentation: In her autobiography, İnan quotes a letter written by herself on the occasion of her graduation from Teachers' School in 1925. According to her own words, during the last days at school, the prospective teachers were asked to write a job application letter. In this letter, as it is quoted in the book, she fictionalizes her life, pretending that the writer of the application—herself—had already graduated from the University of Lausanne and that now she only wants to serve her country. The letter is dated April 31, 1925, which is before she met Atatürk.[70] We cannot prove if she really did write this letter on that occasion, or whether it is a later fabrication. Whatever the case, it fits so well into the overall image that, for example, Nazan Aksoy, in her work on female biographies, takes the text at face value and analyses the character of young Afet İnan based on this "letter" without even pondering its authenticity.[71]

Another well-known story is how İnan convinced Atatürk to introduce the right to vote for women. She repeated it here and there in her publications: when she worked as a teacher at a co-educative school, she had the pupils elect a mayor among themselves to teach them the new law by this applied method. The class elected a girl, but a male classmate refused to accept the result, arguing that the law in force did not include active or passive voting rights for women. İnan continues in her book:

> After the lesson, I felt perturbed. . . . Later in the day, I met Ataturk and Ş. Kaya, the then Minister of the Interior. I explained what had happened at school that day. Ataturk advised me to continue working on this subject. . . . I set to work at once, and after studying the position of women in other parts of the world, I prepared an article on the subject. . . . But although I did work on this subject personally, the holding of the conference, the press coverage, and the publication of my booklet were all done with the approval of Ataturk himself.[72]

The most significant story in the given framework of this article is how she aroused Atatürk's interest in physical anthropology: when she was a student at Notre Dame de Sion in Istanbul, she felt offended by the incorrect information the history textbook provided on races and skin color. According to the book, the white race ruled Western and Northern Asia and consisted of Northern Indians, Iranians, Armenians, and others, while the Turks were part of the yellow or mongoloid race that lived in Eastern and Middle Asia. İnan complained to Atatürk, and he answered: "No, this is not possible. Let's work on this issue."[73] Taking into account that Atatürk had been friends with Pittard much earlier, this focus on her own influence appears somehow overstated.

With the emancipation of gender studies in Turkey from Kemalist state feminism in the 1980s, the sheer enthusiasm for the Kemalist reforms made room for a rather critical deconstruction of the effects of the top-down emancipation process. This critical stance also led to a reevaluation of the exemplary daughters of the Republic such as İnan and her "sibling" Sabiha Gökçen. A paradigmatic case for this new approach is Hülya Adak's publication on "Daughters of the Republic"[74] where she reverses the reading of İnan's story on the female suffrage. Adak summarizes the event under the

heading "Suffrage is daddy's reform," concluding that in the abovemen-
tioned quote from *The Emancipation of the Turkish Women*, İnan did not
mean to relate "the story of how women took their rights, but ... of how
Mustafa Kemal granted them rights"[75] after being inspired by her talks and
publications. Equally harshly comments were made by Yaprak Zihnioğlu on
İnan's submissive navel-gazing, referring to her narrative that the Turkish
women had been restricting themselves to charitable, not political activities
until the time of the Kemalist reforms, and so rights had been granted to the
women, not gained.[76] Independent activists of the First Wave of Feminism
(1923–1935) such as Nezihe Muhiddin (1889–1958) were politically ousted
during the early years of the Republic and replaced by those women who
"accepted Mustafa Kemal Atatürk's leadership unrestrictedly, 'child women'
or 'immature women' who almost adored him. . . . In the eyes of the regime,
Afet Hanım . . . represented [that kind of] 'republican woman,'" Zihnioğlu
concludes.[77]

From Afet to Sabiha?—Women and Violence

Özgür Sevgi Göral qualifies İnan as "Kemalism's girl, committed to and
charged with the duty of (living for) Kemalism,"[78] who hopelessly tried to
repay her debt, her liabilities, to Kemalism throughout her life. This might
be true from a psychological perspective since the duties on the shoulders of
the adopted daughters were so heavy and all-encompassing that there was no
room left for developing an independent, strong personality. Additionally,
İnan's childhood was characterized by several traumatizing events, such
as the early loss of her mother, the escape from her home in the district of
Thessaloniki in 1912 because of the Balkan War, and, finally, the Turkish
Liberation War, which made her an anxious girl, as stated in her biography.[79]

   On the other side, one has to investigate the relation between the female
protagonists and the emphatically military and violent character of the early
Republic. One has to notice the fact that two of the so-called adopted daughters of Atatürk—İnan and Gökçen—took part with total conviction in the
demographic engineering that was violently carried out, that their activities
were immediately related to the control of both the human and the national
body, and that the two did so as women, while at the same time the image of
the Turkish woman as the nurturing and caring mother (of children and nation) was popularized.

   I tend to argue with Nagehan Tokdoğan that the dominant approach in
feminist literature to see women as the passive object and instrument, and
often victim, of nationalism and militarism is neither wrong nor outdated, but
it is a little lopsided since women have, self-evidently, the agency to be active
in and for nationalist, fascist, or racist movements.[80]

İnan's anthropometric fieldwork was carried out from June to December 1937. Unfortunately, we do not know when exactly the team went to Region IX, the region which stretches from Tokat to Hakkari, including Elaziz/Elazığ and Dersim/Tunceli. The map included in the French and the Turkish version of İnan's PhD thesis indicates "Tunceli," but in the text and the statistics, unlike Elazığ, Tunceli is not mentioned.[81] It would be most telling to learn more about the circumstances in which the work was realized in Region IX, during the time of the last armed conflicts between the Turkish state and locals for many decades. March to September 1937 is the time of the First Dersim Maneuver (*İlk Dersim Harekâtı*), a violent conflict on a smaller scale between the army and the Alevi-Kurds of the Dersim region, while the Second Maneuver from June to September 1938 turned into a massacre of the locals. The interference of the Dersim Maneuvers and the anthropometric fieldwork is not just a temporary one; it is the time when the biographies of the two daughters, İnan and Gökçen, intersect. This is not to say that the two came into close personal contact, which they had never been fond of. However, it is the time when the dialectics between state-supported science and military action becomes palpable. While İnan had demonstrated the white supremacy and the racial unity of Turkey's inhabitants, Gökçen was taking part in eradicating the last "abscess"[82] from the otherwise healthy national body when she, as the first female Turkish combat pilot, dropped bombs on Dersim in 1938.

It should also not be forgotten that İnan had one of the *Civilized Knowledge for the Citizen* booklets dedicated to military service. As various scholars have shown, the text was more or less a copy of *Volk in Waffen* (*Nation in Arms*) by Colmar Freiherr von der Goltz, also known as Goltz Pasha,[83] though with Turkish specificities and references to Atatürk and the War of Liberation. A nation needs a strong army, the text says, because only "with the sword in its hand, a nation can remain independent."[84] A qualified commander, we read, needs, among other qualities, "mercilessness," which will protect him on a battlefield covered with blood and with thousands of dead corpses from fear and the usual weakness of the heart.[85]

Atatürk's efforts to push women to the forefront, to support a number of selected girls as legally or metaphorically adopted daughters, is generally taken at face value, as an act of giving "the other half of the society" their rights that they had been deprived of throughout the Ottoman regnum. However, this picture only can be maintained as long as we ignore the independent feminist movement from the late Ottoman era to the early years of the Republic. The moment we draw in the earlier feminists and their activities into the picture, the question arises: Why were they silenced while the "child women," as Zihnioğlu calls them, became the victorious women of the Republic? There are most certainly several answers to this question; for example, the influence of a deeper layer in the society, nurtured by the traditional Mediterranean and

Islamic expectations of female decency and chastity that favored the asexual obeying "partner" over an independent, political individual who claims the right on the own body in every respect. I'd like to take this argument a little further and add an element: From a nationalist perspective, the nation is perceived as a (healthy) body with diverse members carrying out their specific duties. Women are an integral part of this body, with duties of this or that kind, but they are definitely not allowed to question the rules of the male construct. Throughout the history of nationalism, military strength is a most important feature of the national body. While men are, without exception, expected to do military service, women's duties vary between being drafted in the same way as their male fellows, and on the other hand of the sliding scale, being restricted to the home front as nurses and mothers, or in war times as surrogate workers in the industrial sector while men are in combat.

In the Turkish case, military capability was and still is generally considered "an eternal feature of the Turkish race."[86] The inclusion of women in the combat units was an issue that attracted contradictory views in the early Turkish Republic; whereas most "modern" women carried out their tasks as caring, nurturing, and teaching civilians, a small number of women were also more directly included in the outright militarized state, where they defended the national body as racist scientists or combat pilots.[87] The campaign of the Turkish Women's Union in the 1920s was run pro-military service as a sign of equality and a right, whereas in 1935, the first female parliamentarians rejected military service, arguing that women were not fit for such a task.[88] As we can understand from the countless pictures taken of the two daughters (together with Atatürk), their very chaste or non-female sartorial habit helped to strengthen the image of the homogeneous and combat-ready state and the support of the same by the "daughters of the Republic."[89] The image of the soldierly capability of Turkish women that distinguishes them from the women of other nations can be retrieved in later discussions as well: "The Turkish women ... are courageous, self-sacrificing, and devoted to their nation. They have defended their nation in the National Independence War, and they would not hesitate to do the same in future wars," wrote Staff Major Haşmet Alptekin in 1954.[90]

CONCLUSION: DAUGHTERS AND FATHERS

In this chapter, my aim was to unveil the relation between İnan's official biography as a great historian and fighter for women's rights in relation to the ideological backdrop of the time. This backdrop emphasized the importance of female equality as a marker of a successful, civilizing, and Westernizing process; the importance of establishing a Turkish national identity based on a genuine Turkish, pre-Ottoman, history; and the importance of being able to gain and to defend the unique national identity and independence by military means. Surprisingly, from today's perspective, anthropometrics, and particularly craniometrics, played a decisive role in the discursive construction of those basic concepts. While Ottoman intellectuals had been familiar with physical and racist anthropology of the European kind, including the denigrating categorization of the Turks, empirical research aiming at a political "counterstrike" only started in Republican times.[91] In the hands of the Turkish History Institute and İnan, in the 1930s, physical anthropology turned into a tool for "proving" the essential Turkish character of the people and the country. Research culminated in the fieldwork lead by İnan in 1937 when about 64,000 individuals all around Anatolia were measured, and the data was turned into statistics, building the backbone of her PhD thesis. With the shift of the official Turkish foreign policy towards the Allies during the Second World War, however, racist anthropology lost its glamour, and İnan lost her unshakable position inside the Kemalist elite. Although she tried to convince the Turkish public once again by the publication of the Turkish version of her PhD thesis on the Turkish Races in 1947, in the following decades, she had to restrict her activities to lectures on the progress of Turkish women and their empowerment by Atatürk.

The aforementioned prerequisites of a strong state—female equality, national identity based on a genuine Turkish history, and military preparedness—seem, at first glance, to produce the contradictory image of women as tender and caregiving mothers for the future generation on the one hand, and on the other, the glorification of women who use epistemic or military violence to maintain their state. In the case of İnan, violence materialized in her efforts to determine the Turkish character of a citizen by the measures of his/her body and to create an exclusivist category of the white, short-skulled Turkish race. What can be understood from her way of arguing, of interpreting her findings, and of defending her concept is that the construction of the Turkish race by quantitative data was rather a preparation for the second decisive step: What she labored for was the establishment of a discourse community, of a common belief in the existence of and the membership in this white race. From this point of view, her work provided a pretext for the exclusion of non-brachycephalics from the national community. It also justified the punishment of those who, despite "being brachycephalics,"[92] rejected the Turkish civilizational project the way the Alevi Kurds of Dersim did. The place of women in this military society was conceived not as that of an independent self-governing individual but as a servant of the state. While on the one hand, the new Republican women such as İnan and Gökçen had to prove their devotedness and capability through hyperbolic activities, on the other hand, the physical appearance and conduct of these "child women" had to be as desexualized as possible. From this perspective, they were not "women" or "wives," but "daughters" (of Atatürk).

In 2017, a bewildering discussion popped up in the Turkish media: Had Afet İnan been the "unwed First Lady of Çankaya?" Did İnan and Atatürk have a sexual relationship? The heated discussion erupted after Süleyman Yeşilyurt, a popular author of tell-all books, repeated on a television show his well-known opinion that İnan was not an "adopted daughter" but the "unwed First Lady." It had to be that way, Yeşilyurt continued, because İnan had been much too old to be adopted. Their relationship must have been of a different kind. The video of the television show includes the comments of the other male participants: "Good comment," "She was a nice woman," and "Yes, she was a nice woman when she was younger and before she became too fat."[93] After the show, however, Yeşilyurt was severely criticized, and a court case was opened against him because "he had publicly insulted Atatürk's memory and instigated hatred and enmity among the people."[94] It seems that during the last eighty or so years, not much has changed when it comes to the relationship between women's sexuality and the nation, incorporated in the father. Conflict is incited very easily if chastity is in question, though the court does not seek to defend the girl's honor but instead the father's.

Is there really no difference between then and now? We can find a difference where we initially did not expect it: in the significance of femininity in the definition of women's societal position. Women in the early Republic were allowed to join the public sphere as civil servants, teachers, or intellectuals in very decent clothes that cover the body from the neck to the knee, and more often than not included a head cover in the form of a hat or a shawl. Women with naked arms (and legs) could be seen at a few places with strict rules and male control: at dance parties, when playing sports, and in beauty contests. With the increase of political weight and influence of Islamist or Islamic-oriented parties after 1980, we can observe a symbolic feminization of the political area.[95] In opposition to Kemalism, Islam stresses the existence of two genders and the difference between the two. Even if the female body veil covers the individual body shape, it states at the same time: "This is a female person!"

However, if we are to describe the societal place of women in today's Turkey, the requirements for being accepted, for being granted a certain space of freedom or making a career, it is still restricted by the consent and permission of the father, the necessity of obedience to male rules, and the unquestioned over-fulfillment of set expectations. In this tiring battle for a satisfying place in society, it may help to prove that one's skin color is the ideologically preferred one and that one's allegiance to the Turkish race is as obvious as the form of one's skull.

NOTES

1. Historiography on the Ottoman Empire and the Turkish Republic has faced a comprehensive revision, including earlier neglected issues such as the influence of Ottoman political ideologies and practice on the Republican politics and the history of religious and ethnic minorities.

2. Serpil Sancar, *Türk Modernleşmesinin Cinsiyeti. Erkekler Devlet, Kadınlar Aile Kurar* (Istanbul: İletişim, 20174); and Yaprak Zihnioğlu, *Kadınsız İnkılap. Nezihe Muhiddin, Kadınlar Halk Fırkası, Kadın Birliği* (Istanbul: Metis, 2003).

3. Ayşe Gül Altınay, *The Myth of the Military-Nation: Militarism, Gender, and Education in Turkey* (New York: Palgrave Macmillan, 2004); and Rasim Özgür Dönmez, "Coup d'Etats and the Masculine Turkish Political Sphere: Modernization without Strong Democratization," in *Gendered Identities: Criticizing Patriarchy in Turkey*, edited by Rasim Özgür Dönmez and Fazilet Ahu Özmen, 1–32 (Lanham, MD: Lexington, 2013).

4. Murat Ergin, *Is the Turk a White Man? Race and Modernity in the Making of Turkish Identity* (Chicago: Haymarket Books, 2018); and Nazan Maksudyan, *Türklüğü Ölçmek. Bilimkurgusal Antropoloji ve Türk Milliyetçiliğinin Irkçı Çehresi 1925–1939* (Istanbul: Metis 2005).

5. J. Wang, J. C. Thornton, and S. Kolesnik, "Anthropometry in Body Composition: An Overview," *Annals of the New York Academy of Sciences* 904 (2000): 317.

6. Raj Bhopal, "The Beautiful Skull and Blumenbach's Errors," *The British Medical Journal (BMJ)* 335 (2007): 1309.

7. Stephen Jay Gould, *Der falsch vermessene Mensch* (Basel: Springer, 2013), 101.

8. Augustin Weisbach, *Die Schädelform der Türken: mit 3 Tafeln* (Wien: Selbstverl. des Verf., 1873); idem, *Körpermessungen verschiedener Menschenrassen* (Berlin: Wiegandt, Hempel & Parey, 1878); Ivanovsky, *Les Turkmènes et les Turcs d'après les recherches crâniométriques* (Moscou, 1891); Adolphe Bloch, "De l'origine des Turcs et en particulier des Osmanlis," *Bulletins et Mémoires de la Société d'anthropologie de Paris*, VI° Série. Tome 6 fascicule 3 (1915): 158–68; Eugène Pittard, *Les Peuples des Balkans. Esquisses anthropologiques* (Paris: Attinger, 1920); idem, "La taille, l'indice céphalique et l'indice nasal de 300 Turcs osmanlis de la péninsule des Balkans," *Revue Anthropologique* 21 (1911): 488–93; idem, "Comparaison de quelques caractères somatologiques chez les Turcs et chez les Grecs," *Revue Anthropologique* 25 (1915): 447–54.

9. For some more names and examples, see Emmanuel Szurek, "The Sick Man of Europe: A Transnational History of Kemalist Science," in *Kemalism: The Transnational Making of Kemalism in the Post-Ottoman Space*, edited by Nathalie Clayer, Fabio Giomi, and Emmanuel Szurek, 277–79 (London: I.B. Tauris, 2018).

10. Weisbach frankly confesses that he stole the bones "in the benevolent dark of the Cypress wood" (Weisbach, *Die Schädelform der Türken*, 4).

11. Weisbach, *Die Schädelform der Türken*, 5–6. That is to say, that for Weisbach, a Turkish skull was a Turkish skull because it was not a Croatian or Armenian skull.

12. Weisbach, *Die Schädelform der Türken*, 19–20.

13. Szurek, "The Sick Man of Europe," 279.

14. M.Şükrü Hanioğlu, *Bir siyasal düşünür olarak Doktor Abdullah Cevdet ve dönemi* (Istanbul: Üçdal Neşriyat, 1981 [1966]).

15. Afet İnan, *Türk halkının antropolojik karakterleri ve Türkiye tarihi. Türk ırkının vatanı Anadolu. 64.000 kişi üzerinde anket* (Ankara: Türk Tarih Kurumu Basımevi, 1947).

16. An important source of biographical details is, very naturally, Afet İnan's so-called autobiography: Arı İnan (ed.), *Prof. Dr. Afet İnan* (Istanbul: Remzi Kitabevi, 2005). One needs to be aware that this book not only includes the same narrative constrictions as every autobiography does but also contains chapters written by her daughter, Arı İnan, based on earlier works by the mother (İnan, *Prof. Dr. Afet İnan*, 9).

17. İnan, *Prof. Dr. Afet İnan*, 98–99.

18. Afet İnan, *Vatandaş için Medeni Bilgiler* (Istanbul: Devlet Matbaası, 1931).

19. Fatma Gürses provides details on the process of creating the *Medeni Bilgiler* and a list with all themes ("Kemalizm'in Model Ders Kitabı: Vatandaş için Medeni Bilgiler," *Gazi Akademik Bakış* 7 [2010]: 240).

20. Pinar Bilgin and Basak Ince, "Security and Citizenship in the Global South: In/securing Citizens in Early Republican Turkey (1923–1946)," *International Relations* 29, no. 4 (2015): 510.

21. Afet İnan, *Medenî bilgiler ve M. Kemal Atatürk'ün el yazıları* (Ankara: Türk Tarih Kurumu Basımevi, 1988): 7. Quoted after Altınay, *The Myth of the Military-Nation*, 14.

22. Mustafa Kemal Atatürk, *Medeni Bilgiler. Türk Milletin El Kitabı*, edited by Afet İnan, 41–42 (Istanbul: Toplumsal Dönüş Yayınları, 2008). My translation. This is a version of *Vatandaş için Medeni Bilgiler* in modern Turkish where the editor has decided to give the credit of author to Atatürk.

23. Altınay, *The Myth of the Military-Nation*, 15–16.

24. Afet İnan, *Türk Tarihinin Ana Hatları* (Ankara: Devlet Matbaası, 1930).

25. Afet İnan, "Prolegomena to an Outline of Turkish History," in *Modernism: Representations of National Culture: Discourses of Collective Identity in Central and Southeast Europe 1770–1945: Texts and Commentaries*, volume III/2 [en ligne], edited by Ahmet Ersoy, Maciej Górny, and Vangelis Kechriotis, § 8 (Budapest: Central European University Press, 2010). Available online at http://books.openedition.org/ceup/1027.

26. Ibid.

27. Ibid., *§ 9*.

28. Ibid.

29. There is no need to go into all the details of the thesis in the framework of this chapter. Ample literature on the issue provides information on the content, its

influence on academic research, and the emerging critique. E.g., Etienne Copeaux, *Türk Tarih Tezinden Türk Islam Sentezine* (Istanbul: Tarih Vakfi Yurt Yayınları, 2013); or Büşra Ersanlı, İktidar *ve Tarih. Türkiye'de "Resmî Tarih" Tezinin Oluşumu* (1929–1937) (Istanbul: İletişim, 2018).

30. İnan, *Türk Tarihinin Ana Hatları*, 31–34. There is indeed a change of vocabulary from the *Medeni Bilgiler* to the *Ana Hatları*, from *cins* to ırk meaning "race." This may be partly due to the effect of the emerging language "purification," but generally, the use of the anthropological vocabulary is not very consistent in the 1920s and 1930s.

31. Ibid., 31.

32. Ibid., 32.

33. Ibid., 33.

34. Ibid., 34.

35. Ergin, *Is the Turk a White Man?*, 99.

36. Afet İnan, *Tarihten Evvel ve Tarih Fecrinde* (Ankara: Maarif Vekaleti, 1932).

37. Ibid., 31.

38. For further details on Köprülü's approach to Turkish history and racist concepts, see Markus Dressler, "Mehmed Fuad Köprülü and the Turkish History Thesis," in *Ölümünün 50. Yılında Uluslararası M. Fuad Köprülü Türkoloji ve Beşeri Bilimler Sempozyumu Bildirileri*, edited by Fikret Turan, Emine Temel, and Harun Korkmaz), 245–53 (Istanbul: Kültür Sanat, 2017.

39. For a detailed account of this controversy, see Ergin, *Is the Turk a White Man*, 133–38. Zeki Velidi Togan spent four years at German universities. Intriguingly enough, in 1937, he sent from Bonn a letter to İnan, rather a plea letter. After praising her work and Atatürk's immeasurable value, Togan describes his own misery in exile where he is unable to work for the sake of the Republic as fruitful as he could were he in Turkey. He asks İnan to intercede on his behalf and to make Atatürk call Togan back to Turkey (Hüsnü Özlü, "Afetinan'ın Cenevre Günleri ve Tarih Çalışmaları," *Çağdaş Türkiye Tarihi Araştırmaları Dergisi* X, no. 22 (2011): 182–83). On Togan and the First History Congress, see also Ersanlı, İktidar *ve Tarih*, 149. The "restructuring" of the university in Istanbul in 1933 (*tasfiye*) is immediately related to the enforced implementation of the Turkish History Thesis but cannot be discussed in the framework of this chapter.

40. Similar to the denunciation of Köprülü and Togan during the Congress, Professor Avram Galanti (1873–1961), an expert of old-oriental languages, was booed when he questioned the scientific correctness of the Sun Language Theory, and he was likewise excluded from Darülfünun in 1933 (Jens Peter Laut, *Das Türkische als Ursprache? Sprachwissenschaftliche Theorien in der Zeit des erwachenden türkischen Nationalismus* [Wiesbaden: Harrassowitz, 2000], 29).

41. Just one example for the theses' lasting effect in Turkey's cultural heritage: Mehmet Kurtkaya, "I have proven Ataturk's Sun Language Theory!," http://sunlanguage.org/, accessed August 10, 2018.

42. Ergin, *Is the Turk a White Man*, 158.

43. Hans-Lukas Kieser, "Türkische National Revolution, anthropologisch gekrönt. Kemal Atatürk und Eugène Pittard," *Historische Anthropologie* 14, no. 1 (2006): 106.

44. Kieser, "Türkische Nationalrevolution," 107.

45. Ergin, *Is the Turk a White Man*, 160.

46. Kieser, "Türkische Nationalrevolution," 111.

47. Ibid., 112.

48. Eugène Pittard, *Les races et l'histoire: introduction ethnologique à l'histoire* (Paris: La Renaissance du Livre, 1924), 47. Quoted after Kieser, "Türkische Nationalrevolution," 112. In a publication of 1911, Pittard had come to different, not so clear-cut conclusions ("La taille, l'indice céphalique et l'indice nasal de 300 Turcs-Osmanlis de la Péninsule des Balkans", *Revue Anthropologique* 21 [1911]: 488–93). In an earlier period, brachycephaly had been considered a characteristic of the underdeveloped "mongoloid" and "yellow race." As Bloch put it in 1915: "Or, la brachycéphalie des Turcs Osmanlis est, pour nous, un caractère atavique rappelant leur origine mongoloïde, la brachycéphalie étant généralement un caractère propre à la race jaune" (Bloch, "De l'origine des Turcs," 164).

49. The thesis was published in 1941 and was titled *L'Anatolie le Pay de la "Race" Turque*. The quotation marks at *Race* can be related to the influence of Pittard, who still opted for a careful use of the term, much more so than his eager student.

50. There is a persistent rumor that the work was done on skeletons, which is definitely not true.

51. İnan, *Recherches sur les charactères*, 51–52.

52. Ibid., 151–55.

53. Ibid., 162.

54. Ibid., 4–5.

55. Ergin, *Is the Turk a White Man*, 124 and passim.

56. Ibid., 201.

57. İnan, *Recherches sur les charactères*, 50.

58. Ergin, *Is the Turk a White Man*, 202.

59. Sibel Özbudun Demirer, "Anthropology as a Nation-Building Rhetoric: The Shaping of Turkish Anthropology (from 1850s to 1940s)," *Dialectical Anthropology* 35, no. 1 (2011): 126.

60. Suavi Aydın, "Cumhuriyet'in ideolojik şekillenmesinde Antropolojinin Rolü: Irkçı Paradigmanın Yükselişi ve Düşüşü," in *Modern Türkiye'de Siyasi Düşünce*. Cilt II: Kemalizm, edited by T. Bora, M. Gültegingil, and Ahmet İnsel, 344–369, 365 (Istanbul: İletişim Yayınları, 2001).

61. "What the search for a missing Ottoman skull says about Turkish politics," Washington Post, April 26, 2016, https://www.washingtonpost.com/news/world-views/wp/2016/04/26/what-the-search-for-a-missing-ottoman-skull-says-about-turkish-politics/?noredirect=on&utm_term=.dfa374964c99, accessed August 9, 2018. Mimar Sinan (c. 1488–1588) was the chief Ottoman architect and civil engineer for the Sultans of his time. He was a product of the *Devşirme* system, born into a Christian family but raised and educated as Muslim to serve the Ottoman state. In their efforts to include irrefutably significant personalities of the Ottoman history, the authors of the new Turkish history had to find new "proofs" of the Turkish character and body of those personalities. The "retrieval" and measuring of Mimar Sinan's skull is an example of these efforts.

62. Halil Demircioğlu, "Antropoloji ve Tarih. Bir Kitap vesilesiyle," *Ankara Üniversitesi Dil ve Tarih-Coğrafya Fakültesi Dergisi* 6, nos. 1–2 (1948): 52.

63. Ibid., 54.

64. Afet İnan, "Türkiye Tarihi ve Antropolojisi Üzerine," *Ankara Üniversitesi Dil ve Tarih—Coğrafya Fakültesi Dergisi* 7, no. 1 (1949): 203–35.

65. Ayşe Afetinan, *Mimar Koca Sinan* (Ankara: Ankara güzel sanatlar matbaasında, 1956).

66. A. Afetinan, *The Emancipation of the Turkish Woman* (Amsterdam: United Nations, 1962), 60.

67. There is an abundance of similar publications and formulations. To give just one example: İsmail Uzun, "Kadın Haklarının Kazanılmasında Bir Cumhuriyet Kadını: Afet İnan (1908–1985)," *Ahi Evran* Üniversitesi *Sosyal Bilimleri Enstitüsü Dergisi* 3, no. 1 (2017): 73–85.

68. Ece Orhon, "İnançlı bir Cumhuriyet Kadını," *Cumhuriyet Dergi* 606 (November 2, 1997): 4–5.

69. Ercan Dolapçı, "Cumhuriyet kızı: Afet İnan," *Aydınlık*, May 12, 2017, https://www.aydinlik.com.tr/ozgurluk-meydani/2017-mayis/cumhuriyet-kizi-afet-inan, accessed August 3, 2018.

70. İnan, *Prof. Dr. Afet İnan*, 87.

71. Nazan Aksoy, *Kurgulanmış Benlikler. Otobiografi, Kadın, Cumhuriyet* (Istanbul: İletişim Yayınları 2009): 151–53.

72. Afetinan, *The Emancipation of the Turkish Woman*, 55–56. What İnan does not say is that, in 1935, the Turkish Women's Union organized the 12th congress in Istanbul—an international event, this time with women's suffrage as their key topic. The Union was ordered to dissolve itself in the same year (Altınay, *The Myth of the Military-Nation*, 54).

73. İnan, *Prof. Dr. Afet İnan*, 100–1.

74. Hülya Adak, "Suffragettes of the Empire, Daughters of the Republic: Women Auto/biographers Narrate National History (1918–1935)," *New Perspectives on Turkey* 36 (2007): 27–51.

75. Adak, "Suffragettes of the Empire," 44.

76. Zihnioğlu, *Kadınsız İnkılap*.

77. Ibid., 23.

78. Sevgi Özgür Göral, "Afet İnan," *Modern Türkiye'de Siyasi Düşünce. Cilt II: Kemalizm*, edited by T. Bora, M. Gültegingil, and Ahmet İnsel, 220 (Istanbul: İletişim Yayınları, 2001).

79. İnan, *Prof. Dr. Afet İnan*, 71.

80. Nagehan Tokdoğan, "Sevginin ve Nefretin Eğilip Bükülebilirliği: Kadınların Milliyetçiliği," in *Milliyetçilik ve Toplumsal Cinsiyet*, edited by Simten Coşar and Aylin Özman (Istanbul: İletişim, 2015): 111–40.

81. İnan, *Türk halkının antropolojik karakterleri*, 74.

82. For this topos of the Alevi-Kurdish Dersim region as an abscess, in Turkish çıban, in the Turkish body, and the Dersim Maneuvers, see, for example, Hans-Lukas Kieser, "Alevis, Armenians and Kurds in Unionist-Kemalist Turkey (1908–1938)," in *Turkey's Alevi enigma. A comprehensive overview*, edited by Jost Jongerden and

P. J. White (Leiden: Brill, 2003): 177–96; Ayşe Hür, "Dersim hakkında 'kuyruklu' yalanlar," *Radikal,* November 16, 2014, http://www.radikal.com.tr/yazarlar/ayse-hur/dersim-hakkinda-kuyruklu-yalanlar-1232341/, accessed August 4, 2018.

83. Altınay, *The Myth of the Military-Nation,* 14–15.

84. Atatürk, *Medeni Bilgiler,* 234.

85. Ibid., 231.

86. Ayşe Gül Altınay, "Sabiha Gökçen'den Sevgi Soysal'a, Kezbanlardan Kadın Vicdani Retçiler: Militarizmin Feminist Eleştirileri," *Dipnot* 7 (2011): 26.

87. "Sabiha Gökçen's success … also opens the Pandora's Box regarding women's active participation in the development of militarism as a means to solve ethnic and political problems in Turkey" (Altınay, *The Myth of the Military-Nation,* 58).

88. Suat Derviş, "Document 6," in *Rosa Manus (1881–1942): The International Life and Legacy of a Jewish Dutch,* edited by Myriam Everard and Francisca de Haan, 393 (Leiden, Boston: Brill, 2017).

89. In one picture, Sabiha Gökçen poses next to her aircraft with the bombs she is going to drop on Dersim lined up beside her, the biggest bomb standing upright, close to her body and in her arms (Hür, "Dersim hakkında 'kuyruklu' yalanlar"). The picture deserves a broader analysis.

90. Haşmet Alptekin, *Milli Savunma Hizmeti'nde Kadın* (Ankara: E.U. Rs. Basimevi, 1954): 7–8. Quoted after Şule Toktaş, "Nationalism, Modernization and the Military in Turkey: Women Officers in the Turkish Armed Forces," *Oriente Moderno* 23, no. 84 (2004): 257.

91. Özbudun Demirer, "Anthropology as a Nation-Building Rhetoric," 114.

92. For the Turkish state's efforts to "include" the Kurdish population in the civilizational project by means of craniometrics arguments, see Zafer Toprak, "Westphalia'dan Dersim'e Toplum Mühendisliği ve Antropolojik Irk Sorunu," in *Darwin'den Dersim'e Cumhuriyet Antropolojisi,* edited by Zafer Toprak, 563–66 (Istanbul: Doğan Kitap, 20153).

93. "Atatürk'e hakaret eden Süleyman Yeşilyurt ve derin tarihçiler," *YouTube,* https://www.youtube.com/watch?v=HUPzmFeE9oA, accessed August 10, 2018.

94. "Süleyman Yeşilyurt'a Atatürk'e hakaretten hapis cezası," *NTV,* November 1, 2017, https://www.ntv.com.tr/turkiye/suleyman-yesilyurta-ataturkehakaretten-hapis-cezasi,aWHatQjqMEC8jEsu0RYDCw, accessed August 8, 2018.

95. Ayşe Saktanber, "Whose Virtue Is This? The Virtue Party and Women in Islamist Politics in Turkey," in *Right-Wing Women: From Conservatives to Extremists around the World,* edited by by Margaret Power and P. Bacchetta, 59 (New York: Routledge, 2002).

RESOURCES

Adak, Hülya. "Suffragettes of the Empire, Daughters of the Republic: Women Auto/biographers Narrate National History (1918–1935)." *New Perspectives on Turkey* 36 (2007): 27–51.

Afetinan, A. [Afet İnan]. *The Emancipation of the Turkish Woman*. Amsterdam: United Nations, 1962.

Afetinan, Ayşe [Afet İnan]. *Mimar Koca Sinan*. Ankara: Ankara güzel sanatlar matbaasında, 1956.

Aksoy, Nazan. *Kurgulanmış Benlikler. Otobiografi, Kadın, Cumhuriyet*. Istanbul: İletişim Yayınları, 2009.

Altınay, Ayşe Gül. "Sabiha Gökçen'den Sevgi Soysal'a, Kezbanlardan Kadın Vicdani Retçiler: Militarizmin Feminist Eleştirileri." *Dipnot* 7 (2011): 23–42.

———. *The Myth of the Military-Nation: Militarism, Gender, and Education in Turkey*, New York: Palgrave Macmillan, 2004.

Atatürk, Mustafa Kemal. *Medeni Bilgiler. Türk Milletin El Kitabı*, edited by Afet İnan. Istanbul: Toplumsal Dönüş Yayınları, 2008.

"Atatürk'e hakaret eden Süleyman Yeşilyurt ve derin tarihçiler", https://www.youtube.com/watch?v=HUPzmFeE9oA. Accessed August 10, 2018.

Aydın, Suavi. "Cumhuriyet'in ideolojik şekillenmesinde Antropolojinin Rolü: Irkçı Paradigmanın Yükselişi ve Düşüşü." In *Modern Türkiye'de Siyasi Düşünce. Cilt II: Kemalizm*, edited by T. Bora, M. Gültegingil, and Ahmet İnsel, 344–369. Istanbul: İletişim Yayınları, 2001.

Bilgin, Pinar, and Basak Ince. "Security and Citizenship in the Global South: In/securing Citizens in Early Republican Turkey (1923–1946)." *International Relations* 29, no. 4 (2015): 500–20.

Bhopal, Raj. "The Beautiful Skull and Blumenbach's Errors." *The British Medical Journal* 335 (2007): 1308–9.

Bloch, Adolphe. "De l'origine des Turcs et en particulier des Osmanlis." *Bulletins et Mémoires de la Société d'anthropologie de Paris*, VI° Série, Tome 6 fascicule 3 (1915): 158–68.

Copeaux, Etienne. *Türk Tarih Tezinden Türk Islam Sentezine*. Istanbul: Tarih Vakfi Yurt Yayınları, 2013.

Demircioğlu, Halil. "Antropoloji ve Tarih. Bir Kitap Vesilesiyle." *Ankara Üniversitesi Dil ve Tarih-Coğrafya Fakültesi Dergisi* 6, no. 1.2 (1948): 49–67.

Derviş, Suat. "Document 6." In *Rosa Manus (1881–1942): The International Life and Legacy of a Jewish Dutch*, edited by Myriam Everard and Francisca de Haan, 389–394. Leiden, Boston: Brill, 2017.

Dolapçı, Ercan. "Cumhuriyet kızı: Afet İnan." *Aydınlık*. March 12, 2017. https://www.aydinlik.com.tr/ozgurluk-meydani/2017-mayis/cumhuriyet-kizi-afet-inan. Accessed August 3, 2018.

Dönmez, Rasim Özgür. "Coup d'Etats and the Masculine Turkish Political Sphere: Modernization without Strong Democratization." In *Gendered Identities: Criticizing Patriarchy in Turkey*, edited by Rasim Özgür Dönmez and Fazilet Ahu Özmen, 1–32. Lanham, MD: Lexington, 2013.

Dressler, Markus. "Mehmed Fuad Köprülü and the Turkish History Thesis." In *Ölümünün 50. Yılında Uluslararası M. Fuad Köprülü Türkoloji ve Beşeri Bilimler Sempozyumu Bildirileri*, edited by Fikret Turan, Emine Temel and Harun Korkmaz, 245–53. Istanbul: Kültür Sanat, 2017.

210   Béatrice Hendrich

Ergin, Murat. *Is the Turk a White Man? Race and Modernity in the Making of Turkish Identity*. Chicago: Haymarket Books, 2018.

Ersanlı, Büşra. *İktidar ve Tarih. Türkiye'de "Resmî Tarih" Tezinin Oluşumu (1929–1937)*. İstanbul: İletişim, 2018[7].

Gould, Stephen Jay. *Der falsch vermessene Mensch*. Basel: Springer, 2013.

Göral, Sevgi Özgür. "Afet İnan." In *Modern Türkiye'de Siyasi Düşünce. Cilt II: Kemalizm*, edited by T. Bora, M. Gültegingil, and Ahmet İnsel, 220–27. İstanbul: İletişim Yayınları, 2001.

Gürses, Fatma. "Kemalizm'in Model Ders Kitabı: Vatandaş için Medeni Bilgiler." *Gazi Akademik Bakış* 7 (2010): 233–49.

Hanioğlu, M. Şükrü. *Bir siyasal düşünür olarak Doktor Abdullah Cevdet ve dönemi*. İstanbul: Üçdal Neşriyat, 1981 [1966].

Hür, Ayşe. "Dersim Hakkında 'Kuyruklu' Yalanlar." *Radikal*. November 16, 2014. http://www.radikal.com.tr/yazarlar/ayse-hur/dersim-hakkinda-kuyruklu-yalanlar-1232341/. Accessed August 4, 2018.

İnan, Afet. "Prolegomena to an Outline of Turkish History." In *Modernism: Representations of National Culture: Discourses of Collective Identity in Central and Southeast Europe 1770–1945: Texts and Commentaries*, volume III/2 [en ligne],edited by Ahmet Ersoy, Maciej Górny, and Vangelis Kechriotis. Budapest: Central European University Press, 2010. Available online at http://books.openedition.org/ceup/1027.

———. *Medenî bilgiler ve M. Kemal Atatürk'ün el yazıları*. Ankara: Türk Tarih Kurumu Basımevi, 1988.

———. "Türkiye Tarihi ve Antropolojisi Üzerine." *Ankara Üniversitesi Dil ve Tarih—Coğrafya Fakültesi Dergisi* 7, no. 1 (1949): 203–35.

———. *Türk Halkının Antropolojik Karakterleri ve Türkiye Tarihi. Türk Irkının Vatanı Anadolu (64.000 kişi üzerinde anket)* (Türk Tarih Kurumu Yayınlarıdan VII. Seri, No. 15). Ankara: Türk Tarih Kurumu Basımevi, 1947.

———. *L'Anatolie le Pay de la 'Race' Turque. Publication de la Faculté des Sciences Economiques et Sociales de l'Université de Genève*. Genève: Albert Kundig, 1941.

———. *Recherches sur les caractères anthropologique des population de la Turquie* (Thèse présentée à la Faculté des Sciences Economiques et Sociales de l'Université de Genève, pour l'obtention du grade de Dokteur en Sociologie). Albert Kundig : Genève, 1939.

———. *Tarihten Evvel ve Tarih Fecrinde*. Ankara: Maarif Vekaleti 1932.

———. *Türk Tarihinin Ana Hatları*. Ankara: Devlet Matbaası, 1930.

———. *Vatandaş için Medeni Bilgiler*. İstanbul: Devlet Matbaası, 1930–1933.

———. *Prof. Dr. Afet İnan*. İstanbul: Remzi Kitabevi, 2005.

Ivanovsky, n.n. *Les Turkmènes et les Turcs d'après les recherches crâniométriques*. Moscou: n.p., 1891.

Kieser, Hans-Lukas. "Türkische Nationalrevolution, Anthropologisch Gekrönt. Kemal Atatürk und Eugène Pittard." *Historische Anthropologie* 14, no. 1 (2006): 105–18.

———. "Alevis, Armenians and Kurds in Unionist-Kemalist Turkey (1908–1938)." In *Turkey's Alevi enigma. A comprehensive overview*, edited by Jost Jongerden and P. J. White, 177–96. Leiden: Brill, 2003.

Laut, Jens Peter. *Das Türkische als Ursprache? Sprachwissenschaftliche Theorien in der Zeit des erwachenden türkischen Nationalismus*. Wiesbaden: Harrassowitz 2000.

Maksudyan, Nazan. *Türklüğü Ölçmek. Bilimkurgusal Antropoloji ve Türk Milliyetçiliğinin Irkçı Çehresi 1925–1939*. İstanbul: Metis 2005.

Orhon, Ece. "İnançlı bir Cumhuriyet Kadını." *Cumhuriyet Dergi* 606 (November 2, 1997): 4–5.

Özbudun Demirer, Sibel. "Anthropology as a Nation-Building Rhetoric: The Shaping of Turkish Anthropology (from 1850s to 1940s)." *Dialectical Anthropology* 35, no. 1 (2011): 111–29.

Özlü, Hüsnü. "Afetinan'ın Cenevre Günleri ve Tarih Çalışmaları." *Çağdaş Türkiye Tarihi Araştırmaları Dergisi* X, no. 22 (2011): 165–87.

Pittard, Eugène. *Les races et l'histoire: introduction ethnologique à l'histoire*. Paris: La Renaissance du Livre, 1924.

———. *Les Peuples des Balkans. Esquisses anthropologiques*. Paris: Attinger, 1920.

———. "Comparaison de Quelques Caractères Somatologiques Chez les Turcs et Chez les Grecs." *Revue Anthropologique* 25 (1915): 447–54.

———. "La taille, l'indice céphalique et l'indice nasal de 300 Turcs Osmanlis de la péninsule des Balkans." *Revue Anthropologique* 21 (1911): 488–93.

Saktanber, Ayşe. "Whose Virtue Is This? The Virtue Party and Women in Islamist Politics in Turkey." In *Right-Wing Women: From Conservatives to Extremists around the World*, edited by Margaret Power and P. Bacchetta, 59–67. New York: Routledge, 2002.

Sancar, Serpil. *Türk Modernleşmesinin Cinsiyeti. Erkekler Devlet, Kadınlar Aile Kurar*. İstanbul: İletişim, 2017.

"Süleyman Yeşilyurt'a Atatürk'e Hakaretten Hapis Cezası," *NTV*. November 1, 2017. https://www.ntv.com.tr/turkiye/suleyman-yesilyurta-ataturkehakaretten-hapis-cezasi,aWHatQjqMEC8jEsu0RYDCw. Accessed August 8, 2018.

Szurek, Emmanuel. "The Sick Man of Europe: A Transnational History of Kemalist Science." In *Kemalism: The Transnational Making of Kemalism in the Post-Ottoman Space*, edited by Nathalie Clayer, Fabio Giomi, and Emmanuel Szurek, 265–309. London: I. B. Tauris, 2018.

Tokdoğan, Nagehan. "Sevginin ve Nefretin Eğilip Bükülebilirliği: Kadınların Milliyetçiliği." In *Milliyetçilik ve Toplumsal Cinsiyet*, edited by Simten Coşar and Aylin Özman, 111–40. İstanbul: İletişim, 2015.

Toktaş, Şule. "Nationalism, Modernization and the Military in Turkey: Women Officers in the Turkish Armed Forces." *Oriente Moderno* 23, no. 84 (2004): 247–67.

Toprak, Zafer. "Westphalia'dan Dersim'e Toplum Mühendisliği ve Antropolojik Irk Sorunu." In *Darwin'den Dersim'e Cumhuriyet Antropolojisi*, edited by Zafer Toprak, 531–84. İstanbul: Doğan Kitap, 2015.

Uzun, İsmail. "Kadın Haklarının Kazanılmasında Bir Cumhuriyet Kadını: Afet İnan (1908–1985)." *Ahi Evran Üniversitesi Sosyal bilimleri Enstitüsü Dergisi* 3, no. 1 (2017): 73–85.

Wang, J., J. C. Thornton, and S. Kolesnik. "Anthropometry in Body Composition: An Overview." *Annals of the New York Academy of Sciences* 904 (2000): 317–26.

Weisbach, Augustin. *Die Schädelform der Türken: mit 3 Tafeln*, Wien: Selbstverl. des Verf., 1873.

Weisbach, Augustin. *Körpermessungen verschiedener Menschenrassen*. Berlin: Wiegandt, Hempel & Parey, 1878.

Zihnioğlu, Yaprak. *Kadınsız İnkılap. Nezihe Muhiddin, Kadınlar Halk Fırkası, Kadın Birliği*. Istanbul: Metis, 2003.

Chapter Seven

Towards an Islamic Patriarchal Society in Turkey?: Changing Gender Roles in the Secondary School Social Studies Textbooks

Gül Arıkan Akdağ

Gender equality and gender roles have been important dimensions of national identity formation of societies all over the world, including Turkey. In the Turkish literature, the main debate revolves around the different perceptions and policies of the Kemalist versus conservative circles on the issue. In fact, it is identified as an important dimension of the larger debate on religion between the secular and conservative governments in Turkey. As such, the incumbency of the Justice and Development Party (JDP) after the 2002 elections has brought into debate the changing role of women within the society. Although the headscarf issue has been the most politicized dimension of the confrontation that has been evaluated under religious freedoms, more silent dimensions have emerged that seem to be the extension of the patriarchal perception of the Islamist ideology concerning the role of women in the society. Current studies state a dichotomy in the JDP's policies on gender. In the legal field, several ameliorations on gender equality have been done, where lifting the ban on the headscarf being the most important and evaluated as a reform increasing the public presence of covered women. In practice, there is an increasing patriarchy that retreats women from the social, economic, and political sphere and looks to limit them to the domestic sphere. What appears to be a dichotomy, in fact, may not be and can serve to reinforce the basic patriarchal characters of the Islamic society envisioned to be formed by the JDP. The lifting of the ban on the headscarf may not result in the amelioration of individual freedoms that expands the role of the women in the social, economic, and political sphere but can become a means to legitimize patriarchy and exclude these women from these spheres. The major question emerges as to which of these two arguments fit the JDP's gender strategy. This study argues that the lifting of the ban on the headscarf becomes a means to legitimize and increase the existing patriarchy that is present in the Turkish

214 Gül Arıkan Akdağ

Society by giving it an Islamic character. This process may be defined as the Islamization of the patriarchy.

The contribution of this chapter to the book's main objective is its effort to analyze the attempt of the JDP to incorporate the patriarchal relations in the society in its new definition of Islamic nation through the analysis of the secondary school textbooks. Such an analysis is expected to provide a link between the theoretical levels of the nation-building efforts to more concrete policy applications, such as education that directly affects its citizens' national identity formation. Although a considerable number of studies in the sociological and educational field analyzes the changing gender perceptions in school books during the JDP reign, they are limited in the sense that, first, they do not focus on the headscarf issue, which is the most important link to the political sphere. Second, they mostly cover the period when liberalism was an important dimension of the JDP's identity formation, leaving untouched the period where nationalism becomes the main components of its ideology. By linking education policies to political ideology and covering the period after the JDP's increasing nationalist conservatism, the study aims to contribute to the existing literature.

As early education is extremely important in identity formation, the study prefers to conduct its analysis in secondary education social studies textbooks, which are prepared and provided by the Turkish Ministry of National Education. It focuses especially on textbooks distributed for the academic year of 2017–2018, which is when the government applied an extensive change in the content and curricula of these books. The main focus is given to the messages sent indirectly through the illustrations appearing in the textbooks. As such, the study focuses especially on the appearance of the women in these photos. The study chooses to use a quantitative method to perform the analysis by counting and coding the topic where the photo is placed, the number of women/men appearing in the photos, their physical appearance, and their tasks. First, the study bases its basic argument to the existing literature on the JDP's patriarchic perception and its reflection on education policies. Then, the main hypothesis and methodology of the study are evaluated. Lastly, the general findings of the study are revealed and linked to the JDP's patriarchy perception.

NATIONAL IDENTITY FORMATION AND PATRIARCHY: THE JDP'S IDEOLOGY AND THE ISLAMIZATION OF PATRIARCHY

Gender roles and the formation of patriarchy are important dimensions of national identity formation on different societies.[1] The control of women and their sexuality by men was also an important dimension of the nationalization process of Western societies.[2] As such, women were mostly integrated into the nation based on their natural characteristics that made them the primary actor of the private life as wives and/or mothers. As a result, they were mostly excluded from the social, economic, and political spheres. This patriarchal relation was only partly overcome with the increase in feminist movements fighting for women's social and political rights. Albeit having a different path, a similar situation was also present in the nationality formation process of later nationalized, post-colonial states in the Middle East and Africa. Women were used by men as an icon in the fight against colonialism and the legitimization of the modernization process but with their natural characteristics as the mothers of the nation who were responsible of taking care of the next generation and educating them.[3] They were mostly used in the modernization process as the faces of the new modern country, and they were modernly dressed as nurses, teachers, and doctors, yet they still were in roles defined by the men. In fact, the patriarchic relations were left untouched where in reality women were still the main actors of the private life, mostly excluded from the economic and political life. These traditional roles became even stronger once the countries' independence and modernization process have succeeded.[4]

Studies find a similar development in Turkey's modernization and nationalization process. Although women were reflected by the founding fathers of the Turkish Republic as driving actors of modernization, the patriarchal characteristics of the Turkish society and its reinforcement by political actors were still important characteristics of the Turkish nationalization and modernization process. Defined by scholars as "state feminism," the early Republican era was characterized by the projection of women as important actors of the newly founded modern Republic. Within this respect, women were given the right of equal education and economic and political participation. The social and political integration of women became the main dimension of the fight of the secular Republic against the Islamist organization of the state and society. Even still, the main roles of women outside the private sphere were defined by the men of the Turkish Republic, where they were mostly projected with their natural characteristics as breeders and educators of the new generation.[5] With effectuated reforms, the Turkish women were emancipated in the social, economic, and political life, but they were not liberated,[6] since their role in the new nation was firmly defined by the Republican men. Furthermore, these reforms only reached women in large cities and nearly left untouched the large share of women living in the other parts of Turkey.[7] As a result, the Republican reforms far from eliminated the patriarchal character of the Turkish society. Since then, studies indicate the gradual return of women to their traditional roles in the private sphere and the reinforcement of patriarchal relations as more conservative political parties gained political power in Turkey.

The reign of the JDP has increased the debate on gender and patriarchy since the party defines itself in opposition with the secular principles imposed by the Republicans and tries to formulate a new society based on Islamic and conservative values. Authors argue that Turkey is witnessing a gradual Islamization under the rule of the JDP.[8] As such, gender roles become an important dimension of the reformation of the Turkish society by the JDP. However, current studies state a dichotomy in the JDP's policies concerning gender. In the legal field, several ameliorations on gender equality were done where lifting the ban on the headscarf being the most important and evaluated as a reform increasing the public presence of covered women. In practice, there is an increasing patriarchy that retreats women from the social, economic, and political spheres and limits them to the domestic sphere. According to Coşar and Yeğenoğlu,[9] the JDP creates a flexible perception of patriarchy, named as neoliberal-conservative patriarchy, where improvements at the legal level coexists with the retreat of women from the public sphere to the familial sphere. Similar arguments are also developed by other studies. According to them, while the JDP made several amendments regarding individual rights to increase women's freedom, at the same time, it constantly restricted the presence of women to the domestic sphere and sustained their retreat from the social, economic, and political spheres, reinforcing the patriarchal nature of the society.[10]

Concerning the enhancement of women's individual rights, perhaps not the most important, but surely the most politicized one, is the removal of the ban on the headscarf, which gave the Muslim, headscarved women the right to be present in the public sphere.[11] Turkey witnessed an increasing appearance of headscarved women in the social and political realm that demand equal rights with their counterparts. The JDP's amendment of the Constitution increased the public appearance of headscarved women not only as students and teachers in universities but also as functionaries its state institutions.[12] This development detached the traditional Muslim woman from the domestic sphere to different fields of the public life. With the attempts of the government to fulfill the European Union (EU) criteria, there have been legal changes for the protection of women. Among them are changes in the Penalty Code (2004); change in the Law of Municipalities (2005) that obliges municipalities larger than 50,000 inhabitants to open women shelters; and the formation of a parliamentary commission for the equality of opportunity for women and men (2009).[13]

Despite these rights, studies indicates an increase in conservatism, which extends control over women's lives and favors their retreat from social, economic, and political life, limiting their presence to their domestic lives. The main source of this conservatism is the Islamic component of the JDP's ideology, which not only reinforces the patriarchal character of the society but also regulates the physical appearance of women. The main role that Islam and nationalism give to women is to be at home, to raise the next generations, and to ensure happiness in the family.[14] Studies mention that, in the course of Islamisation of Turkey, women retreat from the labor market, and the policies of the JDP fasten this retreat. The amendment in the Social Security and General Health Insurance (2008), the amendments on the ability of women to benefit from their father's insurance, are some of the policies that alienate women from the labor market.[15] Similar policies are also visible in politics where the party refused to incorporate affirmative action in the Constitution and to implement gender quotas in politics.

This study argues that what seems like a dichotomy is, in fact, used as a tool to increase and legitimize the patriarchal characteristics of the society through its Islamization. Reforms effectuated by the JDP to increase the rights of women aim not to socially and political integrate covered or uncovered women in the social and political field but to reinforce their roles as the main actors of the domestic field. For instance, reforms in the penal code and municipal law reinforce the place of women as the main actors of the domestic not social or public sphere. They are not in contradiction with the patriarchic ideology. A similar suggestion can be made for the lifting of the ban on the headscarf. As Nilüfer Göle argues, the headscarf becomes an important symbol of the Islamization of the Turkish society, where, in return, its spread reinforces the patriarchal relations present in the Islamic conception of gender relations.[16] As a result, the increasing appearance of the covered women in social life acts as a mechanism to legitimize Islamic patriarchal codes. As Yeşim Arat points out, the increasing head-covering among women and its legal justification in public institutions play two distinctive roles in the increase of patriarchy.[17] First, she indicates that head-covering came along with restrictive views on women being active outside the home. As a result, the increase in covered women increases the justification of the gender roles among women themselves. Second, it creates an expanding effect on patriarchy, because as the head-covering receives increasing legitimacy, so does the number of women beginning to cover their head to gain this legitimacy. As such, the extension of religious freedoms becomes a mechanism that increases patriarchy by not only defining women's role in the society but also the appropriateness of their physical appearance. What we actually see is the Islamization of the patriarchal relations.

THE ISLAMIZATION OF
PATRIARCHY AND THE EDUCATION SYSTEM

The education system provides an important mean for political parties to shape societies' national identities. The educational system is especially effective in teaching the gender codes to new generations. As such, compulsory public education can become an important tool for the JDP to legitimize the Islamized patriarchy[18]. Although this attempt is mostly evident in the increase in imam-hatip schools that give religious education, the gradual changes realized in the curricula of compulsory education textbooks may also become an equally important means.

Education as a means to legitimize and reinforce patriarchal relations is analyzed by a considerable number of studies in the Turkish context. The analysis of gender roles and patriarchal codes in the compulsory education textbooks is effectuated not only for the JDP but also previous political parties.[19] The results of these studies are in conformity with studies on gender policies of political parties cited in the previous section. Studies analyzing the early Republican era find results in parallel with the "state feminism." Women are not only the equal of men in the private sphere where the latter shares the responsibilities of the housework but also active participants in the social, economic, and political spheres as educated teachers, nurses, doctors, and so on. The same studies indicate the increasing patriarchal characteristics of these textbooks beginning with 1946, which give fewer places for women than men and limit the role of women to the private sphere as wives or mothers and in specific jobs, mostly as teachers or nurses.

There is also a great magnitude of research covering the early JDP era, nearly all of which show similar results.[20] Among them, an important one is Hülya Tanrıöver's discourse analysis of primary and high school textbooks, which was conducted by the History Foundation in 2003 and focuses, generally, on the human rights aspects of the textbooks.[21] Under gender discrimination criteria, Tanrıöver found clear stereotypes concerning domestic role and profession distribution between men and women. Yasemin Esen's research of the textbooks for the academic year of 2005–2006, which was prepared after a serious revision of the curricula by the National Education Ministry, provides a quantitative and qualitative analysis of the illustrations used in the textbooks for ABC, Turkish, Life Studies, and Social Studies in primary school.[22] The important findings of the analysis are as follows. Men and boys are more visible than women and girls, which Esen states is in conformity with previous studies, especially in the case on social studies textbooks. For instance, while working men comprise 49.73 percent of all men, this percentage is lower for women, which is at 35.27 percent. Inversely, the percentage of women in traditional roles such as domestic tasks and mothering is 34.72 percent; for men, it is only 6.14 percent. As such, Esen argues that the patriarchal nature of Turkish society where men are reflected as the primary actors of social life and women as the primary actors of private life is reflected in the textbooks. The finding illustrates that men and women have different professions. Women are portrayed as teachers or doctors while men have higher positions, such as decision-makers, school principles, judges, and so on. Another interesting finding of the research is the sexist approach to the dressing styles of women, who mostly wear skirts and dresses.[23] Esen's research confirms continuity among old and new textbooks on gender issues. Firdevs Gümüşoğlu's qualitative analysis concentrating on the content of the primary school textbooks from 1930 to 2008 successfully portrays the changing role of women throughout Turkish Republic history; where in the 1930s women are seen as the teachers of the society, while in the 1950s, they become the servants of their family[24]. However, in 2001–2002 textbooks, men appear as the supporters of women in housework, but this support clearly becomes invisible in 2005–2006 textbooks. Gümüşçüoğlu indicates a historical fluctuation concerning gender roles. Latife Kırbaşoğlu Kılıç and Bircan Eyüp conducted similar analysis for the sixth-grade Turkish textbook of 2007–2008 of two different publishers, highlighting patriarchal features present in them.[25] The presence of men is more dominant and they are mostly working while women are mostly represented in traditional roles. Similar results are found by Aykaç for the same year life science and social science primary school textbooks. Nevertheless, Aykaç also indicates the increased presence of women outside the house and in professions such as doctors and deputies.[26] Similar results are found by Derya Yaylı and Çınar Kitiş's analysis that covers the illustrations in secondary school Turkish textbooks for the year of 2012–2013.[27] Other recent research that covers the illustrations of the primary school textbooks for religious culture and moral knowledge from 1980–2012 was conducted by Mualla Yıldız.[28] Her analysis finds out that women are portrayed as having more private religious practices such as praying and performing *namaz* and are mostly presented at home. The poor number of women having a profession is illustrated as traditional women professions, such as teacher or nurses.

Although containing valuable information and confirming the increasing patriarchal character of the JDP's national identity, these studies are limited in the sense that, first, their aim is not provide a link to the political realm, since they mostly concentrate on the gender roles in the society, leaving aside the headscarf issue. Second, they mostly cover the period when liberalism was an important dimension of the JDP identity formation, not covering the period of increased Islamization in the party's ideology. When it was founded in 2001, the JDP clearly defined itself as a conservative party similar to its European counterparts, heavily emphasizing its liberal economic policies and commitment to meet the EU membership criteria.[29] However, beginning with the 2010s, there is a transformation in the party's ideology from liberalism to more authoritarian tendencies, with more emphasis on the Islamist national identity and a breakaway from the EU.[30]

The possible effect of the JDP's changing national identity definition that puts more emphasis on traditional values and Islam on its educational policies is not investigated. By linking education policies to political ideology and covering the period after the JDP's increasing Islamism, the study aims to contribute to the existing literature.

Hypothesis and Methodology

This study argues that the lifting of the ban on the headscarf is not used by the JDP to ameliorate individual freedoms, expanding the role of the women in the social and political sphere, but a means to legitimize and increase the existing patriarchy present in the Turkish Society through its Islamization. Within this respect, while this study provides a contemporary analysis of the patriarchal dimension analyzed by previous studies, its main difference from them is its attempt to link educational policies to political ideology by incorporating in the analysis the headscarf as a new dimension of the Islamization of patriarchy. The main arguments of the study are tested through the analysis of the illustrations in the secondary social studies textbooks.

Early education is extremely important in identity formation and in learning social roles.[31] The study prefers to conduct its analysis in secondary school social studies textbooks, which are prepared and provided by the Turkish Ministry of National Education. It especially focuses on textbooks distributed for the academic year of 2017–2018 when the government has applied an extensive change in the contents and curricula of these textbooks. A major difficulty concerning the textbooks is the inaccessibility of the former ones, since they are distributed by the Ministry of National Education free of charge and are forbidden to be sold.[32] This is why the results concerning the traditional variables measuring patriarchy will be compared with former studies. Unfortunately, it will be impossible to compare the data on the covered/uncovered women due to the inaccessibility of previous data and its lack in former studies. Still, this variable is expected to provide important information on the possible effects of the increasing Islamization within society regarding gender inequality. The underlying cause of selecting social studies textbook is very simple. This course's main objective is to teach children the social and political life in the society. As such, it is expected to directly reflect the JDP's perception on the main characteristics of the society it aims to form. Although secondary school is four years in Turkey, the study only focuses in its first three years. The major cause is the difference in the curriculum of the last year where students are given the course of "Revolution History" instead of social studies. It is believed that incorporating this textbook to the data would have misleading results.

In the study, the main focus is given to the messages sent indirectly through the illustrations appearing in the textbooks. As such, each illustration is the unit of analysis of the research. The quantitative method is used to analyze the illustrations where each variable is counted and coded. The total number of coded illustrations are 847, and in 502 of the illustrations, there is at least one individual. The analysis of the variables used as proxies to measure patriarchy is coded from these 502 illustrations.

Previous studies define women and men as two homogeneous groups and compare them concerning variables measuring conservatism. As this study investigates possible differences between covered and uncovered women, it has created a third category for comparison. As such, the three groups that are compared are men, uncovered women, and covered women.

Based on previous studies,[33] the first variable analyzed is the frequency distribution of each group in each illustration. The study believes this variable provides information on the vision of the JDP on the public visibility of each group as social beings. The second variable analyzed is the percentage of each group's appearance on traditional roles, such as being a mother/father or performing housework. The third variable to measure each group's social roles concerns the distribution of the tasks performed by each group categorized as performing traditional roles, working, politically active, and other tasks. The fourth variable classifies the professions of the working individuals according to their sex. Besides revealing the percentage of profession identified with women, the variety of profession would especially give information on the political appearance of women vis-à-vis their male counterparts.

In accordance with the previous studies, first, a comparison of women and men is provided for each variable measuring patriarchy. This would give an idea on the changing magnitude of patriarchy compared with previous studies. Then, covered and uncovered women are compared for each of these variables to understand whether head-cover is a symbol of liberties or the control of men over women.

222 Gül Arıkan Akdağ

Findings

The first part of the findings aim at evaluating the main characteristics of the patriarchal society portrayed in the textbooks and track their change across the years through its comparison with previous studies. Within this respect, there are three sets of variables: frequency distribution of each sex in illustrations, frequency distribution of each sex's activity, and frequency distribution of each sex's profession. These variables are separately analyzed for covered and uncovered women.

Table 7.1 provides information on the public visibility of women and men in the textbooks. The frequency distribution of girls and boys is incorporated in the analysis since their presence is also expected to have an effect on patriarchy. It should be noted that in some illustrations (e.g., crowded streets or squares) it was impossible to count the number of each category; therefore, these illustrations were excluded from the analysis. Table 7.1 shows that in all the textbooks, a total of 1,405 individuals were visible. Among them, the most visible are men, which comprise 61.28 percent of the total individuals. The underrepresentation of women is clearly noticed since they comprise only 15.8 percent of the total population. The frequency of girls and boys is more equally distributed, with 9.54 and 13.38 percent, respectively, despite underrepresentation still being present. When compared with Esen's[34] findings where women represent 13.8 percent of the total individuals, we see that, across the years, the visibility of women in social studies textbooks has slightly increased. A similar situation is present when we analyze the distribution of girls and boys. An interesting finding is the decrease in the number of children, vis-à-vis the adults, which decrease from 43.7 to 22.92 percent. These results sustain previous studies arguments that social life is the arena of mostly adults and males.

The activities performed by women and men are revealed in Table 7.2. The first group among these activities is comprised of traditional women roles, which means performing housework or being a mother/father. The second group consists of individuals working in a working place; while the third group are individuals performing a political activity, such as statesman,

Table 7.1. Frequency Distribution of Each Sex

	Number of individuals	%
women	222	15.80
men	861	61.28
girl	134	9.54
boy	188	13.38
total	1,405	100

Table 7.2.   Frequency Distribution of Each Sex Activity

	women		*men*	
	number	*%*	*number*	*%*
women/men in traditional roles	29	13.06	7	0.81
women/men working	63	28.38	517	60.05
women/men politically active	23	10.36	185	21.49
women/men in the social sphere	107	48.20	153	17.65
total	222	100	862	100

deputy, activist, king, ruler, sultan, and so on. The last category are the rest of the individuals who are performing tasks outside their traditional roles and working, such as shopping, visiting a museum, walking on the streets, and so on. Although the percentage of women in traditional roles seems to be low at 13.06 percent, the percentage of men performing these tasks is even lower at only 0.81 percent. This shows that housework or raising children is perceived as a woman's job. When compared with Esen's study where 6.14 percent of males were performing this task, we see deterioration in the division of labor at home at the expense of women, although their share within the total of women performing traditional activities has decreased from 34.72 to 16.06 percent.

The inequality in the data on working women and men is even more visible. Although 28.38 percent of the women are illustrated as working, working seems to be the main activity of men at a share of 60.05 percent. If political activity is added to the working category, the situation gets even worse since politics is portrayed as mostly male dominated at 21.49 percent of men and only 10.3 percent of women who perform a political activity. When compared with previous studies, these results signal the increasing dominance of men in the work force (the percentage of working men was found to be 49.73 percent in Esen's study). An interesting result is the increasing share of women whose activities are outside their traditional roles, such as shopping, visiting a museum, walking on the street. While this variable is 48.20 percent for women, it is 17.65 percent for men. The findings seems to indicate that women are portrayed as more social actors but still not as working individuals since the share of this group was 26.45 percent in Esen's study. The patriarchal relations seem to be reinforced by increasing the appearance of men as a working individuals.

Different from previous studies, this one also analyzes the frequency distribution of the professions of women and men. The results are revealed in Table 7.3. The six categories are composed purposively as politician (such as president, minister, deputy, mayor, headman, king, ruler, etc.), military

Table 7.3. Frequency Distribution of Each Sex Profession

	women		men	
	number	%	number	%
politician	24	27.27	185	26.35
military	0	0	137	19.52
low-profile jobs	15	17.05	111	15.81
professional jobs	26	29.55	177	25.21
traditional jobs	13	14.77	54	7.7
scientist	8	9.09	38	5.41
total	88	100	702	100

personnel (such as soldier, pilot, etc.), low-profile jobs that do not necessitate any education (such farmer, clerk, office worker, artisan, etc.), professionals jobs that necessitate education (such as doctor, engineer, judge, lawyer, etc.), traditional jobs (such as teacher or nurse for women and police, conductor, train operator, fisherman, or baker for men), and scientists. The first observation is the high diversity of the professions portrayed for men when compared with women, which is in accordance with previous studies. Although the share of politicians among women seems to be higher with 27.27 to 26.35 percent, this situation seems to be the case because of the high visibility of women as activists. When these are excluded from the data, the number of women politicians decrease to 17 percent. As such, women are portrayed as entering politics not through conventional but instead unconventional means. Only two individuals out of 185 are portrayed as entering politics via unconventional means among men. Furthermore, another interesting observation is the presence of women in the lower ranks of politics, such as assisting the rulers, being a headman, and so on. Although there is a considerable number of women entering the military in Turkey, this category is unrepresented in the textbook, while it comprises an important profession for men, which is shown as having a share of 19.52 percent. It is striking that all military personnel are males. There seems to be a slight difference among women and men for low-profile jobs, whose share are 17.05 and 15.81 percent, respectively, whereas women are more portrayed as working in professional jobs requiring an education. Still, women are more identified with traditional women jobs at 14.77 percent than men with traditional men jobs at 7.7 percent. Although their numbers are very low, 9.09 percent of women are visualized as scientists; in contrast, scientist men comprise only 5.41 percent of the male individuals. These results seem to diverge from previous studies, yet it is difficult to make a clear comparison since the quantitative distribution of professions is not available. Nevertheless, the results seem to be in conformity with previous studies concerning the shares of traditional jobs among women and men.

Table 7.4.   Frequency Distribution of Covered/ Uncovered Women

	number	%
covered	70	31.53
uncovered	142	63.96
unknown	10	4.5
total	222	100

The findings based on social studies textbooks sustain the study's main argument that patriarchy is an important element of the JDP's ideology and national identity formation. Economic and political life is mostly seen as the men's domain while there is a considerable decrease in the presence of men at home. However, the presence of women seems to have increased in the social life, although their poor presence remains in the economic and political life.

The patriarchal society envisioned by the party is more visible when women are not taken as a homogenous category but a separation between covered and uncovered women is conducted. Table 7.4 indicates the frequency distribution of covered and uncovered women. An interesting observation is the limited representation of covered women, only comprising 31.53 percent of the female population, given the fact that, in reality, they comprise a higher percent of the Turkish women.[35] The public sphere is seen as a domain where mostly modernized uncovered women take action.

The inequality is even more powerful when these two groups are compared regarding the activities they perform. With 24.29 percent, covered women are more identified with traditional roles such as being a mother or doing housework. This share is only 7.89 percent for uncovered women. Inversely, the covered women are nearly invisible in the working life. Only one woman has been illustrated in the textbook as working who was doing so as a seasonal agricultural worker. Covered women working in different fields of the

Table 7.5.   Frequency Distribution of the Activity of Each Covered/Uncovered Woman

	covered women		uncovered women	
	number	%	number	%
women in traditional roles	17	24.29	12	7.89
working women	1	1.43	62	40.79
women politically active	3	4.28	21	13.82
women in social sphere	49	70	57	37.5
total	70	100	152	100

226 *Gül Arıkan Akdağ*

economic life such as state functionaries, nurses, teachers, and in the private sector have not found places in the textbooks. A similar situation is present concerning political activities. Only three covered women are politically active; two of them are rulers wives illustrated in the pictures from the old Turkish societies. The other woman is as an activist. One probable cause of this situation might be the JDP's caution to not nominate any covered politicians in different ranks of the government apparatus as political representative.[36] Still, given the fact that lots of covered women are actively working in different ranks of the party, such an under-representation seems to be a conscious choice. On the other hand, the data indicates that covered women are still an important part of social life since 70 percent of them are portrayed as being outside the house and the workplace. A more detailed analysis of the illustrations shows that their sociality is due, first, to the role given to them for shopping since they are mostly portrayed in modern or traditional marketplaces. Second, they are seen as active members assisting their male counterparts during the War of Independence. As such, the analysis on the covered/covered women strongly supports this study's main argument that the headscarf is an important means for the JDP to legitimize and strengthen patriarchy in Turkey. The poor role given to covered women in the textbooks indicates the probability of increasing patriarchy as the nation gets more Islamized.

DISCUSSION

The basic aim of this study is to define the patriarchal characteristic present in the JDP's ideology. Previous studies on the patriarchic elements of the JDP's ideology find a dichotomy in the JDP's policy on gender. While the party implemented reforms to increase the individual rights of women, it has also steadily made amendments to retreat women from the economic and political spheres. This study suggest that what seems to be a dichotomy is in fact not one since implemented reforms on individual rights strengthens the position of women in the domestic sphere that they traditionally perform not in the public sphere. As such, the study has two hypotheses. First, it argues that the patriarchic elements found in previous studies steadily continue to exist. Second, it argues that the lifting of the ban on the headscarf does not result with the integration of covered women in the public sphere but with their exclusion from the public sphere, becoming a means to legitimize and strengthen patriarchy. Within this respect, the JDP's policy can be identified as the gradual Islamization of patriarchy.

For this purpose, the study tries to quantitatively analyze the illustrations present in secondary school social studies textbooks used for the academic year of 2017–2018 and compares them with previous studies in the realm of education studies. Besides traditional categories of women and men, the study creates further categories differentiating between covered and uncovered women. For each of the categories, it analyzes their frequency distribution in the illustrations, the tasks they perform, and the distribution of their profession. Two distinct comparisons are done. First, women and men distribution for each variable is measured and compared with previous studies. Second, a comparison of covered and uncovered women is performed for each of the variables.

The findings reveals important information on the patriarchal character of the JDP's ideology while it also indicates the risk of increasing patriarchy as the Islamization of Turkish society increases. Similar to previous studies, the results of the study show poor appearance of women in the textbooks. Although the magnitude of women in the social life outside home and workplace seems to have increased, their poor economic and political presence, when compared to men, is an important characteristic to be taken into account. On the other hand, men are portrayed as the main actors of the economic and political spheres. The comparison of covered and uncovered women clearly indicates that the headscarf is a means to reinforce patriarchy. The covered women are very poorly represented and mostly active in performing traditional tasks. They are not visible in the working or political life. However, an interesting result is their high representation in the social sphere. This indicates that the Islamist patriarchy tolerates the presence of women in the public sphere, but it does not envision them as active members of the economic and political spheres. As such, the spread of Islam is expected to increase the legitimization of patriarchy among Muslim women, creating greater inequalities in gender relations and roles.

NOTES

1. S. A. Martson, "Who are the People: Gender, Citizenship and the Making of the American Nation," *Society and Space* 8 (1990): 444–58; Daniella Coetzee, "South African Education and the Ideology of Patriarchy," *South African Journal of Education* 2, no.4 (2001): 300–4; Patricia Hill Collins, " Its All in the Family: Intersections of Gender, Race and Nation," *Hypatia* 13 no. 3 (1998): 62–82; and Rick Wilford and Robert L. Miller, *Women, Ethnicity and Nationalism: The Politics of Transition* (Routledge: London; New York, 1998).

2. Martson, "Who Are the People"; Collins, " Its All in the Family"; N. Yuval-Davis and F. Anthias. *Women-Nation-State* (Macmillan: London, 1989).

3. Deniz Kandiyoti, "Identity and its Discontent: Women and the Nation," *Dossier* 6 (2004): 45–58; Wilford and Miller, *Women, Ethnicity and Nationalism.*

4. Kandiyoti, "Identity and its Discontent."

5. Şirin Tekeli, "Türkiye'de Feminist İdeolojinin anlamı ve Sınırları Üzerine," *Kadınlar için* (Istanbul: Alan Yayınları, 1988): 307–34 ; Deniz Kandiyoti, "Emancipated but Unliberated? Reflections on the Turkish Case," *Feminist Studies* 13, no. 2 (1987): 317–38; Binnaz Toprak, "Emancipated but Unliberated Women in Turkey: The Impact of Islam," in *Women Family and Social Change in Turkey*, edited by F. Ozbay, 39–50 (Bangkok: UNESCO 1990); Ayşe Durakbasa and Aynur İlyasoğlu, "Formation of Gender Identities in Republican Turkey and Women's Narratives as Transmitters of 'herstory' of Modernization," *Journal of Social History* 35, no.1 (2001):195–203; Yeşim Arat, *The Patriarchal Paradox: Women Politicians in Turkey* (Associated University Press: London, Toronto, 1989); Yeşim Arat, "From Emancipation to Liberation: The Changing Role of Women in Turkey's Public Realm," *Journal of International Affairs* 54, no. 1(2000): 107–23; Bruce H. Rankin and Işık A. Aytaç, "Gender Inequality in Schooling: The Case of Turkey," *Sociology of Education* 79 (2006): 25–43; Nilüfer Göle, *The Forbidden Modern: Civilization and Veiling* (Ann Arbor, MI: University of Michigan Press, 2003).

6. Toprak, "Emancipated but Unliberated Women"; Kandiyoti, "Identity and its Discontent"; Arat, " From Emancipation to Liberation."

7. Saniye Dedeoğlu, "Equality, Protection or Discrimination: Gender Equality Policies in Turkey," *Social Politics* 19, no. 2 (2012): 269–90.

8. Ayhan Kaya, "Islamisation of Turkey under the AKP Rule: Empowering Family, Faith and Charity," *South European Society and Politics* 20, no. 1 (2015):47–69; Buket Türkmen, "A Transformed Kemalist Islam or a New Islamic Civic Morality? A Study of 'Religious Culture and Morality' Textbooks in the Turkish High School Curricula," *Comparative Studies of South Asia, Africa and the Middle East* 29, no. 3 (2009): 381–97; Demet Lüküslü, "Creating a Pious Generation: Youth and Education Policies of the AKP in Turkey," *Southeast European and Black Sea Studies* 16, no. 4 (2016): 637–49.

9. Simtem Coşar and Metin Yeğenoğlu, "New Grounds for Patriarchy in Turkey? Gender Policy in the Age of AKP," *South European Society and Politics* 16, no. 4 (2011): 555–73.

10. Simtem Coşar and Metin Yeğenoğlu, "New Grounds for Patriarchy in Turkey? Gender Policy in the Age of AKP," *South European Society and Politics* 16, no. 4 (2011): 555–73; Yeşim Arat, "Religion, Politics and Gender Equality in Turkey: Implications of a Democratic Paradox?," *Third World Quarterly* 31, no. 6 (2010): 869–84; Saniye Dedeoğlu, "Veiled Europeanisation of Welfare State in Turkey: Gender and Social Policy in the 2000s," *Women's Studies International Forum* 41 (2013): 7–13; Lüküslü, "Creating a Pious Generation"; Ayşe Güneş Ayata and Fatma Tütüncü, "Party Politics of the AKP (2002–2007) and the Predicaments of Women at the Intersection of the Westernist, Islamist and Feminist Discourses in Turkey," *British Journal of Middle Eastern Studies* 35, no. 3 (2008): 363–84.

11. Ayata and Tütüncü, "Party Politics of the AKP."

12. Arat, "Religion, Politics and Gender Equality," 878.

13. Coşar and Yeğenoğlu, "New Grounds for Patriarchy in Turkey," 562; Dedeoğlu, "Veiled Europeanisation of Welfare."

14. Coşar and Yeğenoğlu, "New Grounds for Patriarchy in Turkey," 565; Dedeoğlu, "Veiled Europeanisation of Welfare."

15. Arat, "Religion, Politics and Gender Equality"; Dedeoğlu, "Veiled Europeanisation of Welfare"; Azer Kılıç, "The Gender Dimension of Social Policy Reform in Turkey: Towards Equal Citizenship?" *Social Policy* 42, no. 5 (2008): 487–503.

16. Göle, *The Forbidden Modern.*

17. Arat, "Religion, Politics and Gender Equality."

18. Lüküslü, "Creating a Pious Generation."

19. Ayşe Saktanber, "Muslim Identity in Children's Picture Books," in *Islam in Turkey: Religion in a Secular State*, edited by R. Tapker, 171–88 (London: I B Tauris & Co, 1988); Zeki Dökmen, "Ilkokul Ders Kitaplarının Cinsiyet Rolleri Açısından İncelenmesi," *3P* 3, no. 2 (1995): 38–44; Firdevs Gümüşoğlu, *Ders Kitaplarında Cinsiyetçilik* (İstanbul: Kaynak Yayınları, 1996); Tanju Gürkan and Fatma Hazır, "İlkokul Ders Kitaplarının Cinsiyet Rollerine İlişkin Kalıp Yargılar Yönünden Analizi," *Yaşadıkça Eğitim* 52 (1997): 25–31; Yasemin Esen, *Ders Kitaplarında Cinsiyetçilik: İlköğretim Türkçe Ders Kitaplarında Yapılmış Bir İçerik Çözümlemesi* (Unpublished MA dissertation) (Ankara: A.Ü.S.B.E, 1998); Yasemin Esen and M.Türkan Bağlı, "İlköğretim Ders Kitaplarındaki Kadın ve Erkek Resimlerine İlişkin Bir İnceleme," *A.Ü.E.B.F. Dergisi* 35, nos.1–2 (2003): 143–54.

20. Hülya U Tanrıöver, "Ders Kitaplarında Cinsiyet Ayrımcılığı," in *Ders Kitaplarında İnsan Hakları: Tarama Sonuçları*, edited by B. Çotuksöken, A. Erzan, and O Silier, 106–22 (İstanbul: Tarih Vakfı, 2003); Yasemin Esen, "Sexism in School Textbooks Prepared under the Education Reform in Turkey," *Journal for Critical Education Policy Studies* 5, no. 2 (2007): 465–93; Firdevs Gümüşoğlu, "Ders Kitaplarında Toplumsal Cinsiyet," *Toplum ve Demokrasi* 2, no. 4 (2008): 39–50; Latife Kırbaşoğlu Kılıç and Bircan Eyüp, "İlköğretim Türkçe Ders Kitaplarında Ortaya Çıkan Toplumsal Cinsiyet Rolleri Üzerine bir İnceleme," *Sosyal Bilimler Araştırmaları Dergisi* 2, no. 3 (2011): 129–49; Necdet Aykaç, "Sosyal Bilgiler ve Hayat Bilgisi Ders Kitaplarının Toplumsal Cinsiyet Açısından Değerlendirilmesi," *Hacettepe üniversitesi Eğitim Fakültesi Dergisi* 43 (2012): 50–61; Mualla Yıldız, "Ilkokul ve Ortaokul Din Kültürü ve Ahlak Bilgisi Kitapları Görsellerinin Toplumsal Cinsiyet Açısından İncelenmesi," *Dini Araştırmalar* 16, no. 42 (2013) 143–65; Derya Yaylı and Çınar E. Kitiş, "Ortaokul Türkçe Ders Kitaplarında Toplumsal Cinsiyet," *Turkish Studies* 9, no. 5 (2014): 2075–96.

21. Tanrıöver, "Ders Kitaplarında Cinsiyet."

22. Esen, "Sexism in School Textbooks."

23. Ibid., 478–82.

24. Gümüşoğlu, "Ders Kitaplarında Toplumsal."

25. Kırbaşoğlu Kılıç and Eyüp, "İlköğretim Türkçe Ders."

26. Aykaç, "Sosyal Bilgiler ve Hayat Bilgisi."

27. Yaylı and Kitiş, "Ortaokul Türkçe Ders Kitaplarında."

28. Yıldız, "Ilkokul ve Ortaokul Din Kültürü."

29. Ziya Öniş, "The Triumph of Conservative Globalism: The Political Economy of the AKP Era," Turkish Studies 13, no. 2 (2012):135–52; Ali Çarkoğlu, "Economic Evaluations vs. Ideology: Diagnosing the Sources of Electoral Change in Turkey,

230   Gül Arıkan Akdağ

2002–2011," *Electoral Studies* 31, no. 3 (2012): 513–21; Meltem Müftüler Baç. "Turkey's Political Reforms and the Impact of the European Union," *South European Society and Politics* 10, no. 1 (2005): 17–31.

30. Doğancan, Özsel, Öztürk Armağan, and Hilal Onur Ince, "A Decade of Erdoğan's JDP: Ruptures and Continuities," *Critique* 41, no. 4 (2013): 551–70; Ergun Özbudun, "AKP at the Crossroads: Erdoğan's Majoritarian Drift," *South European Society and Politics* 19, no. 2 (2014): 155–67; William Hale and Ergun Özbudun, *Islamism, Democracy and Liberalism in Turkey* (London and New York: Routledge, 2010).

31. Mehmet Baştürk, "Ders Kitaplarının Tarihçesi," in *Konu Alanı Ders Kitabı İncelemesi*, edited by Özcan Demirel and Kasım Kıroğlu (Ankara: Pegem Yayıncılık, 2008); Mustafa Bayrakçı, "Ders Kitapları Konusu ve İlköğretimde Ücretsiz Ders Kitabı Dağıtımı Projesi," *Milli Eğitim Dergisi* 165 (2005); Wendy M. Tietz, "Women and Men in Accounting Textbooks: Exploring the Hidden Curriculum," *Issues In Accounting Education* 22, no. 3 (2007): 459–80; Kırbaşoğlu Kılıç Eyüp, "Ilköğretim Türkçe Ders."

32. Esen, "Sexism in School Textbooks," 473.

33. Tanrıöver, "Ders Kitaplarında Cinsiyet"; Esen, "Sexism in School Textbooks"; Kırbaşoğlu Kılıç and Eyüp, "Ilköğretim Türkçe Ders"; and Aykaç, "Sosyal Bilgiler ve Hayat Bilgisi."

34. Esen, "Sexism in School Textbooks"

35. Arat, "Religion, Politics and Gender Equality."

36. Ayata and Tütüncü, "Party Politics of the AKP," 370–72.

RESOURCES

Arat, Yeşim. *The Patriarchal Paradox: Women Politicians in Turkey*. London, Toronto: Associated University Press, 1989.

———. "From Emancipation to Liberation: The Changing Role of Women in Turkey's Public Realm." *Journal of International Affairs* 54, no. 1(2000): 107–12.

———. "Religion, Politics and Gender Equality in Turkey: Implications of a Democratic Paradox?" *Third World Quarterly* 31, no. 6 (2010): 869–84.

Arıkan Akdağ, Gül. "Ak Parti'nin Seçim Başarısına Alternatif bir Açıklama: Yerel Örgütlerin Yapı ve İşlevleri." *Alternatif Politika* 4, no.1 (2012): 27–53.

———. *Ethnicity and Elections in Turkey: Party Politics and the Mobilization of Swing Voters*. Milton Park, New York: Routledge, 2015.

Ayata, Ayşe Güneş, and Fatma Tütüncü. "Party Politics of the AKP (2002–2007) and the Predicaments of Women at the Intersection of the Westernist, Islamist and Feminist Discourses in Turkey." *British Journal of Middle Eastern Studies* 35, no. 3 (2008): 363–84.

Aykaç, Necdet. "Sosyal Bilgiler ve Hayat Bilgisi Ders Kitaplarının Toplumsal Cinsiyet Açısından Değerlendirilmesi." *Hacettepe üniversitesi Eğitim Fakültesi Dergisi* 43 (2012): 50–61.

Baştürk, Mehmet. "Ders Kitaplarının Tarihçesi." In *Konu Alanı Ders Kitabı İncelemesi*, edited by Özcan Demirel, Kasım Kıroğlu. Ankara: Pegem Yayıncılık, 2008.

Bayrakçı, Mustafa. "Ders Kitapları Konusu ve İlköğretimde Ücretsiz Ders Kitabı Dağıtımı Projesi." *Milli Eğitim Dergisi* 165, (2005). http://dhgm.meb.gov.tr/yayimlar/dergiler/milli_egitim_dergisi/165/bayrakci.htm.

Coetzee, Daniella. "South African Education and the Ideology of Patriarchy." *South African Journal of Education* 2, no.4 (2001): 300–4.

Collins, Patricia Hill. "It's All in the Family: Intersections of Gender, Race and Nation." *Hypatia* 13, no. 3 (1998): 62–82.

Coşar, Simtem, and Metin Yeğenoğlu. "New Grounds for Patriarchy in Turkey? Gender Policy in the Age of AKP." *South European Society and Politics* 16, no. 4 (2011): 555–73.

Çarkoğlu, Ali. "Economic Evaluations vs. Ideology: Diagnosing the Sources of Electoral Change in Turkey, 2002–2011." *Electoral Studies* 31, no. 3 (2012): 513–21.

Dedeoğlu, Saniye. "Equality, Protection or Discrimination: Gender Equality Policies in Turkey." *Social Politics* 19, no. 2 (2012): 269–90.

Dökmen, Zeki. "İlkokul Ders Kitaplarının Cinsiyet Rolleri Açısından İncelenmesi." *3P* 3, no. 2 (1995): 38–44.

Durakbasa, Ayşe, and Aynur İlyasoğlu. "Formation of gender Identities in Republican Turkey and Women's Narratives as Transmitters of 'herstory' of Modernization." *Journal of Social History* 35, no.1 (2001): 195–203.

Esen, Yasemin. *Ders Kitaplarında Cinsiyetçilik: İlköğretim Türkçe Ders Kitaplarında Yapılmış Bir İçerik Çözümlemesi*. Unpublished MA dissertation. Ankara: A.Ü.S.B.E, 1998.

———. "Sexism in School Textbooks Prepared under the Education Reform in Turkey." *Journal for Critical Education Policy Studies* 5, no. 2 (2007): 465–93.

Esen, Yasemin, and M.Türkan Bağlı. "İlköğretim Ders Kitaplarındaki Kadın ve Erkek Resimlerine İlişkin Bir İnceleme." *A.Ü.E.B.F. Dergisi* 35, nos.1–2 (2003): 143–54.

Göle, Nilüfer. *The Forbidden Modern: Civilization and Veiling*. Ann Arbor, MI: University of Michigan Press, 2003.

Gümüşoğlu, Firdevs. "Ders Kitaplarında Toplumsal Cinsiyet." *Toplum ve Demokrasi* 2, no. 4 (2008): 39–50.

———. *Ders Kitaplarında Cinsiyetçilik*. Istanbul: Kaynak Yayınları, 1996.

Gürkan, Tanju, and Fatma Hazır. "İlkokul Ders Kitaplarının Cinsiyet Rollerine İlişkin Kalıp Yargılar Yönünden Analizi." *Yaşadıkça Eğitim* 52 (1997): 25–31.

Hale, William, and Ergun Özbudun. *Islamism, Democracy and Liberalism in Turkey*. London and New York: Routledge, 2010.

Kandiyoti, Deniz. "Emancipated but Unliberated? Reflections on the Turkish Case." *Feminist Studies* 13, no. 2 (1987): 317–38.

———. "Identity and its Discontent: Women and the Nation." *Dossier* 6 (2004): 45–58.

Kaya, Ayhan. "Islamisation of Turkey under the AKP Rule: Empowering Family, Faith and Charity." *South European Society and Politics* 20, no. 1 (2015): 47–69.

Kılıç, Azer. "The Gender Dimension of Social Policy Reform in Turkey: Towards Equal Citizenship?" *Social Policy* 42, no. 5 (2008): 487–503.

Kırbaşoğlu, Latife, and Bircan Eyüp. "İlköğretim Türkçe Ders Kitaplarında Ortaya Çıkan Toplumsal Cinsiyet Rolleri Üzerine bir İnceleme." *Sosyal Bilimler
Araştırmaları Dergisi* 2, no. 3 (2011): 129–49.

Martson, S. A. "Who are the People: Gender, Citizenship and the Making of the
American Nation." *Society and Space* 8 (1990): 444–58.

Müftüler Baç, Meltem. "Turkey's Political Reforms and the Impact of the European
Union." *South European Society and politics* 10, no: 1 (2005): 17–31.

Lüküslü, Demet. "Creating a Pious Generation: Youth and Education Policies of the
AKP in Turkey." *Southeast European and Black Sea Studies* 16, no. 4 (2016):
637–49.

Özsel, Doğancan, Armağan Öztürk, and Hilal Onur Ince. "A Decade of Erdoğan's
JDP: Ruptures and Continuities." *Critique* 41, no. 4 (2013): 551–70.

———. "Veiled Europeanisation of Welfare State in Turkey: Gender and Social
Policy in the 2000s." *Women's Studies International Forum* 41 (2013): 7–13.

Öniş, Ziya. "The Triumph of Conservative Globalism: The Political Economy of the
AKP Era." *Turkish Studies* 13, no. 2(2012):135–52.

Özbudun, Ergun. "AKP at the Crossroads: Erdoğan's Majoritarian Drift." *South European Society and Politics* 19, no. 2 (2014):155–67.

Rankin, Bruce H., and Işık A.Aytaç,. "Gender Inequality in Schooling: The Case of
Turkey." *Sociology of Education* 79 (2006): 25–43.

Saktanber, Ayşe. "Muslim Identity in Children's Picture Books." In *Islam in Turkey:
Religion in a Secular State*, edited by R. Tapker, 171–88. London: I. B. Tauris &
Co, 1988.

Tanrıöver, Hülya U. "Ders Kitaplarında Cinsiyet Ayrımcılığı." in *Ders Kitaplarında
İnsan Hakları: Tarama Sonuçları*, edited by B. Çotuksöken, A. Erzan, and O Silier,
106–22, İstanbul: Tarih Vakfı, 2003.

Tietz, Wendy M. "Women and Men in Accounting Textbooks: Exploring the Hidden
Curriculum." *Issues In Accounting Education* 22, no. 3 (2007): 459–80.

Toprak, Binnaz. "Emancipated but Unliberated Women in Turkey: The Impact of
Islam." In *Women Family and Social Change in Turkey*, edited by F Ozbay, 39–50.
Bangkok: UNESCO, 1990.

Tekeli, Şirin. "Türkiye'de Feminist İdeolojinin anlamı ve Sınırları Üzerine." *Kadınlar
için*, Istanbul: Alan Yayınları, 1988, 307–34.

Türkmen, Buket. "A Transformed Kemalist Islam or a New Islamic Civic Morality?
A Study of 'Religious Culture and Morality' Textbooks in the Turkish High School
Curricula." *Comparative Studies of South Asia, Africa and the Middle East* 29, no.
3 (2009): 381–97.

Wilford, Rick, and Robert L.Miller,. *Women, Ethnicity and Nationalism: The Politics
of Transition*. London and New York: Routledge, 1998.

Yaylı, Derya, and Çınar E. Kitiş. "Ortaokul Türkçe Ders Kitaplarında Toplumsal
Cinsiyet." *Turkish Studies* 9, no. 5 (2014): 2075–96.

Yıldız, Mualla. "İlkokul ve Ortaokul Din Kültürü ve Ahlak Bilgisi Kitapları Görsellerinin Toplumsal Cinsiyet Açısından İncelenmesi." *Dini Araştırmalar* 16, no. 42
(2013): 143–65.

Yuval-Davis, N., and F. Anthias. *Women-Nation-State*. London: Macmillan, 1989.

Chapter Eight

(Re)construction of Turkish National Identity in Urban Space: Transformation of İstanbul's Panorama Under JDP Rule

Seren Selvin Korkmaz

The Justice and Development Party (JDP) has been ruling Turkey since 2002. Over the course of this period, the JPD has come to hold not only institutional apparatuses of the state, but has also transformed the state and national identity of the country. Through this transformation process, urban space has become the subject of a hegemonic war on different identities.

(Re)construction of urban space has been used as a means of transforming ideologies into a concrete form and consolidating the symbolic power of the state in everyday life. Urban space is not a static but dynamic—*lieux de memoire* (site of memory)—which reproduces the past, constructs the "new," and reflects state–society relations. The new Republic of 1923 used space-politics to create a Westernized, modern, and secular nation-state by detaching the traces of Ottoman past from the urban space. (Re)naming and (re)construction using specific symbols and modern architecture was employed by Kemalists, not only to consolidate the new state identity but also to transform the society. However, counter-hegemonic attacks against the Kemalist policies lay behind the two main political cleavages, the modernists versus traditionalists and Islamists versus seculars dichotomy, has existed throughout the Republican history. Beginning with the 1980s, in tandem with the identity politics of the 1990s, Islamic politics have consolidated its power under the rule of the JDP since 2002. As the hegemony of Kemalist secularism that has been greatly weakened, the visibility of Islamists in society and public life has increased in the JDP era, and a new form of national identity is being created with the support of mass media, architectural designs, and Islamic arts, as well as discursive practices. However, the JDP's interpretation of modernity is different from its pro-Islamist predecessors; rather than rejecting the concept of modernity, the JDP cadres have reinterpreted it by combining with tradition—the Ottoman past.

Istanbul, with its symbolic, geographic, and economic significance, is an ideal field to illustrate the transformation of Turkey's national and state identity in the urban space. As the former capital of the Ottoman Empire and the biggest metropolitan city of Turkey, İstanbul has been the center of hegemonic wars on urban space. Every political group that has held power tried to redesign İstanbul throughout the history of the Republic. The JDP revitalized İstanbul's symbolic power by attributing it as the de facto capital of Turkey. İstanbul's transformation in the last decade, including works such as the construction of the Panorama 1453 Museum as a revival of the Conquest of Istanbul, the boom in mosque construction, and the Çamlıca Mosque Project, the use of Ottoman symbols in public buildings and landscaping, and the renaming of the Boğaziçi Bridge as the "July 15 Martyrs Bridge" are some crucial samples of the JDP's ideological use of spatial politics.

This chapter will argue that the JDP has redefined the national identity and used urban space as a means of consolidating its ideology. I will explain how Islamism, Ottomanism, and the latest growing Turkish nationalism are combined in the national identity and serve as the main pillars of the nation-building process under the JDP rule.

NATIONAL IDENTITY AND SPACE

To explain the relation between national identity and space, I first have to define nation and national identity. Although there are various approaches to nation, I will follow definitions provided by Anthony Smith and Benedict Anderson. According to Smith, a nation is "a named and self-defined human community whose members cultivate shared myths, memories, symbols, values, and traditions, reside in and identify with a historic homeland, create and disseminate a distinctive public culture, and observe shared customs and common laws."[1] Anderson defines nation as imagined community. He argues that printed media and literacy are the focus of this imagination, and through these apparatuses, the idea of nation is disseminated. However, as Tim Edensor argues, in Anderson's definition, other apparatuses of this imagination, such as museums, architecture, popular music, and everyday habits, are not covered.[2] This imagination is not static, but it is changed over time through the use of specific instruments that are mentioned in Smith's definition. Even though the history of the nation is the same, imagination is the key to determining which part of the history or which specific myths are ascribed to in specific periods. As Smith argued, the national identity is "the continuous reproduction and reinterpretation of the pattern of values, symbols, memories, myths, and traditions that compose the distinctive heritage of nations and the identification of individuals with that pattern and heritage."[3] Thus, national identity is exposed to a continuous change in different periods of the national history, and it is used as a means to consolidate the ideologies of governments.

Apart from institutional arrangements, symbolic politics and apparatuses of everyday life have become crucial means used by governments to ensure the reimaging of a nation throughout modern history. Space is an intersectional area where all of these apparatuses operate. Space is not just a geographical space; it is both political and ideological. Henri Lefebvre argues that social and political space is produced and is a product, but it is also producer and reproducer in the maintenance of relations of dominations.[4] Power relations operate in the space. Space also symbolizes culture, socioeconomic status, and political and ethnic identities. [5] Architecture, the layout of the streets, places of worship, designation of neighborhoods, parks, and other symbolic sites represent the language of power.[6] State–society relations are reflected in these micro-spaces. Thus, space, in this context, urban space, has always been in the center of national imagination and is used as a means to create new types of social relations or reconstruct certain identities. Colonial cities that were redesigned by the colonizers provide good samples of this identity formation in the urban landscape.

John R. Gillis emphasized that both identity and memory are political and social constructs, and the relationship between memory and society is historical.[7] The core of the memory of any specific identity is based on the sense of sameness, and the notion of what is remembered is determined by identity politics. Thus, national identity can be reimagined and reconstructed via identity politics. As Amy Mills emphasizes, memory is not a static or pre-determined concept; rather, it is produced and reproduced every day as a process that includes both the past and present.[8] Space is also one of the areas wherein the collective memory turns to collective identity. Ideologies are transformed into concrete forms in the urban landscape where material symbols produce new forms of social relations.[9] In other words, urban space is a *lieux de memoire* (site of memory) that reproduces the past in the context of new power relations. In this context, space becomes a material discourse.

Redesigning of urban space has been used as a means to create alternative histories and national identities throughout the history of the Turkish Republic. While Kemalists aimed to create a national identity severed from Ottoman and Islamic history, the JDP launched the construction of a new type of Turkish national identity by reimagining the Islamic and Ottoman past. Ruling the state and many local municipalities enabled the JDP to reconstruct this new type of identity in the urban space. Although today's neoliberal forms of urban planning cannot be ignored, I will specifically focus on the cultural side of the planning in this chapter.

TURKISH NATIONAL IDENTITY AND ITS
TRANSFORMATION UNDER JDP RULE

It is apparent that fifteen years of JDP rule has certainly changed the Turkish state and its society. However, these changes were not implemented as clear-cut reforms; rather, they have been implemented over time. National identity has also been exposed to transformation under JDP rule. As Jenny White argued, Turkey has never developed a unifying national identity that entirely represents its various constituents.[10] Hence, competing understandings of nationalism existed throughout the Republican history. However, until the JDP consolidated its power in Turkey, the Kemalist understanding of nationalism stood as hegemonic.

The Republic of 1923 was a new nation-state that has been created from the remnants of the multinational and multireligious Ottoman Empire. Hence, the elite cadre of the Republic had to imagine a new national identity. To ensure its legitimacy, first off, the new nation-state attacked the Ottoman legacy and denied the Ottoman past. Kemalism's national identity was gradually shaped during the 1920s and 1930s. This Kemalist imagination of Turkish national identity was based on three pillars: secularism, Westernization, and Turkish nationalism.[11] Soner Çağaptay argues that there were three zones of Turkishness in the 1930s: "an outer territorial one, reserved for the non-Muslims, an inner middle religious one, reserved for non-Turkish Muslims, and [an] inner ethnic one, reserved for the Turks."[12] Being Muslim was one of the main components of Turkish national identity, a signifier that also included non-Turkish Muslims, notably the Kurds. However, a secular understanding of nationalism was adopted. Islam was used as a marker of being, but Islam as a faith was prohibited in the public sphere.[13] This imagination of national identity came together through the top-down control of religion by the state. Religious orders and public displays of religious symbols were banned.[14]

These religious and ethnic tensions in the definition of national identity have remained vivid throughout Republican history. Since national identity is not static, certain cleavages have affected this definition. Different governments and political parties have tried to emphasize one of three components (secularism, Westernization, and Turkish nationalism). Islamist political groups have challenged Kemalist national identity and struggled for the public visibility of Islam; however, until the recent decade, through the institutional apparatuses of Kemalism (the military, the Constitutional Court, education, etc.), the Kemalist notion of national identity had preserved its hegemony. When the JDP came to power in 2002, there was still institutional and ideological Kemalist guardianship within the state. After the JDP consolidated its power in 2007 elections, the party started to transform the state identity by redesigning the state–society relations and reimagining the national identity. This reimaging allows the JDP to pragmatically control the society with ideological indoctrination and mobilized the nation around the party. This transformation has been implemented via an institutional change at the state level and symbolic change in everyday life. Hence, the party consolidated itself as a hegemonic power in Turkish politics.

Within the scope of this chapter, rather than the transformation at the bureaucratic level, I will focus on identity formation. In this sense, there are certain critical junctures that have shaped the national identity formation during the JDP period. First, the end of the Kurdish–Turkish Peace process, known as the "Solution Process," in July 2015; secondly, the failed coup attempt of July 2016. The JDP's attempt to create an alternative national identity goes beyond 2015; however, these critical junctures created certain turning points in the imagination of the nation. As opposed to the Kemalist emphasis on the "secular" pillar of nationalism, the JDP adopted an Islamic emphasis on national identity from the beginning. However, the JDP embraced Turkish nationalism after the failed peace process and consolidated it as a national identity after the failed coup attempt of July 2016.

In the first period of JDP's reign, the party adopted a more Westernized discourse by combining it with an inclusive notion of secularism. The party gradually allowed the public visibility of Islamic symbols. Rapprochement with the European Union (EU) and democratization attempts towards non-Muslim minorities and Kurds prevented the party from adopting an exclusive Turkish nationalist discourse. As the JDP emerged from the conservative Islamic-based Refah Party tradition, Islam had always been on the agenda. However, it was carefully constructed as one of the pillars of national identity. Being Muslim and part of the religious brotherhood was used as a mechanism to solve the historical conflict between the Kurds and the Turkish state. Rather than a secular understanding of nation, the JDP emphasized Muslim identity to show Kurds were part of the *ummah* (Islamic community). After the peace process was collapsed in 2015, the JDP has adopted a more nationalistic discourse.

During the solution process with the Kurds, the JDP adopted a more inclusive understanding of national identity. After the end of the peace process, the JDP adopted more nationalist discourse, and their alignments changed. The July 15 coup d'état is marked as a starting point for the ideology, and it is used as a narrative to consolidate the JDP's power. War policy in Iraq and Syria also created a mass mobilization around the government. Rather than creating a pluralistic state, the JDP created a majoritarian system so that mobilizing the Sunni and nationalist right-wing majority would be enough for the party to remain in power. Thus, identity politics combined with clientelism was implemented. In this chapter, I will try to show the reformulation of national identity as a combination of modernism, Turkish nationalism, Islam versus Kemalist, westernized, secular, Turkish, national identity.

Ottomanism as a Reference to the Islamic Identity

The JDP's imagination and (re)construction of national identity necessitate the answer to the question of "Who are we as a nation?" The answer has been reformulated as "we are all Ottomans" during JDP rule. However, references to Ottomanism are selective concerning the party's policies. While in the first phase of the JDP, this emphasis on Ottomanism included its multiethnic and multi-religious sides to support its Kurdish Solution Process and other policies toward non-Muslim minorities in Turkey. However, after the Solution Process ended and the JDP obtained a more nationalist agenda, its relation to Ottomanism also changed. The Hamidian (Abdülhamid II) era is now more highlighted and adopted, and Recep Tayyip Erdoğan's personality is linked to Abdülhamid as the symbol of the leader of the ümmah and Turks. However, the Islamic emphasis on Ottomanism has not changed. The Kemalist hegemony had undermined the Ottoman Empire to consolidate the new regime and create a new national identity. As a reaction to this Republican ideology, the cleavages in the society have been shaped around this secular–religious dichotomy, with the religious side embracing Ottoman history to represent the Islamic heritage of the country. Islamist political movements of Turkey mostly use this Islamic imaginary of the Ottomans to recreate Islamic identity. This imaginary is not only produced in the media but also in the restoration of Islamic architecture and in redesigning the urban space with Islamic symbols.[15]

For Mill, in Turkey, religion and ethnicity have been employed as markers of political belonging and exclusion; thus, the role of culture is very important in the examination of national identity.[16] In Turkey, official national history carefully separated the Ottoman past from the new Republic (until the JDP dominated the state); however, Islamism, as a reaction to secular Republican ideology, tried to construct Islamic and Ottoman identity by incorporating Ottoman identity into the national identity.[17] As Deniz Kabaağaç claims, Ottomanism enables the JDP to be Islamist without promoting itself as an Islamist party. In addition, this notion of Ottomanism is a kind of globalized version. The JDP, especially in the first phase, did not refuse Western civilization, but it did insist that the concepts of Western philosophical thought, such as democracy and human rights, were actually rooted Ottoman civilization; thus, "we" as Ottomans are accustomed to these concepts.[18] The JDP type of references to Ottomans are more comprehensive in respect to the former Islamists, since they go back either to the Asr-ı Saadet (Asr-ı Saadet refers to Prophet Muhammed's era in the history of Islam) or to the period before Suleiman the Magnificent to make inferences for today. Kemalists also use Ottoman history in a limited context.[19] Kabaağaç claims that there is a double-identification process in the Ottomanist approach of the JDP. The party constituted and instituted the image of Ottomans, and at the same time, the JDP itself is constituted and instituted as a representative of Ottomans with the reconstruction of Ottoman identity. [20]

URBAN SPACE AS A MEANS OF SYMBOLIC POLITICS FROM KEMALISM TO POST-KEMALISM

The JDP emerged as a coalition party that embraced Islamist, center-right, and liberal political figures. Over time, the emphasis on religion increased in the party's policies and discourse of party elites. After the 2011 elections, the party increased the tone of Islam in its agenda.[21] Although the party did not follow an Islamist agenda, it used Islam as a mobilizing agent to ensure its power. The party reinterpreted national identity by using symbolic politics, and Islam became one of the main components of this new identity used to launch its hegemony. Symbolic politics uses narratives, symbols, and spectacles to transform power relations. Gaining control over symbolic politics by using governmental offices also offers opportunities to redefine geographic spaces.[22] Symbolic politics also creates new facts; hence, people can redefine their identities on the basis of those facts.[23] This is a process of the imagination of the identity. Thus, identity construction and symbolic representation are mostly intertwined. As Ulrike H. Meinhof and Dariusz Galasinski remark, identity is a discursive construction, and it exists and is expressed through symbolic representations. [24]

Redesigning of urban space, architectural forms, and naming of public places as a means of symbolic politics are crucial to consolidate national identity in people's everyday lives. When the new Republic was established, the Kemalist state attempted to create a modern and Westernized identity in the public and everyday life of its citizens.[25] The concept of identity requires the definition of "the other" and "we" on the basis of differences. In the Republic's definition of "we," there is a severing from the Ottoman past. Hence, the use of Ottoman symbols was rejected in the urban space, and the urban landscape was to be composed of Western-type buildings, monuments, and museums. This new urban planning, too, implied a rupture from the Ottoman past.[26]

For instance, as Tekeli explains, this symbolic designing of the urban space of Ankara led to the modernization of Anatolia as guidance by representing the success of the Republic.[27] However, this rejection of the Ottoman past and invisibility of Islam in the public sphere has been challenged by the Islamists and has become the center of the main cleavages in Turkey. Beginning in the 1980s, Turkey has witnessed the growth of identity politics, and during the 1990s, Islamist political movements gained increased support in the society. When the JDP came to power in 2002, it was the beginning of a new era for Turkish politics. Hence, the visibility of Islamic symbols in the public life and urban space has increased. Ottoman traditional figures or architectural designs have been revitalized as a challenge to the architectural designs of the Republic. The changing of architectural designs as a "culture war" between secular Kemalists and Islamists has become the status quo during almost sixteen years of the JDP in Turkey. Particularly, gaining the seats of municipalities gives the Islamists the chance to reconstruct Islamic identity by redesigning the urban space.

The JDP did not officially transform the secular characteristics of the state; however, they undermined the secular principles of the state via institutional arrangements and symbolic politics in the public sphere. While the former is beyond the topic of this chapter, I will focus on the latter. The JDP reconsolidated Sunni-Islam in the everyday life of people by using symbolic politics. Art, architecture, media, festivals, and ceremonies are all means that are used to implement symbolic politics. Obtaining municipalities and the government enabled the JDP to promote Islamic values and symbols in public life.[28] Urban space became the instrument of this identity formation in the everyday. Mass construction policies motivated by the neoliberal economic policies of the JDP came together with this identity construction. Those two types of "construction" became the apparatuses of the JDP to reimagine the country by redesigning urban space. The discourse and policy of "building modern cities" includes this dual construction.

HEGEMONIC CLAIMS ON İSTANBUL'S LANDSCAPE

İstanbul is one of the symbolic areas where the aforementioned culture wars of clashing identities have occurred. The city, with its population of 15 million and powerful economy, is accepted as the "heart of Turkey." İstanbul is a transcontinental city that is located both in Asia and Europe. As the capital of the Ottoman Empire and a symbolic center for the Islamic world, the city also carries symbolic meaning. Though the new Republic chose Ankara as the capital, İstanbul was also redesigned with Republican symbols. Nowadays, İstanbul's panorama has been exposed to symbolic change. The city reembraces its Ottoman past, and the public visibility of Islam is now more significant. Actually, the İstanbul municipality has been ruled by conservative Muslims since Erdoğan's gaining the seats of the İstanbul municipality in 1994. However, the city had not been exposed to major changes in an ideological way because of the Kemalist hegemony until the JDP launches its hegemony in the country.

During the JDP period, İstanbul's panorama has certainly changed. This change is not only related to a symbolic, ideological transition, there is also an economic motivation behind it. The construction boom and gentrification projects across the whole country cannot be ignored when we discuss the reconstruction of urban space in Turkey. However, I will focus on the symbolic dimension of this renewed urban space. Museums, architectural designs, landscaping, and renaming are all parts of this symbolic imagination.

SYMBOLS OF THE JDP ERA: İSTANBUL'S NEW MOSQUES

Nowadays, two gigantic mosques are rising in two symbolic places of İstanbul: one is on Çamlıca Hill, the other is in Taksim Square. The construction of these two mosques goes beyond a purely religious motivation. The Çamlıca Mosque project was President Erdoğan's goal. In May 2012, Erdoğan explained that they were planning to construct a huge mosque on Çamlıca Hill, and this mosque will be seen on the hill from every part of İstanbul. This project sparked social debate, and secular opponents criticized the project for its emphasis on the Islamization of space. However, the project was celebrated in Islamic circles. After organizing a competition for architectural design, the construction of the mosque started. As the JDP consolidates its power in Turkey, the Çamlıca Mosque is close to completion. The mosque is located on one of the tallest hills of İstanbul, the farthest place in Anatolia within the city. It is designed as a modern külliye. A *k*ülliye is a social complex that was specifically built in Ottoman and Seljuk eras. *Külliye* includes a mosque located in the center surrounded by other buildings, such as a kitchen, bakery, *madrasa*, and *Dar al-Shifa* (health services). The term külliye for new buildings has come into use after Erdoğan called the presidential palace (built in the JDP era) a *külliye*. Rather than just a praying place, Çamlıca Mosque will be a social complex that includes a conference room, library, art gallery, and a museum on Islamic antiquities. This modernized version of a mosque symbolizes the adoption of Islam as a lifestyle rather than accepting it as just a religious practice.

Çamlıca Mosque also has significance in the sense that an Ottoman tradition is being recreated. İstanbul is known as the "city of seven hills." Actually, this appellation refers to the "old city" (which Çamlıca Hill is not included in); and on each hill, there is a symbolic historical Ottoman mosque. Those mosques are called "*selatin* mosques," *selatin* meaning "sultans" in Arabic. The sultans or their family members built those mosques. The biggest one is the Blue Mosque, which has six minarets. It is the only mosque that has six minarets in İstanbul (in greater Turkey, there is also Mersin's Hz. Mikdat Mosque and Adana's Sabancı Mosque). Now, the Çamlıca Mosque will also have six minarets. It is known as President Erdoğan's project, and it is speculated that the mosque symbolizes the president's power and his rule. On the other hand, Istanbul's minister of environment and city planning explained that the mosque is meant to "represent the era of the JDP."[29] Hence, as in the case of the Ottomans, the JDP will have built a mosque that symbolizes its era.

Another symbolically crucial mosque is rising in Taksim Square, overshadowing the statues of the major figures of the Republic. Taksim has an important symbolic place in the history of İstanbul and Turkey. It is located in the historically Greek and Armenian settlement of Beyoğlu, and currently serves as an entertainment, cultural, and touristic hub of İstanbul. Orthodox and Catholic churches are located around Taksim Square and İstiklal (Independence) Avenue. Although its vibrancy has decreased in recent years, Taksim is still one of the important centers of İstanbul's nightlife. In addition, Taksim is also the habitual place for demonstrations. May Day ceremonies, feminist night marches on March 8, pride marches, and the Saturday Mother's continuing demonstrations are still held in and around Taksim. For the left-wing movement, it has a historical meaning as well. In 1977, during May Day demonstrations, at least thirty-four people were killed. After the 1980 coup d'état, May Day protests in Taksim were officially banned until 2010, and they were again prohibited in 2013. The leftist movement has always had a presence in Taksim during May Day celebrations.

The Gezi Park protests, which became one of the largest social movements of Turkish Republican history, also emerged in Taksim. Demonstrations emerged in response to the planned demolishment of Gezi Park and soon turned to protests against the JDP's crippling authoritarianism and spread over the country. The intended project of the İstanbul municipality to rebuild the *Topçu Kışlası* in Taksim as a shopping mall by demolishing Gezi Park triggered the demonstrations. *Topçu Kışlası* is known as the Taksim Military Barracks or Halil Pasha Artillery Barracks, which were built in 1806 during the reign of Selim III. The barracks were damaged during the March 31 Incidents of 1909 and then converted to a football stadium in 1921. The stadium was closed in 1939, and *Topçu Kışlası* was demolished in 1940 when Taksim Square was redesigned. The current Gezi Park replaced the barracks. In the eyes of Islamists in Turkey, the demolishment of *Topçu Kışlası* symbolized the Committee of Union and Progress (CUP) and Kemalists's attacks towards Ottoman tradition. Hence, the reconstruction of the barracks had political significance. When Gezi Park was slated to be demolished, it sparked countrywide protests. After the protests, the court decision halted the execution of the demolishment of Gezi Park.

Although the JDP was not successful in rebuilding the barracks, after four years of the Gezi protests, construction of a mosque in the center of Taksim was initiated. Now, Taksim Mosque is rising to an equivalent height of the Hagia Triada Greek Orthodox church nearby. The mosque in the symbolic Taksim Square represents the new national identity of Turkey that includes Islam. As Ersin Kalaycıoğlu argues, Taksim Square was also known as "Republic Square" because it was built by the Republic of Turkey's founding fathers to commemorate the war of liberation. Taksim Square is connected to İstiklal (Independence) Avenue and *Cumhuriyet* (the Republic) Avenue, which symbolize the Turkish Republic.[30] While Taksim Mosque is rising, İstanbul's 1960s era Atatürk Cultural Center (known as AKM), an opera house, and an art venue that carries Turkey's founder Mustafa Kemal Atatürk's name has been demolished. AKM had become a giant billboard for anti-government slogans during the Gezi Protests, and it was demolished during the fifth-year celebration of the protests (on May 31, 2018). It was announced that AKM will be replaced with a modern one.[31]

Apart from Çamlıca and Taksim Mosques, the mosque that was built in Rumelihisarı also carries a symbolic meaning. Rumelihisarı is a castle located on the European side of İstanbul and was built by Ottoman Sultan Fatih Sultan Mehmed for the preparation of İstanbul's Conquest. Rumelihisarı has been used as a popular museum open to the public since 1953, and in 1958, an open-air theater was built. Since the 1980s, the castle has served as an open-air venue for seasonal concerts, art festivals, and special events. There were remnants of a minaret in the center of the castle around a mosque that had been demolished in the eighteenth century. The mosque was known as the first mosque in İstanbul. In 2015, the İstanbul Metropolitan Municipality ensured the rebuilding of the mosque in the center of the open-air theater during the restoration of the castle. President Erdoğan also supported this rebuilding project. According to Erdoğan, "to rebuild this mosque means protecting our history; to resist it signifies Turkey's division." Erdoğan actually attributes a symbolic meaning to the mosque and embracing the Ottoman history and Islamic heritage as a pillar of the unified Turkish nation.[32]

It is important to clarify that apart from certain support of the government for construction of mosques, the increasing wealth of the Muslim bourgeoisie is sufficient to carry out these projects. For Muslims, to construct a mosque is really a big charity. The Prophet Muhammed hadith "whoever builds a mosque, Allah would build for him a similar place in paradise" encourages Muslims to build mosques.[33] The government generally does not directly pay for the construction; rather, an association for mosque building or various businessmen are the resources of finance, but they are initiated by the government and municipality. However, this process is also related to the political economy of the JDP that gave way to the rise of Muslim bourgeoisie through patronage relations. İstanbul now has 3,403 mosques, according to the statistics, but rather than numbers, this increase in symbolism is more crucial. Under JDP rule, constructing 13,000 new mosques under the Directorate of Religious Affairs within eleven years is also an important indicator (2006–2017).[34]

REDESIGNING THE URBAN CENTER

İstanbul has also witnessed other symbolic architectural projects that imply Islam, Turkish nationalism, and modernism blended national identity in the JDP era. First of all, not only in İstanbul but in Turkey at large, there is an increasing use of Ottoman and Seljuk motifs and designs in public buildings. For instance, Bağcılar municipality began to renovate school buildings by using Ottoman and Seljuk motifs. The mayor of Bağcılar claimed that these kinds of architectural designs help the mental development of students.[35]

Also, an amendment in the law under the JDP rule lifted the ban on using Ottoman tughras, coat of arms, and epigraphs in public places. In the first years of the Republic, the use of these symbols in public places was banned in order to erase the traces of imperial power. With the current amendment, Ottoman symbols in public places began to be revealed. Both the ban and lifting the ban on Ottoman symbols implies the changing of policies toward Ottomans and explains the differences between the former and new types of national identity. After its restoration, Sultan Abdülaziz's tughra on top of the main entrance of İstanbul University was revealed. The tughra had been concealed with a T. C. banner (Turkish abbreviation for Turkish Republic) until 2014. Its removal created a huge public debate. Opponents argued that the JDP was trying to remove the Turkish Republic's name and recreate an alternative history by recalling Ottoman symbols. Indeed, the JDP's attempts to employ Ottoman symbols began gradually and accelerated, specifically, after the 2011 and 2015 general elections; thus, the JDP felt more confident about creating a new national identity that carries Ottoman and Islamic references.

There are also attempts to use Islamic symbols in urban squares. For instance, in 2015, the Üsküdar Municipality built models of some of Islam's most sacred sites that were originally located in Mecca. The area where replicas were built was called "Asr-ı Saadet Village." Replicas were built for the celebration of the Prophet Muhammed's birthday. The mayor, Hilmi Türkmen, explained the reason for this new site: "We wanted to experience the feeling of Kaaba in our city." However, the model Mecca was not welcomed by the Directorate of Religious Affairs in Turkey and was described as "a great sin." Hence, the municipality removed the replicas within a few days. However, this attempt also shows how the urban center has become the imagination of identity. [36]

REPRESENTING THE FOUNDING MOMENTS IN THE URBAN SPACE

(Re)construction of national identity also necessitates a founding moment. As Alev Çınar explains, the importance of the founding moment for a national identity is as follows: a formation of a nation-state is marked with a beginning, a founding moment. This founding moment creates a turning point that separates the old and the new and the collective memory of the groups; persons are shaped around this linear line where the founding moment is accepted as a new beginning.[37] Also, founding moments generally glorify a triumph of the nation-state against a specific enemy. As Çınar outlined, "there is always an enemy from which the 'nation' is saved, at the 'founding moment' by the 'founders' for the 'people.'"[38] The JDP has also recreated this founding moment of the nation.

The JDP's creation of a new national identity cannot be separated from the recreation of Ottoman identity in the sense that Islamism is implicitly related to Ottomanism in the context of Turkey. May 29, 1453, the day of the Conquest of İstanbul, is the alternative founding moment that represents the Ottoman-Islamic past of the country and Islamists try to reconsolidate this memory of the past by reviving it through the commemoration of May 29.[39]As opposed to the founding moment of the Republic—October 29, 1923—May 29 stands as an alternative moment. The commemoration of the conquest actually began as a Welfare Party's municipality activity in the 1990s (under Erdoğan's mayorship in İstanbul). Although it is not celebrated as an official holiday, the significance of May 29 has increased each year. In 2009, the Panorama 1453 History Museum was opened in İstanbul. The role of the museum in creating identity is very crucial. Museums are the *lieux de memoire* that represents history in a certain way and revive the collective memory of related groups. During the JDP period, museums have also been used as a means for creating a new Islamic identity. Panorama 1453 ensures the revival of the memory of the Conquest of Istanbul by illustrating the moment when the Ottoman soldiers entered the city. The panoramic painting measures thirty-eight meters in diameter and covers an area of 2,350 square meters. The strength of the three-dimensional visual representations and audio effects gives people the embodied experience of that era. The location of the museum is also crucial; it is located across from the Topkapı-Edirnekapı ramparts where the blockade of the city occurred.[40]

This museum is not an ordinary museum, in the sense that its symbolic meaning is very crucial. It symbolizes an alternative history to the secular Kemalist history. The symbolic meaning of the conquest of İstanbul is based on the notion of glorifying the Ottoman past and the prophecy made by the Prophet Muhammed that predicted the conquest of Istanbul. The celebration of the Conquest of Istanbul is embraced by Islamic circles in the sense that it is an alternative history that represents the Islamic and traditional past of the country as an alternative to the secular-national characteristics of Republican history telling.[41] Panorama 1453 also symbolizes the combination of modernity and Islam embraced by the JDP in the sense that is a Western-style modern museum that represents the Ottoman past. On the official website of Panorama 1453, the museum is defined as addressing the prosperity of the Ottoman generation by glorifying the Ottoman past. The wish for visitors to experience the conquest excitement is expressed with the hope that perhaps it would lead to a "Conqueror" of the future. Hence, the founding moment is not only marked by national celebrations and ceremonies, but it is also reimagined in the urban space by creating a *lieux de momoire*.

Another founding moment for the JDP is July 15, 2016. While May 29 represents a historical Islamic-Ottoman founding moment and is used as a re-link with the Ottoman past, July 15 represents the JDP's Turkish nationalism blended with Islamism. On July 15, 2016, a coup attempt was organized by a group of generals linked to the Gulen movement, which was a former ally of the JDP, to overthrow Erdoğan and the JDP. First of all, it was certain that the attempt was poorly organized and failed within hours. Erdoğan appeared on FaceTime on CNN Turk and called his supporters to the streets to protect Turkey's democracy. Religious calls (*salah*) were issued from minarets for hours. Protesters and the government succeeded in preventing the coup. During that night, the Grand National Assembly of the Turkish Republic was bombed. After the control of the coup attempt, Erdoğan announced that, "Realize this: July 15 was a Second War of Independence for the Turkish nation."[42] The coup attempt occurred when the Kurdish solution process ended, and it remobilized the notion of "internal and external enemies of the state and Turkish democracy." After the coup attempt, the JDP increased its authoritarian tendencies and ruled the country under martial law for two years.

July 15 is narrated as the Second War of Independence with a blend of Turkish nationalism and Islamism. The JDP consolidated its new national identity after the July 15 events. While the date stands as a founding moment, it is symbolized in the urban space. İstanbul Boğaziçi Bridge, where the coup attempt started and protesters and soldiers clashed, has been renamed *15 Temmuz Şehitler Köprüsü* (15 July Martyrs Bridge). A monument was built at the entrance of the 15 July Martyrs Bridge. The monument is nine and a half meters tall with an eleven-meter diameter and is covered with limestone. Five arches were built on the five corners of the pentagon dome. Inside the three arches, the names of the 249 people that died in the coup attempt are etched. The architect of the monument, Hilmi Şenalp, explains the symbolic meaning of the monument as follows: "The dome represents a life of eternity for martyrs. It is composed of geometric arms which are a tribute to the unity and togetherness of the nation against the coup. It was this unity that stopped the coup attempt." In front of the monument, visitors hear the *salah* as in the night of coup attempt.

The renaming was used as a crucial means to emphasize the "founding moment" in everyday life. The name of the largest bus terminal in İstanbul was changed from Esenler to "15 July Democracy Bus Terminal." Kısıklı Square's name is now "National Will Square." Also, the names of four parks and fifty-three bus stops were changed and given new names related to July 15 and the martyrs. The overall emphasis of July 15 includes the message of unity of the nation against the internal and external enemies. Being Turkish and Muslim is symbolically emphasized as the main pillars of national identity in the July 15 commemoration. The Turkish flag and *salahs* became the dominant symbols both during the protests and commemoration ceremonies.

As explained previously, İstanbul has become the center of hegemonic claims throughout the Republican history. National identity has been represented in the urban space by using symbolic politics. While Kemalists' urban policy pursued a goal to erase the remnants of Ottoman symbols in the city, the JDP aimed to transform İstanbul's landscape by recalling the Ottoman symbols and constructing new symbolic buildings. Building mosques in Taksim Square, Çamlıca Hill, Rumelihisarı and pursuing an architectural plan that carries Ottoman and Seljuk motifs served to reveal Islamic symbols in the urban space. Museums, monuments, and the renaming related to July 15 and May 29 represents new founding moments of the new national identity that is reimagined by the JDP.

CONCLUSION

National identity is not a static concept, but it is exposed to continuous reproduction and reimagining. This reconstruction process is implemented at an institutional and symbolic level. Space, as both geographic and political area, is used as a means to redesign social and political relations of everyday life. Urban space, as a political and ideological space, became one of the main instruments of the imagination of the national identity. Hence, hegemonic claims over national identity are reflected in the urban space throughout the Republican history in Turkey. The Kemalist imagination of national identity based on secular, Westernized, and Turkish nationalism broke the linkages with the Ottoman history and inhibited the public use of Islamic symbols in the urban space. City squares were redesigned with Westernized architectures; monuments and museums, including Republican symbols, were built. It is apparent that over fifteen years, JDP rule has transformed the national identity of Turkey. This transformation has been implemented both at the institutional and symbolic levels. The party reimagined the nation as a means of ideological indoctrination and mobilized its supporters by creating new myths and founding moments directly related to the JDP era. As opposed to the Kemalist national identity, the JDP has promoted an Islamic and Turkish nationalism-blended identity.

The JDP's ruling at the national level, and holding the seats of most of the municipalities in Turkey, enabled the party to reconstruct the cities not only physically but also symbolically. Renaming and reconstructing in the urban space are implemented as part of the (re)construction of the national identity. Under JDP rule, both at the local and national level, İstanbul, as the capital of the Ottoman Empire, became the center of this new ideological symbolization. The national identity is reimagined with monuments, mosques built in symbolic places, museums, and architectural designs in İstanbul. İstanbul's new mosques are rising as the symbols of the JDP era. The mosques located in Çamlıca Hill, Taksim Square, and Rumelihisarı Castle show that the JDP recalls Ottoman traditions and Islamic symbols in the public space. The party also created an alternative founding moment(s) of the nation. May 29, 1453, the day of the Conquest of İstanbul, is accepted as the alternative founding moment among Islamists. Furthermore, July 15, 2016, the day of a failed coup attempt, is also formulated as the founding moment of the new national identity promoted by the JDP. These alternative founding moments are symbolically represented in İstanbul's landscape. Panorama 1453 Museum, 15 July Martyrs Monument, and other renaming related to July 15 in specific places of İstanbul are all symbols to contribute the reimagining of the nation as the JDP provides.

To conclude, essentially, this chapter explores how the JDP (re)constructed and reimagined Turkish national identity in the urban space of İstanbul. The party promoted a new national identity based on modernism, Islamism, and Turkish nationalism by using both institutional and space politics. The party uses urban space as a means of its ideological indoctrination. İstanbul, as the old capital of the Ottoman Empire and the largest metropolitan city of Turkey, has become an ideal place for hegemonic claims on national identity.

NOTES

1. Anthony D. Smith, *The Cultural Foundations of Nations: Hierarchy, Covenant, and Republic* (Malden, Oxford. Victoria: Blackwell Publishing, 2008), 19.

2. Tim Edensor, *National Identity, Popular Culture and Everyday Life* (Oxford and New York: Berg, 2002), 7.

3. Smith, *The Cultural Foundations of Nations,* 19.

4. Henri Lefebvre, *State, Space, World: Selected Essays,* edited by Neil Brenner and Stuart Elden, 212 (Minneapolis, MN: University of Minnesota Press, 2009).

5. Amy Mills, *Streets of Memory: Landscapes, Tolerance and National Identity in İstanbul* (Athens: University of Georgia Press, 2010), 1.

6. Cihan Tuğal. *Passive Revolution: Absorbing Islamic Challenge to Capitalism* (Stanford, CA: Stanford University Press, 2007), 30.

7. John R. Gillis, ed, *The Politics of National Identity.* Princeton, NJ: Princeton, 1994.

8. See Amy Mills, *Streets of Memory: Landscapes, Tolerance and National Identity in İstanbul* (Athens, GA: University of Georgia Press, 2010), 1.

9. Ibid., 17.

10. Jenny B. White, "Spindle Autocracy in the New Turkey," *Brown Journal of World Affairs* 24, no. 1 (fall/winter 2017): 27.

11. Soner Çağaptay. *Islam, Secularism, and Nationalism in Modern Turkey. Who Is a Turk?* (London/New York: Routledge, 2006), 2.

12. Ibid.,160.

13. Ibid.,162.

14. White, "Spindle Autocracy in the New Turkey," 27.

15. Jenny B. White. *Islamist Mobilization In Turkey: A Study in Vernacular Politics.* (Washington, DC: University of Washington Press, 2002), 53.

16. Mills, *Streets of Memory,* 14.

17. Alev Çınar, "National History as a Contested Site: The Conquest of Istanbul and Islamist Negotiations of the Nation," *Comparative Studies in Society and History* 43, no. 2 (April 2001): 366.

18. Deniz Kabaağaç, "The Imaginary Ottoman: A Examination of 'Ottomanism' among the Islamic Elites in Today's Turkey as an Intellectual Bridge Between the Local and the Global," (MA Thesis, Boğaziçi University, n.d.), 134–40.

19. Ibid., 134.

20. Ibid., 79.

21. Soner Çağaptay, *The New Sultan: Erdogan and the Crisis of Modern Turkey* (New York: I. B. Tauris Press, 2017), 274.

22. Nicole Watts, "Activists in Office: Pro-Kurdish Contentious Politics in Turkey," *Ethnopolitics* 5, no. 2 (June 2006): 147.

23. Ibid.

24. Ulrike H. Meinhof and Dariusz Galasinski, *The Language of Belonging* (New York: Palgrave, 2005), 7–8.

25. See Cihan Tuğal, *Passive Revolution.*

26. See Sibel Bozdoğan, *Modernism and Nation Building* (Washington, DC: University of Washington Press, 2001).

27. Cited in Yıldız Sey, ed., *75 Yılda Değişen Kent ve Mimarlık* (İstanbul: Türkiye İş Bankası& Tarih Vakfı Ortak Yayını, 1998), 41.

28. See Cihan Tuğal. *Passive Revolution*, 48–51, 54–56.

29. https://www.dw.com/en/mosque-construction-sparks-controversy-in-istanbul/a-17041396, accessed July 27, 2018.

30. http://edition.cnn.com/2013/06/07/world/europe/turkey-taksim-square-symbol/index.html, accessed July 27, 2018.

31. https://www.dw.com/tr/geziden-beş-yıl-sonra/a-43961041.

32. https://www.sabah.com.tr/gundem/2015/05/07/erdogandan-mescid-hazimsizligina-sert-cevap, accessed July 23, 2018.

33. Farha Ghannam, *Remaking The Modern: Space, Relocation and the Politics of Identity in a Global Cairo* (London: University of California Press, 2002), 167.

34. https://www.cnnturk.com/turkiye/diyanete-bagli-cami-sayisi-2017de-90-bine-ulasti, accessed July 27, 2018.

35. http://t24.com.tr/haber/kamu-mimarisinde-osmanli-selcuklu-modasi,236720, accessed July 13, 2018.

36. https://www.bbc.com/news/blogs-news-from-elsewhere-32412530, accessed July 25, 2018.

37. Çınar, "National History as a Contested Site," 369.

38. Ibid., 369.

39. Ibid., 366–67.

40. panoramikmuze.com.tr, accessed July 28, 2018.

41. Çınar, "National History as a Contested Site," 366.

42. Çağaptay, *The New Sultan,* 394.

RESOURCES

Akpınar, İpek. "The Rebuilding of İstanbul Revisited: Foreign Planners in the Early Republican Years." *New Perspectives on Turkey* no. 50 (2014): 59–92.

Alaranta, Toni. *National and State Identity in Turkey.* London: Rowman & Littlefield, 2015.

Anderson, Benedict. *Reflections on the Origin and Spread of Nationalism.* London and New York: Verso, 2006.

Azak, Umut. *Islam and Secularism in Turkey: Kemalism, Religion and the Nation State.* London: I. B. Tauris, 2010.

Bilsel, Cana, Kim Esmark, Niyazi Kızılyürek, and Olafur Rastrick, eds. *Constructing Cultural Identity Representing Social Power.* Pisa: Pisa University Press, 2010.

Bozdoğan, Sibel, and Reşat Kasaba, eds. *Türkiye'de Modernleşme ve Ulusal Kimlik.* İstanbul: Tarih Vakfı Yurt Yayınları, 1998.

Bozdoğan, Sibel. *Modernism and Nation Building.* Washington DC: University of Washington Press, 2001.

Bozdoğan, Sibel, and Esra Akcan. *Turkey: Modern Architectures in History.* London: Reaktion Books, 2012.

Carkoglu, Ali, and Binnaz Toprak. *Religion, Society and Politics in a Changing Turkey.* İstanbul: TESEV, 2007.

Çağaptay, Soner. *Islam, Secularism, and Nationalism in Modern Turkey. Who Is a Turk?* London/New York: Routledge, 2006.

Çağaptay, Soner. *The New Sultan: Erdogan and the Crisis of Modern Turkey.* New York: I. B. Tauris Press, 2017.

Çınar, Alev. "National History as a Contested Site: The Conquest of Istanbul and Islamist Negotiations of the Nation." *Comparative Studies in Society and History* 43, no. 2 (April 2001): 364–91.

Doğan, Erhan. "The Historical and Discoursive Roots of the Justice and Development Part's EU Stance." *Turkish Studies* 6, no. 3 (2005).

Edensor, Tim. *National Identity, Popular Culture and Everyday Life.* Oxford & New York: Berg, 2002.

Ergin, Murat, and Yağmur Karakaya. "Between neo-Ottomanism and Ottomania: Navigating State-Led and Popular Cultural Representations of the Past." *New Perspectives on Turkey* 56 (May 2017): 33–59.

Erman, Tahire, Burçak Altay, and Can Altay. "Architects and the Architectural Profession in the Turkish Context." *Journal of Architectural Education* 58, no. 2 (2004): 46–53.

Exploring Architecture in Islamic Cultures 1, "Architectures and Identity." The Aga Khan Award for Architecture: Singapore, 1983.

Ghannam, Farha. *Remaking the Modern: Space, Relocation and the Politics of Identity in a Global Cairo.* London: University of California Press, 2002.

Gillis, John R., ed. *The Politics of National Identity.* Princeton, NJ: Princeton, 1994.

Göle, Nilüfer. *İslamın Yeni Kamusal Yüzleri.* İstanbul: Metis, 2000.

———. *Melez Desenler.* İstanbul: İletişim, 2002.

Gülalp, Haldun. *Kimlikler Siyaseti.* İstanbul: Metis, 2003.

Kabaağaç. Deniz. "The Imaginary Ottoman: A Examination of 'Ottomanism' among the Islamic Elites in Today's Turkey as an Intellectual Bridge between the Local and the Global." MA Thesis, Boğaziçi University, 2011.

Kalaycıoğlu, Ersin. "Justice and Development Party at the Helm: Resurgence of Islam or Restitution of the Right-of-Center Predominant Party?" *Turkish Studies* 11, no. 1 (2010).

Kuru, Ahmet. *Secularism and State Policies toward Religion: The United States, France and Turkey.* New York: Cambridge University Press, 2009.

Lefebvre, Henri. *State, Space, World: Selected Essays*, edited by Neil Brenner and Stuart Elden. Minneapolis, MN: University of Minnesota Press, 2009.

Meinhof, Ulrike H., and Dariusz Galasinski. *The Language of Belonging.* New York: Palgrave, 2005.

Mills, Amy. *Streets of Memory: Landscapes, Tolerance and National Identity in İstanbul.* Athens, GA: University of Georgia Press, 2010.

Prakash, Gyan, and K. Kruse. *The Spaces of the Modern City: Imaginaries, Politics and Everyday Life.* Princeton, NJ: Princeton, 2008.

Sa'di, Ahmad H. "Catastrophe, Memory and Identity: Al-Nakbah as a Component of Palestinian Identity." *Israel Studies* 7, no. 2 (2002): 175–98.

Sey, Yıldız, ed. *75 Yılda Değişen Kent ve Mimarlık.* İstanbul: Türkiye İş Bankası& Tarih Vakfı Ortak Yayını, 1998.

Shankland, David. *Islam and Society in Turkey.* Cambridge: The Eothen Press, 1999.

Silverstein, Brain. *Islam and Modernity in Turkey.* New York: Palgrave, 2010.

Somer, Murat. "Moderate Islam and Secularist Opposition in Turkey: Implications for the World, Muslims and Secular Democracy." *Third World Quarterly* 28, no. 7 (2007): 1271–89.

Smith, Anthony D. *The Cultural Foundations of Nations: Hierarchy, Covenant, and Republic.* Malden, Oxford. Victoria: Blackwell Publishing, 2008.

Tajbakhsh, Kian. *The Promise of the City: Space, Identity, and Politics in Contemporary Social Thought.* Berkeley: University of California Press, 2001.

Toprak, Binnaz. "Islam and Democracy in Turkey." *Turkish Studies* 6, no. 2 (2005): 167–86.

Tuğal, Cihan. *Passive Revolution: Absorbing Islamic Challenge to Capitalism.* Stanford, CA: Stanford University Press. 2007

Turam, Berna. *Türkiye'de İslam ve Devlet: Demokrasi, Etkileşim, Dönüşüm.* İstanbul: Bilgi Üniversitesi Yayınları, 2011.

Turam, Berna. "The Primacy of Space in Politics: Bargaining Rights, Freedom and Power in an İstanbul Neighborhood." *International Journal of Urban and Regional Research* 37, no. 2 (March 2013): 409–29.

Watts, Nicole. "Activists in Office: Pro-Kurdish Contentious Politics in Turkey." *Ethnopolitics* 5, no. 2 (June 2006).

White, Jenny B. *Islamist Mobilization in Turkey: A Study in Vernacular Politics.* Washington, DC: University of Washington Press, 2002.

———. *Muslim Nationalism and the New Turks.* Princeton and Oxford: Princeton University Press, 2013.

———. "Spindle Autocracy in the New Turkey." *Brown Journal of World Affairs* 24, no. 1 (fall/winter 2017): 23–37.

Yıldırım, Ergun, Husamettin Inac, and Hayrettin Ozler. "A Sociological Representation of the Justice and Development Party: Is it a Political Design or a Political Becoming?" *Turkish Studies* 8, no. 1(2007).

ONLINE SOURCES

BBC: bbc.com
BirGün: birgün.net
CNN Türk: www.cnnturk.com
Deutche Welle: www.dw.com

Diyanet İşleri Başkanlığı: diyanet.gov.tr
İstanbul Büyükşehir Belediyesi: www.ibb.istanbul
Panorama 1453: panoramikmuze.com
Sabah: sabah.com.tr
T24: t24.com.tr
T.C. Cumhurbaşkanlığı: tccb.gov.tr

Conclusion

Islam has always been the most prominent element of Turkey's national identity since the beginning of the Ottoman Empire, and it was used to bound multiethnic and religious societies within the state. Unlike its European empire correspondents, Islam and the bureaucracy dominated over other religions since the beginning of the Empire. Thus, Islam was used to legitimize the state rather than serve as a dominant doctrine and to close the center–periphery dichotomy. As Rasim Özgür Dönmez stated, the Ottoman center used profoundly organized Islamic orders in the society to bind the periphery.

The losing lands of the Ottoman Empire were forced to be a nation-state located in the Westphalian system because of nation-building. It emanated from the question, "How do we rescue the society?" and came to the high sectors of international society as they were in the past. This question was asked to all non-European ex-empires, such as Japan and Russia. They became a permanent "outsider" of the European international system, thus stigmatizing these countries and their elites. As Büke Koyuncu and Dönmez stated, their answer to this question was to adopt Western modernity by separating from Western culture and imperialism.

However, the state attempted to create a religiously heterogeneous Ottoman identity patterned on equal citizenship with Tanzimat reforms to adopt the Ottoman Empire to international society but did not succeed. Afterward, the Ottoman diplomats began to defend a national identity patterned on Muslim identity. The first Islamists were young Ottoman journalists, such as Şinasi and Namık Kemal, belonged to European mason lodges supporting Islam, and compromised Islam with Western-oriented concepts, such as freedom, liberty, and justice. Their attempts can be presumed as the Empire's visions of nation-building and nationalization; hence, the Empire would adopt itself to the international community.

However, the Ottoman diplomats understood that Islam could not be the sole element of national identity, particularly after the independence of Albania and the emergence of Arab nationalism. Turkism became the dominant ideology of the Committee of Union and Progress (CUP), which shared political power with the sultanate. World War I (1914–1918) and the Turkish War of Independence (1919–1923) transformed the Empire to a nation-state patterned on Turkism. Turkism indicated all Muslim citizens of the country by excluding non-Muslims from the system.

However, the new state inherited two essential features from the Ottoman Empire: the center–periphery dichotomy and a strong state tradition. Islam and laicism fundamentally bound these. As Edgar Şar stated, laicism became a symbolic capital that provided modernity and loyalty to the political system. As Beatrice Hendrich claimed, this new system envisioned an ideal citizenship by "white Turks," signifying a secular, modern, moral, and patriotic, Westernized, masculine identity that erased the Ottoman past of the country. These visions gave women the subsidiary role of men.

Subsequently, the pious Islamic networks and ethnic and traditional sectors of society, particularly in rural areas, were excluded from the new citizenship regime that opened the distance in the center–periphery dichotomy. As Bourdieu and Zarakol remarked, political and social actors in advantageous positions are likely to protect their places by not allowing newcomers to enter their social field. The 1960 military coup that resulted from banning the Democrat Party and executing their leaders opened this dichotomy.

Strong state tradition also continued in this new system. The state did not withdraw from the religious sphere that its policies were patterned on to control Sunni Islam. As Ali Yaman and Edgar Şar claimed, the elites set up the Turkish Presidency of Religious Affairs to control Sunni Islam and legitimize Turkey's government policies to continue the Ottoman political culture.

However, well-organized Sunni orders penetrated the political system, transforming the single-party system to a multiparty one. The central-right parties cooperated with these networks during the elections. Turkey's entry into NATO and the struggle against Communism led these Islamic networks to gain important places in state-making and set up parallel social and economic universes. Their ideologies began to spread against the "communism threat" by the state. The 1980 coup d'état and the 1981 Constitution indicating to transform state-led development to the free-market economy led Islamists to pattern nation-building on nationalism, modernization, Turkish-Islamic values, and masculinity. However, the secular establishment was still dominant in the political system, and the center–periphery dichotomy still continued.

The JDP's rising to power opened a new era for nation-building. This indicated the victory of the periphery against the center. The JDP elites perceived to govern the country as the struggle against the center, and Seren Selvi Kork-maz claimed this at an institutional and symbolic level and that urban space was a prominent political and ideological arena for this struggle. According to Korkmaz, as opposed to the Kemalists breaking the Ottoman past, the JDP emphasized the Ottoman heritage as a strategy to use Islamic symbols in public without being marked as Islamists. Thus, Istanbul became the center of this new ideological symbolization, embodying itself with monuments, mosques built in symbolic places, museums, and architectural designs.

The authors within this book generally divided the JDP period in two: the first period comprising the alliance of the party with the liberals and the Sufi orders, and the second comprising the alliance of the JDP with the national-ists. Although the JDP continued the nation-building process of the secular establishment, there were two important differences from the secular estab-lishment. As Edgar Şar stated, while the JDP was cautious in the first period for laicism and interpreted it as the state objectivity to all religions, it tried to desecularize the political and social system, particularly in the second period.

This also strongly reflected gender issues. Gül Arıkan Akdağ wrote about how gender was defined in the JDP period, particularly the role of women in social life, and concluded that women were highly restricted to work in the ideological sphere of the party compared with the previous governments. Senem Kurt Topuz supported this hypothesis but concluded that unlike the secular establishments of women as schoolteachers, pilots, and others, good housewives replaced women with unsecured jobs. However, a patriarchal understanding of the government continued definitely.

With the JDP period, nation-building continued, patterning on Muslim na-tionalist understanding. Although this study did not analyze a specific place, the demographic changes in the country will probably change nation-build-ing. There are approximately three million Syrian refugees, and a majority of them will be permanent residents of the country. The conflicts in the Middle East and Asia would bolster this migration flow to Turkey. Unfortunately, the center–periphery dichotomy seems to open day by day.

Can Turkey transform itself from community to society—*gemeinschaft* to *gesellschaft*? Can Turkey minimize the center–periphery dichotomy?

Index

About the Authors

Rasim Özgür Dönmez is a professor of politics in international relations department of Abant Izzet Baysal University. He is the founder and the editor of the journal *Alternatif Politika/Alternative Politcs*. He works on nationlism, political violence, and dynamics of conflicts. Some of his studies were *Waves of Social Movement Mobilizations in the Twenty-First Century: Challenges to Neo-liberal World Order and Democracy* (2015), *Gendered Identities in Turkey: Criticizing Patriarchy in Turkey* (2013), *Societal Peace and Ideal Citizenship in Turkey* (2011), and *Türkiye'de Politik Değişim:Neo-Osmanlıcılığın Sosyo-Politiği (The Political Change in Turkey: The Socio Political Dynamics of Neo-Ottomanism)* (2014).

Ali Yaman received his MA in political history and PhD in international relations from Istanbul University. Both of his dissertations were on the transformation of Alevism and Bektashism. He also conducted fieldwork in Central Asia and worked at Ahmet Yesevi Kazak-Turk University as a lecturer and senior researcher in Turkology Institute from 2002–2005. He currently works as a professor in the International Relations Department of Bolu Abant İzzet Baysal University. He is co-editor of *Journal of Alevism-Bektashism Studies*. His research interests include Alevism, migration, the European Union, and political anthropology.

Gül Arıkan Akdağ is working as an assistant professor at the department of Political Science and Public Administration at Katip Çelebi University. After she graduated from the department of Political Science and International Relations at Boğaziçi University, she got her master degree in International Relations from Sorbonne University and holds a PhD in political science from Sabancı University. Her research interests include political parties, political

266 About the Author

mobilization, voting behavior, clientelism, Turkish political life, and Turkish foreign policy. She is the author of *Ethnicity and Elections in Turkey: Party Politics and Mobilization of Swing Voters* (2014). She is also the author of several articles published in respectable political science journals.

Béatrice Hendrich is assistant professor at the University of Cologne, Turkish Studies. Her main research areas are the religious landscape of Turkey, Turkish literature, gender history of Turkey, and the colonial history of the Turkish community in Cyprus. She is the author of numerous articles, including "Träume, Reime, Laptops. Die Medialisierung religiöser Erfahrung in drei türkischen Romanen" (Dreams, Verses, Laptops: Medialization of Religious Experience in Three Turkish Novels).

Seren Selvin Korkmaz is a lecturer and doctoral researcher in the Department of Asian, Middle Eastern, and Turkish Studies at Stockholm University. Seren got her BA and MA degrees from the Department of Political Science and International Relations at Boğaziçi University, Turkey. She spent the 2017–2018 academic year as a Fox International Fellow in the Middle Eastern Council of MacMillan International and Area Studies at Yale University where she has completed a non-degree graduate program. Her research interests include the political economy of exclusion, populism, space politics, identity politics, migration, state–society relations, and Turkish politics. Seren has also contributed to the studies and administration of various NGOs and research centers; and participated in various congresses, workshops, and seminars as speaker and organizer. She co-founded Political and Social Research Institute of Europe (PS:EUROPE), an Austria- and Turkey-based research institute and served as Director of Turkey Office of the institute in 2015–2017. Seren is the co-founder and executive director of İstanbul Political Research Institute (İstanPol), an independent, policy-oriented research institute with a particular focus on Turkey and the Euro-Mediterranean zone.

Büke Koyuncu was born in 1979 in İstanbul. After graduating from Üsküdar American Academy, Koyuncu completed her graduate studies at Marmara University, Economics and Administrative Sciences Faculty, Department of Public Administration (in French). She received her MA from Istanbul University, Institute of Social Sciences, Department of Women Studies, and her PhD from Mimar Sinan Fine Arts University, Institute of Social Sciences, Department of Sociology. Her PhD thesis was published by İletişim under the title "Benim Milletim . . . AK Parti İktidarı, Din ve Ulusal Kimlik" in 2014. Her research interests mainly cover sociology of politics, religion, and morality. Currently, she teaches at Mimar Sinan Fine Arts University, in the Department of Sociology.

Edgar Şar is currently a doctoral researcher in political science at Boğaziçi Unversity. He graduated *cum laude* and received his BA degree in political science and international relations from Marmara University and received his Masters degree in political science from Bogazici University with his thesis "The Relationship between Secularism and Democracy: The Case of Turkey in the 2000s." In his current researches, he specifically focuses on the meanings of secularism in the contemporary political theory and state–religion–society relations and their impact on democratization in Turkey and the Middle East. His research interests include theories of secularism and democracy, democratization, sociology of relations, Turkish politics, and constitutional law. Şar, who is currently a content and opinion contributor at Medyascope.tv, worked as co-director of Academic Studies at Political and Social Research Institute of Europe (PS:EUROPE) during 2015–2018. Şar is co-founder of İstanbul Political Research Institute (İstanPol).

Senem Kurt Topuz is an associate professor in the Department of Public Administration at Abant Izzet Baysal University, Bolu, Turkey. She received her PhD degree from Gazi University in the field of politics and social sciences in 2010. She did her post-doctoral studies at the University of Manchester and Manchester Metropolitan University, UK. Her research focuses on gender studies, poverty, discrimination, and social policy. She has publications on citizenship, capability approach, women poverty, and women's freedom in Turkey.